INDIA AND THE FRONTIER STATES OF AFGHANISTAN, NIPAL AND BURMA

INDIA AND THE FRONTIER STATES OF AFGHANISTAN, NIPAL AND BURMA

VOLUME - II

By

JAMES TALBOYS WHEELER, EDGAR SALTUS

GYAN

ISBN : 978-81-212-1688-3(Set)

ISBN : 978-81-212-1690-6(HB)

First Published, 1880

Published, 2018

Published by

Gyan Publishing House
5, Ansari Road
Daryaganj, New Delhi-110002
Phone: 011-47034999, 9811692060
www.gyanbooks.com
E-mail: books@gyanbooks.com

GYAN

Printed at: G. Print Process, Delhi.

THE BATTLE OF CUDDALORE

Frontispiece, vol. two.

CONTENTS

PART III

BRITISH INDIA

(CONTINUED)

CHAPTER VII

LORD CORNWALLIS AND SIR JOHN SHORE. (A.D. 1785 TO 1798) . 448

CHAPTER VIII

MYSORE AND CARNATIC—WELLESLEY. (A.D. 1798 TO 1801) . . 467

CHAPTER IX

MAHRATTA WARS—WELLESLEY. (A.D. 1799 TO 1805) . . . 492

CHAPTER X

CONCILIATION—LORD CORNWALLIS, SIR GEORGE BARLOW, AND LORD MINTO. (A.D. 1805 TO 1813) 514

CHAPTER XI

NIPAL HISTORY—GHORKA CONQUEST. (A.D. 1767 TO 1814) . . 531

CHAPTER XII

NIPAL WAR—LORD MOIRA (HASTINGS). (A.D. 1814 TO 1816) . . 543

CHAPTER XIII

PINDHARI WAR, AND FALL OF THE PEISHWA—LORD HASTINGS. (A.D. 1815 TO 1818) 549

CHAPTER XIV

MAHRATTA CONQUEST—LORD HASTINGS. (A.D. 1817 TO 1823) . . 560

CHAPTER XV

BURMAN HISTORY—AVA AND PEGU. (A.D. 1540 TO 1823) . . . 575

CHAPTER XVI

BURMESE AND BHURTPORE WARS—LORD AMHERST. (A.D. 1823 TO 1828) 593

CHAPTER XVII

NON-INTERVENTION—LORD WILLIAM BENTINCK. (A.D. 1828 TO 1835) . 600

CHAPTER XVIII

CENTRAL ASIA—AFGHAN HISTORY. (A.D. 1747 TO 1838) . . . 619

CHAPTER XIX

AFGHAN WAR—LORDS AUCKLAND AND ELLENBOROUGH. (A.D. 1839 TO 1842) 635

CHAPTER XX

SINDE AND GWALIOR—LORD ELLENBOROUGH. (A.D. 1843 TO 1844) . 647

CHAPTER XXI

WAR DECADE—BURMA AND NIPAL. (A.D. 1839 TO 1849) . . . 653

CHAPTER XXII

SIKH HISTORY—RUNJEET SINGH, ETC. (*Ante* A.D. 1845) . . . 671

CHAPTER XXIII

TWO SIKH WARS—LORDS HARDINGE AND DALHOUSIE. (A.D. 1845 TO 1849) 679

CHAPTER XXIV

MATERIAL PROGRESS—LORD DALHOUSIE. (A.D. 1848 TO 1856) . . 691

CHAPTER XXV

SEPOY MUTINIES—LORD CANNING. (A.D. 1856 TO 1858) 712

CHAPTER XXVI

IMPERIAL RULE—CANNING—ELGIN—LAWRENCE—MAYO—NORTHBROOK AND LYTTON. (A.D. 1858 TO 1880) 756

SUPPLEMENTARY CHAPTER

LORD RIPON—AFGHANISTAN—THE MARCH FROM KABUL TO KANDAHAR—LORD DUFFERIN AND KING THEEBAW—THE ANNEXATION OF UPPER BURMA—THE MARCH OF EMPIRE—LORD CURZON INSTALLED (A.D. 1879 TO 1899) 777

CHRONOLOGICAL TABLES OF INDIAN HISTORY 807

INDEX 817

LIST OF ILLUSTRATIONS

INDIA

Frontispiece—THE BATTLE OF CUDDALORE . . . .

HYDER ALI'S DEFEAT AT PLASSY . . . .

DEATH OF TIPPU SAHIB AT SERINGAPATAM . . . .

SEPOY REBELS BEING SHOT FROM THE MOUTHS OF THE CANNON . .

LIST OF MAPS

	PAGE
INDIA IN THE TIME OF CORNWALLIS	447
INDIA IN THE TIME OF WELLESLEY	469
INDIA IN THE TIME OF LORD HASTINGS	545

A SHORT HISTORY OF INDIA

PART III—BRITISH INDIA
(CONTINUED)

CHAPTER VII

LORD CORNWALLIS AND SIR JOHN SHORE

A.D. 1785 TO 1798

IN 1785 the British empire in India comprised Bengal and Behar in eastern Hindustan; a very little area round Bombay in the western Dekhan; and a larger area round Madras in the eastern Peninsula. There were also two protected princes, namely, the Nawab Vizier of Oude, and the Nawab of the Carnatic. Outside the area of British supremacy were the three native powers who were the bugbear of English statesmen—Nizam Ali, Tippu Sultan, and the Mahrattas.

The Mahrattas were regarded as the most formidable power in India. The heart of the Mahratta empire was weak and palpitating; half shattered by domestic commotions and its recent struggles against the English. The Peishwa at Poona was an infant, and the council of regency was in mortal fear of Tippu Sultan. The real head of affairs at Poona was Nana Farnavese, an able Brahman but no soldier. But the feudatory princes of the Mahratta empire were strong and nominally subordinate to the Peishwa's government. The Gaekwar of Baroda, Sindia, and Holkar in Malwa, and the Bhonsla Raja of Berar, although practically independent, admitted, one and all, their obligations to obey the Peishwa as suzerain of the Mahratta empire; and the confirmation of the Peishwa was necessary to the validity of every succession to a feudatory state or throne.

Of all these feudatory princes, Mahadaji Sindia was the most powerful and the most ambitious. Whatever prestige he had lost during the Mahratta war he had recovered during the negotiations which ended in the treaty of Salbai. Being a neutral at the conclusion of the treaty, he had acted as the representative of all the Mahratta princes, from the Peishwa downward; and he was the sole guarantee for the fulfilment of the treaty. To crown all, an English Resident, named Anderson, was sent to his camp to transact all business between the English and the Mahrattas.[1]

The lot of Mahadaji Sindia was cast in a revolutionary era. His career was marked by restlessness and cunning, and by those sudden changes of fortune which befall the leading actors in Oriental revolutions. He was swayed to and fro by conflicting motives. He was afraid of the English but proud of his connection with them. He was anxious to exercise a paramount ascendency at Delhi as well as at Poona; indeed, he could not rivet this ascendency in either court unless he was master at both. He could not be supreme at Delhi unless he was backed up by the Peishwa's government; and he could not be supreme at Poona unless he was backed up by the authority of the Great Moghul.

For years the Moghul court at Delhi had been the scene of distractions, intrigues, and assassinations at once tedious and bewildering. Shah Alam was a weak prince, who clung to the name and dignity of sovereignty, but was without authority or power. The government was carried on by a prime minister, or lord protector, who was known as the Amir of Amirs, a title higher than that of Vizier, and implying the guardianship of the Padishah. The Amir of Amirs for the

---

[1] Mr. Mostyn, the English Resident at Poona, had died just before the first Mahratta war, and no one had been sent to supply his place.

time being collected revenue and tribute by force of arms, and carried on petty wars with Rajputs, Jats, and other neighboring chieftains. In 1784 there had been a crisis. The ruling Amir of Amirs had obtained his post by the murder of his predecessor, and was in mortal fear of being murdered in his turn. Accordingly he invited Mahadaji Sindia to Delhi, and Shah Alam joined in the invitation.

It is difficult to realize the horrible complications which must have prevailed at Delhi to induce the Muhammadan minister and Muhammadan sovereign to invite the help of a Mahratta chieftain, who was at once a Hindu and an idolater, an alien in race and religion. Mahadaji Sindia, on his part, was only fearful of offending the English, and having duly sounded the English Resident, and ascertained that the English rulers at Calcutta would not interfere in his doings at Delhi, he left Poona and proceeded to the Moghul court. Shortly afterward it was reported that the Amir of Amirs had been murdered at the instigation of Mahadaji Sindia; and that the Mahratta chieftain had taken Shah Alam under his protection, and assumed the administration of the relics of the Moghul empire.[1]

Mahadaji Sindia would not accept the title of Amir of Amirs; it would have clashed with his position at Poona. He artfully procured the title of "deputy of the Padishah" for his nominal sovereign the Peishwa; and then procured

---

1 The following summary of events may suffice to explain the position of affairs on the arrival of Mahadaji Sindia at Delhi. Before Shah Alam returned to Delhi in 1771, the Rohilla Afghan, Najib-ud-daula, had filled the post of Amir of Amirs; but this man died in 1770, and was succeeded by his son, Zabita Khan, who fled from Delhi at the approach of Shah Alam . A Persian named Najaf Khan then came to the front. He had been in the service of Shah Alam at Allahabad, and accompanied him to Delhi in command of his army. Then followed an obscure intrigue in which the Mahrattas expelled Najaf Khan and restored Zabita Khan to the post of Amir of Amirs. Next another intrigue, in which Zabita Khan fled to the Jats, and Najaf Khan took a part in the war against the Rohillas. Najaf Khan formed an alliance with the Nawab Vizier of Oude, and was appointed deputy Vizier. Then followed fresh plots and fresh wars between Najaf Khan and Zabita Khan. Najaf Khan died in 1782. His son, Afrasiab Khan, is the Amir of Amirs mentioned in the text, who murdered his predecessor, and was subsequently murdered by Mahadaji Sindia. The details are told at length in Mr. Keene's Fall of the Moghul Empire.

for himself the title of "deputy of the Peishwa." Thus for the nonce he appeared at Delhi as the deputy of the Peishwa. In this capacity Mahadaji Sindia performed all the duties of an Amir of Amirs, administered the government at Delhi and Agra, commanded the rabble army of the empire, and collected tribute from Rajputs and Jats in the name of the Great Moghul.

In reality Mahadaji Sindia was founding a new Mahratta kingdom between the Ganges and Jumna, and extending Mahratta influence over an unknown region to the westward. He was raising battalions of regular sepoys, who were being trained and disciplined by a Frenchman, celebrated in after years as General De Boigne. He became inflated with his own greatness, and once again called upon the British government to pay chout for Bengal and Behar. In reply he was told that the demand was a violation of the treaty of Salbai. The rebuff smote him with apprehension; and both Sindia and Shah Alam sent a solemn disavowal of the demand to Calcutta under their respective seals.

At this time the dominant feeling of the English was alarm at the French. The war between Great Britain and France had been brought to a close in 1784 by the treaty of Versailles; but there was constant expectation of a renewal of hostilities; and for many years the English were discovering or imagining French intrigues at almost every court in India. A French agent was already residing at Poona. Accordingly an English agent, Mr. Charles Malet, was posted to Poona to look after English interests and frustrate French designs.

The dignity of Mahadaji Sindia was hurt by this proceeding. He had been guarantee to the treaty of Salbai, and considered himself the sole agent in all transactions between the Mahrattas and the English. He was quieted by the assurance that Mr. Malet would send all correspondence between the Peishwa and the Governor-General through the Resident in attendance at his camp. Moreover, in order to smooth the ruffled feathers of the Mahratta, Mr. Malet was

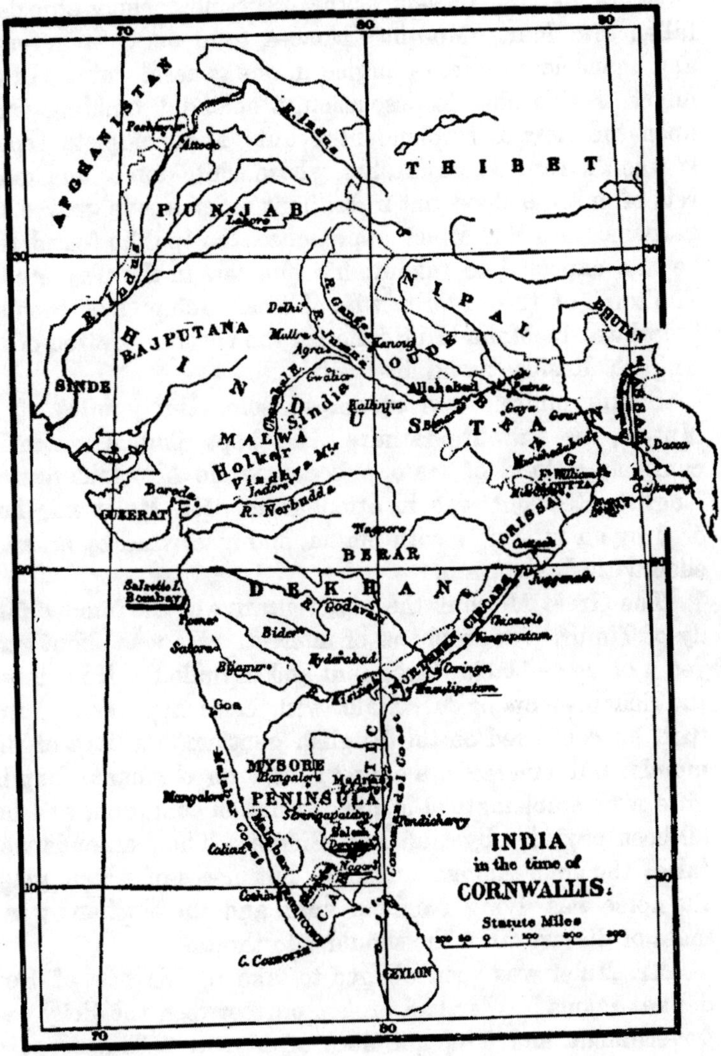

INDIA in the time of CORNWALLIS.

sent to the camp of Sindia, in the neighborhood of Agra, to arrange matters with Mr. Anderson.

Agra in 1785 presented the most melancholy objects of fallen grandeur. Mosques, palaces, gardens, caravanserais, and mausoleums were mingled in one general ruin. In the midst of this chaotic desolation, a splendid building burst upon the view in resplendent beauty and complete repair. It was the famous Taj Mahal, whose white domes and minarets of marble stood out in brilliant relief above groves and gardens. As Mr. Malet approached the spot he found that he was expected to take up his quarters in the Taj Mahal. The tomb of the favorite wife of Shah Jehan had been appropriated by Mahadaji Sindia for the accommodation of the English Resident and his retinue.

Sindia himself was encamped some thirty miles off at Muttra, the ancient Mathura. He kept Shah Alam in his camp as a kind of state prisoner, while Mr. Anderson as English Resident was in attendance. Mr. Malet was honored by an interview with Sindia, and afterward by an audience with Shah Alam.

The Great Moghul, the representative of the famous family of Timur, was an object of interest. He was about sixty years of age—placid, benignant and dignified. He received the rich presents of Mr. Malet with calm approval. In return he conferred on the English gentleman a tiara of diamonds and emeralds, a charger, and an elephant; but his gifts were emblematical of his own fallen condition, and had all been provided by Mahadaji Sindia. The diamonds were false; the emeralds were nothing but pieces of green glass; the horse was dying from old age; and the elephant was a mass of disease from the shoulder to the tail.

Mr. Malet was soon obliged to take up his post of Resident at Poona. War had broken out between the Peishwa's government and Tippu, Sultan of Mysore. The dread of Tippu was very strong, and the Brahman government of the Peishwa formed an alliance with Nizam Ali against Tippu; and Nizam Ali, notwithstanding his Muhammadan faith, eagerly helped the Mahrattas against the dangerous Sultan of Mysore. It was expected that the British government would furnish help in like manner. But the English were bound by the treaty of Salbai not to help the enemies of the Mahrattas; and they were equally bound by the treaty of Mangalore not to help the enemies of Tippu. The question of the day was, whether Tippu Sultan had not himself broken the treaty of Mangalore by forming an alliance with the French, who were the avowed enemies of the English; and this question was not solved until a later period in the history.

When Hastings returned to England in 1785, he left a Mr. Macpherson to act as Governor-General. At this time it was decided that the future Governor-General should not be a servant of the Company, but a nobleman of rank. Lord Macartney was offered the post, but declined it; and in 1786 Lord Cornwallis landed at Calcutta as Governor-General and Macpherson passed away.

The introduction of an English nobleman in the place of a merchant ruler produced beneficial results. Vansittart and Hastings had been powerless to effect reforms which touched the pockets of the servants of the Company. Indeed, Hastings had been often driven to distribute contracts and sinecures in order to secure personal support. But Lord Cornwallis was strong enough, by virtue of his rank as an English peer, to abolish all such abuses. He even forced the Court of Directors to replace the system of perquisites by that of large salaries. At the same time his respectability of character elevated the tone of English society at Calcutta. Under Warren Hastings there had been painful scandals in high quarters; while gambling had risen to such a pitch that within one month Philip Francis won twenty thousand pounds at whist from Barwell. But under the severe and stately morality of Lord Cornwallis excesses of every description were discountenanced; and the increasing number of ladies from Europe introduced a refinement and decorum which had long been wanting.

Lord Cornwallis carried out a startling change in the land settlement. He abolished the system of leases, granted the lands in perpetuity to the Zemindars, and fixed a yearly rental for the several estates which was never to be enhanced. The details of this important measure were worked out by Mr. Shore, afterward known as Sir John Shore and ultimately as Lord Teignmouth. Mr. Shore argued, however, that a change which was to last for all futurity should not be made irrevocable until further inquiries had been made as to the value of the land, the nature of the different tenures, and the rights of landlords and tenants as represented by Zemindars and Ryots. He proposed that the settlement should be made for ten years, and then declared permanent if it proved satisfactory. Lord Cornwallis's views, however, were referred to the ministers in England, and after some delay the perpetual settlement became the law of the land.

To this day the good and evil effects of the perpetual land settlement are matters of controversy. It raised the condition of Zemindars from that of tax collectors to that of landed proprietors; but it did not raise them to the position of a landed aristocracy, capable of administering patriarchal justice among their tenantry, or of legislating for the welfare of the masses. It proved an immediate relief to the Zemindars, but opened out no prospects of relief to Ryots or farmers. Worst of all, as the rental of land is the backbone of the Indian revenue, it fixed the limit of the recepits of government, without making provision for the future requirements of the country, when military defences would call for a larger expenditure, and the wants of advancing civilization would be pressed upon the attention of government. Consequently the permanence of the landed settlement tended to fossilize the people of Bengal, until an English education broke the trammels of ages, and opened out new careers of advancement to the rising generation.

Lord Cornwallis carried out a thorough reform in the administration of justice. He separated the judicial branch from the revenue branch by restricting the English collectors to their fiscal duties, and appointing a separate class of English magistrates and judges. He appointed magistrates to towns and districts to deal with civil and criminal cases. He established courts of appeal in the four cities of Calcutta, Dacca, Murshedabad, and Patna; each court consisting of a judge, a registrar, and qualified assistants. These courts of appeal disposed of all civil cases, with a final appeal to the Sudder court at Calcutta, which was nominally composed of the Governor-General and members of council. The same courts also held a jail delivery twice every year, by going on circuit in their several circles for the trial of criminal cases committed by the district magistrates.

Meanwhile Mahadaji Sindia received a check in Hindustan. Shah Alam suddenly left the camp at Muttra and returned to Delhi. The Muhammadan party at Delhi persuaded the imbecile old prince that his imperial sovereignty had been insulted by the Mahrattas. They stirred up the Rajput princes to revolt against Sindia. They carried on secret intrigues with the Muhammadan officers in Sindia's army. The result was that when Mahadaji Sindia attempted to suppress the Rajput revolt, the Muhammadans in his army deserted him in a body and joined the Rajput rebels. In a moment he lost all his acquisitions between the Jumna and the Ganges. He was reduced to worse straits than when he had fled from the battle of Paniput more than a quarter of a century before. He had no alternative but to fall back on Gwalior, and implore Nana Farnavese to send him reinforcements from Poona.

But Shah Alam had soon cause to lament the absence of Mahratta protection. Zabita Khan, the Rohilla ex-Amir of Amirs, died in 1785. In 1788 his son, Gholam Kadir, entered Delhi with a band of freebooters, and took possession of the city and palace. The atrocities perpetrated by these miscreants in the palace of the Great Moghul reduced the wretched pageant and his family to the lowest depths of misery and despair. Gholam Kadir plundered and insulted the aged Padishah, smoked his hookah on the imperial throne, forced princesses to dance and play before him, and scourged and tortured princes and ladies in the hope of discovering hidden treasures. In one mad fit of passion at the supposed concealment of money or jewels, he threw Shah Alam on the ground and destroyed his eyes with a dagger. For two months this infamous ruffian and his barbarous followers ran riot in the palace, and there was no one to deliver the helpless family of the Great Moghul from their unbridled excesses.[1]

Nana Farnavese at Poona was agitated by conflicting passions. He was jealous of the growing power of Mahadaji Sindia, but anxious to maintain the Mahratta ascendency to the northward. He determined to play Holkar against Sindia. He sent reinforcements to Sindia under the command of Tukaji Holkar, accompanied by a kinsman of the infant Peishwa, named Ali Bahadur;[2] but he insisted that all territories acquired to the northward of the Chambal river should be equally shared by the Peishwa and Holkar, as well as by Sindia.

Thus reinforced Mahadaji Sindia marched to Delhi with the allied army of Mahrattas, and was hailed by the Muhammadan population with the greatest joy. The wretched inmates of the imperial palace were delivered from their

---

[1] It is to be hoped that Gholam Kadir and his followers are not fair types of the Rohilla Afghans, who were so much praised by Lord Macaulay. Gholam Kadir was the son of Zabita Khan and grandson of Najib-ud-daula. The outrages which he committed at Delhi were the outcome of the struggle for supremacy at the Moghul court between the families of Najib-ud-daula the Rohilla, Najaf Khan the Persian, and Mahadaji Sindia the Mahratta. See ante, p. 379, note.

[2] The kinship between a Muhammadan like Ali Bahadur and a Brahman like the Peishwa is the outcome of the laxity of Mahratta courts. The father of Ali Bahadur was the son of Baji Rao, the second Peishwa, by a Muhammadan woman. According to Hindu law, the offspring of such illicit unions belonged to the same caste as their mother; and in this case caste was equivalent to religion.

Ali Bahadur was associated with a military Guru, or soldier-saint, named Himmut Bahadur, who commanded a large force of Gosains, or religious devotees, in the army of Mahadaji Sindia. Subsequently Ali Bahadur deserted Sindia, and was instigated by Himmut Bahadur to attempt the conquest of Bundelkund. Ultimately Himmut Bahadur, the spiritual teacher and military leader of the army of yellow-robed Gosains, went over to the English during the second Mahratta war.

misery. Gholam Kadir fled at the approach of the Mahrattas, but was captured and put to death with horrible tortures.

About this time the proceedings of Tippu of Mysore began to excite the serious alarm of the English. This prince, unlike his father Hyder Ali, was a bigoted Muhammadan of the persecuting type. He committed horrible ravages in the Malabar country, and converted thousands of Hindus and Brahmans to the Muhammadan religion by forcibly subjecting them to the rite of circumcision. He asserted a sovereign authority far beyond that of any other native ruler in India. The Nawab Vizier of Oude, and even the Peishwa of the Mahratta empire, continued to acknowledge the Moghul Padishah as the suzerain of Hindustan. But Tippu threw away every pretence of dependence on the Great Moghul, and boldly assumed the independent and sovereign title of Sultan of Mysore.

In 1787 Tippu Sultan took fright at some military reforms of Lord Cornwallis, and hastily made peace with the Mahrattas and Nizam Ali. At the same time he was known to be a bitter enemy of the English, and to be in secret communication with the French at Pondicherry; and he was naturally regarded by the English as a dangerous enemy, who was not to be bound by treaties, and who might at any moment take advantage of a war with France to invade and plunder the Carnatic as his father had done before him.

By the treaty of Mangalore the Hindu Raja of Travancore, to the south of Malabar, had been placed under British protection. But the Raja was in terror of Tippu Sultan. He purchased two towns from the Dutch on his northern frontier, and built a wall of defence which was known as "the lines of Travancore." Tippu declared that the two towns belonged to the Raja of Cochin, who was his vassal. The Raja of Travancore refused to resign them, and applied to the British government for protection. Lord Cornwallis ordered an inquiry to be made into the merits of the case, and Tippu to be informed that the British government would defend the rights of the Raja; and at the same time he desired the Madras government to make the necessary preparations for war.

Unfortunately the Madras government was at this time as corrupt and demoralized as it had been in the days of Hyder Ali. A Company's servant named Holland had been appointed Governor of Madras. Holland was deeply implicated in loans to the Nawab of the Carnatic; and he set the Governor-General at defiance, refused to make preparations for the coming war, and appropriated the revenues of the Carnatic to the payment of the Nawab's debts. Finally he wrote to the Raja of Travancore, offering to help him with a British detachment, on condition of receiving a present for himself of a lakh of pagodas, or some thirty-five thousand pounds sterling.

Meanwhile Tippu attacked the lines of Travancore, but, to his utter surprise, he was repulsed by the Hindu army of Travancore. Accordingly he ordered a battering train from Seringapatam, and called for reinforcements from every quarter. At this news Lord Cornwallis resolved to take the field. But Holland was incorrigible. He provided no cattle, but proposed to appoint commissioners to settle all differences with Tippu. Lord Cornwallis was much exasperated, and Holland fled from his post and embarked for England.

Lord Cornwallis now resolved on forming alliances with Nizam Ali and the Mahrattas against Tippu; but the British authorities in India were prohibited by Mr. Pitt's bill of 1784 from making any more alliances with native princes. Lord Cornwallis violated the letter of the act, but respected its spirit by providing that the treaties should cease to have effect after the conclusion of the war.

Negotiations with Nizam Ali were comparatively easy. He was anxious for the humiliation of Tippu, and he was still more anxious for British protection against the Mahrattas, who claimed vast sums of money from him, under the head of arrears of chout. He would gladly have secured the permanent protection of the English government against the Mahrattas; but this could not be granted by the English government, without giving mortal offence to the Mahrattas. Accordingly Nizam Ali was obliged to be content with the British guarantee for the protection of his territories until the conclusion of the war; and in return he promised to join the English army with ten thousand horsemen.

The Peishwa's government professed equal readiness to join the English army against Tippu with another body of ten thousand horsemen. But Nana Farnavese secretly played a double game. He entertained Tippu's envoys at Poona, and delayed the march of the Mahratta contingent for several months, in the hope of inducing Tippu to purchase the neutrality of the Peishwa's government by a large cession of territory.

Mahadaji Sindia was equally anxious to render the war against Tippu subservient to his own individual interests. He offered to join the confederation against Tippu, provided the British government would guarantee him in possession of the territories he had acquired in Hindustan, and help him to conquer the princes of Rajputana. Lord Cornwallis was obviously unable to accede to such conditions. Accordingly Mahadaji Sindia refused to take any part in the war against Tippu.

In 1790 the war began with a campaign under General Medows, who had been appointed Governor of Madras and commander-in-chief of the Madras army. But its operations were futile, and Lord Cornwallis proceeded to Madras and took the command in person. Meanwhile Tippu had desolated the Carnatic, and proceeded toward the south in the hope of procuring a French force from Pondicherry.

In 1791 Lord Cornwallis advanced through the Carnatic to the Mysore country, and captured the fortress of Bangalore. Up to this date neither of his native allies had joined him. Nizam Ali would not leave his frontier until he heard that Tippu had gone away to the south; and then, when he entered Mysore, it was not to fight but to plunder. When he heard of the fall of Bangalore, he joined the force of Lord Cornwallis. His cavalry had good horses and showy costumes, but were disorderly, undisciplined, and unfitted for field duties; and they only helped to consume the grain and forage. Meanwhile, for reasons stated, the Mahratta contingent of the Peishwa never appeared at all.

The result of the campaign of 1791 was that Lord Cornwallis advanced toward Seringapatam, and was then compelled to retreat from sheer want of supplies and carriage bullocks. Shortly afterward he was joined by a Mahratta force under Hari Pant. Had the Mahrattas come up a week earlier they might have changed the fate of the campaign. They had abundance of supplies, but were imbued with the spirit of hucksters, and refused to part with grain or provisions of any kind to their English allies excepting at exorbitant prices. They had done nothing but rob and ravage the Mysore country from the day they left their frontier; and the bazar in their camp was stored with the plunder of towns—English broadcloths, Birmingham cutlery, Kashmir shawls and costly jewelry, as well as with oxen, sheep, and poultry. Yet Hari Pant pleaded poverty, and demanded a loan of fourteen lakhs of rupees; and Lord Cornwallis was forced to give him the money, not on account of his services, but to prevent the Mahratta contingent from deserting to Tippu.

In 1792 Lord Cornwallis renewed the campaign in Mysore on a scale which had not been seen in India since the days of Aurangzeb. He engaged large numbers of Brinjarries, the hereditary carriers of India, who have already been described under the name of Manaris.[1] His infantry, battering train, field-pieces, and baggage moved in three parallel columns, followed by a hundred wagons loaded with liquors, and sixty thousand bullocks loaded with provisions. The resources of the English struck the natives of India with awe; and Tippu is said to have exclaimed, "I do not fear what I see, but what I do not see."

Lord Cornwallis was soon joined by the gaudily dressed horsemen of Nizam Ali, and a small force of Hari Pant's

[1] See ante, p. 224.

Mahrattas; and after a long march at last drew up his artillery on a rising ground which commanded Seringapatam. Tippu had constructed three lines of earthworks, protected by three hundred pieces of cannon, and covered by a bound hedge of thorny plants. British valor carried the defences by storm, and British cannon were soon playing on the fortifications of Seringapatam.

Tippu was bewildered and confounded. His losses in killed and wounded were severe, and the levies whom he had pressed into his service deserted him in large numbers. He saw that nothing but prompt submission could save his throne. He suddenly accepted the terms which had been offered by Lord Cornwallis, namely, to cede a moiety of his territories, to be equally divided between the English, the Nizam, and the Peishwa; to pay three millions sterling toward the expenses of the war; and to deliver up his two sons as hostages for the fulfilment of the terms. In after years it was discovered that the sudden submission of Tippu had defeated the treacherous intentions of the Mahrattas and Nizam Ali. Both were engaged in a clandestine correspondence with Tippu, but both were checkmated by the arrival of his sons as hostages in the camp of the English army.

The Mysore war marks a change in the policy of the British government. Lord Cornwallis had undertaken it to protect the Raja of Travancore from the Mysore Sultan, but his main objects were to cripple the power of Tippu, to sever his connection with the French, and to shut him out of the Carnatic. The policy of political isolation, which had been enjoined by the English parliament, the Board of Control, and the Court of Directors, had proved a failure. Accordingly Lord Cornwallis proposed to go a step further: to keep the peace in India in the same way that it was supposed to be kept in Europe, namely, by a balance of power. With this view he sought to convert the confederation of the English, the Nizam, and the Peishwa against Tippu into a basis for a balance of power, in which the British government should hold the scales.

But there was a fatal obstacle to such a political system. There was not a government in India, excepting that of the British, that cared for the maintenance of the public peace, or hesitated to disturb it at any moment for the promotion of some immediate and individual advantage. Indeed Warren Hastings had reported, ten years before, that the want of faith among native states, and the blind selfishness with which they pursued their individual schemes of aggrandizement, regardless of the obligations of treaties or the interests of allies, had rendered such a balance of power as was possible in Europe altogether impossible in India.

The result of Lord Cornwallis's negotiations was that Nizam Ali was willing to join in any confederation which would protect him from the Mahratta claims; while the Mahrattas refused to join in any alliance which would hamper their demands for chout upon Nizam Ali or any one else. But English statesmen at home had been charmed with the scheme for keeping the peace in India by a balance of power. They could not abandon the political idea; and for years it haunted their imaginations, and perverted public opinion as regards the government of India.

As if further to show the impossibility of a balance of power, Mahadaji Sindia and Nana Farnavese took opposite views of the British government. Sindia contended that the English had become too powerful in India, and that it would be necessary to support Tippu as a counterpoise. The Nana, on the other hand, was anxious to gain the help of the British government against Mahadaji Sindia; but he insisted on the right of the Peishwa to claim arrears of chout, not only from Nizam Ali, but from Tippu Sultan. Lord Cornwallis was thus obliged to abandon his political project in despair.

In 1792 Mahadaji Sindia had grown to enormous power. He had augmented his French battalions under De Boigne, and raised his standing forces to eighteen thousand regular infantry, six thousand irregulars, two thousand irregular horse, and six hundred Persian cavalry, besides a large train of artillery. This military power was accompanied by territorial aggrandizement, for it was maintained by formal grants of land revenue in the Doab, to the westward of Oude, which Sindia procured from Shah Alam as the Great Moghul.[1] At the same time Agra was becoming a most important fortress in the hands of Mahadaji Sindia; it was a depot of cannon and arms, and a stronghold which commanded upper Hindustan.

In 1792 Mahadaji Sindia marched an army from Delhi to Poona to confer the hereditary title of "deputy of the Great Moghul" upon the young Peishwa. Nana Farnavese tried to prevent the Peishwa from accepting the post; it was opposed, he said, to the constitution of the Mahratta empire. It was indeed a strange anomaly for the Brahman suzerain of the Mahratta confederacy to accept the post of deputy to an effete Muhammadan pageant like Shah Alam. But Sindia insisted, and Nana Farnavese was obliged to give way. The empty ceremony was accordingly celebrated with the utmost pomp and magnificence at Poona.

Mahadaji Sindia sought to allay all suspicions of his ambitious designs by a mock humility which imposed on no one. His father, Ranuji Sindia, claimed to be the hereditary head man, or Patell, of a village; and he had been originally appointed to carry the slippers of one of the former Peishwas. Accordingly Mahadaji Sindia refused to be called by any other title but that of Patell, and ostentatiously carried the slippers of the young Peishwa at the ceremony of his installation as deputy of the Great Moghul.

But the would-be Patell and slipper holder had a keen eye for his own interests. Mahadaji Sindia demanded payment from the Peishwa's government of the expenses he had incurred in extending the Mahratta empire to the northward; and he requested that Tukaji Holkar and Ali Bahadur, who

---

[1] The Doab, or region between the two rivers, might be called the Mesopotamia of Hindustan. It lies between the Jumna and Ganges, just as Mesopotamia lies between the Tigris and Euphrates. It is impossible to draw a line of strict demarcation at this period between the territories of the Great Moghul and those of the Nawab Vizier of Oude.

had been sent to his assistance after his retreat to Gwalior, might be recalled from Hindustan to Poona.

But Mahadaji Sindia met his match in Nana Farnavese. The Brahman statesman, who had been schooled in diplomacy at Poona, was not to be foiled by the son of a Patell. Nana Farnavese called upon Mahadaji Sindia to produce the revenue accounts of the territories in the Doab and elsewhere, which he had acquired for his sovereign master the Peishwa. Sindia had conquered these territories with the utmost ease, and enjoyed them for a considerable period; and the astute Mahratta minister urged, with some show of reason, that it was high time that the servant should pay the revenue into the treasury of his master.[1]

While Sindia and the Nana were plotting against each other at Poona, hostilities were breaking out between the armies of Sindia and Holkar in Hindustan. There had been a quarrel over some plunder, and Tukaji Holkar had been defeated by De Boigne, the French general in the service of Sindia, and compelled to retire to his capital at Indore. At this crisis the rivalry between Mahadaji Sindia and Nana Farnavese was brought to a close by death. Mahadaji Sindia expired at Poona in February, 1794, and was succeeded by a boy of fourteen, afterward known as Daulat Rao Sindia. Thus Nana Farnavese was left without a rival in the Mahratta empire.

Meanwhile there was peace and prosperity in Bengal. In 1793 the permanent land settlement was promulgated, and Lord Cornwallis returned to England, leaving Sir John Shore, the servant of the Company, to succeed him in the post of Governor-General. Important events were occurring

---

[1] The rivalry between Sindia and Nana Farnavese furnishes a strange instance of the instability of native alliances. Sindia had rescued the Nana from the grasp of the conspirators, including Tukaji Holkar and his confederates, who were plotting to restore Rughonath Rao to the throne of the Peishwa. Since then Tukaji Holkar had been appointed, as the faithful ally of Nana Farnavese, to the command of the troops which were at once to support Sindia and to check his growing power. In reality Holkar was sent because of his known rivalry to Sindia; and it will be seen from the text that this rivalry culminated in a battle between Tukaji Holkar and Sindia's force under De Boigne.

in Europe; Great Britain had declared war against France and the French revolution; and the British authorities in India took possession of Pondicherry for the third time in Indian history.

Sir John Shore was a model Indian civilian, free from all suspicion of corruption—honorable, honest, high-minded, and of undoubted industry and capacity. He was the real author of the land settlement, for Lord Cornwallis can only claim the credit of making it perpetual. The British ministry were so impressed with his merits that he was knighted, and appointed to succeed Lord Cornwallis as Governor-General. But he knew little of the history of the world, and was apparently blind to the significance of political events in India.

At this time the progress of affairs at Poona and Hyderabad was exciting universal alarm. The Mahrattas insisted on a final settlement of their claims on Nizam Ali for arrears of chout. They had been put off for years by the war against Tippu, and the evasions and procrastinations of Nizam Ali; and after the conclusion of peace with Tippu they became more pressing in their demands for an immediate settlement. Nizam Ali could neither pay the money, nor hope to repel the Mahratta invasion. In sore distress he implored the help of the English against the Mahrattas, but Sir John Shore declined to interfere. Indeed the British parliament and Court of Directors had strictly enjoined a policy of non-interference. Sir John Shore was fully alive to existing dangers. He saw that, without the interference of the British government, Nizam Ali would be crushed by the Mahrattas. He also saw that the destruction of Nizam Ali would remove the last check on the growing power of the Mahrattas, and leave the British government without an ally of any weight to resist Mahratta encroachments. But Sir John Shore was the last man to disobey orders; and he persistently refused to protect Nizam Ali.

Nizam Ali, losing all hope of help from the English, had

naturally sought it from the French. Forty years before, his elder brother, Salabut Jung, owed his throne to the French, and maintained himself against the Mahrattas, as well as against all domestic rivals, solely by the aid of Bussy and the French. Accordingly Nizam Ali entertained a Frenchman, named Raymond, who had originally served in the army of Hyder Ali, and who raised a force of sepoy battalions, trained and disciplined by French officers. In the beginning of 1795 Nizam Ali possessed an army of twenty-three battalions of regulars commanded by Raymond. He was now independent of the English, and ceased to be afraid of the Mahrattas.

The Peishwa's government demanded arrears of chout to the amount of nearly three millions sterling. The accounts were swelled by high rates of interest and other exasperating items. They were drawn up with much precision and nicety by Mahratta Brahmans, and were perplexing, if not unintelligible, to every one else. A Mahratta envoy carried the accounts to Hyderabad, and requested payment. The Muhammadan minister of the Nizam treated the Mahratta with haughty insolence. He told the envoy in open durbar that Nana Farnavese must come in person to Hyderabad to explain the items; and that if he refused to come he must be brought. This threat was regarded by both sides as a declaration of war.

Nizam Ali was puffed up with hopes of victory. The dancing-girls glorified his triumphs in prophetic songs. The soldiers boasted that they would sack and plunder Poona. The minister at Hyderabad was a Muhammadan like his master; and he bragged that no treaty should be concluded with the Mahrattas until the Brahman Peishwa had been sent on pilgrimage to Benares, to mutter his incantations on the banks of the Ganges, with a cloth about his loins and a pot of water in his hand.

The Mahrattas were one and all eager for the war. All the feudatories of the empire—Sindia and Holkar, the Gaekwar and the Bhonsla; and even the smaller chieftains of the southern Mahratta country—were burning to share in a settlement of the Mahratta claims. For the last time in Mahratta history the summons of the Peishwa was obeyed throughout the length and breadth of the Mahratta dominion.

The decisive battle was fought near the small fortress of Kurdla in March, 1795. The Nizam's cavalry were routed with rockets and artillery, but the French battalions under Raymond stood their ground. Nizam Ali, however, was seized with a panic from the outset. He fled to the fortress of Kurdla, repeatedly calling on Raymond to follow him. The bulk of his troops dispersed in all directions, plundering the baggage of their own army as they fled from the field. The banditti in the Mahratta army, known as Pindharies, rushed after the fugitives and stripped them of their ill-gotten spoil; while the Mahrattas swarmed round the fortress of Kurdla, animated by the thought that the Nizam and all his treasures were within their grasp.

Nizam Ali held out for two days in the fortress of Kurdla; then yielded to every demand. He surrendered his offending minister, ceded nearly half his territory, and pledged himself to liquidate the whole of the Mahratta claims.

The victory of Kurdla raised Nana Farnavese to the height of prosperity; but within six months he was plunged in a vortex of distractions, which wellnigh worked his ruin.

The Peishwa, Mahdu Rao Narain, had reached his twenty-first year. He had all his life been kept in galling tutelage by Nana Farnavese, and saw no hope of throwing off the yoke and exercising his sovereign rights as Peishwa of the Mahratta empire. In a fit of despair he threw himself from a terrace of the palace, and died two days afterward.

The nearest kinsman was Baji Rao, son of the Rughonath Rao whom the English had supported in the first Mahratta war. Baji Rao was at this time a young man of twenty; but had long been kept in confinement by Nana Farnavese.

He was too old and too cunning to be a puppet; and the unscrupulous minister was anxious to override his claims by prevailing on the widow of the dead Peishwa to adopt a son. But Baji Rao, within the walls of his prison, was already engaged in a counter-plot. He tried to play Sindia against Nana Farnavese. He secretly opened a correspondence with the young Daulat Rao Sindia, and promised to cede him a large territory if Sindia would place him on the throne of Poona as the Peishwa of the Mahrattas.

Nana Farnavese discovered the plot and forestalled Sindia by releasing Baji Rao and declaring him to be Peishwa. But the minister could not trust the new Peishwa, and the new Peishwa could not trust the minister, until Nana Farnavese had taken the most solemn oaths on the tail of a cow to be faithful to Baji Rao, and Baji Rao had taken oaths equally solemn to keep Nana Farnavese at the head of the administration.

The plots which followed are tortuous and bewildering. Daulat Rao Sindia marched an army to Poona. Nana Farnavese fled to Satara, under pretence of procuring the insignia of investiture from the pageant Maharaja. Baji Rao came to terms with Daulat Rao Sindia by promising to pay him a sum of two millions sterling. All this while, in spite of oaths and promises, and in spite of his being a Hindu and a Brahman, Baji Rao sent messengers to Nizam Ali, the Muhammadan ruler at Hyderabad, imploring his help against both Sindia and the Nana, and promising to restore all the territory ceded after the battle of Kurdla, and to forego the balance due on the Mahratta claims.

These plots threw the city of Poona into tumult and anarchy. Nana Farnavese was induced to return to Poona, and to pay a visit to Daulat Rao Sindia; but he was treacherously seized and thrown into prison with all his chief partisans. Parties of Mahratta soldiers were sent off to plunder the houses of the imprisoned chieftains. They found the doors barricaded, and the inmates posted with arms at the windows and on the roof. The firing was incessant and spread universal alarm; and there was nothing but uproar, plunder and bloodshed throughout the city.

Sindia next demanded his two millions of Baji Rao, and was told to plunder Poona. Sindia took the hint and plundered the capital of his suzerain without mercy. All the wealthy inhabitants were scourged and tortured until they had given up their hoarded treasures. In the end Baji Rao made an attempt to entrap Sindia, by inviting him to the palace for the purpose of murdering him; but his heart failed him at the last moment, and he hesitated to give the necessary signal to the assassins. Accordingly Sindia left the palace without injury, but not without suspicions; and henceforth he was more distrustful than ever of the good faith of Baji Rao.

Sir John Shore was not the man to deal with such distractions. The Mahratta empire was breaking up, and non-intervention would not solve the problem. A statesman of European experience and original genius was required to deal with the crisis; a man of stronger brain and firmer will. At the same time a dangerous disaffection broke out in the English army in Bengal. Sir John Shore was devoid of all military experience, and found that he had not nerve enough to suppress the growing disorders, and he requested the Court of Directors to send out a successor.

Before Sir John Shore returned to England, he was forced to give his attention to the state of Oude. The administration was at once weak and oppressive. The money wrung from the Ryots was withheld by the Talukdars,[1] or squandered in wasteful luxury at the capital; while nothing but the presence of the British battalions prevented the whole country from being overrun by the Mahrattas. Sir John Shore remonstrated with the Nawab Vizier, but only wasted his words. Asof-ud-daula died in 1797, and Sir John Shore

---

[1] The Talukdars of Oude corresponded generally to the Zemindars in Bengal, but in some cases they were mere collectors of revenue, while others corresponded to a feudal nobility. Under the rule of a Nawab Vizier it is impossible to say what they were.

recognized a certain Vizier Ali as his successor. Subsequently it turned out that Vizier Ali was illegitimate, and that Saadut Ali, the brother of the late ruler, was the legitimate and rightful Nawab Vizier. Accordingly Vizier Ali was pensioned off and sent to reside at Benares. Saadut Ali was placed upon the throne and effected a change in the aspect of affairs. He devoted his energies to hoarding up the revenues which his predecessors had been accustomed to squander on their pleasures.

In March, 1798, Sir John Shore, now Lord Teignmouth, embarked at Calcutta for Europe. Meanwhile a Governor-General was coming out to India of a very different stamp. At first he was only known as Lord Mornington, but, in the history of British India, he is more widely known by his later title of Marquis of Wellesley.

CHAPTER VIII

MYSORE AND CARNATIC—WELLESLEY

A.D. 1798 TO 1801

LORD MORNINGTON landed at Calcutta in the thirty-eighth year of his age. At the time he left England he had three objects in view; namely, to drive the French out of India, to revive the confederacy with Nizam Ali and the Peishwa against Tippu of Mysore, and to establish the balance of power which Lord Cornwallis had failed to create and which was still the darling object of the English ministry.

At this time the hatred of the British nation toward the revolutionary government in France had risen to fever heat. The reign of terror, the horrors of the guillotine, the execution of Louis the Sixteenth and Marie Antoinette, the rise of Napoleon, and the threatened invasion of England, had stirred up depths of antagonism which later generations can scarcely realize. The new Governor-General shared in the national sentiment, but his wrath was mingled with alarm as he heard that one army of French sepoys was in the service of Nizam Ali; that another French army was in the service of Daulat Rao Sindia; and that Tippu Sultan, the hereditary enemy of the British nation, was entertaining French officers, and courting a French alliance which might endanger British power in India.

But Lord Mornington soon discovered that while it was possible to revive the old confederation against Tippu, it was utterly impossible to frame a network of alliances which would establish a balance of power, and maintain the peace of India on the basis of international relations. Indeed the progress of events had rendered such a task still more hopeless in 1798 than it had been in 1792. In 1792 the Nizam and the Peishwa were at any rate substantive states, although they could not be formed into trustworthy allies. But in 1798 the power of the Nizam was shattered by his humiliation at Kurdla; while the Peishwa's government was distracted by the dissensions between Baji Rao, Daulat Rao Sindia, and Nana Farnavese. Accordingly, the idea of a balance of power was abandoned; and Lord Mornington saw that the work before him was to secure the disbandment of the French battalions and to revive the confederation against Tippu.

Lord Mornington began with the Nizam. There was little difficulty, except what arose from the alarms, the prevarications, and the fickle temperament of Nizam Ali himself. In the end, Nizam Ali agreed to disband his French battalions, and to maintain an English force in their room, with the understanding that the British government would mediate in the Mahratta claims, and, if necessary, protect him against the Mahrattas. Nizam Ali further pledged himself to take no Frenchman or other European into his service without the consent of the British government. Finally, he promised to furnish a contingent force to serve in the coming war against Tippu.

The disbandment of the French battalions at Hyderabad was attended with anxiety, but carried out without bloodshed. An English force was on the ground. The disbandment was proclaimed, and then the French sepoys broke out in mutiny for arrears of pay, and the French officers fled for protection to the English lines. The French sepoys were reassured by the discharge of their pay and arrears, and submitted to their fate; and within a few hours the French battalions had melted away.

Lord Mornington also opened negotiations with the Mahrattas, but he found them impracticable. Baji Rao and Nana Farnavese had become reconciled; for both were Brahmans, and both were threatened by Daulat Rao Sindia. But they

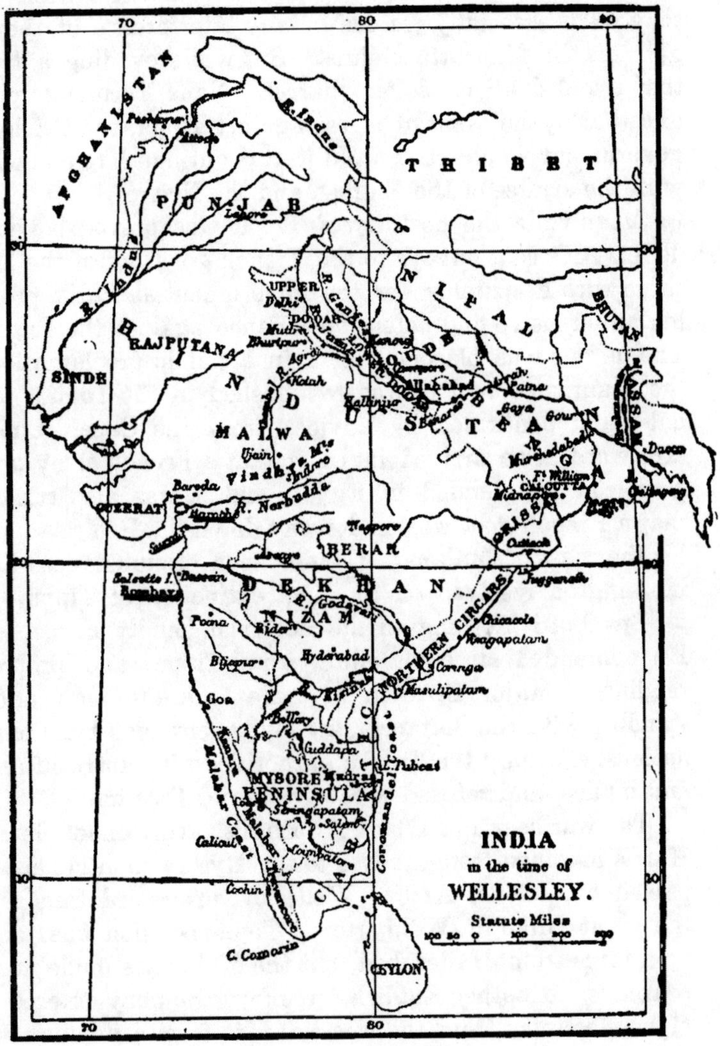
AFGHANISTAN
Peshawur
Attock
R. Indus
THIBET
PUNJAB
Lahore
NIPAL
BHUTAN
UPPER
Delhi
DOAB
R. Ganges
R. Jumna
Muttra
Bhurtpur
RAJPUTANA
HINDUSTAN
SINDE
Agra
Kanouj
OUDE
Cawnpore
Allahabad
Patna
Kotah
Kallinjur
Benares
Gaya
Gour
MALWA
Ujjain
Vindhya Mts
Indore
Dacca
Ft. William
CALCUTTA
Midnapore
Chittagong
Baroda
GUZERAT
R. Narbudda
Nagpore
BERAR
ORISSA
Cuttack
Juggernath
Salsette I.
Bassein
Bombay
DEKHAN
R. Godavari
NIZAM
Poona
Bider
Chicacole
Vizagapatam
Hyderabad
Coringa
NORTHERN CIRCARS
R. Kistna
Masulipatam
Goa
Bellary
Cuddapa
Pulicat
Malabar Coast
Coromandel Coast
MYSORE
Madras
PENINSULA
Seringapatam
Salem
Calicut
Coimbatore
Cochin
Travancore
C. Comorin
CEYLON
INDIA
in the time of
WELLESLEY.
Statute Miles
70
80
90
30
20
10

would not form a close connection with the English; they were jealous of the English alliance with the Nizam; and they were especially jealous of any interference of the English in the Mahratta claims. But while evading a treaty they avoided all cause for quarrel. Nana Farnavese promised that in the event of a war against Tippu, the Peishwa's government would send a Mahratta contingent to co-operate with the armies of the English and the Nizam.

Meanwhile the hostility of Tippu was proved beyond a doubt. He sent envoys to the French governor of the Mauritius with despatches for the government at Paris, proposing an offensive and defensive alliance against the English. The matter was blazoned forth in a public proclamation at the Mauritius; and it was republished in the Indian journals, and confirmed by advices from the Cape. Shortly afterward news arrived in India that a French army under Napoleon had landed in Egypt; and it was also rumored that a French fleet was on its way down the Red Sea bound for the coast of Malabar. Under such circumstances Lord Mornington resolved on the final extinction of Tippu.

But Lord Mornington did not rush blindly into a war. He demanded an explanation from Tippu, and proposed sending a Major Doveton to come to a thorough understanding with the Sultan. But Tippu sent back lame explanations, charging the French authorities with untruthfulness and malice, and refused to receive Major Doveton.

The war began in 1799. An English army under General Harris marched from Madras to the Mysore country, accompanied by Colonel Arthur Wellesley, afterward famous as the great Duke of Wellington. The expedition was joined by a force from Hyderabad, but the Mahrattas made no appearance. Another English force from Bombay entered the Mysore country from the westward, to form a junction with the Madras army.

Tippu made some efforts at resistance, but was routed and compelled to fall back on his famous capital and stronghold at Seringapatam. He seemed bewildered and infatuated as the forces from Madras and Bombay closed around him. He sued for peace, and was required to cede half his remaining territories, and to pay a sum of two millions sterling. The terms were hard, but the hearts of the English were steeled against him. They remembered his cruelties toward his English prisoners, and were enraged at his intrigues with the French. Tippu spurned the proffered conditions. "Better," he said, "to die like a soldier, than to end my days as a pensioned Nawab."

In May, 1799, the fortifications of Seringapatam were taken by storm. Tippu himself was found dead in a gateway; his remains were treated with becoming respect, and buried with funeral honors in the mausoleum of his family.

Thus fell the dynasty of Hyder Ali after a brief existence of forty years. The downfall of Tippu and capture of Seringapatam thrilled through India like the victory at Plassy. Every Englishman felt a relief; every native prince was alarmed at the rapid success of the conquerors. There were few in India to lament the fate of Tippu, excepting the members of his own family and the Muhammadans of Mysore. He was denounced as a cruel persecutor of Hindus and Christians; as a foe of the English and a friend of the French. He was not a born genius like his father Hyder Ali, but he was more zealous and consistent as a Muhammadan.

Territorial conquest in India was distasteful to the people of England. Lord Mornington was hailed as the conqueror of Tippu, and rewarded with the title of Marquis of Wellesley; but, like Lord Clive, he deemed it prudent to veil his conquest from European eyes. A part of Mysore was formed into a Hindu kingdom; and an infant representative of the extinct Hindu dynasty was taken from a hovel and placed upon the throne as Maharaja. The remaining territory was divided into three portions; one to be retained by the English; one to be given to the Nizam, who had joined in the war; and the third, under certain conditions, to be made over to the Peishwa, who had taken no part in the hostilities.

Picturesque glimpses of the Carnatic and Mysore in the year 1800 are furnished by Dr. Buchanan, who was deputed by Lord Wellesley to undertake a journey through the newly opened territories of Mysore and Malabar.

Dr. Buchanan left Madras in April, 1800, and marched toward Arcot. His journey in the first instance lay through the Company's Jaghir; and it is curious to note the changes which the Jaghir had undergone. It had been ceded to the East India Company by Muhammad Ali, Nawab of Arcot, many years previously, in return for the services rendered by the English. It extended along the Coromandel coast, north and south, from Pulicat lake to the river Palar, and inland from Madras to Conjeveram. It was thus about a hundred miles long and forty broad.

The Company's Jaghir was twice ravaged by Hyder Ali with fire and sword. The devastation was so complete that at the end of the war in 1784, there were few signs that the country had been inhabited, beyond the bones of those who had been murdered, and the naked walls of houses, temples, and choultries that had been burned. The havoc of war was succeeded by a destructive famine, which drove many of the wretched survivors to emigrate from the country.

In 1794, ten years after the war, the Company's Jaghir was formed into a collectorate under the management of Mr. Place, who was long remembered by the natives. Mr. Place retired in 1798. Two years later Dr. Buchanan was on his way from Madras to Mysore.

Dr. Buchanan found the weather very hot and dry, as is generally the case in April. After leaving the plain occupied by the white garden houses of the Europeans, Dr. Buchanan entered a level country covered with rice-fields. The roads were good, and many of the mud huts were covered with tiles, and consequently appeared better than those in Bengal.

Dr. Buchanan was struck with the resting-places and choultries which had been built for the accommodation of travellers by rich native merchants of Madras. The resting-places were mud walls four feet high, on which porters deposited their loads during intervals of rest, and took them up again without stooping. The choultries were square courts enclosed by low buildings, divided into apartments in which the poorest travellers obtained shelter from sun or rain, and a draught of water or milk without expense. In some choultries provisions were sold; in others they were distributed gratis, at least to Brahmans or other religious mendicants. The village choultry was also the place of assembly for all the head men and elders, when they met together to settle disputes or discuss other public matters.

In collecting rents in the Company's Jaghir, the crops were not kept on the ground until the rent was paid, as was the case in Bengal. On the contrary, the grain was cut, threshed, and stacked, and then sealed with clay bearing a stamp, until the cultivator paid his rent in coin or kind.

The great water-tank of Saymbrumbaukum on the road to Conjeveram was then as now an object of wonder. It was not dug like the tanks in Bengal, but was formed by shutting up, with an artificial bank, an opening between two natural ridges. The sheet of water was seven or eight miles in length and three in width. During the rains it was filled by neighboring rivers, and during the dry season it was let out in small streams. In the event of the rains failing, it sufficed to water the lands of thirty-two villages for a period of eighteen months.

Mr. Place, the English collector,[1] had repaired this tank, and given great satisfaction to the cultivators while augmenting the revenue. Mr. Place had also caused every village to be surrounded by a hedge of bamboos, which served to keep off small parties of horsemen during a hostile invasion, while extending the cultivation of bamboos.

Buchanan halted at Conjeveram, or Kanchi-puram, about forty miles from Madras. To this day Conjeveram is a type

---

[1] In Madras the civil officers are termed collectors and deputy-collectors; in Bengal and elsewhere they are termed commissioners and deputy-commissioners.

of the Hindu cities in the Peninsula. The streets were tolerably broad and lined with cocoanut trees, and crossed one another at right angles. The houses were built of mud in the form of a square, with a small court in the centre. They appeared much more comfortable than the houses in the country towns in Bengal.

There was a large temple at Conjeveram dedicated to Siva and his wife. Three miles off was another temple dedicated to Vishnu. There were a hundred Brahman families and a hundred dancing-girls employed in the service of these temples. Twice a year the images of Vishnu and his family were carried in procession on a visit to Siva; but Siva returned the visit only once a year. On those occasions there were frequent disputes between the worshippers of Siva and those of Vishnu, leading to abusive language and blows, which the English collectors were sometimes obliged to put down with the bayonet.

The Brahmans of Southern India were divided into three leading sects, namely, the Smartal, the Vaishnava, and the Madual.

The Smartal was the most numerous and comprehended half the Brahmans in the Lower Carnatic. Its members were followers of Sankhara Acharya. They were commonly said to be worshippers of Siva, but they considered Brahma, Vishnu, and Siva to be the same god assuming different persons as the creator, preserver, and destroyer of the universe. They believed their own souls to be portions of the divinity, and did not believe in transmigration as a punishment for sin. They were readily distinguished by three horizontal stripes on the forehead made with white ashes.[1]

Buchanan met with a Smartal Brahman, who was a fair type of his class. He was reckoned a man of learning, but

[1] Sankhara Acharya, the apostle of the Smartals, was a Namburi Brahman of Malabar, who flourished about the eighth century of the Christian era. His disciples taught that he was an incarnation of Siva, who appeared on earth to root out the religion of the Jains and regulate and reform the Brahmans. In 1871 a representative or successor of this apostle was still living. His name was Narsingh Acharya. He was called by his disciples the Jagat Guru, or teacher of the world. See larger History of India, vol. iii. chap. viii.

he denied all knowledge of Jains, Buddhists, or other sects, beyond having heard them mentioned. He considered the doctrines of all sects, save his own, to be contemptible and unworthy of notice. He believed in a supreme god, called Narayana, or Para Brahma, from whom proceeded Siva, Vishnu, or Brahma; but he regarded all of them, individually and collectively, as one and the same god. His sect prayed to Siva and Vishnu, as well as to many of their wives, children, and attendants, among whom were the Sakhtis, or destructive powers. Siva, however, was the principal object of their worship; for they considered him to be a most powerful mediator with Narayana, who was rather too much elevated to attend to their personal requests. They abhorred bloody sacrifices, but did not blame the Sudras for practicing such a form of worship; they said it was the custom of the Sudras, and that it was a matter of very little consequence what such low people did. The Smartals believed that when a good Brahman died, his spirit was united to God; but that the soul of a bad Brahman was punished in purgatory, and then passed through other lives, as an animal or as a person of low caste, until at last he became a Brahman and had another opportunity by the performance of good works to become united to God.

The followers of Ramanuja Acharya were the most numerous sect of Brahmans, next to the Smartals, and formed about three-tenths of the whole. They were called Vaishnava and A'yngar, and were readily known by three vertical marks on the forehead, connected by a common line above the nose, and formed of white clay. They abhorred Siva, calling him the chief of the Rakshasas, or devils; and they worshipped only Vishnu and the gods of his family. They formed two sects; those who believed in transmigration and those who did not.[1]

[1] Ramanuja Acharya, the apostle of the Vaishnavas and A'yngars, flourished about the twelfth century. He made Conjeveram his headquarters, but undertook missionary circuits over the whole of the Peninsula. One of his disciples, named Ramanand, founded another celebrated sect at Benares, who worshipped Vishnu through his incarnations of Rama and Krishna, and threw off all ties of caste. See larger History of India, vol. iii. chap. viii.

The Maduals formed the remaining two-tenths of the Brahmans. They wore the vertical marks on the forehead, which were appropriate to the followers of Vishnu, but they also worshipped Siva. They believed in the generation of the gods in a literal sense, thinking Vishnu to be the father of Brahma, and Brahma to be the father of Siva.

The proper duty of a Brahman was meditation on things divine; and the proper mode of procuring a livelihood was by begging. But the common people were not so charitable as in a former age, nor so willing to part with their money. Accordingly most of the Brahmans in the Lower Carnatic followed secular professions. They filled the different offices in the collection of revenue and administration of justice; and were extensively employed as guides and messengers, and as keepers of choultries. They rented lands, but never put their hands to the plow, and cultivated their farms by slaves who belonged to the inferior castes.[1] Hence arose the distinction between the Vaidika and Lokika Brahmans: the Vaidika devoting their days to study, contemplation, and the education of younger Brahmans; while the Lokikas engaged in the government revenue and other worldly concerns. The mercenary Brahmans who officiated in pagodas for a livelihood were despised alike by Vaidikas and Lokikas.

Throughout both Carnatics, except at Madras and some other exceptional towns, the Brahmans appropriated to themselves a particular quarter, generally that which was the best fortified. A Sudra was not permitted to dwell in the same street as a Brahman, and Pariahs and other low-castes were forbidden to dwell in the same quarter as the Sudras. Indeed the Pariahs, and others of the same stamp, generally lived in wretched huts about the suburbs, where a Brahman could not walk without pollution.

[1] The lower-castes, or rather outcasts, were by far the most hardy and laborious people in the Carnatic, but the greater number were slaves. Hyder Ali was alive to their value, and during his incursions in the Carnatic he sought to carry them away to Mysore, where he settled them down in farms. They are divided into numerous tribes or castes, distinguished by a variety of names, but are best known to Europeans by the general term of Pariahs. Properly speaking, the Pariahs or Pareyars form only a single tribe.

Buchanan paid a passing visit to Arcot and Vellore. He saw nothing remarkable except the Muhammadan women, who rode about on bullocks, and were entirely wrapped up in white veils. He ascended the Eastern Ghats and entered Mysore. The country was exceedingly bare and the population scanty. All the houses were collected in villages; the smallest villages of five or six houses were fortified with a wall six feet high, and a mud tower on the top to which the only access was by a ladder. If a plundering party approached the village, the people ascended the tower with their families and valuables, and drew up the ladder, and defended themselves with stones, which even the women threw with great force and dexterity. The larger villages had square forts, with round towers at the angles. In towns the defences were still more numerous; the fort served as a citadel, while the town or pettah was surrounded by a weaker defence of mud. The inhabitants considered fortifications as necessaries of existence, and incurred the whole expense of building them and the risk of defending them. Indeed for a long series of years the country had been in a constant state of warfare; and the poor inhabitants had suffered so much from all parties that they would not trust in any.

Buchanan halted at Bangalore, which has since become a favorite resort of the English in India. Bangalore was founded by Hyder Ali, and during his reign was an emporium of trade and manufactures. Hyder built the fort at Bangalore after the best fashion of Muhammadan military architecture; but Tippu destroyed it after he found that it could not resist English valor. Tippu also ruined the town by prohibiting all trade with the subjects of the Nawab of Arcot and Nizam of Hyderabad, whom he held in detestation.[1] It was plundered during the Mysore war of 1791–92 by the forces of Lord Cornwallis and his native allies, and the inhabitants fled in all directions. Subsequently Tippu

[1] Tippu sought to punish both the Nawab and Nizam by stopping the trade with Arcot and Hyderabad, much in the same way that the first Napoleon tried to punish England by the Berlin decrees.

induced the refugees to return with the wreck of their fortunes; and then, having got them under his thumb, he fleeced them of all they possessed, down to the most trifling ornaments, on the pretence that they had favored the English. Since the fall of Tippu in 1799 the inhabitants began once more to flock into Bangalore under the assurance of British protection.

At Seringapatam Buchanan saw the palace of Tippu Sultan. It was a large building surrounded by a wall of stone and mud. Tippu's own rooms formed one side of the square, while the three remaining sides were occupied by warehouses. Tippu had been a merchant as well as a prince; and during his reign he filled his warehouses with a vast variety of goods, which the Amildars, or governors of provinces, were expected to sell to the richer inhabitants at prices far in excess of their real value. Much corruption and oppression resulted from this forced system of trade. Those who bribed the Amildar were exempt from making large purchases. Those poor wretches who were unable to bribe were forced to buy; and as they were equally unable to pay, they were stripped of all they possessed, and written down as debtors to the Sultan for the outstanding balances.

Tippu persecuted Hindus, and especially Brahmans, as bitterly as Aurangzeb; but his bigotry rarely stood in the way of his interest. He might be unmerciful toward the temple Brahmans, but he spared the seculars. Indeed, the secular Brahmans were the only men in his dominions who were fitted for civil administration. His Dewan, or financial minister, was a Brahman of singular ability, named Purnea. Tippu was anxious that Purnea should become a Muhammadan; but Purnea was so horrified at the idea that the intention was abandoned.

All this while the Brahmans were so avaricious and corrupt that Tippu would gladly have displaced them could he have found capable men of other castes to fill their posts. He tried to check their malpractices by appointing Muhammadan Asofs, or lord-lieutenants, to superintend the administration in the provinces; but this measure only aggravated the evil. The Asofs were indolent, ignorant, and self-indulgent; and hungered after money bribes to supply their wants. Consequently the Brahmans doubled their exactions in order to satisfy the Asofs. Every native supposed to be rich was exposed to false charges, and there was no escape except by bribery.

Under the new government introduced by the Marquis of Wellesley, Purnea remained in the post of Dewan, and conducted the administration of Mysore under the supervision of an English Resident. He was a Brahman of the Madual sect, a good linguist, and well versed in the affairs of the country. The revenue establishments were largely reduced, and consequently the Brahmans were the loudest in their complaints against the new government. Those who were retained in the public service were paid liberal salaries to place them above temptation, but the result was not satisfactory. The people of Mysore acknowledged that they were delivered from the licentiousness of Tippu's soldiery, and the arbitrary exactions of his government; but they complained that the Brahman officials took more money than ever.

Buchanan explains the remarkable distinction which prevails in the two Carnatics between the left and right "hands." This distinction is confined to the Pariahs and low-castes generally. The "left hand" comprised nine tribes or castes, including blacksmiths, carpenters, masons, gold and silversmiths, oil-makers, hunters, shoemakers, and some others. The "right hand" comprised eighteen tribes, including Pariahs properly so called, calico-printers, shepherds, potters, washermen, palanquin-bearers, barbers, painters, cowkeepers, and others. The Pariahs proper were the chief tribe of the "right hand."

The origin of this division of the Hindu low-castes was involved in fable. It was said to have been carried out at Conjeveram by the goddess Kali. It was also said that the rules to be observed on either side were engraved on a copper plate, and preserved in the great temple of Siva. The existence of the plate, however, was more than doubtful. The pretensions of both hands were diametrically opposed, yet both appealed to the plate as an authority, and no one produced a copy. The antagonism originated in claims to the exclusive possession of certain honorary distinctions, such as the privilege of using twelve pillars to the temporary building under which the marriage ceremonies were performed; the right of riding on horseback in processions; or the claim to carry a flag painted with the figure of the monkey god Hanuman.[1]

Buchanan saw something of the working of Gurus and Swamis in the Brahmanical hierarchy.[2] They were the bishops of their respective sects, exercising a jurisdiction in all things relating to religion or caste. The Gurus and Swamis performed certain ceremonies of initiation and confirmation in their respective sects. They imparted to every disciple a mysterious sentence, known as the Upadasa, which was to be uttered orally in their devotions, and was never to be written down or revealed. Sometimes a Guru gave a Upadasa and some images to a favorite disciple, and appointed him as a kind of deputy to manage affairs at a distance. In the Vaishnava sect every disciple was branded with the spear of the god Vishnu. This ceremony was

---

[1] The division between the left and right "hands" is unknown in Hindustan, but prevails throughout the Peninsula and a great part of the Dekhan. The disputes among the low-castes at Masulipatam (ante, p. 228) were connected with this distinction. The English at Madras and the French at Pondicherry were often troubled in the last century by disputes between the left and right "hands," which sometimes were productive of bloodshed, and necessitated the interference of the military. Abbe Dubois relates a remarkable instance at which he himself was present. A terrible feud had broken out between the Pariahs and Cobblers, which spread through a large district. Many of the timid inhabitants began to remove their effects and leave their villages, as if they had been threatened by a Mahratta invasion. Fortunately matters did not come to an extremity, as the chief men came forward to mediate between the vulgar castes, and to disband the armed ranks just as they were awaiting the signal for battle. The cause of this dreadful commotion was a trifle. A Cobbler had stuck red flowers in his turban at a public festival, and the Pariahs insisted that none of his caste had a right to wear them.

[2] See ante, part i., chap. iv., p. 84.

known as the Chakrantikam.[1] The spear was made hot and applied to the shoulder so as to burn the skin. The Upadasa was imparted to the disciple only once during life; but the Chakrantikam or branding was performed several times.[2]

The Gurus were entirely supported by the contributions of their disciples; but these were so burdensome that a Guru seldom continued long in one place. The contributions of a rich town like Madras would not support a Guru or Swami for more than one or two months; and the visits of a Guru were often regarded with dread like the incursions of a Mahratta.[3]

The Gurus travelled in great state, with elephants, horses, palanquins, and an immense train of disciples, the least of whom considered himself as elevated far above ordinary mortals by his superior sanctity. They generally travelled at night in order to avoid their Muhammadan or European conquerors, who would not show them that veneration, or adoration, to which they considered themselves entitled. On the approach of a Guru to any place, all the inhabitants of the higher castes went out to meet him; but the lower castes were not admitted to his presence. The Guru was conducted to the principal temple, and bestowed Upadasa, or Chakrantikam, on such as had not received those ceremonies, and also distributed holy water. He then inquired into matters

---

[1] This branding ceremony was not practiced by the Smartal sect who worshipped Siva.

[2] At the Madras Presidency College, many years ago, the author often heard educated Hindus speak of the ceremonies described by Buchanan. He believes that the Upadasa imparted to the higher castes corresponded to the Gayatri, or invocation of all the Vaidik deities as represented by the sun. The Upadasa imparted to Sudras and others was nothing more than the name of some particular god, which was to be constantly repeated by the worshipper. The ceremony of branding was sometimes a subject of mirth to those who were not required to submit to it.

[3] A hundred pagodas a day, or about thirty-six pounds sterling, were as little as could be offered to a Guru on his tour, and the Raja of Tanjore was said to have given his Guru something like ninety pounds a day whenever the great spiritual teacher honored him with a visit. There is reason, however, to believe that the disciples exaggerated the value of past gifts in the hope of exciting the emulation of current worshippers.

of contention, or transgressions against the rules of caste; and having settled or punished all such offences, he heard his disciples and other learned men dispute on theological subjects. This was the grand field for acquiring reputation among the Brahmans.

Besides the Gurus, however, there were popular forms of ecclesiastical government. Throughout every part of India, wherever there was a considerable number of any one caste or tribe, there was usually a head man, and his office was generally hereditary. His powers were various in different sects and places; but he was commonly intrusted with authority to punish all transgressions against the rules of caste. His power was not arbitrary; as he was always assisted by a council of the most respectable members of his tribe. He could inflict fines and stripes, and above all excommunication, or loss of caste, which was the most terrible of all punishments to a Hindu.

While Gurus, and Brahmans generally, were held in such outward veneration, an undercurrent of antagonism occasionally found expression in the language of revolt. Satirical songs were current, showing up the incapacity of the Gurus; and sarcastic tales were told of the vanity or stupidity of Brahmans. Abbe Dubois has preserved a specimen of these compositions, which sufficiently illustrates the popular sentiments, and may be reproduced in a condensed paraphrase:

"Once upon a time four Brahmans were going on a journey, when they met a soldier, who cried out—'Health to my lord!' All four replied with a benediction, and then quarrelled among themselves as to which of the four had been saluted by the soldier. Accordingly they ran back and put the question to the soldier, who replied that his salutation had been intended for the greatest fool of the four.

"The four Brahmans next quarrelled as to which of them was the greatest fool. Accordingly they proceeded to the choultry of a neighboring village, and put the question to the elders who were assembled there; and in order to arbitrate on this knotty point, each Brahman was called upon in turn to prove his claim to the salutation.

"The first Brahman said that a rich merchant had given him two of the finest pieces of cloth that had ever been seen in his village. He purified them by washing, and hung them out to dry, when a dog ran under them; and neither he nor his children could tell whether the dog had touched them so as to render them impure. Accordingly he crawled under the clothes on his hands and knees without touching them; but his children decided that the trial was of no avail, as the dog might have touched them with his turned up tail, while their father had no such appendage. This decision so exasperated the Brahman that he tore the cloths to rags, and was then laughed at as the greatest fool in the village, because he might have washed the cloths a second time, or at any rate have given them to a poor Sudra.

"The second Brahman then told his story. His head had been shaved by a barber, but his wife had given the man two annas instead of one, and the barber refused to give back the extra anna. After much wrangling the barber agreed to shave the head of the Brahman's wife for nothing. The husband agreed, but the wife screamed with terror, for shaving her head was equivalent to charging her with infidelity. However, the Brahman was determined not to lose his anna, and the wife was shaved by force. The result was that the wife ran away to her parents, while the husband was railed at as the greatest fool in the world.

"The third Brahman next put in his claim. One evening he remarked that all women were prattlers. His wife replied that some men were greater prattlers than women. After some disputing it was agreed that the one who spoke first should give a leaf of betel to the other. The night passed away without a word. Morning came, but neither would speak or rise. The village was alarmed, and a multitude of Brahmans, men and women, gathered round the house fearing that the inmates were murdered. At last the carpenter broke down the door. The husband and wife were still lying on the couch, and neither would speak or move. Some of the bystanders declared that the pair were possessed of devils; and a magician was called in, but his incantations had no effect. At last a wise old Brahman brought a bar of red-hot gold in a pair of pincers, and applied it to the feet of the husband; but the man bore the torture without a word. Next the bar was tried on the wife, with a different effect; she rose up with a shriek and gave her husband a leaf of betel. The man took the leaf, saying—'Was I not right when I said that all women were prattlers?' The multitude looked on with amazement, but when they discovered that the husband had aroused the whole village for the sake of a leaf of betel they declared that he was the biggest fool they had ever seen.

"At last the fourth Brahman asserted his right to be regarded as the greatest fool of the four. For some years he had been betrothed to a girl, and at last she was old enough to be his wife. His mother would have fetched the damsel from her father's house, but was too sick to go. Accordingly she sent her son, but knowing him to be a brute, she implored him to be careful in his behavior. The father of the damsel entertained his son-in-law with all hospitality, and then dismissed him with his bride. The day was excessively hot, and the road ran through a desert which scorched their feet. The damsel had been tenderly brought up, and fainted with the heat, and lay down upon the ground and declared that she wished to die. A rich merchant came up, and offered to save her life by carrying her away on one of his bullocks; he also offered twenty pagodas to her husband as the value of her ornaments. Accordingly the bridegroom parted from his bride, and went home with the twenty pagodas. When his mother heard the story she overwhelmed him with curses. Presently the wife's relations came to the village, and would have murdered him had he not fled to the jungle. As it was, the chiefs of the caste fined him two hundred pagodas, and prohibited him from ever marrying again.

"Meanwhile the elders at the choultry had been convulsed with laughter at the stories of the four Brahmans, and so had all the people who had gathered around to hear what was going on. When the fourth Brahman had finished his tale, the elders delivered their judgment. They decided that each of the four Brahmans might consider himself entitled to the salutation of the soldier; and thereupon all four rushed out of the choultry in great delight, each one declaring that he had won the cause."

The foregoing tale cannot be regarded as history proper; but it is a specimen of folk-lore, and reveals the current of feeling which was running through Peninsular India at the beginning of the present century, and is still flowing. It will now be necessary to resume the thread of the narrative, which has been interrupted ever since the Mysore war was brought to a close by the destruction of Tippu and downfall of Seringapatam.

The conquest of Mysore was followed by vital changes in Tanjore and the Carnatic, similar to those which Lord Clive had carried out in Bengal and Behar some thirty-five years before, but without the sham of Moghul suzerainty. English administration was introduced into both countries in the place of native rule; and the Raja of Tanjore and Nawab of the Carnatic were reduced to the condition of titular princes like the Nawab Nazim of Murshedabad. How far Lord Wellesley was justified in carrying out such radical reforms may be gathered from the following facts.

The Hindu Raj of Tanjore had been favored by nature beyond all the other principalities in the Peninsula. It has already been described at the delta of the Koleroon and Kaveri; a well-watered garden, vying in fertility with the delta of the Nile, and forming the granary of Southern India. It had been conquered in the seventeenth century by a Mahratta prince of the house of Sivaji; but it was cut off from the homes of the Mahratta-speaking people in the western

Dekhan by the intermediate territories of the Carnatic Nawab.[1]

Tanjore had suffered much from the encroachments of the Moghuls, but was otherwise an independent principality. Isolated from the Mahratta empire, the Mahratta Rajas of Tanjore paid no such allegiance to the Maharajas at Satara, or Peishwas at Poona, as was paid by Sindia or Holkar, the Gaekwar or the Bhonsla of Berar. For many years the frontiers of Tanjore were oscillating, like those of the Mahratta empire; but during the eighteenth century they became fixed, and the Raj of Tanjore is described as a compact territory, seventy miles long from north to south, and sixty miles from east to west. It was bounded on the north by the Koleroon, on the east by the Bay of Bengal, on the south by the Marawar country,[2] and on the west by Trichinopoly and the Tondiman's country.[3]

---

[1] Tanjore was originally a province of the old Hindu empire of Vijayanagar. After the battle of Talikota, the Hindu viceroy or Naik became an independent Raja. Then followed intermittent wars between Tanjore and Trichinopoly. The Tanjore Raja was overpowered, and called the Mahrattas to his help. In 1680 the Mahrattas helped him with a vengeance. They saved him from destruction and then overran his territory, and took possession of his kingdom in payment for their services. See ante, p. 211.

[2] The Marawar country is a relic of Hindu antiquity, and closely associated with the legendary wars of Rama and Ravana. The people were primitive, and included the caste of Kalars, or hereditary robbers. In modern times the tract fell into the possession of the Rajas of Sivaganga and Ramnad, the former of whom was known as the little Marawar, while the latter was known as the great Marawar. The Ramnad estate was granted to the ancestors of the great Marawar, with the title of Sethıpati, or "Commander-in-chief," for the defence of the road and protection of pilgrims resorting to the sacred pagoda of Ramisseram.

[3] The Tondiman was originally a Zemindar, who rendered great services to the East India Company during the wars in the Carnatic, and was rewarded by the title and dignity of Raja. One incident in the family history is suggestive of old Hindu life. There was an ancient dispute between the Tondiman and Sivaganga Rajas respecting a small tract of land about ten miles long. Generation after generation fought for this land, so that four-fifths of it became jungle, while the remainder was sowed sword in hand, and reaped with bloodshed. Many attempts were made to settle the dispute, but without avail. At last a Major Blackburne, Resident at Tanjore, summoned the representatives on either side to bring all their documents and vouchers. After six weeks' laborious investigation, Major Blackburne discovered beyond all doubt that most of them were forgeries. Both parties, seeing that the fact was patent, admitted that every document of importance had been fabricated for the occasion; but they confidently appealed to the boundary stones, which they swore had been set up from a remote antiquity. On inquiry, however, Major Blackburne found that

Swartz, the missionary, was favorably disposed toward the Raja who was reigning in 1775 when Tanjore was restored by Lord Pigot. Indeed the Raja had permitted him to preach and establish schools. But the evidence of Swartz reveals the agony of Tanjore. The people were groaning under oppression and misgovernment. The Raja was a slave in the hands of Brahmans; he lived immured in the recesses of the palace, surrounded by a multiplicity of wives, and left the administration in the hands of a rapacious minister. The cultivators were at the mercy of renters, who took sixty or seventy baskets of rice out of every hundred; and sometimes the entire harvest was reaped by the servants of the Raja, while the cultivators looked helplessly on. In 1786 it was reported that sixty-five thousand of the inhabitants had fled from Tanjore; and that many of those who remained refused to cultivate the lands unless there was a change in the administration.

Unfortunately the English government at Madras was more or less responsible for this tyranny. When Lord Pigot restored Tanjore to the Raja, he engaged that there should be no interference for the future in the administration. The Madras government could consequently only remonstrate with the Raja, and its advice was thrown away. At last a committee of inspection was appointed, and Swartz was nominated a member. The Raja appealed to the pledges given him by Lord Pigot, and promised to amend his administration; but he did little or nothing, and the Madras government left matters to drift on.

The Raja died without issue in 1787. His death was followed by a disputed succession. There was an adult half-brother, named Amar Singh, and an adopted son, aged ten,

---

four years previously none of the stones had been in existence. Major Blackburne then decided the case on his own authority by dividing the land equally between the Tondiman and Sivaganga Rajas, and setting up new boundary stones under the seal of the British government. By so doing he offended both parties, but he put an end to the interminable wars, and before long the whole jungle was brought under cultivation. This measure, in the eyes of natives, was one of the oppressions of British rule.

named Serfoji. The recognition of the Madras government, as the superior authority in the Peninsula, was necessary to settle the case. Accordingly, the Madras government nominated twelve Pundits, who decided against the adoption, on the ground that the boy was disqualified by reason of his age, and by being the only son of his natural father. Under such circumstances Amar Singh, the half-brother, was placed upon the throne of Tanjore by the Madras government.

The administration of Amar Singh was as oppressive as that of his predecessor. He placed the boy Serfoji in close confinement, together with the widows of the deceased Raja. After some delay, and repeated complaints, the Madras government insisted on the liberation of the prisoners, and Serfoji and the widows were removed to Madras. Then followed a petition from Serfoji, claiming the throne of Tanjore by the right of adoption. More Pundits were consulted, who decided in favor of the adoption. The Madras government, after long and careful consideration, determined that a mistake had been made, and resolved on dethroning Amar Singh in favor of Serfoji.

Amid the contradictory interpretations of Sanskrit law, and the conflict of authority on the part of the Pundits, it is impossible to say who was the rightful Raja. Indeed, it is impossible to say how far the Pundits on either side may have been swayed by undue influences. Swartz intimates pretty plainly that the Tanjore Pundits were bribed by Amar Singh; while it is equally probable that the Madras Pundits were bribed by Serfoji. Lord Wellesley solved the problem by placing Serfoji on the throne on the condition that the entire administration should be transferred to the Company's officers. Accordingly Serfoji was put in possession of the town and fort of Tanjore and maintained by a yearly grant of thirty-five thousand pounds, together with one-fifth of the revenues of the Raj; while a yearly stipend of about nine thousand pounds was awarded to the ex-Raja Amar Singh.

Carnatic affairs had drifted into still greater confusion.

The introduction of British administration had become a crying necessity, not only for the deliverance of the people from oppression, but for the security of the East India Company's possessions in the Peninsula. In the war against Tippu in 1791–92 Lord Cornwallis had followed the example set by Lord Macartney during the invasion of Hyder Ali, and assumed the entire management of the Carnatic, as the only safeguard against underhand practices and failure of supplies. After making peace with Tippu in 1792, Lord Cornwallis concluded a treaty with Nawab Muhammad Ali, under which the Company was to assume the management of the Carnatic in all future wars, and the Nawab was pledged to carry on no correspondence whatever with any other state, native or foreign, without the sanction of the British government.

Muhammad Ali died in 1795, and was succeeded on the throne at Arcot by his eldest son, Umdut-ul-Umra. In 1799 Lord Wellesley prepared for the conquest of Mysore; but as he purposed to make short work with Tippu, he would not hamper his operations by taking over the Carnatic. He soon regretted his forbearance. The Nawab and his officers created such obstructions at critical moments that it was impossible to avoid the suspicion that they were guilty of systematic treachery.

After the capture of Seringapatam the treachery came to light. A clandestine correspondence was discovered which had been carried on with Tippu by both Muhammad Ali and his son Umdut-ul-Umra. Some sympathy between a Muhammadan prince at Arcot and another at Seringapatam was perhaps to be expected; although the Carnatic had been ravaged and plundered by Tippu only a few short years before. But the primary duty of Lord Wellesley was to secure the safety of the Company's rule in India; and it was impossible for him to overlook deliberate treachery, which threatened the existence of the Company, and which certainly violated the treaty of 1792, and put an end to all confidence in the future good faith of the Carnatic family.

Umdut-ul-Umra was on his deathbed. Lord Wellesley refused to disturb his last moments; and nothing was done beyond investigating the correspondence until after his death in July, 1801. The family was then told of the treachery which had been discovered, and the resolution of the Company, that henceforth the Carnatic was to be brought under the same system of government as Tanjore and Bengal. The dynasty was not to be subverted. There was to be a titular Nawab of Arcot in the same way that there was a titular Nawab Nazim of Murshedabad; but he was no longer to exercise any civil or military authority, and the entire administration was to be transferred to the servants of the Company. There were two claimants of the throne, a son and a nephew; and the nephew was said to have a better claim to the succession because the son was illegitimate. In the first instance the throne was offered to the son of Umdut-ul-Umra, but he refused the proffered terms. It was then offered to the nephew and accepted. An allowance of about fifty thousand pounds a year was assigned to the new Nawab for his personal expenses; and a yearly grant of one-fifth of the revenues of the Carnatic was set apart for the maintenance of the family.[1]

By these autocratic measures Lord Wellesley put an end to the anarchy and oppression which had prevailed for centuries in Southern India. At the same time he established the British government as the dominant power in the Peninsula. British administration was introduced into the Moghul Carnatic, and into the newly-acquired territories in Mysore, from the Kistna to the Koleroon, and from the Bay of Bengal to the frontier of the Mysore Raj. It was also introduced into the countries to the south of the Koleroon; and not only Tanjore and Trichinopoly, but Tinnevelly and

[1] The Nawab of the town of Surat on the side of Bombay was equally dependent on the British government, equally helpless in defending the place, and equally incompetent to manage its internal affairs. In 1800 the dynasty of Surat shared the fate of that of the Carnatic. Advantage was taken of a disputed succession to assume the government and revenues of Surat, and to reduce a favored claimant to the position of a titular pensioner.

Madura became British territory.[1] Further to the west, on the Malabar side, Malabar proper and Kanara were in like manner brought under British administration; while the states of Coorg, Cochin, and Travancore were brought into feudatory relations with the British government, which have continued, with the exception of Coorg, down to our own time.[2] Thus the Madras Presidency, which was originally restricted to a sandy tract on the Coromandel coast of six miles in length and one inland, was extended westward to the coast of Malabar, northward to the Kistna and Godavari, and southward to Cape Comorin.

---

[1] The English collectorate of Madura includes Dindigul and the two Marawars, Sivaganga and Ramnad.

[2] The general character of these feudatory relations will be sufficiently described in the next chapter. In 1834 the Raja of Coorg declared war against the British government, and was speedily reduced by British arms. His country, at the expressed and unanimous desire of the people, was then brought under the Company's rule. The incident belongs to the administration of Lord William Bentinck, and will be told hereafter.

CHAPTER IX

MAHRATTA WARS—WELLESLEY

A.D. 1799 TO 1805

THE Mysore war did something more than establish the British government as the dominant power in the Peninsula. It put an end to the phantom of a balance of power in the Dekhan and Hindustan. The Nizam was helpless; his very existence depended on the British government. The Peishwa's government was faithless; it sent no contingent to join the forces of the English and the Nizam, and kept the envoys of Tippu at Poona long after the war began, in order to carry on underhand negotiations with the enemy. Henceforth it was for the British government, and for that government alone, to keep the peace of India by the exercise of a paramount power.

The political system contemplated by the Marquis of Wellesley lies in a nutshell. The native states were to surrender their international life to the British government in return for British protection. They were to make no wars, and to carry on no negotiations with any other state whatever, without the knowledge and consent of the British government. They were not to entertain Frenchmen or any other Europeans in their service, without the consent of the British government. The greater principalities were each to maintain a native force commanded by British officers for the preservation of the public peace; and they were each to cede certain territories in full sovereignty to meet the yearly charges of this force. The lesser principalities were to pay tribute to the paramount power. In return the British government was to protect them, one and all, against foreign enemies of every sort or kind. This system had already been carried out as regards the petty Hindu principalities of Travancore and Coorg, which had been left intact in the Peninsula. Its extension was now to be urged on the greater powers of the Dekhan and Hindustan.

The Nizam of Hyderabad was the first to enter into the new political system; the first to become a feudatory of the British government. Nizam Ali agreed to the maintenance of a native force under British officers, known as the Hyderabad Subsidiary Force; and he ceded back to the British government all the territories which had been given him after the Mysore conquests in 1792 and 1799, to meet the charges of the Hyderabad Subsidiary Force. This was the beginning of the new political system of a British empire over native feudatories.[1]

Lord Wellesley next tried to bring over the Peishwa's government to the subsidiary system. He offered to make over the remaining share of the Mysore country, provided the Peishwa would agree to the same terms as the Nizam. Baji Rao and Nana Farnavese were anxious for the proffered territory, but would not accept the conditional treaty. They urged that the Peishwa was endowed with the inherent right to collect chout for the whole of the Mysore territory; and they tried to convince Lord Wellesley that it would be politic to make over the proposed share of the Mysore conquest to the Peishwa as an equivalent for the collection of the chout throughout the whole of the Mysore territory. They met all other proposals by diplomatic evasions. The Peishwa would help the English against the French, but would not dismiss the Frenchmen in his service. He would take English battalions into his pay provided he might employ them against his refractory feudatories. But he would not accept the mediation of the English in the claims of the Mahrattas against the Nizam, nor pledge himself as regards wars or negotiations with other states or principalities.

---

[1] A distinction must be made between the Hyderabad Subsidiary Force and the Hyderabad Contingent. The Contingent was a later creation.

Daulat Rao Sindia was still more refractory. He was barely nineteen years of age, but he exercised a preponderating influence in the Mahratta empire, and was puffed up with exaggerated ideas of his own importance and power. Lord Wellesley refrained from exciting his suspicions by any premature disclosure of his larger political views, and only attempted to engage him in a defensive alliance against the Afghans. Lord Wellesley himself was in some alarm about the Afghans. Zeman Shah, the reigning sovereign of Afghanistan, was a grandson of the once famous Ahmad Shah Abdali, and longed to tread in the footsteps of his illustrious progenitor. In 1796 he had advanced into the Punjab as far as Lahore; but was compelled to return to Kabul the following year on account of distractions in his own territories. Later on he sent a letter to Lord Wellesley announcing his intention to invade India, and inviting the British government to help him to drive the Mahrattas out of Hindustan. Lord Wellesley forwarded this letter to Daulat Rao Sindia, and proposed an alliance between the English and Mahrattas against Zeman Shah. But Daulat Rao Sindia was not to be terrified by an Afghan invasion. The slaughter of the Mahrattas at Paniput in 1761 had died out of the memory of the rising generation. Accordingly Daulat Rao Sindia treated the letter of Zeman Shah as the idle vaporings of a distant barbarian; and refused to hamper himself with an English alliance for resisting an invasion which might never be attempted.[1]

Lord Wellesley was exasperated at the apathy of Daulat Rao Sindia, for he was seriously afraid of the Afghans. He knew nothing of their domestic wars and endless feuds; he only knew that they had more than once established a do-

---

[1] In a previous generation, when the Afghan armies of Ahmad Shah Abdali were overrunning the Punjab, and threatening Hindustan, neither the Moghuls nor the Mahrattas ever troubled themselves about the Afghans until the invaders reached Delhi. Since then thirty years had passed way. Ahmad Shah Abdali died in 1773, and his sons were too much occupied in fighting one another for the throne to attempt a renewal of their aggressions on Hindustan.

minion in Hindustan, and must be anxious to recover their lost power. He was in great alarm lest the Afghans should invade Oude; for Oude had nothing to protect her but a few English battalions, and a rabble army, in the pay of the Nawab Vizier, that would be worse than useless in the event of an invasion.

Under these circumstances Lord Wellesley called on the Nawab Vizier of Oude to disband his own army, and devote the money thus saved to the maintenance of a larger number of the Company's battalions. The Nawab Vizier refused to do anything of the kind. Lord Wellesley was imperious and peremptory; he was not disposed to give in to the Nawab Vizier as he had given in to the Peishaw and Daulat Rao Sindia. He considered that unless Hindustan was in a sufficient state of defence against the Afghans, the British empire in India would be in peril. Accordingly he compelled the Nawab Vizier to cede half his territories and revenues for the protection of the remaining half; and he devoted the additional income thus acquired to the permanent defence of Hindustan.

As a matter of fact, the threatened invasion of Zeman Shah turned out a bugbear. In 1800 the would-be conqueror of Hindustan was dethroned and blinded by one of his brothers, and ultimately compelled to seek a refuge in British territory. But Lord Wellesley had no means of knowing what was going on. Kabul in those days was associated with the invasions of Timur, Nadir Shah, and Ahmad Shah Abdali; and for aught Lord Wellesley knew to the contrary, hosts of Tartars and Afghans might have rushed into Hindustan like a destroying flood. Moreover, no help was to be expected from native princes. The Mahrattas would have held aloof and played a waiting game. The Muhammadans expected Zeman Shah to deliver them from the English. The Rajputs expected him to deliver them from the Mahrattas. Then again there was no knowing what the French might be doing in the background. Under such circumstances Lord Wellesley was driven by the instinct of self-preservation to take extreme measures for the permanent defence of Hindustan against foreign invaders.

Meanwhile Lord Wellesley turned an anxious eye toward Persia. During the anarchy which followed the assassination of Nadir Shah in 1747, the old trade between Bombay and Persia had dwindled away. Persia was the theatre of bloody struggles between the Persian and the Turkoman, otherwise known as the Zend and the Kajar. For a brief interval the Zend gained the mastery, but in 1794 was compelled to succumb to the Kajar, amid massacres and atrocities too horrible for description. A Kajar dynasty was founded by Agha Muhammad Khan. For a brief interval it was exposed to Russian aggression.[1] Subsequently there was reason to suspect that it might be made an instrument of French intrigue. Accordingly, having got rid of Tippu as a creature of the French in the southern Peninsula, it was natural that Lord Wellesley should provide against any possible danger that might be brewing to the northwest of Hindustan.

In 1800 Lord Wellesley sent Captain John Malcolm on a mission to Persia, to create a diversion against Zeman Shah on the side of Khorassan, and to counteract any designs that might be entertained by France. The mission has left no mark in history; but Malcolm was a man of his time, and destined to play an important part in the later affairs of India. He distinguished himself in Persia by a lavish distribution of presents among the Shah and his courtiers, who were equally poor, vain, and mercenary; and he concluded a treaty, under which the Shah agreed to act, if necessary, against Zeman Shah, and to exclude all Frenchmen from his dominions.[2]

---

[1] The Kajar conqueror, Agha Muhammad Khan, was extending his conquests to the eastward, when he was called away by Russian aggression in Georgia; but he was saved by the death of Catherine the Second in 1796, and the unexpected recall of the Russian army by her son and successor the Emperor Paul. In 1797 Agha Muhammad Khan was assassinated, and, after another interval of wars and distractions, was succeeded by his nephew, Futih Ali Shah, the second sovereign of the Kajar dynasty, who died in 1834.

[2] John Malcolm belonged to the old military school of political officers. In 1783 he landed at Madras as a boy ensign of fourteen. In 1784 he took charge

Meanwhile the progress of Mahratta affairs had engaged the anxious attention of Lord Wellesley. In 1800, Nana Farnavese, the famous Mahratta minister, was gathered to his fathers. He was a Brahman statesman of the old Hindu type. For many years he had grasped the real power, and treated the late Peishwa, Mahdu Narain Rao, as a child; but Baji Rao, the successor of Mahdu Narain, was older, more experienced, and consequently more troublesome, and was forever intriguing against his authority. The death of Nana Farnavese released Baji Rao from a state of ministerial thraldom, but exposed him more than ever to the galling dictation of Daulat Rao Sindia. Shortly afterward Sindia was called away to the northward by disorders which had broken out in Holkar's territory; and Baji Rao was left alone at Poona to follow his own devices without any interference whatever.

The dominion founded in Malwa by Mulhar Rao Holkar was at this period passing through a crisis, which tempted the interference of Daulat Rao Sindia. Ailah Bai, the daughter-in-law of Mulhar Rao, had carried on the civil administration of the state ever since his death in 1767.[1] She had transformed the village of Indore into a wealthy capital; and henceforth the name of Indore was applied to the state as well as to the capital. She died in 1795, leaving the state of Indore in the sole possession of her commander-in-chief, Tukaji Holkar.

Tukaji Holkar died in 1797, leaving two legitimate sons, one of whom was an imbecile. Daulat Rao Sindia hurried away from Poona to Indore, and played the part of a suzerain. He placed the imbecile son of Tukaji Holkar on the throne, and put the other in prison and eventually murdered

---

of the prisoners surrendered by Tippu after the treaty of Mangalore, and caused some amusement on the occasion by reason of his extreme youth. In 1791 he distinguished himself in the Mysore war under Lord Cornwallis. In 1798 he took an active part in the disbandment of the Nizam's French battalions. He was only thirty-one when he was sent by Lord Wellesley on his mission to Persia.

[1] See ante, p. 397.

him; his object being to render his own influence paramount at Indore. But an illegitimate son of Tukaji appeared upon the scene under the name of Jaswant Rao Holkar. This man had no pretensions to the throne, for they were barred by the baseness of his birth. He had professed to be the partisan of the half-brother whom Sindia had set aside; but when the half-brother was murdered, Jaswant Rao fled to the jungles and turned outlaw and freebooter after Rajput fashion. He was joined by a host of the predatory rascals who infested Central India at this period—Bhils, Pindharies, Afghans, and Mahrattas. In this fashion he became so formidable that Daulat Rao Sindia was compelled to march against him with a large army and attempt to suppress him by main force.

The army of Jaswant Rao Holkar was reckoned at twenty thousand men, all of whom were maintained by plunder. It is needless to dwell upon the details of rapine, desolation and bloodshed which characterized his proceedings, and rendered him the pest of Malwa and Berar. In October, 1801, he was attacked and routed by Sindia and his French battalions; but defeat in those days was of little avail in suppressing a freebooting chief, whose name alone was a tower of strength for outlaws and refugees of every kind, and a rallying point for all the brigands and blackguards in Central India.

Meanwhile Baji Rao was free from all restraint. Nana Farnavese was dead, and Daulat Rao Sindia was busied in establishing his influence over the territory of the Holkar family in Indore. Accordingly, the young Peishwa at Poona pursued a wild career of revenge upon all his enemies, real or supposed. It would be tedious to dwell on his acts of savage ferocity; a single instance will serve as a type. A brother of Jaswant Rao Holkar had given some offence, or committed some crime, and was condemned to die by being dragged through the streets of Poona tied to the foot of an elephant. Baji Rao was not only deaf to the humblest prayers for mercy, but revelled in the sufferings of his victim. He looked on with delight while the wretched man was being dragged by the elephant from the palace yard, and filling the air with his shrieks at the prospect of a death of lingering agony.

Baji Rao had soon reason to repent of his cruelty. News arrived at Poona that Jaswant Rao had reassembled his scattered forces, inflicted some small defeats on Daulat Rao Sindia, and was marching to Poona to be revenged on the Peishwa for the tortures which had been inflicted on his brother.

Baji Rao was in great consternation. He was half inclined to agree to the treaty with the English, and accept their protection. Sindia, however, prevented the British alliance for a while by despatching a large force to reassure the Peishwa. In October, 1802, the decisive battle of Poona changed the fate of the Mahratta empire. The united armies of Sindia and the Peishwa were defeated by Jaswant Rao Holkar; and Baji Rao fled for his life to the western coast, and escaped on board an English ship to the port of Bassein, about twenty miles to the northward of Bombay.

Baji Rao was paralyzed by the disaster. Another Peishwa was set up by Jaswant Rao Holkar at Poona, and Baji Rao saw nothing before him but ruin. In this extremity he agreed to sign the obnoxious treaty, provided the English restored him to his throne at Poona. Accordingly the treaty of Bassein was concluded on the last day of December, 1802.

By the treaty of Bassein Baji Rao severed all the ties which bound the Mahratta princes to him as Peishwa, lord paramount, and suzerain. He absolutely abdicated the headship of the Mahratta empire. He pledged himself to hold no communication with any other power, not even with the great feudatories of the empire, such as Sindia and Holkar, the Gaekwar and the Berar Raja, without the consent of the British government. He also ceded territory for the maintenance of a Poona Subsidiary Force. He thus secured his restoration to the throne of Poona; but, as far as treaties were binding, he had ceased to be lord paramount of the Mahratta empire; he had transferred his suzerainty to the

East India Company; and henceforth was bound hand and foot as a feudatory of the British government.

The treaty of Bassein is a turning-point in the history of India. It established the British empire as the paramount power in India, but it rendered a Mahratta war inevitable. It was impossible for a Mahratta prince of Baji Rao's character and surroundings to fulfil the obligations involved in such a treaty; he was certain, sooner or later, to attempt to recover the lost headship of the Mahratta empire. It was equally impossible for Daulat Rao Sindia to respect the terms of a treaty which shut him out from the grand object of his ambition, namely, to rule the Mahratta empire in the name of the Peishwa.

In 1803 Baji Rao was conducted by a British force from Bassein to Poona. The Madras army under Colonel Wellesley, and the new Hyderabad Subsidiary Force under Colonel Stevenson, were moving up from the south in the same direction for his protection. Yet at this very time Baji Rao was secretly imploring Daulat Rao Sindia and the Bhonsla Raja of Berar to march to his assistance, and deliver him from the English supremacy.[1]

Sindia and the Bhonsla had each taken the field with a large army, and were restlessly moving near the western frontier of the Nizam's dominions. They were closely watched by Wellesley and Stevenson, but they were stupefied by the treaty of Bassein, and knew not what to do. They had no particular regard for Baji Rao; indeed they were opposed in theory to the supremacy of the Brahman Peishwas. Daulat Rao Sindia had long been intriguing to gain the ascendency at Poona, and rule the Mahratta feudatories in the name of the Peishwa; while every successive Raja of Berar nursed the design of overthrowing the Brahmanical supremacy, and seizing the throne at Poona as the representative of Sivaji. But both Sindia and the Bhonsla preferred the

[1] Mudaji Bhonsla died in 1788, and was succeeded on the throne of Berar by his eldest son Rughoji Bhonsla, who reigned twenty-eight years, and died in 1816. Baji Rao was imploring the help of Rughoji Bhonsla.

Brahman sovereignty to the British; and they hesitated to conclude treaties with Lord Wellesley, or to begin a war.

Meanwhile both Sindia and the Bhonsla used every effort to induce Jaswant Rao to join them. They were prepared to make any sacrifice; to ignore the legitimate branch of Holkar's family, and to acknowledge Jaswant Rao as Maharaja of Indore. But Jaswant Rao was richly endowed with the craft and cunning of his race. He was profuse in promises to join the allies against the English; and by these means he procured from Sindia and the Bhonsla all the recognition and countenance he wanted; and then he went back to Indore, to strengthen his position and await the result of the expected collision with the English. At Indore he received repeated invitations from Sindia and the Bhonsla; but he replied to all with seeming frankness, "If I join you in the Dekhan, who is to take care of Hindustan?"

All this while Lord Wellesley was full of alarms at the presence of Sindia's French battalions between the Jumna and the Ganges. De Boigne had returned to Europe, and was succeeded in the command by a violent French republican named Perron, who was known to be hostile to the English. Perron collected the revenues of the Doab for the maintenance of his French battalions; and the imagination of Lord Wellesley was so fired by his fear and hatred of the French that he pictured Perron as a French sovereign of upper Hindustan, with the Great Moghul under his thumb, and unbounded resources at his command.

The state of affairs in Europe gave a fresh impetus to these alarms. Napoleon's expedition to Egypt had revealed the vastness of his ambition. The young Corsican was prepared to march in the footsteps of the great Macedonian from Egypt to Persia, and from Persia to Hindustan. The peace of Amiens in 1802 was only an interval of preparation for grand designs. News of a renewal of the war between Great Britain and France was expected by every ship from Europe; and many besides Lord Wellesley imagined that the imperial dreamer at the Tuileries was still longing to outdo Alexander by conquering the Oriental world from the Mediterranean to the mouths of the Ganges.

Lord Wellesley brooded over the map of India with a jealous eye. He pondered over every vulnerable spot on the coast of India where a French armament could anchor. He was especially alarmed at the convenient position of Baroche on the western coast to the northward of Surat. Baroche was a port belonging to Sindia, situated at the mouth of the Nerbudda river. Accordingly, the fevered imagination of Lord Wellesley was again at work. He pictured a French armament sailing down the Red Sea, and across the Indian Ocean, to Sindia's port of Baroche; a French flotilla going up the Nerbudda river from Baroche to the neighborhood of Indore; a French army marching through Malwa, followed by a host of Mahrattas and Rajputs, joining Perron at Agra and Delhi, and pretending to conquer India in the name of the Great Moghul.[1]

At this time, General Lake, commander-in-chief of the Bengal army, was posted at Cawnpore on the frontier of Oude. He was told by Lord Wellesley that a Mahratta war was impending; and that directly the war note was sounded he was to march toward Delhi, break up Sindia's French battalions, and occupy the whole territory between the Jumna and the Ganges.

Meanwhile Colonels Wellesley and Stevenson continued to watch Sindia and the Bhonsla in the Dekhan. Sindia was still waiting to be joined by the recreant Jaswant Rao Holkar, but his language as regards the British government and its allies was more hostile. He threw out hints to the British Resident, who accompanied his camp, that he meant to collect chout in the Nizam's territory. He was doubtful, he said, whether there would be peace or war between the Mahrattas and the English; and he could arrive at no decis-

---

[1] Baroche, or Broach, had fallen into the possession of the English, together with other territories in Guzerat, during the first Mahratta war in the days of Warren Hastings, but had been needlessly and heedlessly made over to Mahadaji Sindia at the treaty of Salbai in 1782. See ante, p. 436.

ion on this point until he had talked the matter over with the Bhonsla Raja of Berar.

Sindia had a meeting with the Bhonsla, but nothing was decided. The two chiefs professed to be the friends of the British government, but naturally cavilled at the treaty of Bassein. They said they ought to have been consulted before it was concluded, and that many of the articles required more discussion.

In August, 1803, Colonel Wellesley put an end to these vacillations. "If," he said, "Sindia and the Bhonsla are such friends of the British government as they profess to be, let them prove their sincerity by marching back their armies to their respective dominions." Sindia replied that the English ought to set the example; in other words, that the English were to leave Sindia and the Bhonsla with their armies of freebooters to threaten the frontier of the Nizam, while Wellesley returned to Madras and Stevenson withdrew to Hyderabad. Sindia forgot that he had threatened to plunder the Nizam's dominions, and had doubted whether there was to be peace or war. Sindia was accordingly told that it was he, and not the British government, who had broken the peace, and that therefore he must take the consequences.

Thus began the second Mahratta war. The Resident left Sindia's camp. Sindia and the Bhonsla moved toward the southeast, as if to threaten Hyderabad; but their operations were feeble and undecided. They marched and countermarched more to delay action than to carry out any definite plan.

At last Wellesley and Stevenson agreed to make a combined attack on the united armies. By some accident Wellesley alone came upon the enemy near the village of Assaye on the Nizam's frontier, and resolved to fight a battle single-handed. His force only numbered four thousand five hundred men, while that of the Mahrattas numbered fifty thousand. The battle of Assaye was fought on the 23d of September, 1803. The Bhonsla Raja fled at the first shot, and Sindia soon followed his example. The Mahratta artillery, however, worked great execution; and Wellesley only won the battle by cavalry and infantry charges. It was the clashing of a fiery few of Europeans against a host of Mahrattas; and the fiery few won the day.[1] The victory was decisive, but one-third of the European force in the British army lay dead or wounded on the field.

The victory of Assaye was followed by the capture of fortresses, and another victory at Argaum. It would be tedious to dwell on the details of the military operations, which, however much they redounded to the credit of the youthful Wellesley, were destined to be overshadowed by the glories of the Peninsula and Waterloo. It will suffice to say that by the end of the year 1803 the Dekhan campaign was over, and Sindia and the Bhonsla sued for peace.

Meanwhile General Lake had carried on another brilliant campaign in Hindustan. He left Cawnpore in August, 1803, defeated Perron's cavalry at Alighur, and captured the Alighur fortress. He next marched on to Delhi, defeated the French infantry, and entered the capital of the Moghuls as a hero and a conqueror. More than forty years previously the last representative of the dynasty of the Great Moghul, the unfortunate Shah Alam, had fled from Delhi to Bengal, and taken refuge with the English. Ten years later he fled back from his protected retreat at Allahabad to the city of his fathers under the wing of the Mahrattas. In 1803 he was pondering over his deliverance from the Mahrattas, and the advent of his English protectors at the capital of Aurangzeb and tomb of Humayun.

The imperial family were much excited by the arrival of the English army. Some finery and tinsel were furbished up to enable the blind and aged Shah Alam to give a reception to the English general. The tottering descendant of Aurangzeb then placed himself under British protection;

---

[1] "This is he that far away
Against the myriads of Assaye
Clash'd with a fiery few and won."
Ode on the Death of the Duke of Wellington: TENNYSON.

and was left to dwell in the palace, supported by a liberal pension from the British government.

General Lake left the city of Delhi in charge of Colonel Ochterlony, and brought the campaign to a close by the capture of Agra and victory at Laswari. The battle of Laswari broke up the French battalions forever, and put the English in possession of the whole of upper Hindustan.

The fate of Perron was somewhat extraordinary. At the very beginning of the campaign he appeared as a suppliant to the English general. He was in bad odor with Sindia; his life was in danger; and he was anxious to retire to British territory with his private fortune. Permission was granted, and Perron ultimately took up his abode in the French settlement at Chandernagore, and then dropped into oblivion.

Sindia and the Bhonsla had no alternative but to accept the dictation of the British government. Accordingly they concluded treaties on the basis of the treaty of Bassein. Sindia renounced all pretensions to the regions northward of the Jumna and westward of the Chambal; all hold on the Great Moghul; all claims to collect chout or plunder from the Rajputs, Jats, or other native princes. To all appearance his power for mischief had gone forever.[1] The Bhonsla

[1] The negotiations with Daulat Rao Sindia were conducted by Major Malcolm and General Wellesley. Sindia's prime minister was a veteran Brahman and born diplomatist, with a sour, supercilious, inflexible countenance, which nothing could disturb. The most startling demand or unexpected concession was received without the movement of a muscle. Malcolm said that he never saw a man with such a face for a game of brag; and henceforth the gray-haired Mahratta went by the name of "Old Brag." Years passed away, and Wellesley returned to Europe and became Duke of Wellington. Malcolm met him and asked him about Talleyrand. Wellington replied that he was very much like "Old Brag," but not so clever.

Negotiations under such circumstances were not easy. Malcolm went to Sindia's camp, and found the young Maharaja almost as grave as his minister. A meeting took place in a large tent amid a storm of rain. Suddenly a volume of water burst in torrents through the canvas, and fell upon an Irish officer named Pepper. The Maharaja screamed with laughter at the catastrophe, and all present joined in the chorus. All gravity was at an end. The rain was followed by a storm of hail, and the diplomatists and their followers fell to work at collecting the hailstones, which are as refreshing as ices in the hot plains of India.

But nothing could stop the pertinacity of "Old Brag." On a subsequent

Raja belonged to a smaller fry. He ceded Cuttack on the east and Berar on the west; and was henceforth known as the Raja of Nagpore. But Lord Wellesley was afraid to vaunt his conquests in the eyes of the people of England, unless he could prove that they were necessary for protection against the French. He kept possession of Cuttack because it was the only vulnerable tract on the Bay of Bengal that was open to invasion from the sea; but he made over the territory of Berar proper as a free gift to the Nizam of Hyderabad.

In 1804 Lord Wellesley had completed his political scheme for the government of India. The Gaekwar of Baroda accepted the situation, and ceded territory for the maintenance of a Subsidiary Force. The Rajput princes and the Jat Raja of Bhurtpore gladly surrendered their old international life, with all its wars and feuds, for the sake of protection against the Mahrattas. The cession of Cuttack by the Berar Raja removed the only break on the British line of seaboard from Calcutta to Comorin. Only one power of the slightest moment remained outside the pale of the new political system; and that was Jaswant Rao, the Mahratta freebooter who had usurped the throne of Holkar.

In those days the British government had no interest or concern in the rightness or wrongness of Jaswant Rao's pretensions. It was in no way responsible for his usurpation, for that had begun before the subsidiary treaties were concluded with the other Mahratta powers. The British government might have arbitrated, but it could not force the people of Indore, nor the Mahratta princes in general, to accept its arbitration. It could not conclude any subsidiary or protec-

---

occasion he demanded that an article should be inserted in the treaty that out of respect for the caste of Brahmans of which the Peishwa was a member, and out of friendship for Maharaja Sindia, and for the purpose of increasing its own reputation, the British government should prohibit the slaughter of cows throughout Hindustan. Such a wholesale demand was perilous to the well-being of European soldiers, to say nothing of Englishmen in general, who are supposed to owe their superiority to beef. Accordingly the proposition was rejected as inadmissible.

tive treaty, which would guarantee Jaswant Rao Holkar in the dominions of the Holkar family; because, according to the common understanding of the Mahratta states, Jaswant Rao Holkar was a rebel against the Peishwa, and an illegitimate son of the late ruler, while the legitimate heir was still alive. But Lord Wellesley was willing to leave Jaswant Rao alone, provided only that he abstained from all aggressions upon the territories of the British government, or upon those of its allies.

But Jaswant Rao was a free lance of the old Mahratta type; a man of the stamp of Sivaji with the instinct of a freebooter running in his blood. He did not aspire to be a warrior and hero like the Sindias. He preferred plunder to political power; and consequently took more delight in commanding loose bodies of predatory horsemen, like another Sivaji, than in directing the movements of drilled battalions of infantry, like Mahadaji Sindia or Daulat Rao. It was the boast of Jaswant Rao Holkar that his home was in the saddle, and that his dominions extended over every country that could be reached by his horsemen.

In 1803, while English and Mahrattas were engaged in wars in the Dekhan and upper Hindustan, Jaswant Rao Holkar collected a golden harvest in Malwa and Rajputana. Subsequently he was joined by deserters or fugitives from Sindia and the Bhonsla; and but for the presence of the English in Hindustan might have become the most formidable predatory power in Central India.

But Jaswant Rao Holkar was ill at ease. He was an Esau among the Mahratta powers, without fear or love for any one of them. He was alarmed at the victories of the English. It was obvious to his mind, molded by Mahratta culture, that he had an inherent right to collect chout, which the English were bound to respect. As a matter of fact, he could not keep his forces together without plunder or chout. But he feared that the English were unable or unwilling to recognize the sacred rights of the Mahrattas, and were bent on putting a stop to his future expeditions.

Jaswant Rao proceeded to work upon the English with all the wariness of a Mahratta. He wrote an arrogant letter to General Lake, full of pretensions as regards what he called his rights, but still professing much friendship. He continued the work of collecting chout and plunder from the protected allies in Rajputana, and at the same time he urged them to throw off their dependence on the British government. He was told by General Lake that the English had no desire to interfere with him, but that it was absolutely necessary that he should withdraw to Indore territory, and abstain from all aggressions on the British government or its allies.

Jaswant Rao then took a more decided tone. He requested permission to levy chout according to the customs of his ancestors. He offered to conclude a treaty, provided the British government would guarantee him in the possession of Indore territory. But he refused to withdraw from Rajputana until the English complied with his demands. He wrote letters still more peremptory to General Wellesley in the Dekhan, threatening to burn, sack, and slaughter by hundreds of thousands in the event of refusal. He invited Daulat Rao Sindia to join him in an attack upon British possessions; but Sindia was already disgusted with his duplicity, and not only refused to have anything more to do with such a faithless chieftain, but reported Jaswant Rao's proffered alliance to the British authorities.

There was no alternative but to reduce Jaswant Rao to submission. General Lake was ordered to move southward into Rajputana, while General Wellesley moved northward from the Dekhan; and Jaswant Rao would then have been hemmed in between the two armies, and compelled to surrender at discretion. But there was a famine in the Dekhan; the rains had failed, and the country had been ravaged by the armies of Sindia and the Bhonsla. General Wellesley could not move from the Dekhan, but ordered Colonel Murray to march from Guzerat toward Malwa with a sufficient force to co-operate with any force which might be sent by

General Lake. Daulat Rao Sindia also offered to co-operate with the English for the reduction of Jaswant Rao, whom he declared had forfeited all claim to consideration from his treacherous refusal to join the allied Mahratta armies before the battle of Assaye.

In April, 1804, General Lake moved an army into Rajputana, and sent a detachment in advance under Colonel Monson. Jaswant Rao beat a hasty retreat through Rajputana toward Indore territory in the south. In May the English force captured Holkar's fortress of Rampoora, known as Tonk-Rampoora. The rains were now approaching, and General Lake left Colonel Monson to keep Jaswant Rao in check, and then returned to cantonments.

The force under Colonel Monson consisted of five battalions of sepoys, a train of artillery, and two bodies of irregular horse, one under a Lieutenant Lucan, and the other under Bapoji Sindia, a kinsman of Daulat Rao. In June Monson crossed the river Chambal and reached Kotah, and was joined by a body of troops in the service of the Rajput ruler of Kotah, who was anxious for the friendship of the British government. Monson was daily expecting to be joined by Murray with the force from Guzerat, as well as by a force which Daulat Rao Sindia promised to send from Ujain. Accordingly he advanced through the pass of Mokundra into Holkar's territory, and continued his march some fifty miles further to the southward.

In the beginning of July Colonel Monson was staggered by a succession of untoward events. His supplies were running very low. Treachery was in his camp of which he was ignorant; Bapoji Sindia was sending secret messages to Jaswant Rao to turn back and advance against the English brigade. Next Monson heard that Colonel Murray had taken fright and was retreating to Guzerat; and that Jaswant Rao had stayed his onward flight and turned back, and was marching against him with overwhelming forces, and a vast train of artillery.

Colonel Monson ordered a retreat to Mokundra pass, leaving the irregular horse to follow. Shortly afterward Bapoji Sindia came up with a story that Jaswant Rao had routed the irregular horse, and that Lucan was taken prisoner. Monson reached the Mokundra pass; and Bapoji Sindia filled up the measure of his iniquity by deserting the English and going over bodily to Jaswant Rao with all his horsemen. Shortly afterward Monson was attacked by the whole army of Holkar, but succeeded in repulsing the enemy.

Unfortunately, instead of holding out at the Mokundra pass, Colonel Monson continued his retreat to Kotah. The ruler of Kotah lost heart at seeing the fugitives, and shut his gates against them. The rainy season was at its height. Colonel Monson continued his retreat toward the north, but his supplies were exhausted, and his guns sank hopelessly in the mud. He was obliged to spike his guns and destroy his ammunition to prevent their falling into the hands of the enemy. Sindia's commander came up to join him with the expected detachment from Ujain; but when the Mahratta saw the wretched state of the fugitives he turned his guns upon the English force and went over to Jaswant Rao. It is needless to dwell on further details of disasters in crossing rivers, and privations and sufferings beneath the pitiless rains. The retreat became a disorderly rout, during which the English sepoys were constantly exposed to the charges and surprises of Jaswant Rao Holkar. About the end of August, 1804, the shattered remains of Monson's brigade managed to reach Agra.

Monson's retreat was one of those disasters which will upset the designs of the ablest statesmen. The political system of Lord Wellesley was in imminent danger. For a brief interval British prestige vanished from Hindustan. Jaswant Rao Holkar was exaggerated into a Mahratta hero, and was joined by most of the predatory bands of Central India. Even the Rajput and Jat princes, the protected allies of the British government, were shaken in their allegiance by the successes of the victorious Mahratta.

Jaswant Rao took possession of Muttra, and then with

happy audacity hastened to Delhi, to seize Shah Alam, and plunder Hindustan in the name of the Great Moghul. He was beaten off from Delhi by a small force under Ochterlony; but meanwhile a new ally had sprung up in his rear. The Jat Raja of Bhurtpore threw off his dependence on the British government, and declared in favor of Jaswant Rao Holkar. The fortress of Bhurtpore was the strongest in Hindustan. The huge walls of hardened mud rose round the city like a rampart of mountains. They were a godsend to Jaswant Rao. He sent his guns and infantry within the walls, and began to ravage the Doab with his army of horsemen, like a Tartar Khan of the olden time.

General Lake took the field with his cavalry, and soon routed and dispersed the Mahratta horse. The English captured the fortress of Deeg, which also belonged to the Bhurtpore Raja. But then, instead of completing the destruction of Jaswant Rao, General Lake advanced against Bhurtpore, and endeavored to capture the impregnable fortress without even a siege-train. For a period of four months, from January, 1805, to the following April, he wasted the strength of the English army in trying to storm these enormous earthworks. To make matters worse, Daulat Rao Sindia threw off his allegiance to the British government, and declared for Jaswant Rao Holkar.

The fortunes of the English soon began to brighten. The Raja of Bhurtpore grew frightened, and was restored to the protected alliance on paying a fine of two hundred thousand pounds to the British government. Subsequent defeats inflicted on Jaswant Rao brought Daulat Rao Sindia to his senses. Difficulties were being removed, and tranquillity was about to be restored, when negotiations were upset by the home authorities. At the end of July, 1805, Lord Cornwallis landed at Calcutta, and took up the office of Governor-General, and the policy of the British government underwent an important change. Shortly afterward Lord Wellesley returned to England.

Lord Wellesley was a statesman of the highest order, who brought the political experiences of western culture to bear upon the conditions of Asiatic rule. His genius was untrammelled by the narrow ideas which grew out of a trading monopoly, and which swayed the better judgment of Robert Clive and Warren Hastings. He valued the security and prestige of the British empire in India at a higher rate than the commercial privileges of the East India Company; and consequently he raised up a host of enemies who could not appreciate his comprehensive foresight. But, in the teeth of all opposition, he established the sovereignty of the British government over the greater part of India, and put an end forever to the English-born fantasy of a balance of power.

Lord Wellesley has been compared with Akbar. Consciously or unconsciously, he sought to build up a British empire in India on similar foundations to those of the Moghul empire of Akbar. He avoided, however, the spirit of Oriental intrigue, which balanced one element of race or religion against another; and he labored to provide for the peace and security of India by establishing the British government as a paramount power over Moghuls and Mahrattas, and protecting the chieftains of Rajputana against the predatory incursions of Sindia and Holkar. He formed a school of political officers, whose aspirations were linked with the well-being of the British empire rather than with the maintenance of the Company's monopoly; and thus he led to the identification of British interests with those of India, which has been the main work of the nineteenth century. Small in stature and imperious in will, he was known to his admirers as the "glorious little man"; and as long as the Anglo-Indian empire retains a place in history, the name of the Marquis of Wellesley will rank among its most illustrious founders.

Lord Wellesley was led into errors, but they were the errors of genius—the outcome of a foresight which credits enemies with the entertainment of designs beyond their power of execution. Wellesley gauged the ambition of the first Napoleon, and foreshadowed the dreams which would have carried a French army from the Mediterranean to the Ganges; but he overrated the resources as well as the prescience of the imperial dreamer, and he underrated the obstructions and difficulties which beset Napoleon in Europe, and checked his advance in the footsteps of Alexander. He provided for the defence of India against plans which had no real existence, excepting in his own imagination, but which nevertheless might have proved substantial dangers had Napoleon been a Wellesley, or Wellesley a Napoleon.

Lord Wellesley was the founder of the Indian Civil Service on its existing footing. The old servants of the Company were emphatically merchants; and he rightly considered that mercantile training is of small use to civil administrators in comparison with a knowledge of history, law, political economy, and Indian languages. Moreover, during the old commercial period, money-making too often became a master passion, and certainly exercised an undue influence on the Indian rulers of the eighteenth century. With these views Lord Wellesley founded a College on a grand scale at Calcutta, with a competent staff of professors, for the special education of young civilians fresh from Europe; and although his plans were dwarfed for a while into insignificance by the Court of Directors, yet in the end they led to the establishment of a College at Haileybury, which served as a training-school for Indian civil servants until the introduction of the competitive system in comparatively modern times.

CHAPTER X

CONCILIATION—LORD CORNWALLIS, SIR GEORGE BARLOW, AND LORD MINTO

A.D. 1805 TO 1818

THE second coming of Lord Cornwallis to India was the result of a political reaction. The British nation was alarmed at Lord Wellesley's conquests, and his large assumption of political power. It was always averse to territorial aggrandizement except for colonial purposes, or to humble France; and it was especially averse to conquests in India, which provided no outlet for the superfluous population of England, but only transferred large provinces from the government of native princes to that of the servants of the East India Company. The Directors themselves were equally alarmed at the extension of their dominion and responsibilities; for they had learned by bitter experience that wars and conquests only added to the expenditure, without increasing the profits of the Company, or otherwise promoting the interests of trade. Above all, neither the British nation nor the Company could understand the new political dogma, that India could only be governed in peace by reducing her princes to the condition of feudatories, and setting up the British government as the paramount power. The policy of Lord Wellesley savored too much of that of Napoleon to be acceptable to the people of England; and it was accordingly attacked on all sides tooth and nail.

The real fact was that the native powers in India were not states after the European model. They were for the most part new and crude principalities, which had grown up within the previous half century.[1] Rebel Muhammadan Viceroys had thrown off their dependence on the Great Moghul, and converted their provinces into kingdoms. Mahratta freebooters had created an empire over feudatory princes on the basis of plunder; and their dominions had been consolidated by Brahmans, who played the part of ministers, accountants, and collectors of revenue. There were no political constitutions or hereditary aristocracies in either the Moghul or the Mahratta empires; nothing but bodies of officials, organized chiefly for the collection of revenue, bound by no national ties, and only held together by a system of red-tape and routine, which in times of revolution or disaster was either broken up or dwindled into hereditary names and sinecures.

The older states of Europe may have been created in a similar fashion; but they have endured for a thousand years, and the traditional experiences of a past history have converted subject populations into nationalities, and rude warrior barons into landed nobilities. The kingdoms of India, with the exception of the Rajput principalities, were things of yesterday, without national life or organization. The kingdoms of Europe had undergone a political training under kings and emperors, parliaments, popes, and priests, which had molded them into substantive states, quickened them with international life, and fitted them for the exercise of political power within their respective circles, and the observance of their obligations and duties in the European states system.

The princes and nobles of India required the same training as the old feudal kings and barons of Europe. The Great Moghul, the last symbol of imperialism, had shrivelled into a feeble pageant. The little vitality that remained in the name had died out under a Vizier, or an Amir of Amirs, who might be Moghul or Mahratta, Afghan or Arab, accord-

---

[1] The only exceptions of importance were the Rajputs, and they were overrun by Mahrattas, and were as shattered as the Nizam after the battle of Kurdla.

ing to the daily game of revolutions and shuffling of factions at the Moghul capital. Lord Wellesley was a generation in advance of his age. He saw, with that true genius which is rarely understood or recognized by contemporaries, that a new paramount power was necessary for the salvation of India; and that such a power could be exercised by the British government and by that government alone.

But Lord Wellesley made mistakes, like all other statesmen who are dealing with a present which is imperfectly known and a future that can only be conjectured. He had overrated the strength of the Mahrattas, and the danger of Sindia's French battalions. Since then he had underrated the powers of mischief which were still left in the hands of the Mahratta princes. He was consequently taken aback at the outbreak of Jaswant Rao Holkar; especially when it was followed up by the defection of Sindia and the protected Rajas of Rajputana.

The result of the imbroglio was that the home authorities resolved to reverse the policy of Lord Wellesley, and revert to that of Sir John Shore; to abandon the system of subsidiary and protective alliances, and return to that of neutrality and isolation; and, above all, to conciliate the Mahratta princes to British ascendency by the restoration of conquered territories, and surrender of captured fortresses.

That Lord Wellesley was bitterly mortified by this decision may well be imagined; but every statesman who is in advance of his generation must be prepared to see his ideas ignored, misunderstood, or held up to derision, until popular errors are corrected by public disasters, and the foregone conclusions of those in power are educated by a larger experience to a right understanding of the evils and their cure.

Lord Cornwallis was prepared to go extravagant lengths in the way of conciliation and neutrality. He would have withdrawn the Great Moghul and all his family to Bengal, and made over Delhi to Daulat Rao Sindia, with liberty to recover his lost territories between the Ganges and the Jumna. He would have abandoned the protective treaties with the Rajput and Jat princes, and left them to the tender mercies of the Mahrattas.

Fortunately for the interests of philanthropy, Lord Cornwallis did not live to carry out these reactionary intentions. He was sixty-seven years of age; he had landed at Calcutta at the end of July to be exposed to the damp heats of a Bengal August, when every breeze from the south was laden with the feverish malaria of the Sunderbunds. In the month of September, the most trying month in the plains, he was travelling toward the northwest; and the fatal result might have been foreseen. The anxious veteran became weak in mind and body, sank into a state of insensibility, and, finally, died on the 5th of October, 1805, before he had been ten weeks in the country.

The successor of Lord Cornwallis was a man of a different culture. Sir George Barlow was not an independent nobleman, educated in European politics; but a civil servant of the Company, pliant under superior authority, but self-willed in his own sphere of action. He had been a member of council in the time of Lord Wellesley, and had steadily supported Wellesley's imperial policy. Subsequently, however, he accepted the policy of conciliation and neutrality, which Lord Cornwallis was preparing to carry out in accordance with the will of the home authorities.

The political apostasy of Barlow has been much condemned, but perhaps without sufficient cause. He adopted the imperial system of Lord Wellesley when that nobleman was in power; but it was impossible for him to resist the reaction in public opinion which had recalled Lord Wellesley and placed Lord Cornwallis at the head of affairs. Such open rebellion against all the home authorities, including both houses of parliament, would have been an unwarrantable assumption, and have ended in a political suicide from which nothing was to be gained.

By the end of 1805, Lord Lake had pursued Jaswant Rao Holkar into the Punjab, and forced him to come to terms. A half-hearted treaty was concluded by Sir John Malcolm with the Mahratta adventurer, which satisfied no one. There was enough concession to the new policy of conciliation to exasperate Lord Lake, and enough spice of Wellesley's policy of imperialism to exasperate Sir George Barlow. All Holkar's territories were restored to Jaswant Rao, except the fortress of Tonk Rampoora; but he was bound over not to commit any aggressions on the British government, or on any of its allies, including the Rajput Rajas.

This unexpected liberality revived the audacity of Jaswant Rao. He claimed the territories in Hindustan and the Dekhan, which he had demanded from Lake and Wellesley before the beginning of the war. He claimed a right to collect contributions from the Raja of Jaipur. Lord Lake was so disgusted with these arrogant demands on the part of a prostrate foe that he stopped the negotiations; and then, of course, Jaswant Rao Holkar gave in, and withdrew all demands, and accepted the proffered terms.

But Sir George Barlow was not satisfied with this treaty. He ordered the fortress of Tonk Rampoora to be restored to Jaswant Rao. The recovery of the fortress was most gratifying to the faithless Mahratta, and he naturally thought he could do as he pleased. Accordingly he broke all his pledges, and exacted enormous sums from the Jaipur Raja; while Lord Lake, who had returned to headquarters to save the expense of his field force, was prevented from putting a stop to his depredations.

Sir George Barlow next annulled the protective treaties which had been concluded with the chiefs of Rajputana. He declared that the chiefs had forfeited British protection by the countenance they had subsequently given to Jaswant Rao Holkar during the retreat of Colonel Monson. The Rajput chiefs had certainly deserted the English and helped Holkar when they saw Monson running away. But in like manner they deserted Holkar and helped the English when they saw Jaswant Rao running away. The question in dispute, however, became a matter of personal quarrel between Lake and Barlow. Lake had promised to restore the Raja of Jaipur to the protective alliance provided he resisted the advance of Holkar. The Raja performed his part, but Barlow annulled the protective treaty with Jaipur, and Lake was naturally indignant that his pledges should be ignored. But Barlow was deaf to all the protests of Lake, and abandoned the Rajputs to the irregular demands of the Mahrattas, with the exception of the Rajput state of Ulwar and the Jat state of Bhurtpore, whose claims to protection could not be set aside.

But the violence of the reaction against the policy of Lord Wellesley went too far for even Sir George Barlow. The home authorities proposed to restore all the territories which had been acquired by Lord Wellesley during the Mahratta war. Barlow replied that such a restitution would be most dangerous. Instead of inducing the Mahrattas to keep the peace, it would only tempt them to renewed efforts for the subversion of the British power in India, and a return to the wars and anarchy of the eighteenth century. Meanwhile the Mahratta feudatories heard of the proposal, and were puzzled by the restoration of territory and fortresses to Jaswant Rao Holkar. The Raja of Nagpore especially demanded the restoration of Cuttack and Berar, although Cuttack was essential to the maritime defence of British India, and Berar had been ceded to the Nizam. The Raja of Nagpore, however, was a true Mahratta; and down to his death, in 1816, he never ceased to implore the British government for compensation on account of Cuttack and Berar.

For a brief interval the policy of non-intervention appeared to be a success. The predatory powers confined their depredations to Malwa and Rajputana, and respected the territories of the British government and its allies. There were frequent rumors of confederacies against the British power, but they were generally discredited. To all outward appearance the Peishwa was politically dormant, or too much engaged in trying to reduce the smaller refractory feudatories within his own dominions, to attempt to carry on secret intrigues with other powers outside his frontier. At the same time Sindia and Holkar were afraid of each other, and chiefly busied themselves with exacting revenue and chout for the maintenance of their overgrown armies.

In 1806 there was a great alarm in the Madras Presidency. There was a sudden rising of the sepoys at Vellore, and the Madras army was said to be disaffected. The fortress of Vellore, which had been the scene of many tragedies in the past history of the Carnatic, had been turned into a residence for the Mysore princes of Tippu's family. It was held by a garrison of about four hundred European soldiers, and fifteen hundred sepoys. The sepoys arose in the night, and attacked the European barracks, firing through the Venetian windows until half the force were killed or wounded. Other parties of sepoys attacked the European houses and shot down thirteen English officers, who had rushed out to learn the cause of the uproar. All this while the Mysore princes and their followers were in active communication with the mutineers, supplied them with provisions, and hoisted the flag of Mysore over the fortress.

Unfortunately the Europeans had no ammunition, but the survivors made a sally from the barracks, and managed to maintain a position on a gateway under cover of a bastion. Every officer was killed, but a gallant resistance was maintained by a Sergeant Brodie, who was the hero of the day. Meanwhile news of the outbreak was carried to Arcot, eight miles off, where Colonel Gillespie was in command. Relief was soon at hand. Colonel Gillepsie galloped to Vellore with a troop of European dragoons, and two field guns. Gillespie rode far in advance of his men, and reached the gateway, amid a furious fire, just as Brodie and his small party were burning their last cartridge. A chain of soldiers' belts was let down by Brodie, and Gillespie dragged himself to the top of the gateway, and placed himself at the head of the survivors, who welcomed him as their deliverer. At his word of command the soldiers promptly formed, and drove back the enemy with the bayonet. Presently the dragoons came up with the galloper guns. The gates of the fortress were blown open; the soldiers rushed in; four hundred mutineers were cut down; others were taken prisoners; and a few only escaped by dropping from the walls.

A searching inquiry was made into the cause of the mutiny. It was ascertained that the military authorities at Madras had issued orders forbidding the sepoys from appearing on parade with earrings or caste marks, and requiring them to shave their beards and trim their mustaches. Above all, an obnoxious headdress had been introduced, which was totally unlike the beloved turban, and bore a closer resemblance to the European hat, which has always been an eyesore to Orientals.

These innovations had rankled in the hearts of the Madras sepoys, and exposed them to taunts and derision. At Vellore the disaffection was aggravated by the presence of the Mysore princes, and the fact that many of Tippu's old soldiers were serving in the English garrison. Moreover, alarming rumors were whispered abroad that the new army regulations were only a preliminary to the forcible conversion of the sepoys to Christianity. The prompt action of Colonel Gillespie put a stop to further troubles; but there were some disturbances at Hyderabad, which showed that the disaffection was widely spread.

The Court of Directors were so alarmed at this sepoy mutiny that they recalled Lord William Bentinck, the Governor of Madras, as well as Sir John Craddock, the commander-in-chief of the Madras army, for having sanctioned such dangerous innovations. Lord William Bentinck protested against his removal, but the Directors were inexorable. Twenty years afterward he obtained tardy redress by being appointed Governor-General of India.

In 1807 Sir George Barlow was succeeded at Calcutta by Lord Minto. The new Governor-General was strongly impressed with the wisdom of the policy of non-intervention. He was bent on eschewing the errors of Lord Wellesley and walking in the ways of Lord Cornwallis. Moreover, Great Britain was engaged in wars against Napoleon, and peace in India was to be maintained at any price.

Immediately after Lord Minto's arrival in Bengal, attention was called to the state of affairs in Bundelkund; and he discovered to his surprise and disappointment that the policy of non-intervention was sometimes not only inexpedient but impossible. The territory of Bundelkund stretches to the southward of the Jumna from Behar to Malwa. It was parcelled out among a number of turbulent chieftains, who had been partly conquered by Ali Bahadur,[1] but who were supposed to acknowledge the suzerainty of the Peishwa. A large tract of Bundelkund had been ceded by the Peishwa to the British government for the maintenance of the Poona Subsidiary Force; but it was found that the country had never been completely subjected by the Peishwa, and that territory had been ceded which had never acknowledged his suzerainty. Bundelkund was overrun with military freebooters. A hundred and fifty fortresses were held by as many chiefs of banditti, who were permitted on the principles of non-intervention to settle their disputes by the sword.

Sir George Barlow had sacrificed revenue and prestige rather than violate the new policy; but Lord Minto resolved to take action. Military operations were undertaken with the usual success. The result was that peace and order were established in Bundelkund; and the turbulence and anarchy which had prevailed in these jungle tracts since the days of Aurangzeb were banished out of the land under the protective influence of British rule.

The Punjab next attracted the attention of Lord Minto. A Sikh chieftain, named Runjeet Singh, had brought the Sikh Sirdars under his authority, and established a sovereignty which kept down rebels and bandits by the iron heel of military despotism. The territories of Runjeet Singh included the old battle-grounds where Alexander fought against Porus; and fears were entertained that Napo-

---

[1] See ante, p. 452.

leon would march in the steps of the great Macedonian and attempt the conquest of Hindustan.[1]

In 1807 Runjeet Singh was making aggressions on the Sikh principalities of Sirhind, between the Sutlej and the Jumna. These Cis-Sutlej Sikhs had paid allegiance to the British government ever since the campaign of Lord Lake; and they now applied for British protection against Runjeet Singh. The case was a difficult one, for it was necessary to conciliate Runjeet Singh as regards French invasion, while maintaining British supremacy on the banks of the Sutlej.

In 1808 Lord Minto sent a young civilian, named Charles Metcalfe, to conduct the negotiations with Runjeet Singh; and by firmness on the part of the envoy, and the advance of a military force to the Sutlej, Runjeet Singh was induced to give in, and withdraw his troops to the westward of the river. Mr. Metcalfe established his reputation for tact and discretion by his able conduct of the mission, and lived to play an important part in Indian history.[2]

Later on, the affairs of Jaswant Rao Holkar fell into disorder. His subjects rebelled against him as a usurper, and he sought to retain the throne by murdering his legitimate brother and nephew. Next he took to drinking brandy, until at last he was pronounced to be insane, and placed in confinement; and his wife Tulsi Bai assumed the government of Indore with the help of an Afghan adventurer named Amir Khan.

---

[1] According to the latest orthography "Runjeet" is spelled "Ranjit," and this spelling has been adopted in dealing with Ranjit Singh, the Jat Raja, who is unknown to European readers. But the name of Runjeet Singh, the "Lion of Lahore," has become classical.

[2] Besides Metcalfe's mission to the Punjab, Lord Minto sent a mission, under Colonel Malcolm, to the court of Persia, and another, under Mr. Mountstuart Elphinstone, to the court of Kabul, to counteract the supposed designs of the Emperor Napoleon. Neither mission was followed by any practical result, and both might be passed over as obsolete. It is, however, curious to note that Elphinstone never reached Kabul, but met Shah Shuja, the nominal sovereign of Afghanistan, at Peshawar. By this time the Afghan empire, founded by Ahmad Shah Abdali, was broken up; the whole country was distracted by civil wars, and Shah Shuja was driven into exile shortly after Elphinstone left Peshawar.

The career of Amir Khan, the founder of the Tonk principality, reveals the wretched condition of Rajputana and Malwa. Originally Amir Khan was a leader of bandits, and as such he had been an associate of Jaswant Rao Holkar. His banditti grew into an army, maintained by forced contributions and robberies. When Jaswant Rao became insane, Amir Khan interfered in the affairs of Indore; he professed to protect the state of Holkar, while exacting large grants of territory and revenue from the weak government of Tulsi Bai.

Amir Khan, like all the predatory powers at this period, was constantly in want of means to support his lawless soldiery. Rajputana and Malwa were exhausted, and he was compelled to look abroad. He revived some dormant claim of Holkar against the Bhonsla Raja of Nagpore, and invaded Nagpore territory with a large army

Lord Minto sent a force to protect Nagpore, and the result was that Amir Khan was forced to retire to his own territories. But Lord Minto felt that this interference was a violation of the policy of non-intervention; and he explained to the Court of Directors that he had interfered in behalf of the Raja of Nagpore as a measure of self-defence, to prevent any alliance between two Muhammadan powers, like Amir Khan and the Nizam. By this time, however, the home authorities were awakening to the fact that war, brigandage, and anarchy were on the increase in Central India; and they not only approved of what Lord Minto had done, but expressed a wish that he had made an end of Amir Khan.

One episode will suffice to reveal the horrible state of turmoil which prevailed in the fertile regions of Rajputana. Every Rajput chieftain was anxious to marry a daughter of the Rana of Udaipur. The reigning Rana had only one daughter, and she had been betrothed at an early age to the Raja of Jodhpur. The Raja died, and was succeeded by a prince named Man Singh. Meanwhile the princess had been betrothed to the Raja of Jaipur; but Man Singh claimed her hand on the ground that she had been betrothed to the throne of Jodhpur, and not to the mere occupant for the time being.

From 1806 to 1810, Rajputana was convulsed by this domestic struggle between Jodhpur and Jaipur. Nearly all the chiefs in Rajputana took a part in the war, just as their forefathers had fought on either side in the war of the Maha Bharata.

Amir Khan went from one side to the other with his army of banditti, as best suited his own interests. Originally he was bought over by Jaipur, and helped to defeat Man Singh, and shut him up in his fortress of Jodhpur, while ravaging the surrounding country. Next he was bought over by Man Singh, who offered to pay him a yearly tribute of some half a million sterling. Meanwhile Amir Khan was guilty of treacheries and wholesale assassinations, which alone would suffice to brand his character with infamy.

All this time the Rana of Udaipur took no part in the war; but his territories were exposed to the ravages and depredations of Daulat Rao Sindia and Amir Khan. The marches of the Mahratta and Afghan armies were to be traced by blazing villages and ruined harvests; and whereever they encamped they turned the garden of Rajputana into a desert and desolation.

In this extremity the Rana of Udaipur claimed the protection of the British government as the paramount power. He offered to cede half his territories for the defence of the other half. The rival princes of Jodhpur and Jaipur joined in the solicitation. They declared that there always had been a paramount power in India to protect the weak against the strong; and as the East India Company had become the paramount power it was bound to fulfil its duties.

The interference of the British government would have put an end to all this frightful anarchy; but it would have been an open and undisguised violation of the policy of non-intervention. The Rana of Udaipur was refused all help. Driven by despair, he bought the protection of Amir Khan by the cession of a quarter of his dominions; and stooped to the ignominy of exchanging turbans with the Afghan freebooter.

Still the war was raging between Jodhpur and Jaipur. Amir Khan proposed to stop it by taking the life of the innocent cause of the quarrel; and he threatened to carry off the princess, and make her over to Man Singh of Jodhpur, unless his advice was followed. The miserable Rana gave his consent to the murder of his child; and the Rajput maiden accepted her doom, and drank the poison which was to put an end to her existence. The terrible tragedy filled western India with shame and horror; and there was not a chieftain in Rajputana who did not lament the fate of the unhappy princess, and execrate all concerned in the heartless atrocity.

But other causes were at work, besides the policy of non-intervention, to prevent Lord Minto from interfering in western India. The war between Great Britain and France was being fought in eastern waters. The Mauritius was a depot for French frigates and privateers, which swept the seas from Madagascar to Java. The merchants of Calcutta alone estimated their losses at two millions sterling since the beginning of the war, while, in one year, the East India Company estimated their losses at half a million.[1]

In 1810 Lord Minto sent an expedition against the Mauritius and captured the island. In 1811 he sent expeditions against the Dutch settlements in India, which had passed into the hands of Napoleon. The island of Java was captured and occupied by the English down to the end of the war with France; but eventually it was restored to the Dutch, and irretrievably lost to the British nation.

Lord Minto accompanied the expedition to Java, but returned to Calcutta in 1812. Anarchy still prevailed in Malwa and Rajputana. Jaswant Rao Holkar died in 1811, and was succeeded by an infant, named Mulhar Rao Hol-

[1] The merchants at Calcutta chiefly confined their trading to the eastern seas, and consequently suffered most severely. The East Indiamen from Europe were armed like men-of-war.

kar, who had been adopted by his widow Tulsi Bai. This, however, was a matter of small moment in comparison with the dark clouds which threatened India in the shape of organized battalions of bandits under Amir Khan, and the loose bands of marauders who were known by the dreaded name of Pindharies.

The Pindharies were a low class of freebooters, who had been attached to the Mahratta armies during the desolating wars of the eighteenth century. Their origin is lost in obscurity, but one body, as already seen, joined the Mahratta host that fought at Paniput.[1] The Mahratta horsemen of any respectability affected to look down upon the Pindharies; but it was only a difference between regular and irregular banditti; between gentlemen highwaymen who were ready to fight, and pickpockets and pilferers who were ready to run away.

Before the Mahratta wars of 1803 and 1804 the Pindharies had been distributed among different Mahratta chieftains. One body was known as Sindia's Pindharies; another body as Holkar's Pindharies; and lands were assigned by Sindia and Holkar to different Pindhari leaders for the maintenance of their respective hordes. When the wars were over the Pindharies still formed separate and independent bodies, but followed the fortunes of any turbulent chieftain or lawless adventurer. They were not divided by differences of race and religion, but were the riffraff of Hindus and Muhammadans bound together by no tie save that of plunder.

Two notorious Pindhari leaders were known by the names of Chetu and Khurim. There was no union between the two; on the contrary, they were jealous of each other, and often at open enmity; and they were entirely wanting in the military strength and organization which characterized the army of Amir Khan.

At first the Pindharies confined their depredations to Rajputana and Malwa. Sometimes they made raids on the

---

[1] See ante, p. 392.

territories of Sindia and Holkar. On one occasion Daulat Rao Sindia captured the two Pindhari leaders, and kept them in confinement; but was at last induced to liberate them on payment of a ransom of a hundred thousand pounds sterling. Subsequently, they extended their raids into the Dekhan, and invaded the territories of the Peishwa, the Nizam, and the Raja of Nagpore.

In 1809–10, Captain Sydenham, the Resident at Hyderabad, described the proceedings of the Pindharies. Their incursions, he said, were as regular as the periodical monsoons. They seemed to wait with malicious pleasure until the crops were ripe upon the ground, and then robbed the unfortunate husbandmen of the fruit of their labors at the moment they expected to reap them. Every villain who escaped from his creditors, or was expelled for flagrant crimes, or was disgusted with an honest and peaceable life, fled to Central India and enrolled himself among the Pindharies.

The Pindharies generally invaded a country in bands varying from one thousand to four thousand men. On reaching the frontier they dispersed in small parties of two or three hundred. They advanced with such rapidity that the story of their depredations was generally the first news of their approach. They were not encumbered with tents or baggage, but carried only their arms, and slept on their saddle-cloths. Both men and horses were accustomed to long marches, and they never halted except to refresh themselves, to collect plunder, or to commit the vilest outrages on the female population. They subsisted on the grain and provisions which they found in the villages; took everything that was valuable; and wantonly destroyed all that they could not carry away.

Lord Minto left India in 1813, and was succeeded as Governor-General by Lord Moira, afterward Marquis of Hastings. One of the last acts of Lord Minto's administration was to impress on the Court of Directors the necessity for adopting large measures for the purpose of suppressing the Pindharies; and thus from an early period the attention of Lord Moira was directed to the annual depredations of these organized banditti.

Lord Moira landed at Calcutta in the fifty-ninth year of his age. Before he left England he had denounced the ambitious policy of Lord Wellesley in seeking to establish the British government as the paramount power in India. But his attention had already been directed to the yearly expeditions of the Pindharies; and soon after his arrival in Bengal he began to modify his political views. He reported to the Court of Directors that the battalions of Amir Khan and hordes of Pindharies numbered some fifty thousand men; that they subsisted by plunder alone, and extended their ravages over an area as large as England. He emphatically declared that the affairs of the Company would never prosper until the British government was placed at the head of a league which embraced every native state in India, and was enabled to bring the whole strength of the league to bear upon any single power that disturbed the public peace.

This sudden conversion of Lord Moira from the policy of non-intervention to that of a paramount power had no effect upon the home authorities. There was still the same morbid dread of the Mahrattas, which misled the British nation at the beginning of the century. Daulat Rao Sindia was still regarded as a dangerous power like Chenghiz Khan or Timur. In reality he was a prince in sore distress, worried by an army which was in frequent mutiny from want of subsistence, and paralyzed by a terror of the English which never left him after the battle of Assaye. He had been anxious to follow the advice of the British Resident, who still accompanied his camp; but the Resident was a victim to the policy of non-intervention, and refused to advise Sindia. Thus in India and in England every one, save Lord Moira, was a strict adherent to the policy of non-intervention. Accordingly, Lord Moira was told by the Directors that no league was to be formed, or any step taken for the suppression of the Pindharies, that was likely to embroil the British government with the Mahrattas, or to give offence to Daulat Rao Sindia.

Meanwhile black clouds were gathering over the Himalayas. For years the Ghorka rulers of Nipal had been making systematic encroachments on British territory. The English in Bengal remonstrated in vain. They were anxious for peace at any price short of abject submission; but the Ghorkas were beyond all bearing: appropriating villages and districts without a shadow of a claim, and turning a deaf ear to all representations, or stubbornly insisting that the abstracted territory had always belonged to Nipal. Lord Minto sent an ultimatum to Khatmandu before he left Bengal, and Lord Moira sent another shortly after his arrival. The result was the Ghorka war of 1814 and 1815; but before describing the military operations it will be as well to review the history of the Ghorka conquest of Nipal.

CHAPTER XI

NIPAL HISTORY—GHORKA CONQUEST

A.D. 1767 TO 1814

NORTHWARD of Hindustan, a square mass of territory extends over the Himalayas beyond the British frontier toward the great desert of Gobi or Shamo, the terror of Marco Polo.[1] On the west, this irregular quadrangle is bounded by Kashmir and the upper streams of the Sutlej and Ganges; on the east by China proper and the courses of rivers which are as yet unfamiliar to modern geographers. The southern side of the quadrangle, immediately to the northward of British territory, is occupied by the mountain range of the Himalayas, which includes the valley of Nipal and heights of Bhutan. Northward of the Himalayas the flat tableland of Thibet stretches over little known tracts toward the great desert. Southern Thibet is watered by the Brahmaputra river, which coils like a huge serpent round the northern slopes of the Himalayas, and finally flows southward through Assam, and helps to form the delta of the Ganges.

A veil of religious mystery hangs over the Himalayan mountains and the Thibetan tableland beyond. Buddhism, which once overshadowed Hindustan, was driven northward between the eighth and twelfth centuries of the Christian era by the great Brahmanical revival which was associated with the reformed worship of Vishnu and Siva. The monasteries and the monastic colleges, which once flourished on the banks

---

[1] It was known to Marco Polo as the desert of Lop, and was said to be haunted by evil spirits or goblins.

of the Ganges and Jumna, reappeared amid the mountain scenery of the Himalayas and pathless wastes to the northward. But Hindustan was never forgotten. The memories of the holy land of Behar and Gaya, sanctified by the footsteps of Sakya Muni and his disciples, were treasured in the hearts of the inmates of every monastery, from the boy néophyte of twelve or fourteen to the venerable Lama or abbot, who ruled as lord and master. To this day pious legends of Magadha and Benares are still the subjects of religious thought and teaching in those remote regions, which are a *terra incognita* to the European.[1]

Buddhism, like Christendom, has its bishops and its heresies. The city of Lhassa, seated on the southern bank of the Brahmaputra, forty days' journey from Pekin, is the Rome of Thibetan and Chinese Buddhism. At Lhassa a succession of Great Lamas, the supposed incarnations of Sakya Muni, exercise a spiritual dominion resembling that of the Holy See. At Digarchi, ten days' journey to the westward of Lhassa, the Teshu Lama is worshipped and protected by the emperors of China as their spiritual father.[2]

The valley of Nipal is located in the southern slopes of the Himalaya range. It is shut out from Hindustan by the lower shelves and precipices of the Himalayas; while the still lower range of mountains, at the base, is guarded by a broad belt of dense forest, from which a low marshy plain stretches out toward the south, the whole being known as the Terai. Nipal has rarely been invaded by Muhammadans

---

[1] The holy land of Magadha is identical with the modern Behar or Vihar. The word Vihar signifies a Buddhist monastery.

[2] Both the Great Lama of Lhassa and the Teshu Lama of Digarchi are pontiffs of the yellow sect, the orthodox and reformed Buddhism of the court of Pekin. But the followers of the red sect, who retain much of the old devil-worship and incantations in their religious observances, continue to maintain monasteries and Lamas of their own in Thibet and Bhutan.

Thibet is nominally subject to the Chinese emperor, but little is known of the extent of Chinese jurisdiction in that quarter. Lhassa is the capital of what is called Chinese Thibet, and is the abode of a Chinese viceroy as well as of the Great Lama.

or Moghuls, and to this day the Muhammadans form no part of its population.[1]

From a remote period this fertile and secluded valley has been inhabited by a peaceful and industrious race of Hindu Buddhists, known as Newars. Like India, the whole country was parcelled out into petty Hindu kingdoms, each having its own Raja; but in the early half of the eighteenth century the whole were absorbed in three kingdoms, of which Khatmandu was the chief. Indeed, at this period the Newar Raja of Khatmandu was always treated by the East India Company as the ruler of Nipal.

In those early times the valley of Nipal might have been likened to the happy valley of Rasselas. The Newars were devoted to agriculture and trade, and pursued the even tenor of their way under the mild influence of Buddhism. The East India Company carried on a profitable trade with Nipal; and numerous commodities, including quantities of gold from Thibet, were imported into Behar and Bengal.

About 1767, ten years after Plassy, the Ghorkas of Kashmir, a race of Rajputs and Brahmans, invaded the happy valley of Nipal. There was no apparent cause of quarrel. The Ghorkas were a military people, hungering after territory and revenue; and the valley of Nipal, with its peaceful population of Buddhist Newars, was open to their inroads. They preserved the usages of caste, and worshipped the same gods as the Rajputs of Hindustan; and the Ghorka conquest may have been a later wave of the great Brahmanical revival which convulsed India in mediæval times and drove Buddhism out of Hindustan.

The Newars were as helpless to resist the Ghorkas as sheep when attacked by wolves. The Newar Raja of Khatmandu abandoned his territories to the invaders, and shut himself up in his capital, and implored the help of his mercantile friends in Bengal. Strange to say, the English rulers responded to his prayers. Their trade was slack, their

---

[1] Muhammad Tughlak sent an army over the Himalayas in the fourteenth century, but it perished miserably. See ante, p. 109.

revenues were falling away, and specie itself was vanishing from Bengal. Moreover, the spirit of Clive was still abroad, and the Company's servants were burning with military glory as well as commercial enterprise. A small force was sent to the Himalayas under a Captain Kinloch to deliver the Newar Raja from the Ghorkas, and reopen the outlets of gold from Thibet. Unfortunately Kinloch set out at the worst season of the year. He made a desperate effort to march through the Terai in the middle of the rains, but was beaten back by malaria and want of provisions; and the Newars and their Rajas were abandoned to their doom.

Maharaja Prithi Narain was the hero and sovereign of the Ghorkas. He conquered the Nipal valley by the aid of his Bharadars or barons. He made a great slaughter of the Newar Rajas, and massacred every Newar of distinction throughout the country. The horrors of the Ghorka conquest were beyond all telling. A European eye-witness, Father Guiseppe, describes Prithi Narain as a monster of inhumanity—as crafty, treacherous, and bloodthirsty as any Tartar conqueror of the olden time. Atrocities and outrages were committed which must be left to the imagination. At one city, six miles from Khatmandu, the whole of the inhabitants were deprived of their lips and noses in punishment for their long and obstinate resistance to the invaders.

The Ghorka conquest throws valuable light on the ancient constitution of the Rajputs. The valley of Nipal was parcelled out among the Ghorka Bharadars, much in the same way that England was parcelled out among the Norman barons under William the Conqueror. The Maharaja reigned at Khatmandu as sovereign and despot; but the Bharadars claimed for themselves and families an exclusive right to all offices and commands, as well as a voice in the national councils. Accordingly the Maharaja selected his ministers exclusively from the Bharadar aristocracy; and in times of national emergency all the Bharadars in the kingdom were summoned to a council of state at Khatmandu.

The strength of the Ghorkas lay in their military organization. They maintained three armies at the expense of one, each army numbering about twelve thousand men. About the end of every year the existing army returned to civil life, while a new army was enrolled, which generally consisted of old soldiers. Thus three trained armies could be brought into the field in cases of emergency, while only one army was kept on military duty, and drew military pay.

The old army was disbanded and the new army was enlisted at a yearly festival known as the Panjani. At every Panjani there was a redistribution of all offices and commands among the Bharadars and their families. Indeed, under the old Ghorka constitution the Panjani was the great institution of the year, when there was a change of ministers as well as officers and generals, and nothing remained permanent excepting the Maharaja.

Prithi Narain, the hero founder of the Ghorka dynasty in Nipal, died in 1771, leaving two sons. The elder succeeded to the throne, but died in 1775, leaving an infant son, a babe in arms. Then followed the usual complication. The baby grandson of Prithi Narain was placed upon the throne under the name of Run Bahadur. The uncle of the infant, the younger son of Prithi Narain, became regent and guardian. But the queen-mother also claimed to be regent and guardian; and for some years there was a struggle for supremacy between the queen-mother and the uncle—a struggle which used to be common to every Hindu court in India.[1] In 1786, when the boy Maharaja was eleven years of age, the queen-mother died, and the uncle became supreme. Henceforth the uncle surrounded the boy with all the young profligates of the court, and permitted him to indulge in every species of vice and cruelty, in the hope of

[1] Such rivalries and jealousies between a minister and a queen-mother have been frequent in all Oriental courts from a remote antiquity. Sometimes the quarrel is prevented by a criminal intimacy between the two parties. In India the British government arbitrates as the paramount power, and all quarrels about a succession or a regency are thus nipped in the bud.

thereby perpetuating his own authority as regent. It will be seen hereafter that he sowed the wind and reaped the whirlwind.

Meanwhile the Ghorkas were troublesome and aggressive toward all their neighbors—westward toward Kashmir and the Punjab, and eastward toward Sikhim and Bhutan. One Ghorka army invaded Thibet and plundered the temples at Lhassa and Digarchi. The audacity and sacrilege kindled the wrath of the Chinese emperor and court of Pekin; and in 1792 a Chinese army of seventy thousand men advanced against Nipal.

The Ghorkas were wild with alarm, and began to make advances to the English. Hitherto they had affected to disdain trade and traders, and had displayed a haughty and exclusive spirit in their dealings with the Bengal government. But the victories of the English in the first Mahratta war had inspired them with respect, and they hungered for the help of British arms and soldiers.[1] They hastily offered to negotiate a treaty of commerce and friendship with the English Resident at Benares; and a treaty was concluded in 1792, under which certain privileges were granted to traders from British territories, and a fixed duty of two and a half per cent was to be charged by either government on all commodities imported on either side.

The commercial treaty was a blind. The Ghorkas amused the Bengal government with hopes of a revival of trade, and then asked for British help against China. Lord Cornwallis replied that the English had no quarrel with the Chinese emperor, but would willingly mediate between Nipal and China; and for this purpose he sent Colonel Kirkpatrick on a mission to Khatmandu.

Before Kirkpatrick left Patna the Ghorkas were routed by the Chinese and driven back to Nipal through the snows

---

[1] The old trade between Bengal and Behar had died out under the military despotism of the Ghorkas, and every effort to recover it had hitherto proved a failure. In 1774 Warren Hastings sent a mission to Thibet under Mr. Bogle; and in 1783 he sent another under Mr. Turner; but there was no practical result.

of the Himalayas. The Chinese army advanced to Nayakote, within a day's march of Khatmandu, and dictated their own terms. The Ghorka regency was compelled to restore all the plunder that had been carried from the temples, and to pay tribute for the future to the court of Pekin.

The Ghorkas were now disgusted with their treaty with the English, and only anxious to keep the English out of Nipal. Kirkpatrick was met by messengers, who announced the peace with China, and tried to induce him to go back. But the Bengal government was anxious to establish friendly relations with the Ghorka government, and Kirkpatrick pushed on to Khatmandu. He was received with every show of courtesy and respect, but thwarted in every attempt at negotiation. He soon found that his presence at Khatmandu was useless and dangerous, and returned to Bengal. Henceforth the treaty was a dead letter.

In 1795 there was a revolution at Khatmandu. Maharaja Run Bahadur had reached his twentieth year. He had been nurtured in the worst possible school, and the natural ferocity of his temper had been encouraged rather than controlled. At last he cunningly worked the destruction of his uncle. He suddenly announced in open durbar that he had assumed the sovereignty; and the Bharadars hailed the declaration with a burst of loyalty. The regent uncle was powerless to contend against the voice of the nobles, and compelled to give place to his nephew. For a few months he was treated with decent respect, but was then arrested, loaded with chains, and thrown into a dungeon. Nothing more was heard of him. Some said that he was starved to death; others that he was assassinated by his royal nephew.

Run Bahadur reigned over Nipal like another Nero. Day by day he took a savage joy in beholding tortures, mutilations, and executions. His marriages and amours were the scandal of Khatmandu. His chief wife was childless. His second wife gave birth to a son, and was then neglected. Run Bahadur, in spite of his Kshatriya caste, was bent on securing a Brahmani bride. He carried off a young Brahmani widow from her father's house in the plains, and made her his queen, in violation of the laws against widow marriages and the mixture of castes; and a son was born of the Brahmani queen, who was destined to change the fortunes of the dynasty.

Run Bahadur was deeply enamored of his Brahmani bride. She was his prime favorite, the idol of his soul. She was seized with smallpox, and Run Bahadur was frantic with grief and alarm. He spent vast sums on offerings to the gods at the different temples. He summoned the ablest physicians from Benares to attend the sick lady. But prayers and medicines were of no avail, and the Brahmani queen was soon numbered with the dead.

Run Bahadur was driven to madness by the loss of his Brahmani queen. He broke out in fits of ungovernable fury, which spread a wild terror through the court and capital. He flogged the physicians, cut off their noses, and sent them back to Benares. He wreaked his vengeance on the gods of Nipal by firing cannon at the sacred statues in the temple of Pusput Nath, the great national shrine of Siva and Parvati in the suburbs of Khatmandu. He threw up the sovereignty, and vowed to spend the remainder of his days in religious seclusion at Benares; and he actually placed the little son of his dead queen on the throne of Nipal, and called on the Bharadars to swear allegiance to the infant. He sought to smooth matters by appointing his second wife to be regent, and her young son to be prime minister. The result was a baby sovereign aged four, a child premier aged six, and a regent stepmother. But Run Bahadur remained at Khatmandu. He had abdicated the throne, but persisted in exercising supreme authority.

The abdication of Run Bahadur was a mere caprice of insanity. He wished to honor his dead queen by placing her son upon the throne; but he continued to wreak his ferocity on those around him. Some officers of government were scourged; others were hung up by the heels to branches of trees. In a word, the sovereign was dangerous to his subjects; and neither rank, age, nor caste could protect any one from his blind anger.

Meanwhile the Bharadars began to conspire against the headstrong Maharaja; and Damodur Pandey, the head of the once famous Pandey family, was the moving spirit of the conspiracy. The Bharadars urged that their allegiance had been solemnly transferred to the infant son, and they called on Run Bahadur to complete his abdication of the throne by going into exile. Damodur Pandey had already gained over the army; indeed, he was a type of those Hindu ministers who, at different intervals, have dragged their country and its princes at the heels of a military car. A civil war broke out, and Run Bahadur was worsted. He saw that his life was in sore peril, and suddenly left Khatmandu in the night time, and fled to Benares, accompanied by his neglected chief queen and a young Bharadar named Bhim Sein Thapa, who was the head of the Thapa family, and bitter rival of the Pandeys.

The flight of Run Bahadur placed Damodur Pandey at the head of affairs. He was appointed prime minister to the infant Maharaja and regent stepmother; and he filled all the ministerial posts with members of the Pandey family. Henceforth there were constant plottings at Benares for the destruction of the Pandeys and restoration of Run Bahadur to the throne of Nipal; and at the same time constant counterplots at Khatmandu for the forcible detention of the royal exile in British territory, and the destruction of Bhim Sein Thapa.

At this period Lord Wellesley was Governor-General of India. The sudden appearance of the ex-Maharaja of Nipal within British territory stirred up that active nobleman to attempt the recovery of the lost trade. Run Bahadur was received by the British authorities at Benares with every mark of honor and distinction. Money from the Company's treasury was advanced for his support. A Captain Knox was appointed Political Agent, to carry on all communication with the royal exile, and to open up negotiations in his behalf with the regency at Khatmandu.

The government of the East India Company was conducted on mercantile principles. It was therefore deemed necessary to apply to the Ghorka government for a repayment of the moneys advanced to the ex-Maharaja, and also for a suitable pension for his future maintenance. Accordingly Captain Knox was sent to Khatmandu in 1802 to make the necessary arrangements, and also to establish a cordial friendship with the ruling powers, and open up a trade through Nipal with Thibet and Bhutan. Knox was welcomed at Khatmandu with respect and courtesy, but soon found that he was hedged around with spies, and played upon by mendacious intriguers. There was a great show of business and much pretended negotiation, but nothing was concluded. At heart the Ghorkas were as jealous and exclusive as ever, and evidently imagined that Lord Wellesley was scheming to restore Run Bahadur, overthrow the Ghorka dominion, and take possession of Nipal. After much prevarication and vacillation they agreed to pay certain yearly allowances to the ex-Maharaja, as long as he was detained in British territory. In return, the ex-Maharaja pledged himself to devote the remainder of his life to the worship of the Supreme Spirit at Benares, under the religious title of "Swami." But the money was never sent to Benares, and Run Bahadur only professed to be a Swami until a way was opened for his restoration to the throne at Khatmandu.

Suddenly the chief queen left the ex-Maharaja at Benares and made her way to Nipal. She was resolved to oust the second queen from the regency, and take the government into her own hands. Her approach threw the court of Khatmandu into confusion. Cannon were drawn up before the city gates; guards were posted in every avenue; ammunition was served out; and hurry, noise and disorder prevailed in every quarter. Damodur Pandey began to vacillate, and went out to make terms with the chief queen. In his absence the second queen fled from the palace with the infant Maharaja, and took refuge in the temple of Pusput Nath. Meanwhile the chief queen was joined by Damodur Pandey, and entered Khatmandu in triumph, and assumed the post of regent. The infant Maharaja was then brought back from the temple, and placed upon the throne; and the second queen saved her life by timely submission to her older rival.

The new government was profuse in promises to Captain Knox, but only to cajole and thwart him. The new queen-regent evaded the terms which had been accepted by her predecessor; and Knox left Khatmandu in disgust as Kirkpatrick had done ten years previously. Accordingly Lord Wellesley formally announced to the new government that the alliance with Nipal was dissolved, and told the ex-Maharaja that he might leave Benares, and go where he pleased.

In 1804 Run Bahadur returned to Nipal accompanied by Bhim Sein Thapa. Damodur Pandey came out to meet him at the head of the Ghorka army, prepared to join him or fight him as occasion might arise. But the Ghorka soldiery were still loyal at heart toward the ex-Maharaja. Run Bahadur fearlessly advanced toward the opposing column, and threw his royal bonnet into the air, exclaiming, "Now, my Ghorkas, who is for me, and who is for the Pandeys?"

At once the whole army received their sovereign with acclamations. Damodur Pandey was arrested on the spot, loaded with chains, and carried off to Khatmandu, and beheaded with many of his adherents. The chief queen resigned the government into the hands of her husband; but Run Bahadur dared not assume the title of Maharaja. The army had sworn fidelity to the son of the Brahmani queen; and Run Bahadur was obliged to be content with the post of regent, and to carry on the government in the name of his son, with Bhim Sein Thapa for his prime minister.

The revolution, however, was not yet over. The air of Khatmandu was heavily charged with plots and intrigues. Many Bharadars had supported the Pandeys, and they now dreaded the resentment of the Thapas. A conspiracy was formed under the leadership of the brother of Run Bahadur for the overthrow of the new government, and the destruction of the Thapas; but the scheme exploded before it was ripe for execution.

Bhim Sein Thapa discovered the plot, and made his arrangements accordingly. By his advice Run Bahadur ordered his brother to attend the durbar, and then directed him to join the Ghorka army on the western frontier. The brother returned an insolent reply, and was ordered off to immediate execution. The brother drew his sword before he could be arrested, and slaughtered Run Bahadur on the spot, but was then cut to pieces on the floor of the hall.

The bystanders were horror-stricken at the double murder. Every man was cowed, and thought only of his own safety. Bhim Sein Thapa alone was master of himself and the situation. By his orders every enemy of the Thapa family was put to the sword on the charge of being implicated in the murder of Run Bahadur. Fifty officers of the army are said to have been executed amid the general massacre. Meanwhile the remains of the dead sovereign were carried off to the place of burning; and his second queen, the deposed regent-mother, was forced to immolate herself on the funeral pile.

The deeply laid plot of Bhim Sein Thapa was soon revealed to the people of Khatmandu. It turned out that he was the secret paramour of the chief queen. Accordingly the chief queen resumed her post of regent-mother, and Bhim Sein Thapa continued to hold the post of prime minister, while he was virtually the sole ruler of Nipal. For some years there was a lull in the domestic politics of the Ghorkas, but meanwhile the Ghorka rulers were forcing the British government into a war against Nipal.

CHAPTER XII

NIPAL WAR—LORD MOIRA (HASTINGS)[1]

A.D. 1814 TO 1816

IN 1813, eight years after the elevation of Bhim Sein Thapa, Lord Minto resigned the post of Governor-General of India into the hands of Lord Moira. Ever since the dissolution of the alliance by Lord Wellesley in 1804, there had been constant wrangling between the two governments. The Ghorka authorities had been gradually absorbing British territory along the whole line of frontier to the north of Hindustan, from the neighborhood of Darjeeling to the neighborhood of Simla. Sir George Barlow had remonstrated, and Lord Minto had remonstrated, but to no purpose. Each Governor-General in turn had overlooked the aggressions in order to avoid a war; until at last it was discovered that within the previous quarter of a century more than two hundred British villages had been added to Nipal territory; and it was obvious that the aggressions were conducted on a regular system, having for its object the extension of Nipal dominion to the banks of the Ganges.

At last two large districts were annexed by the Ghorka authorities, respecting which there could not be a shadow of doubt. At this date Lord Minto was still Governor-General, and he invited the Nipal government to send a commissioner to investigate the claim to the two districts, in association with a British commissioner. The investigation lasted over a year. In the end it was ascertained that the districts in question had always belonged to Oude; and that they formed

---

[1] Lord Moira was not created Marquis of Hastings until after the Nipal war, but he is best known to history by the latter title.

a part of the territory which the Nawab Vizier had ceded to the British government in 1801. The Nipal commissioner was unable to disprove this fact, or to show that his government had any claim whatever to the disputed territory.

The Nipal government dealt with the case in characteristic fashion. They recalled their commissioner and stoutly maintained that the investigation proved their right to the two districts. Lord Minto then brought matters to a crisis. He sent an ultimatum to the effect that unless the districts were restored they would be recovered by force. The answer was not received until after the arrival of Lord Moira; it was to the effect that the districts belonged to Nipal, and would not be surrendered.

Lord Moira followed up the action of his predecessor by sending another ultimatum, fixing the day on which the districts were to be restored. The Nipal government allowed the time to pass; and a British detachment took possession of the districts without opposition, and set up police stations for their protection.

But although the Ghorka government had treated the ultimatum with apparent contempt, the letter of Lord Moira had nevertheless created a profound sensation, and led to a division of parties in Nipal. Bhim Sein Thapa foresaw that the local dispute about frontier districts was broadening into a question of peace or war. He summoned the Bharadars to a council of state at Khatmandu, and twenty-two Bharadars assembled to discuss the question.

Amar Singh, the most renowned general in the Ghorka army, was opposed to the war. He had faced Runjeet Singh, the "lion" of the Punjab; and he knew something of the fighting powers of Englishmen, and the resources of the British government. "Fighting against the Newars," he said, "was like hunting deer; but fighting against Englishmen would be like battling with tigers." Other chiefs joined Amar Singh in deprecating a collision with the British government; but Bhim Sein Thapa held a different opinion. "What power," he asked, "can fight against us in Nipal?

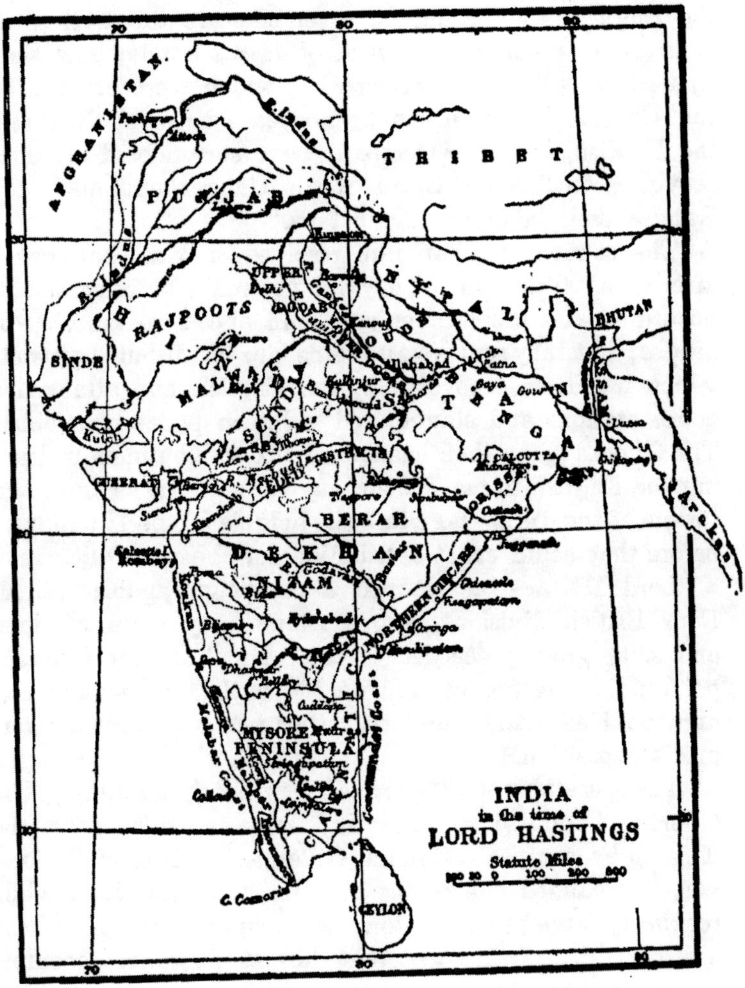
INDIA
in the time of
LORD HASTINGS
Statute Miles
AFGHANISTAN
PUNJAB
TIBBET
NEPAL
BHUTAN
RAJPOOTS
SINDE
MALWA
UPPER DOAB
Delhi
Allahabad
Patna
CALCUTTA
GUZERAT
BERAR
DEKKAN
NIZAM
Hydrabad
NORTHERN CIRCARS
MYSORE
PENINSULA
C. Comorin
CEYLON
Arakan

Not even the great Alexander of Macedon could carry his rams into our mountains.[1] Our hills and fastnesses are the work of God, and are not to be taken by mortals. As for the English, they could not even capture the fortress of Bhurtpore, which is the work of men's hands; how then shall they reduce our strongholds, which were created by the Almighty? There can be no peace between Nipal and the English, until the Company have surrendered all their provinces to the northward of the Ganges, and made the Ganges their boundary against us."

The council of Bharadars resolved on war; but a war after Oriental fashion. They did not make a declaration of hostilities, and prepare for a solemn appeal to the God of battles; but they sent a large force into the disputed districts which had been recovered by the English, and attacked a police station, and slaughtered eighteen police constables. The Ghorka army then hastened back to Khatmandu, leaving the English to make their way through the swamps and forests of the Terai and climb the heights of the Himalayas, before they could exact retribution for the cowardly crime.

Lord Moira soon planned a campaign against Nipal. Four British divisions, aggregating thirty thousand men and sixty guns, proceeded to enter Nipal at four different points: the western column on the Sutlej, the eastern column on Khatmandu, and the other two columns on intermediate positions.

The operations of 1814 proved very nearly a failure. The Ghorkas exhibited a pluck and bravery which took the English by surprise. General Gillespie, the hero of Vellore, who commanded one of the columns, was shot dead while recklessly attempting to storm a mountain fortress without a siege train. Other generals showed a strange incompetency, and one of them on setting out was so alarmed at the

---

[1] Alexander the Great is known to Asiatics by the name of Sekunder. Bhim Sein Thapa alluded to him as Sekunder, but the name would convey no idea to English readers, and has accordingly been modified in the text.

density of the forests in the Terai that he galloped back to Dinapore, leaving his division behind him.

General David Ochterlony, who commanded the division advancing by the way of the Sutlej and Ludhiana, was pitted against Amar Singh, the Ghorka general who had deprecated the war. Ochterlony was a Company's officer of the old heroic type. In his younger days he had fought against Hyder Ali in the Carnatic under Sir Eyre Coote. At a later day he had held Delhi against the Mahratta army under Jaswant Rao Holkar. His advance up the Himalayas was a marvel of caution and audacity. Those who have visited Simla will realize the difficulties of his march along shelves and precipices, dragging up eighteen-pounders, and opening roads by blasting rocks, and battering down obstructions with his field guns. For five months, at the worst season of the year, in the teeth of snowstorms and mountain blasts, he carried one fortress after another, until not a stronghold was left in the hands of the enemy excepting Maloun.

The fortress of Maloun was situated on a shelf of the Himalayas, with steep declivities of two thousand feet on two of its sides. Amar Singh was shut up in Maloun. After a desperate attack on the British works, he held out till the British batteries were about to open on his stronghold, and then came to terms, and was permitted to march out with the honors of war.

The fall of Maloun shook the faith of Bhim Sein Thapa in his heaven-built fortresses, and he sent commissioners to make terms with the British government. He ceded all the conquests of the Ghorkas to the westward of the Kali river, together with the whole of the Terai; and he also agreed to receive a British Resident at Khatmandu; but nothing was said about a subsidiary force.

The negotiations were closed; Lord Moira had even signed the treaty; when a question arose as to whether the Terai, which had been ceded to the English, included the forest on the lower slopes of the Himalayas, or only the marshy plain at the foot of the mountain. At this moment Amar Singh returned to Khatmandu, and persuaded the Bharadars to defend their mountain territory to the last, and if conquered to retire toward China, rather than yield to the demands of the British government.

Lord Moira, who had been honored with the title of Marquis of Hastings, at once prepared to renew the war. In the beginning of 1816, General Sir David Ochterlony, who had been made a baronet, advanced toward Khatmandu with an army of twenty thousand men, and defeated the Ghorka army within fifty miles of the capital. The original treaty was then concluded in hot haste by the Thapa regent; the red seal was attached; peace was concluded at Segowlie, and the British army was withdrawn from Nipal. But the difference about the Terai was renewed in other forms with a tenacity peculiar to the Ghorka character; it ended by the British government tacitly abandoning its rights rather than renew the war. The other mountain territory ceded by the treaty has, however, proved a valuable acquisition; it has furnished sites for the principal hill stations in India—for Simla and Mussoorie, Landour, and Nynee Tal.

CHAPTER XIII

PINDHARI WAR, AND FALL OF THE PEISHWA —LORD HASTINGS

A.D. 1815 TO 1823

IN 1815-16, while Sir David Ochterlony was bringing the Nipal war to a close, the Pindharies began to make raids on British territories. One horde of eight thousand horsemen swept the Nizam's territories as far south as the Kistna river. Another and a larger horde of twenty-five thousand Pindharies entered the Madras Presidency and plundered three hundred villages on the coast of Coromandel. A third band of five hundred horsemen rode through the Peishwa's dominions, and plundered the villages along the coast of Malabar for a distance of two hundred miles, and then returned up the valley of the Tapti river to their homes in Malwa.

Lord Hastings determined, in spite of all orders to the contrary, to take steps for the extermination of these execrable miscreants. Other Pindhari raids were carried out in the cold weather of 1816 and 1817, and confirmed him in this resolution. He tried to form such a league with the Mahratta powers as would at least prevent them from interfering in behalf of the Pindharies. At the same time he secretly and silently made his own preparations for a campaign on such a large scale against the homes of the Pindhari hordes as would insure their destruction once and forever.

Meanwhile the horrible details of Pindhari atrocities were

told in England, and created a revulsion of public opinion. Even the Mahrattas were forgotten in the stern resolution to punish the Pindharies and put an end to their cruel raids. Stories were related of villages surrounded by swarms of savage banditti; of fire and sword, rapine, murder, torture, and outrage, which spread universal alarm, and were proved by unquestionable testimony. At the approach of the Pindharies, fathers were known to pile firewood round their dwellings, and perish with all their families in flames kindled by their own hands; and in some cases the whole female population of a village threw themselves into wells rather than fall into the hands of such merciless marauders. Under such circumstances the home authorities violated their own policy of non-intervention, and hastened to sanction the most vigorous measures for the protection of British subjects. The British cabinet concurred with the Court of Directors in authorizing hostilities against Sindia, Holkar, or any other native power, that should venture to protect the Pindharies against the just resentment of the British government.

At this moment, and indeed for some years previously, the British government was aware that certain secret intrigues were being carried on at Poona by Baji Rao Peishwa, and his minister Trimbukji Dainglia, with Sindia and Holkar's governments, and even with the Pindhari leaders. The main object of these intrigues was to re-establish political relations with Sindia and Holkar contrary to the treaty of Bassein; to restore the Peishwa to the headship of the Mahratta empire; and to form a general confederacy of native powers for the overthrow of the British government.

The objects which the Peishwa and his minister had in view might possibly be justified as patriotic efforts to throw off a foreign yoke; but the underhand means employed to carry them out were of a nature to provoke the hostility of the British government. The Peishwa had certain money claims against the Nizam of Hyderabad and the Gaekwar of Baroda; and these claims were to have been settled by the arbitration of the British government in accordance with the treaty of Bassein. But the Peishwa evaded all such arbitration, and it was discovered that these claims were used as a cover for carrying on secret negotiations with the Nizam and the Gaekwar, like those which had been carried on with Sindia, Holkar, and the Pindhari leaders.

In 1815 it was proposed that the Gaekwar should send his minister to Poona to settle the claims of the Peishwa against Baroda. This minister was a Brahman of high caste, named Gungadhur Shastri. His sacred character would have insured his safety in any other court in India; but the unscrupulous treachery of Baji Rao was notorious, and the Shastri would not go to Poona until the British government guaranteed his safety.

Gungadhur Shastri was coldly received at Poona. He was suspected of being a friend of the British government, and was treated with so much reserve and covert hostility that he prepared to return to Baroda. His departure, however, would have put an end to all further communications with the Gaekwar. Accordingly the Peishwa and his minister turned round, and won him over by flattery and cajolery. The Shastri was told that the Peishwa had been so much struck by his talents that he was to be appointed minister at Poona directly the claims against Baroda were settled. Moreover, a marriage was arranged between the son of the Shastri and a sister-in-law of the Peishwa.

The result of this cajolery was that Gungadhur Shastri was brought to agree to a settlement of the claims which was more favorable to the Peishwa than to the Gaekwar. The proposals were sent to Baroda for ratification, but the Gaekwar was very angry and sent no reply. The Shastri became alarmed; he was afraid that the Gaekwar would think that he had neglected his master's interests in order to form a marriage connection with the Peishwa. Accordingly he broke off the marriage.

The Peishwa was mortally offended at this proceeding,

but betrayed no sign of anger to the Shastri. On the contrary, the Shastri was treated with more kindness and cordiality than ever. He was invited to accompany the Peishwa and his minister on a pilgrimage to the temple of Punderpore. He was warned of danger, but was too much puffed up with the deference paid to him to take any heed. He went to Punderpore, dined with the Peishwa, proceeded to the temple, performed his devotions, took leave of the Peishwa and minister on the veranda of the temple, and set out to return to Poona. He had scarcely gone three hundred yards from the temple gateway when he was attacked and cut to pieces by assassins who had been hired by the minister, Trimbukji Dainglia.

There was no doubt of the guilt of Trimbukji Dainglia. Mr. Elphinstone, the British Resident at Poona, investigated the case, and found that it was Trimbukji who hired the assassins. The general voice of the country pronounced that Trimbukji was the murderer of the Brahman. There was no moral doubt that the Peishwa was also implicated, but that was allowed to pass. The British government had guaranteed the safety of the Shastri, and the Peishwa was called upon to surrender the murderer. The Peishwa tried to evade the demand, but was at last terrified into compliance; and Trimbukji was placed under confinement in the fortress of Thanna on the island of Salsette, near Bombay.

Trimbukji Dainglia was confined at Thanna from September, 1815, to December, 1816. To prevent the possibility of escape, his guard was composed entirely of Europeans. He felt that his case was hopeless. He admitted to the officers of his guard that he had planned the murder of the Shastri, but declared that he only acted under the orders of the Peishwa. Subsequently Baji Rao managed to communicate with his favorite. A Mahratta horsekeeper in the service of one of the officers of the garrison passed the window of the prisoner every day with his master's horse. He carelessly sung a Mahratta song under the window, which the European guards neither understood nor suspected, but which told the ex-minister how to escape.[1] A number of Mahratta horsemen were lying in wait in the neighborhood, and one night Trimbukji Dainglia was missing. He had escaped over the wall, joined the party of horsemen, and fled northward to the hills and jungles of Kandeish, where he found refuge among the Bhils. No one doubted that Baji Rao had abetted the escape of his favorite; but nothing could be proved, and the matter was allowed to drop.

All this while, however, the Peishwa was actively but secretly negotiating with Sindia, Holkar, Amir Khan, and the Pindhari leaders, against the British government. He was enlisting troops in all directions, and sending large sums of money to Trimbukji Dainglia to enable him to raise a force in like manner. Subsequently Mr. Elphinstone discovered that Trimbukji had assembled an army within fifty miles of Poona. The Peishwa denied all knowledge of the fact, but continued to aid and abet his exiled favorite, and encouraged him to make war on the British government.

The conduct of Baji Rao Peishwa at this crisis was as provoking to Lord Hastings as the conduct of Jaswant Rao Holkar had been to Lord Wellesley. It threatened to interfere with his plans for the extermination of the Pindharies. Lord Hastings had been most anxious to avoid a breach with Baji Rao, and had consequently ignored the Peishwa's connivance at the murder of the Shastri and escape of the min-

---

[1] Bishop Heber turned the Mahratta ballad into English verse as follows:

"Behind the bush the bowmen hide
The horse beneath the tree.
Where shall I find the knight will ride
The jungle paths with me?

"There are five-and-fifty coursers there,
And four-and-fifty men;
When the fifty-fifth shall mount his steed,
The Dekhan thrives again."

—*Heber's Journal.*

ister. But Baji Rao was enlisting large bodies of troops in spite of the Resident's remonstrances; and he was placing his forts in a state of preparation, and sending his treasures out of Poona. At the same time the number of rebels under Trimbukji was increasing daily. It was obvious that the Peishwa was engaged in a conspiracy against the British government in order to effect the restoration of Trimbukji Dainglia to power, and possibly to carry out designs of a more serious character.

At last in April, 1817, Mr. Elphinstone told the Peishwa that unless he put a stop to his hostile preparations, active measures would be taken against him by the British government. The Peishwa was now alarmed, and made a show of disbanding troops; but all this while he was raising fresh levies, and re-enlisting the disbanded troops in other quarters. In May the Resident sent an ultimatum; and after endless evasions and delays the Peishwa came to terms, and delivered up three important fortresses as pledges of his future good behavior. In June, 1817, a treaty was concluded at Poona, under which the Peishwa ceded a considerable territory, and pledged himself to hold no further communication with any power whatever, Mahratta or otherwise, excepting the British government.

Lord Hastings was at this time completing his military preparations; he was assembling the largest army that had ever appeared in India under British colors. Lord Cornwallis brought thirty thousand men to bear against Tippu. Lord Wellesley assembled nearly sixty thousand during the second Mahratta war. Lord Hastings called together the armies of the three Presidencies, which, together with native contingents and irregular troops, numbered nearly a hundred and twenty thousand strong. He was resolved not only to exterminate the Pindharies, but to take decisive measures with the three predatory powers—Sindia, Holkar, and Amir Khan.

Lord Hastings planned a campaign for placing the Pindharies between two fires; between the Bengal army from the north under his own command, and the Madras army from the south under Sir Thomas Hislop. On the north four Bengal divisions were to march from the Jumna, and to close round Malwa from the side of Bundelkund, Agra, and Rajputana. At the same time four Madras divisions were to move from the south, cross the Nerbudda, and drive the Pindharies out of their haunts toward the river Chambal, where a Bengal force was lying in wait to receive them.

The three predatory powers were aware of the movements of the Madras army from the southward, but they had no inkling of the decisive operations which Lord Hastings proposed to carry out on the northward from the side of Bengal. They imagined that the greater part of the British forces on the Madras side were to be employed in defending the frontiers of the Nizam, the Raja of Nagpore, and the British possessions. They expected that a British detachment would make a push upon the homes of the Pindharies to the northward of the Nerbudda; but they calculated that the Pindharies would hide themselves for a while, either by enlisting in the predatory armies of the three powers, or by retiring to remote villages. Moreover, they chuckled over the idea that when the storm had blown over, and the British troops had returned to cantonments, the Pindharies would revenge the British attack on their homes by still more savage and extensive raids on British territories.

Daulat Rao Sindia was the most decided supporter of the Pindharies. As far back as 1816 he engaged to help in the expulsion of the Pindharies; but he hoped to evade his promise by some delusive action against the Pindharies, which might be managed in concert with their chiefs. He permitted the British to establish posts in his territories for operations against the Pindharies, but made no attempt to co-operate with the British officers for the destruction of his old retainers. On the contrary, his officers maintained cordial relations with the Pindhari leaders, in spite of the remonstrances of Captain Close, the British Resident.

In 1817, at the beginning of the campaign, Daulat Rao Sindia was asked to issue orders for the friendly reception of the Madras army, which was crossing the Nerbudda into his territories in order to dislodge the Pindharies from his dominions. He was thunderstruck at the demand, and said that it required time for consideration. He was told by Captain Close that deliberation was out of the question; that the Madras forces were hastening northward on the faith that he was acting in concert with them for the extirpation of the Pindharies; and that these movements were combined with those of the Bengal army, which was about to cross the Jumna under the command of the Governor-General in person.

Sindia saw that he was outwitted, and in imminent danger of being overwhelmed. He was overawed by the threatened approach of the Bengal army under Lord Hastings. Next day he sent to say that he had despatched orders to his officers for the friendly reception of the British troops within his own territories.

Lord Hastings was fully alive to the fact that the sympathies of the three predatory powers were with the Pindharies; and that the Pindharies looked to them for refuge and protection during the coming storm. Consequently he foresaw that the mere expulsion of the Pindharies from their haunts would not secure the peace of India, or prevent the revival of the predatory system. Accordingly he resolved to disarm the three predatory powers before rooting out the Pindharies.

Daulat Rao Sindia soon felt that his powers for mischief were ebbing away. He was told that he had violated existing treaties by carrying on secret negotiations with the Peishwa, as well as with Runjeet Singh, the ruler of the Punjab. Nevertheless Lord Hastings was willing to leave him in possession of his territories, but was determined to deliver the Rajput states out of the clutches of the predatory powers by reviving the protective treaties that had been annulled by Sir George Barlow.

At this crisis Daulat Rao Sindia was singularly unlucky. While solemnly protesting that he had carried on no negotiations contrary to treaty, two of his messengers were arrested on the road to Nipal conveying letters to the Ghorka government at Khatmandu. Other letters were discovered between the leaves of a Sanskrit book, which had been glued together, and concealed among the baggage of the messengers. The contents proved that Daulat Rao Sindia was making proposals to the Thapa ministry for a combined attack of Ghorkas and Mahrattas on the British government.

Lord Hastings, however, was not inclined to press matters too hardly upon the Mahratta. He directed the British Resident to make over the documents to Daulat Rao Sindia in open durbar, briefly stating what they were and what they contained. Sindia was dumb with astonishment and alarm; he could make no defence whatever. He agreed to a new treaty under which the Rajput states, and all other native states that desired it, were taken under British protection. He also pledged himself to co-operate for the expulsion of the Pindharies, and to prevent the future formation of any predatory gangs in his dominions.

Negotiations were next opened with Amir Khan, through Mr. Charles Metcalfe, the British Resident at Delhi. The Afghan freebooter was growing old, and could not contend against the British government. He agreed to a treaty which converted a leader of bandits into a prince, and turned a predatory power into a native state under the guarantee of the British government. In return, Amir Khan engaged to abstain from all depredations for the future; to reduce his troops to a specified number; to surrender his artillery to the British government at a certain valuation; to refrain from all foreign conquest and aggrandizement; to exclude Pindharies and plunderers of every kind from his dominions; and to oppose to the utmost of his power the revival of the predatory system. Amir Khan thus appears in history as the founder of a Muhammadan dynasty which is represented to this day by the Nawab of Tonk in Rajputana.

The territories of Holkar were in a different condition to those of Sindia or Amir Khan. The government had been rapidly declining ever since the insanity of Jaswant Rao; and after his death it had fallen into a state of imbecility, and was literally at the mercy of the so-called army of Holkar. The best provinces were usurped by military chiefs, or mutinous bodies of armed men. The regent-mother, Tulsi Bai, and the young prince, Mulhar Rao Holkar, had sought refuge in a remote fortress from the outrages of the turbulent soldiery, who were clamoring for arrears of pay. Under such circumstances the regent-mother was naturally anxious for British protection against the army.

In October, 1817, Lord Hastings left Cawnpore and began to cross the Jumna; and the different divisions of his army took up the positions assigned them. Meanwhile the Pindharies had been dislodged from their haunts by the Madras army, and fled with their wives and families to the northward; and now found themselves checkmated by the Bengal forces, and barred out of Rajputana and Bundelkund. They were panic-stricken at the open defection of Sindia, and knew not where to go. All their anxiety was to avoid a conflict with the British troops. One body managed to escape in a southerly direction, with the loss of nearly all its baggage; the rest were forced to abandon their horses and hide themselves in the jungles, where numbers perished miserably. The body that escaped toward the south received a severe defeat, and suffered so much in smaller encounters that in the end it was completely dispersed. Many were slain in these actions and the subsequent flight; and many fell by the hands of the villagers in revenge for their former cruelties.

In this state of misery and despair some of the Pindhari leaders threw themselves upon the mercy of the conquerors. Khurim was provided with a landed estate in British territory, and permitted to reside there with his family. Chetu was killed in the jungles by a tiger. Several of the subordinate chiefs, and some of their followers, were settled in agricultural pursuits in the territories of the Nawab of Bhopal, and converted into peaceful and profitable subjects. Others who survived the conflict mingled with the population and melted away, insomuch that after a very few years not a trace of the Pindhari gangs remained.

CHAPTER XIV

MAHRATTA CONQUEST—LORD HASTINGS

A.D. 1817 TO 1823

FROM the very beginning of the Pindhari war the attention of Lord Hastings was distracted by untoward events. He had hoped to suppress the predatory system in India, without disturbing one of the established principalities, or adding a rood of land to the British empire. This politic intention was thwarted by sheer force of circumstances. While he was advancing against the Pindharies, Daulat Rao Sindia and Amir Khan remained true to their engagements, but the Peishwa, the Raja of Nagpore, and the army of Holkar, broke out in open hostilities to the British government, and his hopes of maintaining the existing political system were at an end.

Baji Rao Peishwa could no more keep the treaty of Poona than he could keep that of Bassein. It was equally opposed to his nature as a Mahratta, his culture as a Brahman, and his experiences as a Peishwa. It was just as reasonable to suppose that he could remain at Poona content with the loss of his suzerainty, as to suppose that the first Napoleon would have remained at Elba content with the loss of his empire.

Meantime Baji Rao Peishwa was playing his old game of duplicity. He had signed the treaty of Poona in June, 1817, and he then tried to throw dust in the eyes of the British Resident by pretending to disband his army. He discharged large bodies of cavalry, but gave the officers seven months' pay in advance, and sent them to their respective villages with orders to return to Poona with their

HYDER ALI'S DEFEAT AT CONJERVAM

India, vol. two.

friends and followers directly they received his summons. In July he left Poona, and went on a pilgrimage to the temples of Punderpore, the scene of the murder of Gungadhur Shastri. From Punderpore he went to another sacred place, named Maholi, which was situated near Satara, the later capital of the dynasty of Sivaji.

At this crisis Sir John Malcolm was at Poona, busied with political arrangements connected with the approaching Pindhari war. Malcolm knew the Peishwa well, having accompanied him on his restoration to Poona in 1803. Accordingly Malcolm received a pressing invitation from Baji Rao to visit him at Maholi, and readily accepted it in the hope of reconciling the Peishwa to his new situation. Baji Rao welcomed Malcolm most cordially, spoke of his restoration in 1803, declared that John Malcolm and Arthur Wellesley were his best friends, and dilated on his lasting gratitude to the English. But he was evidently smarting under the treaty of Poona. He bitterly complained of his loss of position and territory, and especially harped upon the three fortresses which he had been forced to surrender as pledges of his good faith.

An officer of Malcolm's experience ought to have known that Baji Rao was only cajoling him, in the hope of getting back the three fortresses before committing himself to a war. But Malcolm believed in the sincerity of the Peishwa, and tried to soothe him with promises of future reward and consideration. He explained the coming operations against the Pindharies, and exhorted the Peishwa to co-operate heartily with the English during the campaign. He then returned to Poona, so convinced of the good faith of the Peishwa that he actually induced Mr. Elphinstone to restore the three fortresses.

Elphinstone however had lost all faith in Baji Rao. He restored the fortresses because he would not throw cold water on Malcolm's hopes; but he was by no means carried away by Malcolm's generous enthusiasm, and events soon proved that Elphinstone was in the right.

Baji Rao returned to Poona in September, and took enormous numbers of horsemen into his pay, declaring that he was going to make war on the Pindharies. Elphinstone was not deluded, for Baji Rao was enlisting double the number of troops that could possibly be required. Moreover, Baji Rao evaded sending any troops to the northward, although their presence was urgently required on the Nerbudda. At the same time he was putting his fortresses into a state of defence, strengthening the garrisons, and storing them with provisions and treasure. It was also discovered that he was trying to seduce the English sepoys from their allegiance by bribes and promises; sending secret emissaries to the Raja of Nagpore, as well as to Sindia, Holkar, and Amir Khan; and planning to assassinate Elphinstone, either by treacherously inviting him to an interview, or by surrounding the Residency with a rebel force under Trimbukji Dainglia.

Elphinstone knew pretty well what was going on, but was anxious not to precipitate a rupture, and accordingly proceeded very cautiously with his preparations for defence. The Poona Subsidiary Force under General Smith had gone to the northward to join in the operations against the Pindharies; but a detachment remained at Poona, and Elphinstone obtained the services of a European regiment from Bombay. The whole British force at Poona only numbered two thousand sepoys and eight hundred European soldiers; and it was deemed expedient to remove the troops from Poona to Khirki, a village about four miles from the British Residency.

The arrival of the European regiment from Bombay was the one thing above all others which disconcerted Baji Rao. For more than sixty years the presence of a European regiment had been regarded with terror by every native prince. Accordingly, on the arrival of the Europeans, Baji Rao feigned to be alarmed at the intentions of the British government. He threatened to withdraw from Poona unless the European regiment was sent back to Bombay. The removal of the British force to Khirki reassured him; he ascribed it to fear. On the 5th of November Elphinstone himself left the Residency and joined the force at Khirki.

Baji Rao was at this time buoyed up by false hopes. He believed that Daulat Rao Sindia and Amir Khan had taken the field against the British government. He knew that the Raja of Nagpore and the army of Holkar were preparing to support him. Accordingly on the afternoon of the day that Elphinstone left the Residency, Baji Rao attacked the British force at Khirki with an army of eighteen thousand horse, eight thousand foot, and fourteen pieces of artillery. Notwithstanding these overwhelming numbers, he was repulsed with the loss of five hundred killed and wounded. That same night the Residency was plundered and burned, and Elphinstone lost a magnificent library which no money could restore.

The Subsidiary Force under General Smith, which had been sent to co-operate against the Pindharies, had already been recalled to Poona. It soon made its appearance, and prepared to attack the Peishwa's army on the morning of the 17th of November. But the heart of Baji Rao had already failed him. He left Poona on the night of the 16th, and thus surrendered his dominions without a blow. The British troops occupied Poona, and General Smith set out in pursuit of Baji Rao.

Meanwhile the Raja of Nagpore secretly made common cause with the Peishwa. Rughoji Bhonsla died in 1816; his son and successor was an idiot, and his nephew Appa Sahib became regent. The idiot was murdered by Appa Sahib, and the regent became Raja without any discovery of his crime. Appa Sahib conciliated the English by concluding a subsidiary treaty. At the same time he secretly maintained an active correspondence with the Peishwa, and played the same game as the Peishwa. He was somewhat sobered by the treaty of Poona, which Baji Rao had been compelled to accept in June; but he soon renewed his secret negotiations with the Peishwa, and began to levy troops on a large scale. When news arrived of the attack on the British Residency at Poona, Appa Sahib talked at great length to Mr. Jenkins, the Resident at Nagpore, on the treachery of Baji Rao, and the impossibility that he should ever be induced to follow so bad an example; yet all this while Appa Sahib was preparing to falsify every protestation by making common cause with the Peishwa against the British government.

The story reveals the double-faced duplicity of the Mahratta. In November, 1817, when Baji Rao was already at war with the English, he appointed Appa Sahib to the honorable but nominal post of commander-in-chief of the army of the Peishwa. Such empty dignities had been common enough in the palmy days of the Mahratta empire, and often served to revive the fading loyalty of a disaffected feudatory, and bind him in closer allegiance to his suzerain. But such an appointment in November, 1817, was a gross violation of the treaties of Bassein and Poona, and was obviously made for the purpose of drawing Appa Sahib into hostilities with the British government.

On the night of the 24th of November Appa Sahib sent word to Mr. Jenkins that he had accepted the post of commander-in-chief of the army of the Peishwa, and was to be invested with the insignia of office on the following morning in the presence of all his troops; and he invited Mr. Jenkins to be present on the occasion, and requested that a salute might be fired by the English in honor of the investiture. Mr. Jenkins declined having anything to do with the ceremony, and warned the Raja that it might lead to dangerous consequences.

Next morning Mr. Jenkins discovered that treachery was abroad. All communication between the city of Nagpore and the Residency had been interdicted by the Raja; and the Raja and his ministers were sending their families and valuables out of the city. He foresaw that an attack would be made on the Residency; and he ordered up the British troops from the neighboring cantonment, and posted them on the Sitabuldi hill, between the Residency and the city of

Nagpore. On the following evening the Raja brought up all his forces and began the attack on the hill.

The battle of Sitabuldi is famous in the annals of British India. The English had no European regiment on the spot, as they had at Khirki; they had scarcely fourteen hundred sepoys fit for duty, including three troops of Bengal cavalry, and only four six-pounders. Appa Sahib had an army of eighteen thousand men, including four thousand Arabs, the best soldiers in the Dekhan; he had also thirty-six guns. The battle lasted from six o'clock in the evening of the 26th of November until noon the next day. For many hours the English were in sore peril; their fate seemed to hang upon a thread. The Arabs were beginning to close round the Residency, when a happy stroke of British daring changed the fortunes of the day.

Captain Fitzgerald, who commanded the Bengal cavalry, was posted in the Residency compound and was anxious to charge the Arabs; but he was forbidden by the commander of the British forces. Again he implored permission, but was told to charge at his peril. "On my peril be it!" cried Fitzgerald, and gave the word to charge. Clearing the enclosures, the Bengal cavalry bore down upon the enemy's horse, captured two guns, and cut up a body of infantry. The British sepoys posted on the hill hailed the exploit with loud huzzahs, and seeing the explosion of one of the enemy's tumbrels, they rushed down the hill, driving the Arabs before them like sheep. The victory was won, but the English had lost a quarter of their number in killed and wounded.

Foiled in this treacherous attempt, Appa Sahib sent envoys to Mr. Jenkins to express his sorrow, and to deny having authorized the attack. Reinforcements were now pouring in from all directions; but Mr. Jenkins affected to believe the statement of the Raja, and even promised to be reconciled, provided he disbanded his troops. But Appa Sahib was still playing his old game. He continued his correspondence with the Peishwa, and stirred up his own chiefs to rebellious outbreaks, in order to keep his territories in a state of alarm and disorder.

At this juncture it was discovered that Appa Sahib had been guilty of the murder of his predecessor. Under these circumstances he was arrested, and sent as a prisoner to Allahabad; but on the way he managed to bribe his guards and make his escape. Henceforth Appa Sahib was a fugitive; and after a precarious existence for many years in the Vindhya and Satpura mountains, he finally found refuge in the territories of the Raja of Jodhpur.[1]

An infant grandson of Rughoji Bhonsla, aged nine, was then placed upon the throne of Nagpore. He was a son of Rughoji's daughter, but was formally adopted by Rughoji's widow in order that he might take the name of Bhonsla. The widow was appointed regent, but her authority was nominal, as the whole administration was placed in the charge of Mr. Jenkins until the boy Raja attained his majority.

Affairs in Holkar's state of Indore ran nearly in the same groove as at Nagpore, but the circumstances were different. The regent-mother, Tulsi Bai, was no longer anxious to place the infant, Mulhar Rao Holkar, under the protection of the British government. The Peishwa had reduced the army of Holkar to obedience by discharging all arrears of pay out of his own treasury. The regent-mother and her ministers recovered their ascendency over the soldiery, avowed themselves the partisans of the Peishwa, and led the army toward the south to make war upon the British government in support of the Peishwa.

At this moment, the Madras army, under Sir Thomas

---

[1] The Raja of Jodhpur was called upon to surrender Appa Sahib to the British authorities, but pleaded that he would be disgraced in the eyes of his brother chieftains in Rajputana, if he gave up a fugitive who had found an asylum within his territories. As Appa Sahib had not committed an offence which placed him outside the bar of mercy, and as he was powerless for further mischief, the plea was admitted on the Jodhpur Raja becoming responsible for his good behavior. In the end a provision was made for the support of the wretched exile, and his latter days were soothed by the medical attendance of the English doctor at the Jodhpur Residency.

Hislop, was moving northward in pursuit of the Pindharies. In December, 1817, it met the army of Holkar near Ujain; and Sir John Malcolm, who accompanied the Madras army in a diplomatic capacity, opened up negotiations with the regent-mother and her ministers. The latter seemed inclined to come to an arrangement with the British government; but the military chiefs were bent on war, and suspected that the ministers and regent-mother were making secret terms with the British authorities. Accordingly the army rose against their rulers, put the ministers under confinement, and carried off the regent-mother to a neighboring river and cruelly beheaded her on the bank, and threw her remains into the stream.

The barbarous murder of a woman and a princess cut off all hope of pacification. An action was inevitable; indeed, the army of Holkar began operations by plundering the English baggage. The battle was fought at Mehidpore on the 21st of December, 1817. Sir John Malcolm commanded the English troops on that occasion, and gained a complete victory. The army of Holkar was utterly routed, and all their guns and military stores fell into the hands of the English.

The Mahratta powers were thus prostrate, and Lord Hastings prepared to construct the new political system, which has continued without material change down to the present day. The arrangements with Sindia, Amir Khan, and the infant Raja of Nagpore, were already completed, or were in course of completion. It may, however, be added, that Sindia was required to cede the territory of Ajmir in Rajputana; as it was deemed essential to the security of the public peace in India to shut out all Mahratta influences from Rajputana. The only princes remaining to be dealt with were Baji Rao Peishwa and Mulhar Rao Holkar.

The Peishwa had fled from Poona southward toward Satara. He sought to strengthen his hereditary claims on the allegiance of the Mahratta powers by causing the pageant Raja of Satara to be brought to his camp. His movements, however, were little more than desperate efforts to avoid a collision with the British forces in pursuit; and all hope of recovering his position as suzerain of the Mahratta empire died out of his restless brain, and reduced him to the depths of despair.

The glorious defence of Korygaum belongs to this interval; it was regarded as the most brilliant exploit of the war, and is celebrated to this day in Mahratta songs in all parts of the Dekhan. A detachment of Bombay sepoys and irregular horse, not exceeding eight hundred men, reached the village of Korygaum, on the bank of the river Bhima, under the command of Captain Staunton. There were only ten English officers and twenty-four European artillerymen with two six-pounders. Suddenly Staunton saw the whole army of the Peishwa drawn up on the opposite bank, to the number of twenty-five thousand horsemen and about six thousand Arab and Gosain infantry. Staunton at once occupied the village of Korygaum, and prepared for defence. The enemy surrounded the village with horse and foot, while three picked bodies of infantry attempted to storm the English position with rockets. Then followed a series of charges and repulses which lasted till nightfall. Without provisions, and without water—for all access to the river was cut off—the Bombay sepoys and their European officers fought with a pluck and desperation which broke the spirit of the enemy. Staunton lost a third of his sepoys, and eight out of his ten officers; but the Mahrattas left six hundred killed and wounded on the field. Baji Rao witnessed the whole action from a neighboring hill, and was beside himself with anger and mortification. Next morning his army refused to renew the fight, and rapidly disappeared from the scene.

For six months longer Baji Rao remained at large, but his career was run. There was another battle at Ashti, but he cowardly fled at the first shot, leaving his army to be defeated by General Smith, while the pageant Raja of Satara fell into the hands of the English. Indeed, from a very early period, the defection of Daulat Rao Sindia, the destruction of the Pindharies, the crushing defeat of the army of Holkar, and the deposition of Appa Sahib at Nagpore, had combined to deprive Baji Rao of all hope of recovering his throne, and to render his capture a mere question of time.

The Peishwa was doomed to extinction. The treaty of Bassein had failed to break up the Mahratta confederacy; it had failed to prevent the Mahratta states from regarding the Peishwa as their lawful suzerain, and leaguing under his authority against the British government. Nagpore and Holkar had waged war against the British government in obedience to the call of the Peishwa; and Sindia would probably have done the same had he not been taken by surprise, and bound over to keep the peace before committing himself to a suicidal war.

It was thus obvious to Lord Hastings that the abdication of Baji Rao would have proved wholly insufficient to secure the peace of India. To have set up another Peishwa in his room would only have led to a revival of the old intrigues against the British government. To have transferred the territories of the Peishwa to a prince bearing another title would have proved equally dangerous and delusive. The other Mahratta powers would still have deemed it their duty to award to the new prince the indefeasible right of the Peishwa to command their armies, in spite of the change of name; and Poona would have continued to be the rallying point for disaffection, not only to every Mahratta feudatory, but possibly to every Hindu prince in India. Accordingly, Lord Hastings determined that henceforth the Mahrattas should be without a Peishwa.

It was a question whether the Raja of Satara might not have been raised from the condition of a pageant to that of sovereign of Poona. But the representative of Sivaji had long been shut up as an idol at Satara, and was now a forgotten idol. The traditions of the once famous Bhonsla family had lost their hold on the Mahrattas. The dynasty of Sivaji had been superseded by the dynasty of Brahmans; and the descendant of Sivaji could no more have been restored to sovereignty than the descendant of the Great Moghul. Accordingly, Lord Hastings resolved to abolish the Peishwa, annex his territories, and reduce Baji Rao to the condition of Napoleon at St. Helena. He delivered the Raja of Satara from the thraldom of generations, and assigned a territory for his support out of the possessions of the Peishwa.

In June, 1818, Baji Rao was surrounded by British troops under the command of Sir John Malcolm, and had no alternative but to die sword in hand, or throw himself on the mercy of the British government. The terms offered by Malcolm were so liberal as to excite much controversy. While the great Napoleon was condemned to pass his last days on a solitary rock in the southern ocean, with a comparative pittance for his maintenance, the ex-Peishwa was permitted to live in luxury in the neighborhood of Cawnpore on a yearly stipend of eighty thousand pounds. Trimbukji Dainglia was captured shortly afterward, and was doomed to spend the remainder of his days in close confinement in the fortress of Chunar.

Lord Hastings refused to annex Holkar's territories. The hostile action of the army of Holkar had compelled the British government to treat the shattered principality of Indore as an enemy; but Lord Hastings had no desire to annihilate the remains of Holkar's government, or to dethrone the family of Jaswant Rao. Accordingly the Holkar state was required to cede certain territories, and to confirm the grants it had already made to Amir Khan; it was also required to surrender its international life, and become a subsidiary state under the guarantee of the British government. But in all other respects the infant Mulhar Rao Holkar was treated as an independent prince, and the administration was left in the hands of the ministers and durbar, aided by the advice of the British Resident.

The policy of Lord Hastings did not meet with the full approval of his contemporaries, but its success is proved by the after history. From the extinction of the Peishwas in 1818, and the suppression of the Pindharies, there has been no serious attempt at an armed confederation of native states against the British government. Possibly had Lord Wellesley extinguished the Great Moghul as thoroughly as Lord Hastings extinguished the Mahratta Peishwa, the mutinies of 1857 might never have occurred, Delhi might have been as loyal as Poona, and any outbreak of deluded sepoys would have hurt no one but themselves.

In other directions the administration of Lord Hastings marks a new era in the history of India. He was the first Governor-General that countenanced and encouraged the education of the native populations. Previous to his time it had been the popular idea that the ignorance of the natives insured the security of British rule; but Lord Hastings denounced this view as treason against British sentiment, and promoted the establishment of native schools and native journals. In so doing he was in advance of his time, and consequently he was condemned in his generation.

The dealings of Lord Hastings with the Nizam's government have been much criticised. The Nizam profited by the extinction of the Peishwa more than any other native prince in India, for he was relieved by the British government from the Mahratta claims for arrears of chout, which had hung like a millstone on the necks of the rulers of Hyderabad for the greater part of a century. But the Nizam eschewed all business, and cared only for his pleasures. A Hindu grandee named Chandu Lal was placed at the head of the administration, and found it necessary to keep on good terms with both the Nizam and the British government, much in the same way that Muhammad Reza Khan in a previous generation had tried to secure his hold on the administration of Bengal. The result was that nothing flourished but corruption. Every public office was put up for sale; judicial decrees could only be purchased by bribes; the revenues of the state were farmed out to the highest bidders; and the farmers became all-powerful in the districts, and were left to practice every species of oppression and extortion without control. In the end the people were driven by exactions to become rebels and bandits; villages were deserted; lands fell out of cultivation, and provisions rose to famine prices.

In 1820, Mr. Charles Metcalfe was appointed Resident at Hyderabad. Having made a tour of the country, he deemed it expedient to place his political assistants, and British officers of the Nizam's Contingent,[1] in charge of different districts, in order to superintend a new revenue settlement, check oppression, and control the police. There is no question that this measure contributed largely to the improvement of the country and well being of the people; but it was naturally unpalatable to the Nizam and Chandu Lal, and in 1829 the supervision of British officers was withdrawn.

Meanwhile as far back as the year 1814, a bank had been established at Hyderabad by a firm known as Palmer & Co. It received loans from deposits bearing twelve per cent interest, and lent the money to the Nizam at twenty-four per cent on the security of assignments of land revenue. According to act of parliament all such transactions were prohibited to British subjects without the express sanction of the Governor-General; but this sanction had been obtained from Lord Hastings, who believed that such dealings were better in the hands of European bankers than in those of native money-lenders. Moreover, one of the partners had married a ward of Lord Hastings; and thus, under a variety of circumstances, the Governor-General was enabled to throw the veil of his authority over the transactions of Palmer & Co.

Mr. Metcalfe reported that this bank had become a source of corruption. In 1820, Chandu Lal had obtained the sanction of the British government to a new loan of sixty lakhs of rupees, or six hundred thousand pounds sterling, nominally to pay off and reduce public establishments, to make

---

[1] The Nizam's Contingent was a body altogether different from the Nizam's Subsidiary Force. By the treaty of 1800 the Nizam was bound to furnish a Contingent of fifteen thousand troops in time of war, but those which he supplied during the Mahratta war of 1803 were little better than a rabble. Subsequently the force was reduced in numbers, and its efficiency was increased by the employment of British officers; and it was retained by the Nizam as a permanent force in time of peace for the reduction of refractory Zemindars and other domestic purposes.

advances to the ryots, and to clear off certain debts due to native bankers. Mr. Metcalfe, however, discovered that the new loan was a sham. Eight lakhs of the money was transferred as a bonus to the partners in Palmer & Co.; while the remainder was appropriated to paying off money lent to the Nizam, or said to have been lent to him, without the knowledge of the British government. In a word, the new loan of sixty lakhs was a deception, which filled the pockets of interested parties without liquidating the real claims; while, in consequence of the sanction inconsiderately given by Lord Hastings, the British government was more or less compromised in the matter. Accordingly it was resolved to pay off all debts due by the Nizam to the bank, and put an end to the relations between the Nizam's government and Palmer & Co. The matter ended in the insolvency of the firm.

The money for paying off the Nizam's debts was provided for in a peculiar fashion. Some half a century previously the East India Company had agreed to pay the Nizam a yearly rent of seventy thousand pounds sterling for the Northern Circars; and in spite of political changes this yearly sum had been regularly paid down to the time of Lord Hastings. Accordingly the rent was capitalized, and the money was devoted to the payment of the Nizam's debt to Palmer & Co.

The error of judgment committed by Lord Hastings in sanctioning the money dealings of Palmer & Co. blotted his reputation in the eyes of his contemporaries, and is only worthy of record as containing a useful political lesson for all time.

Lord Hastings left India on the 1st of January, 1823, at the advanced age of sixty-eight. His last years were embittered by the reproaches of the Court of Directors; but he will live in history as the Governor-General who carried the imperial policy of Lord Wellesley to its legitimate conclusion, and established the British government as the paramount power in India.

Lord Amherst was appointed Governor-General in succession to Lord Hastings, but he did not reach India until August, 1823. During the interval Mr. Adam, a civil servant of the Company, acted as Governor-General; but his short administration is only remarkable for his sharp treatment of the public press. An obnoxious editor named Buckingham had written unfavorably of government officials in a Calcutta newspaper, and was forthwith deprived of his license, and sent to England.[1] Nothing further is known of Mr. Adam; he perished at sea on his return voyage to England.

The all-important event in Lord Amherst's administration was the first Burmese war of 1824–25; but before describing the military operations, it may be as well to bring the country and people of Burma under review.

---

[1] Before the year 1833 no European was permitted to reside in India unless he was in the service of the late East India Company, or had obtained a license from the Court of Directors. These restrictions were removed on the renewal of the charter of the late East India Company in 1833.

CHAPTER XV

BURMAN HISTORY—AVA AND PEGU

A.D. 1540 TO 1823

BURMA is an irregular oblong, lying west and east between Bengal and China, and between the Bay of Bengal and the kingdom of Siam. On the north it touches Assam and Thibet. On the south it runs downward in a long narrow strip of seaboard, like the tail of an animal, and terminates at the Siamese frontier on the river Pak Chan.

Burma includes the valley of the Irawadi, which is destined at no distant period to play as important a part in the eastern world as the valley of the Ganges. Burma proper, or Ava, comprises only the upper valley. The lower valley, although included in the general term of Burma, is better known as Pegu.[1]

The people of Burma belong to the Indo-Chinese race, having Mongolian features, with tolerably fair complexions, varying from a dusky yellow to a clear whiteness. They

---

[1] Ava, or Burma proper, is an inland country entirely cut off from the sea by the territory of Pegu. It has no outlet to the sea excepting by the river Irawadi, which runs through Pegu, and forms a Delta toward the Gulf of Martaban. In ancient times, and down to the middle of the last century, Ava and Pegu were separated into different kingdoms, and were often at war with each other. Indeed, there was some obscure antagonism of race, the people of Ava being known as Burmans, and the people of Pegu as Talains. Besides Ava and Pegu there are two long strips of coast territory facing the Bay of Bengal, which are respectively known as Arakan and Tenasserim; but they also formed independent kingdoms, and had no political connection with either Ava or Pegu until a recent period. Arakan runs northward from the Delta of the Irawadi toward the frontier of Bengal on the river Naf. Tenasserim runs southward toward the frontier of Siam, on the river Pah Chan. Tenasserim is the "territorial tail" indicated in the opening paragraph to the present chapter.

are Buddhists in religion; converts from the old Vedic worship of Indra, Brahma, and other gods, which still lingers in the land. They are without caste, without hereditary rank save in the royal family, without nobility save what is official and personal, and without any of the prejudices which prevail in India as regards early marriages and the seclusion of females. They are a joyous race in comparison with the grave and self-constrained Hindus; taking pleasure in dramatic performances, singing, music, dancing, buffoonery, boat-racing, and gambling. They revel in shows and processions on gala days, at which young and old of both sexes mingle freely together. They indulge in much mirth and practical joking at the water festival and other feasts which have been handed down from the old nature worship of Vedic times. They are imbued with military sentiments akin to those of Rajputs; and leave all menial appointments to slaves and captives.

Burma is a land of sun and rain. There are no cold blasts from the Himalayas like those which sweep over Hindustan during the winter season; and the southwest monsoon, which begins early in May and lasts till September, empties its torrents on the soil far more abundantly than on the plains of India. The villages are generally on the banks of rivers. They consist of wooden huts built on piles, so as to be raised above the floods during the rainy season. The ordinary villagers seem to saunter through life, caring only for their cattle and harvests, their fields, fisheries, and fruit-trees; knowing nothing of the outer world, and caring for nothing, except as regards famous pagodas or renowned places of pilgrimage. All real business is generally transacted by wives and daughters, who attend to the cares of the household, and often carry on a traffic in the bazar, and are most exemplary in the discharge of their religious duties.

In every village throughout Burma there is at least one Buddhist monastery built of wood or brick, with a separate building for a monastery school. There are no endowments of money or land of any sort or kind. Every morning the monks go their rounds through the village, clad in yellow robes, and carrying bowls to receive the alms of the villagers in cooked food, after the manner of Gotama Buddha and his disciples. The daily alms are never wanting, for every Burmese man and woman is imbued with the faith that by such acts of benevolence and loving-kindness they secure a higher and better life in the next existence in the chain of transmigrations. When the monks return to the monastery, they take their breakfast, which with them is the chief, if not the only, meal of the day. The younger monks then engage in teaching reading, writing, and arithmetic to a daily gathering of village boys; while the older monks are teaching the sacred language of Pali to more advanced neophytes, or studying Pali scriptures, or pondering over the mysteries of life and transmigrations of the soul.

In Burma the pagodas of Buddhists are to be seen everywhere, and are sometimes substantial buildings of masonry. Statues of Buddha are to be found in all parts of the building, or in neighboring chapels. There are figures squatting on the ground, representing Gotama about to become a Buddha; and there are horizontal figures representing Gotama in the act of dying, or entering into the sleep of Nirvana. Sometimes miniature figures are placed in small niches; sometimes there is a colossal statue many feet high. The images are covered with gilding, or are painted red, or are made of white alabaster, with the features tinted in gold and colors. On festival days the pagodas are decked with flags and garlands, and thronged with people of both sexes and all ages, who prostrate themselves before some great statue of Gotama Buddha, and chant his praises in sacred verses. Fathers and mothers go with all their families. Infants are carried about, sometimes in arms, but generally in baskets yoked to the shoulders like milk-pails. Old men and matrons march along with grave countenances, mingled with swaggering young men in gay attire, and demure damsels with graceful forms, radiant in divers colors and bright adornments, with flowers of every hue lighting up their coal-black hair. All go trooping up the aisles of the pagoda, to make their prostration to Buddha; and then they go out into the temple enclosure to hammer at the pagoda bells with antelopes' horns, as part of some mystic rite of which the meaning is forgotten.

There is one institution in Burma which reveals the marked contrast between Hindus and Burmese. In India marriages are contracted by the parents between boys and girls of a tender age, when the children themselves can have no voice in the matter. In Burma marriages are brought about by mutual liking, which is developed by an innocent custom of pastoral simplicity. The interval between sunset and retiring to rest is known as courting-time. Any young daughter of a house who is desirous of receiving visitors, attires herself in her best, adorns her hair, takes a seat on a mat, and places a lamp in her window as a hint that she is at home. Meantime all the young men of the village array themselves in like manner, and pass the hours of courting-time in a round of visits, at which there is always much talking and laughing. Sometimes the hour may be a little late; sometimes there may be a little quarrelling between jealous rivals; but as a rule the party breaks up at a suitable time without any serious incident to mar the pleasure of the evening. In this way young men and maidens meet and exchange their sentiments in a perfectly innocent and natural manner, until partners are selected for life, marriages are celebrated, and for them the courting time is over.

This richly favored country has been exposed from a remote period to cruel oppressions and bloody wars. It was anciently parcelled out, like India, among petty kings, who waged frequent wars on each other. There was constant rivalry between the Burmese people of Ava on the upper valley of the Irawadi and the Talains of Pegu on the lower valley.[1] Other kings warred against each other in like man-

[1] See ante, p. 575, note.

ner; while ever and anon an invading army from China or Siam swept over the whole country, and deluged the land with blood. Sometimes there were insurrections under a rebel prince or schismatic monk, followed by sack and massacre without a parallel in recorded history, except among Tartar nations. To this day the whole region of Pegu and Ava bears the marks of these desolating contests; and vast tracts of cultùrable lands lie utterly waste from sheer want of population.

In the sixteenth century many Portuguese adventurers and desperadoes found a career in Burma. They were for the most part the skum of Goa and Malacca: renegade priests or runaway soldiers, who had thrown off the restraints of church or army to plunge in the wild license of Oriental life, and to reappear as pirates, bravos, or princes in the remoter eastern seas. One Portuguese deserter got possession of the island of Sundiva at the entrance to the Sunderbunds, and created a fleet of pirate-galleys, which was the terror of Arakan and eastern Bengal. He was followed by an Augustine monk known as Fra Joan. Another scoundrel got possession of a fort at Syriam, over against Rangoon, and was the terror of the Burmese kings on the Irawadi. Others entered the service of different kings of Burma, and often changed the fortunes of war by their superior physique and firearms.

About 1540 a Burmese warrior, named Byeen-noung, rose to the front, and became a conqueror of renown.[1] Originally he was governor of Toungoo;[2] then he made himself king of the country; and subsequently he marched an army of Bur-

---

[1] Byeen-noung is so named in Burmese annals. He was known to the Portuguese as Branginoco. See Faria y Sousa's Portuguese Asia.

[2] Toungoo, the Portuguese Tangu, lies in the interior of Burma, between Pegu and Ava. In the present day it is the frontier district of British Burma. In the sixteenth and seventeenth centuries it was sometimes a province of Ava, sometimes an independent kingdom, and sometimes the seat of a Burmese empire; indeed, at one time the city of Toungoo is said to have been the capital of Upper Burma or Ava. Such shifting of provinces, kingdoms, empires, and capitals is one of the conditions of old Burmese history.

mans toward the south, and conquered the Talain kingdom of Pegu and slew the Talain king.

Byeen-noung next resolved on the conquest of Martaban. This kingdom lay to the eastward of Pegu, between Pegu and Tenasserim; it was separated from Pegu by an arm of the sea, known as the Gulf of Martaban. Byeen-noung raised a large army of all nations, in addition to his army of Burmans, by promising them the sack of Martaban, and with these united forces he invested Martaban by land and sea.

The siege lasted six months. The king of Martaban had married the daughter of the slaughtered king of Pegu and the queen and all her ladies spurred on the king and his generals to resist Byeen-noung to the uttermost. The people of Martaban were starved out and driven to eat their elephants. The king had taken several hundred Portuguese into his service, but they had all deserted him, and entered the service of Byeen-noung. The king was reduced to such extremities that at last he offered to make over his kingdom to Byeen-noung, provided he might retire from Martaban with his queen and children; but Byeen-noung was furious at the obstinate resistance he had encountered, and burning to be revenged not only on the king, but on the queen and all her ladies, and he demanded an unconditional surrender.

The king of Martaban was in despair. He called his generals to a council of war, and one and all pledged themselves to die like warriors; to slaughter all their women and children, throw their treasures into the sea, set the city on fire, and rush out and perish sword in hand. But when the council broke up, one of the chief commanders turned traitor or coward, and fled away to the camp of Byeen-noung. Then the rest of the generals lost heart, and threatened to open the gates of the city to Byeen-noung, unless the king gave himself up without further parley.

Accordingly the king of Martaban held out a white flag on the city wall. He then sent a venerable Buddhist priest to Byeen-noung to request that he might be allowed to turn monk, and spend the rest of his days in a monastery. Byeen-noung was very reverential toward the priest, and promised to forget the past, and provide an estate for the king of Martaban, but no one could trust his word.

Next morning there was a great parade of soldiers and elephants, music and banners, throughout the camp of Byeen-noung. A street was formed of two lines of foreign soldiers from the tent of Byeen-noung to the gate of the city; and all the Portuguese soldiers were posted outside the gate, with their captain, Joano Cayeyro, in their midst; and many of the Burmese princes and nobles of Byeen-noung went into the city, with a host of Burmese guards, to bring the king of Martaban in a great procession to the feet of his conqueror.

The scene is thus described by an eye-witness:[1] "At one o'clock in the day a cannon was fired as a signal. After a while the procession from the palace inside Martaban approached the gate of the city. First came a strong guard of Burmese soldiers, armed with harquebuses, halberts, and pikes. Next appeared the Burmese grandees mounted on elephants, with golden chains on their backs, and collars of precious stones round their necks. Then at a distance of nine or ten paces came the Roolim of Mounay, the sovereign pontiff of Burma, who was going to mediate between the king of Martaban and the high and mighty conqueror Byeen-noung. After him the queen of Martaban was carried in a chair on men's shoulders, together with her four children—two boys and two girls—of whom the eldest was scarcely

---

[1] Fernam Mendez Pinto. Modern writers have doubted the veracity of Pinto, but his truthfulness was never doubted by his contemporaries, and the author has resided long enough in Burma to vouch from his own personal knowledge for the credibility of Pinto's accounts of that country. In fact, Pinto, like Herodotus and Marco Polo, is trustworthy about what he saw, but he was simple enough to believe any absurd fable that he was told. His stories of Byeen-noung are confirmed by Burmese annals and Portuguese historians. It should be added that the passages in the text marked with inverted commas are not taken from Pinto's original narrative, which is tedious and prolix to the last degree; they are extracted from a reproduction of Pinto's travels and adventures, with notes and commentaries.

seven. Round about the queen were thirty or forty young ladies of noble birth, who were wonderfully fair, with cast-down looks and tears in their eyes, leaning on other women. After them walked certain priests, like the capuchins in Europe, with bare feet and bare heads, praying as they went, with beads in their hands, and ever and anon comforting the ladies, and throwing water upon them when they fainted, which they did very often. Presently the king appeared, mounted on a little elephant, in token of poverty and contempt of life. He wore a cassock of black velvet; and his head, beard, and eyebrows were all shaven; and there was an old cord round about his neck by which to render himself to Byeen-noung. He was about sixty-two years of age, and tall in stature; and although his countenance was worn and troubled, he had all the bearing of a generous sovereign.

"A great throng of women and children and old men were gathered round the city gate; and when they beheld their king in his garb of woe, they set up a terrible cry, and struck their faces with stones until the blood ran down. The spectacle was so horrible and mournful that even the Burmese guards were moved to tears, although they were men of war and the enemies of Martaban.

"Meanwhile the queen fainted twice, and her ladies fainted around her; and the guards were fain to let the king alight, and go and comfort her. Whereupon, seeing the queen upon the ground in a swoon, with her children in her arms, the king kneeled down upon both his knees, and cried aloud, looking up to heaven, 'O mighty power of God, why is thy divine wrath spent upon these innocent creatures?' This said, he threw water on the queen and brought her round.

"After a while the king was remounted on his elephant, and the procession moved through the gate. Then the king saw the Portuguese deserters dressed in their buff coats, with feathers in their caps, and harquebuses in their hands; while their captain, Cayeyro, stood in front apparelled in carnation satin, making room for the procession with a gilt partisan. The king withdrew his face from the Portuguese deserters, and exclaimed against their base ingratitude; and the Burmese guards fell foul of the Portuguese, and drove them away with shame and contumely.

"After this the king of Martaban went through the street of soldiers until he came to the tent where the conqueror, Byeen-noung, was sitting in great pomp surrounded by his lords. The king threw himself upon the ground, but spake never a word. The Roolim of Mounay stood close by, and said to Byeen-noung, 'Sire, remember that God shows his mercy to those who submit to his will. Do you show mercy likewise, and in the hour of death you will clear off a load of sins.' Byeen-noung then promised to pardon the king; and all present were greatly contented; and Byeen-noung gave the king and queen in charge of two of his lords.

"Now Byeen-noung was a warrior of great craft; and he posted Burmese captains at all the twenty-four gates of the city of Martaban, and bade them let no one in or out on pain of death, as he had promised to give the sacking of the city to his foreign mercenaries. Meanwhile, and for the space of two days, he brought away all the treasures of the king of Martaban, including very many wedges of gold, and strings of precious stones of inestimable value. When he had carried away all that he wanted, he abandoned the city to the soldiery. A cannon was fired as a signal, and they all rushed in pell-mell, so that many were stifled to death at the gates; and for three days such horrible murders and wickedness were committed that no man can imagine or describe.

"While the city of Martaban was being sacked, Byeen-noung left his quarters in the Burmese camp, and pitched his tent on the hill Beidao, which was close by. One morning, when the work of plunder and destruction was nearly over, twenty-one gibbets were set up in stone pillars on the hill, and guarded with a hundred Burmese horsemen. Presently there was a great uproar in the Burmese camp, and troops of horsemen came out with lances in their hands, and formed a street from the camp to the hill, crying aloud, 'Let no man approach with arms, or speak aloud what he thinks in his heart, on pain of death!'

"Then the marshal of the camp came up with a hundred elephants and a host of foot soldiers. Next followed bodies of cavalry and infantry, and in their midst were a hundred and forty ladies bound together four and four, accompanied by many priests, who sought to comfort them. After them marched twelve ushers with maces, followed by horsemen, who carried the queen of Martaban and her four children on their horses.

"The hundred and forty ladies were the wives and daughters of the chief captains of Martaban, on whom the tyrant Byeen-noung was wreaking his spite because they had persuaded their husbands and fathers to hold out against him. They were for the most part between seventeen and twenty-five years of age, and were all very white and fair, with bright auburn hair, but so weak in the body that oftentimes they fell down in a swoon; and certain women on whom they leaned endeavored to bring them to, presenting them with comfits and other things, but they would take nothing. Indeed, the poor wretches were so feeble and benumbed that they could scarcely hear what the priests said to them, only now and then they lifted up their hands to heaven.

"Sixty priests followed the queen in two files, praying with their looks fixed on the ground, and their eyes watered with tears; some ever and anon saying one prayer in doleful tones, while others answered weeping in like manner. Last of all three or four hundred children walked in procession, with white wax lights in their hands, and cords about their necks, praying aloud with sad and lamentable voices, saying, 'We most humbly beseech thee, O Lord, to give ear unto our cries and groans, and show mercy to these thy captives, that with a full rejoicing they may have a part of the graces and blessings of thy rich treasures.' Behind this procession was another guard of foot soldiers, all Burmans, armed with lances and arrows, and some with harquebuses.

"When the poor sufferers had been led in this fashion to the place of execution, six ushers stood forth and proclaimed with loud voices that the ladies were condemned to death by the king of Burma, because they had incited their husbands and fathers to resist him, and had caused the death of twelve thousand Burmans of the city of Toungoo.

"Then at the ringing of a bell all the officers and ministers of justice, pell-mell together with the guards, raised up a dreadful outcry. Whereupon, the cruel hangman being ready to put the sentence of death into execution, these poor women sobbed and embraced each other, and addressed themselves to the queen, who lay at that time almost dead in the lap of an old lady. One of them spoke to the queen in the name of all the others, and begged her to comfort them with her presence while they entered the mournful mansions of death, where they would present themselves before the Almighty Judge, and pray for vengeance on their wrongs. To this the queen, more dead than alive, answered with a feeble voice, 'Go not away so soon, my sisters, but help me to sustain these little children.' This said, she leaned down again on the bosom of the old lady, without speaking another word.

"Then the ministers of the arm of vengeance—for so they term the hangmen—laid hold of those poor women, and hung them all up by the feet with their heads downward upon twenty gibbets, namely, seven on each gibbet. Now, this death was so painful that it made them give strange and fearful groans and sobs, until at length in less than an hour the blood had stifled them all.

"Meantime the queen was conducted by the four women on whom she leaned to the remaining gibbet; and there the Roolim of Mounay made some speeches to her to encourage her the better to suffer death. Then, turning to the hangman, who was going to bind her two little boys, she said, 'Good friend, be not, I pray you, so void of pity as to make me see my children die; wherefore put me first to death, and refuse me not this boon for God's sake.' She then took her children in her arms, and kissing them over and over in giving them her last farewell, she yielded up the ghost in the lady's lap upon whom she leaned, and never stirred afterward. On this the hangman ran to her, and hanged her as he had done the rest, together with her four little children, two on each side of her, and she in the middle.

"At this cruel and pitiful spectacle the whole multitude set up a hideous yell; all the soldiers of the army that belonged to Pegu broke out in mutiny; and Byeen-noung would have been murdered had he not surrounded himself with the Burman soldiers he had brought from Toungoo. Even then the tumult was very great and dangerous throughout the day, but at last night set in and quieted the fury of the men of Pegu.

"That same night the king of Martaban was thrown into the river with a great stone tied about his neck, together with sixty of his male captives, whose wives and daughters had been executed a few hours before on the hill Beidao."

The remaining adventures of Byeen-noung may be told in a few words. After the desolation of Martaban, he returned to Pegu, and advanced up the river Irawadi and conquered Prome, and attempted the conquest of Ava.[1] Two years later he invaded Siam with a large army, but was suddenly called back by rebellion in Pegu.

Here it should be explained that when the king of Pegu was put to death by Byeen-noung, his brother turned monk and became the most famous preacher in all that country. Accordingly, while Byeen-noung was gone away to Siam, this royal monk ascended the pulpit in the great pagoda at Pegu, and harangued a vast audience on the sufferings of the Talains, and the crimes committed by the Burmans from

---

[1] Some sickening tragedies were perpetrated at Prome, but enough has been said about such horrors.

Toungoo on the royal house of Pegu. The sermon threw the whole congregation into an uproar. The people seized their arms and rose as one man against the Burmese yoke. They slaughtered every Burman in Pegu, and carried the monk to the palace, and placed him in possession of all the treasures, and hailed him as their king.

Byeen-noung was furious at the tidings. He hurried back his army with all speed to Pegu, and put down the revolt with his Burmese soldiers, and secured possession of the city; while the royal monk fled from Pegu to the kingdom of Henzada. But the spirit of insurrection could not be quenched by force of arms. At Pegu Byeen-noung was assassinated, and his foster-brother was deserted by the mercenaries, and compelled to fly back to Toungoo. At Martaban the people rose up against the Burmese garrison, slaughtered them to a man, and declared for the royal monk.[1] Finally the royal monk was joined by many nobles and great men in the kingdom of Henzada. He raised a mighty host, and returned to Pegu in triumph and was again crowned king.

Meanwhile the foster-brother of Byeen-noung enlisted a large army among the barbarous hillmen round about Toungoo, and promised to give them the plunder of Pegu if they would help him to recover the city. He marched his army toward the south, as Byeen-noung had done before him, and scattered the army of the monk; and he entered Pegu in triumph, while the monk fled for his life to the mountains between Pegu and Arakan. But his successes led to great perplexities. He had promised to give the plunder of Pegu to his mercenary army; but the people of Pegu had submitted to his yoke, and he was horrified at the idea of abandoning them to the tender mercies of the barbarians from the hills. The mercenaries demanded the fulfilment of his

---

[1] The resuscitation of a town in Burma in the course of a few weeks or days is by no means surprising. The houses are built of wood, and can be set up very quickly.

pledge, and when he explained why he would not bear the burden of the crime, they broke out into mutiny. He fled from the camp and took refuge in a pagoda, and protected himself for a while with his Burmese soldiers. At last he held a parley with the ringleaders from the walls of the pagoda; and after much debating, it was agreed that he should distribute among the mercenaries a large sum from his own treasures as ransom for the city of Pegu.

After a while the fugitive monk was taken prisoner. He had thrown off his monastic vows, and married the daughter of a mountaineer; but he had discovered his rank to his wife, and her parents betrayed him to the Toungoo king, for the sake of the reward offered for his capture.

The execution of the royal monk was a piteous spectacle. He was taken out of his dungeon; dressed in rags and tatters; crowned with a diadem of straw garnished with mussel-shells, and decorated with a necklace of onions. In this guise he was carried through the streets of Pegu, mounted on a sorry jade, with his executioner sitting behind him. Fifteen horsemen with black ensigns proclaimed his guilt, while fifteen others in red garments were ringing bells. He was strongly guarded in front and behind by a long array of horse and foot and elephants. He was led to the scaffold; his sentence was read aloud to the multitude; and his head was severed from his body by a single blow.

During the revolt at Pegu, one of the Portuguese soldiers who had been in the service of Byeen-noung met with a fearful doom. His name was Diego Suarez. When Byeen-noung was alive and at the height of his prosperity and power, he took a great liking to Diego Suarez, and appointed him governor of Pegu. The man thus became puffed up with pride and insolence, and did what he pleased without regard to right or wrong, keeping a bodyguard of Turks to protect him in his evil ways. One day there was a marriage procession in the streets of Pegu, and Diego Suarez ordered his Turks to bring away the bride. A great tumult arose, and the bridegroom was slain by the Turks, while the bride strangled herself with her girdle to save her honor; but the father escaped with his life, and swore to be revenged upon the wicked foreigner who had brought such woe upon his household.

Years passed away, but the wretched father could do nothing but weep. Diego Suarez rose into still higher favor with Byeen-noung, and was honored with the title of "brother of the king." At last the people of Pegu broke out in revolt, and the father saw that the time had come for wreaking his vengeance on the wicked man from Portugal. He rushed into a pagoda, carried away the idol, and harangued the multitude, telling aloud the story of his wrongs. The people of Pegu rose up in a wild outbreak of fury. The officers of justice were forced to arrest Diego Suarez, and, in spite of prayers and bribes, to deliver him up to the mob; and he was then stoned to death in the market-place of Pegu, while his house was demolished so that not a tile remained.

The story of Byeen-noung is typical. It tells of a forgotten conqueror who flourished in the sixteenth century; but it also reveals the general conditions of life in Burma, from a remote antiquity down to our own times. Byeen-noung was but the type of Burmese warriors who have arisen at intervals in that remote peninsula; played the part of heroes; conquered kingdoms and founded dynasties; crushed out rebellions by wholesale massacres; and have been followed in their turn by other kings of smaller genius, but equally cruel and tyrannical.

In the middle of the eighteenth century, more than two hundred years after Byeen-noung, there was a warrior of the same stamp who founded the dynasty of Burmese kings still reigning at Mandalay. During the earlier years of that century the Talain kings of Pegu gained the mastery of the kings of Ava, and the people of upper Burma groaned under Talain domination. But about 1750 a deliverer appeared in the person of a man of low origin, known as Alompra the hunter.[1] He headed a popular insurrection, which at first only numbered a hundred men, but was soon joined by multitudes. Alompra and his newly created army threw off the Talain yoke, and swept down the Irawadi, subverted the Talain dynasty in Pegu, and founded a maritime capital at Rangoon. The English at that time had a factory at Negrais, off the coast; and the merchants were weak enough to court the friendship of Alompra, while selling powder and ammunition to the Talains. A French adventurer informed Alompra of their misdeeds, and the result was that nearly every Englishman at Negrais was massacred by the Burmese.

The successors of Alompra followed in his steps. Bhodau Phra, his third son, was the sixth sovereign of the dynasty. He reigned from 1779 to 1819, and is regarded by the Burmese as the hero of the line next to his illustrious father. He conquered Arakan as far as the boundary of Bengal, and Martaban and Tenasserim as far as the frontiers of Siam. His cruelties were boundless, and were the outcome of the same savage ferocity as those of Byeen-noung. He not only put his predecessor to death, but ordered all the women and children of his victim to be burned alive. On another occasion, on discovering that a plot had been hatched against him in a particular village, he collected together the whole population of the village, including women, children, and Buddhist monks, and burned them all alive in one vast holocaust. Father Sangermano, a Catholic missionary who was in Burma about the same time, has left authentic details of the horrible cruelties perpetrated by Bhodau Phra.

The successor of Bhodau Phra was Phagyi-dau, who brought on the Burmese war of 1824–25; but the story of his reign belongs to the after history.

The kings of Burma from Alompra downward were rude despots of the old Moghul type. They generally maintained large harems; and every high official was anxious to place a sister or a daughter in the royal household, to watch over

[1] Alompra is the most familiar name to English readers: properly it should be Alompara, or Alom Phra.

his interests and report all that was going on. Kings and queens dwelt in palaces of brick and stucco painted white and red; with roofs, walls, and pinnacles of carved timber covered with gilding and dazzling as picture-frames; with durbars, reception halls, thrones, canopies, and insignia of all kinds, radiant with bits of looking-glass and gilding. Sometimes they went on water excursions in large vessels shaped like huge fishes, and covered with gilding; and they were accompanied by long war-boats, each one covered with gilding, and rowed or paddled by fifty or sixty men. Sometimes a king went on a royal progress through his dominions, like the old Moghul sovereigns of Hindustan, carrying his queens, ministers and law courts with him. Each king in turn was constantly exposed to insurrection or revolution, in which he might be murdered, and all his queens and children massacred without regard to age or sex; while a new king ascended the throne, and removed the court and capital to some other locality, in order to blot out the memory of his predecessor. Thus during the present century the capital has been removed from Ava to Amarapura and back again; and at this present moment it is fixed in the comparatively new city of Mandalay. The kings of Burma have always been utterly ignorant of foreign nations; regarding Burma as the centre of the universe, and all people outside the Burman pale as savages and barbarians.

The despotic power of the sovereign, however, was kept in check by an old Moghul constitution, which seems to have been a relic of the remote past. The aristocracy of Burma consists only of officials, who have spread a network of officialism over the whole kingdom. There are heads of tens and hundreds; heads of villages, districts, and provinces; and all are appointed, punished, or dismissed at the mere will of the sovereign. But the ministers and officials at court exercise a power in their collective capacity, to which a king is sometimes obliged to bend; for there have been critical moments when a king has been deposed by the ministers, and another sovereign enthroned in his room.

Four chief ministers, with the king or crown prince as president, sit in a great hall of state within the palace enclosure, known as the Hlot-dau. This collective body forms a supreme legislative assembly, a supreme council of the executive, and a supreme court of justice and appeal. There are also four under-ministers, and a host of secretaries and minor officials, who conduct the administration at the capital in the name of the king, but under the orders of the Hlot-dau.

Besides the Hlot-dau, or public council of state, there is a privy council, sitting within the palace itself, and known as the Byadeit. This council is supposed to advise the king privately and personally, and to issue orders in his name, whenever it is deemed inexpedient to discuss the matter in the Hlot-dau.

The real working of these councils has always been obscured by Oriental intrigues. It is, however, obvious that they lack the authority of a hereditary assembly, such as the council of Bharadars at Khatmandu; while the bare fact that they are exclusively composed of officials, nominated by the king, and depending for their very existence on the king's favor, deprives them of any authority they might otherwise have exercised as popular or representative bodies.

CHAPTER XVI

BURMESE AND BHURTPORE WARS—LORD AMHERST

A.D. 1823 TO 1828

THE difficulties of the British government with Burma began about the end of the eighteenth century. Bhodau Phra had conquered Arakan, but the people rebelled against him, and some of the rebels fled into eastern Bengal. The Burmese governor of Arakan demanded the surrender of the fugitives. Sir John Shore was weak enough to comply rather than hazard a collision; but his successor, Lord Wellesley, refused to deliver up political refugees who had sought an asylum in British territory, and who would probably be tortured and executed in Burmese fashion the moment they were surrendered to their oppressors.

Meanwhile every effort was made to come to a friendly understanding with the Burmese government. Colonel Symes was sent on a mission to Ava; and after him a Captain Canning and a Captain Cox. But the Burmese court was impracticable. Bhodau Phra and his ministers were puffed up with pride and bombast. They despised the natives of India, and had been ignorantly led to believe that the English were traders without military capacity, who paid the black sepoys to fight their battles.

At last the Burmese authorities grew violent as well as insolent. They repeated their demands for the surrender of political refugees who had escaped into British territory; claimed possession of an island on the English side of the frontier at the Naf river; and threatened to invade Bengal unless their demands were promptly conceded.

The wars of Lord Hastings had secured the peace of India, but had been vehemently denounced in England. Lord Amherst was therefore most reluctant to engage in a war with Burma; he was ready to make any concession, short of acknowledgment of inferiority, to avert the threatened hostilities. But the Burmese refused to listen to reason, and were resolutely bent on a rupture. In 1822 their general Bundula invaded the countries between Burma and Bengal; conquered the independent principalities of Assam and Munipore, and threatened Cachar. Subsequently Bundula invaded British territory, and cut off a detachment of British sepoys. Lord Amherst was thus forced into hostilities, and in 1824 an expedition was sent against Rangoon under the command of Sir Archibald Campbell.

Meanwhile the Burmese were inflated by the successes of Bundula, and looked forward with confidence to the conquest of Bengal. Bundula was ordered to bind the Governor-General in golden fetters, and send him as a prisoner to Ava. But the British expedition to Rangoon took the Burmese by surprise. They purposed invading Bengal, and they may have expected to encounter a force on the frontier; but they never reckoned on an invading army coming to Rangoon by sea. At the same time the English invaders were almost as much surprised as the Burmese. They had been led to expect a foe worthy of their steel; but they soon discovered that the Burmese army was the most despicable enemy that the British had ever encountered. It was composed of raw levies, miserably armed, without either discipline or courage. Their chief defence consisted in stockades, which were, however, constructed with considerable skill and rapidity.

In May, 1824, the English expedition arrived at Rangoon. The Burmese had constructed some strong stockades, but they were soon demolished by British artillery. The troops were then landed, and found that Rangoon was empty of population and provisions. The Burmese governor had ordered the whole of the inhabitants—men, women, and children—to retire to the jungle with all their flocks and herds and stores of grain. As for the Burmese soldiery, they had fled in terror at the first discharge of British guns. Shortly after the landing the rains began; and the British army was forced to remain at Rangoon, and to depend for its subsistence on the supplies that arrived from Madras and Calcutta.

In December, 1824, Bundula approached Rangoon from the land side with an army of sixty thousand men. Within a few hours the Burmese soldiery had surrounded the British camp with stockades, and then burrowed themselves in the earth behind. But Bundula was attacked and defeated; his stockades were carried by storm; and he fled in a panic with the remains of his army to Donabew, a place further up the river Irawadi, about forty miles from Rangoon.

Bundula was resolved to make a stand at Donabew. He constructed field-works and stockades for the space of a mile along the face of the river. He sought to maintain discipline by the severity of his punishments; and one of his commanders was sawn asunder between two planks for disobedience of orders.

Early in 1825 the British force advanced up the river Irawadi toward Ava, leaving a detachment to capture Donabew. The detachment, however, was repulsed by the Burmese, and the main army returned to Donabew and began a regular siege. A few shells were discharged to ascertain the range of the British mortars, and next morning the heavy artillery began to play upon the works, but there was no response. It turned out that one of the shells on the preceding evening had killed Bundula. The brother of Bundula was offered the command of the army, but was too frightened to accept it; and he then made his way with all speed to Ava, where he was beheaded within half an hour of his arrival. Meanwhile the Burmese army at Donabew had dispersed in all directions.

The British expedition next proceeded to Prome. All the mad women in Ava, who were supposed to be witches or to have familiar spirits, were collected and sent to Prome to unman the British soldiers by their magic arts. Another Burmese army was sent to attack Prome, but was utterly defeated. The court of Ava was frantic at its losses, but could not realize its position, and showed itself as arrogant as ever. A brother of the king, named Tharawadi, bragged that he would drive the English to the sea, and left Ava for the purpose, but soon returned in the greatest terror.

The British expedition left Prome, and advanced toward Ava; and the court of Ava, and indeed the Burmese generally, were panic-stricken at the invaders. It was noised abroad that the white foreigners were demons, invincible and bloodthirsty; that European soldiers kept on fighting in spite of ghastly wounds; and that European doctors picked up arms and legs after an action and replaced them on their rightful owners.[1]

Early in 1826 a treaty of peace was concluded at Yandabo. The whole country from Rangoon to Ava was at the mercy of the British army. Phagyi-dau, king of Ava, engaged to pay a crore of rupees, about a million sterling, toward the expenses of the war; and the territories of Assam, Arakan, and Tenasserim, were ceded to the British government. The king was left in possession of the whole of Pegu and Upper Burma, and was even permitted to retain the maritime city of Rangoon; while the British headquarters were fixed at Moulmein in Tenasserim.

Later on Mr. John Crawfurd was sent to Ava to conclude a commercial treaty with the king. But the Burmese had already forgotten the lessons of the war, and entertained but little respect for an English envoy after the British army had retired from the scene. Accordingly Crawfurd could effect nothing of any substantial importance to either government.

---

[1] Fytche's Burma, Past and Present. General Albert Fytche's work contains many interesting facts in connection with Burmese history.

He found the Burmese officials ignorant, unprincipled, and childish, and in no instance endowed with the artifice and cleverness of Hindus and other Asiatics. Some of them had risen from the lowest ranks of life by the favor of the king; one had been a buffoon in a company of play-actors, while another had got a living by selling fish in the bazar. They did not want any treaty whatever. They evaded every proposition for a reciprocity of trade, and only sought to cajole the envoy into restoring the ceded territories and remitting the balance still due of the money payment. The country was only sparsely cultivated, and there were few if any indications of prosperity. Phagyi-dau was in the hands of his queen, the daughter of a jailer, who was older than her husband, and far from handsome. She was known as the sorceress, as she was supposed to have rendered the king subservient to her will by the power of magical arts and charms.

The first Burmese war is forgotten now by the princes and chiefs of India; but in 1824 and 1825 the current of events was watched with interest and anxiety by every native court. The different chiefs and princes of India had not quite settled down under the suzerainty of the British government; and many restless spirits among the warriors and freebooters of a previous generation would gladly have hailed the defeat of the British troops in Burma, the overthrow of order in India, and the revival of the predatory system of the eighteenth century.

Suddenly, in the crisis of the campaign in Burma, there was a fiasco in the Jat state of Bhurtpore on the British frontier near Agra, which had been under the protective alliance of the British government ever since the days of Lord Wellesley. The Raja of Bhurtpore died in 1825, leaving a son aged seven, named Bulwant Singh. The British government recognized the succession of Bulwant Singh under the guardianship of his uncle; but a cousin of the infant Raja, named Durjan Sal, corrupted the army of Bhurtpore, put the guardian to death, imprisoned the little prince, and took possession of the principality.

Sir David Ochterlony, the Resident at Delhi, was agent of the Governor-General for Rajputana and Malwa. He belonged to the once famous school of soldier-statesmen, which began with Robert Clive, and boasted of men like Sir Arthur Wellesley and Sir John Malcolm. His Indian experiences were perhaps larger than those of any living English officer. He had fought against Hyder Ali in the old days of Warren Hastings and Sir Eyre Coote; and ten years previous to the fiasco at Bhurtpore he had gained his crowning laurels in the Nipal war. He saw that a conflagration was beginning in Bhurtpore that might spread over Central India; and he ordered a force to advance on his own authority to maintain the peace of Hindustan, support the rights of the infant Raja, and vindicate the offended suzerainty of the British government.

Lord Amherst considered that the military preparations were premature. He doubted the right of the British government to interfere in the Bhurtpore succession; and he was alarmed at the strength of the great fortress of clay, which had resisted the assaults of Lord Lake, and had long been deemed impregnable by every native court in India. Accordingly he countermanded the movement of the troops.

Sir David Ochterlony was much mortified at this rebuff. In the bitterness of his soul he resigned his appointment, and died within two months, feeling that an illustrious career of half a century had been brought to an inglorious close.

The vacillation of the British government induced the usurper to proclaim that he would hold the fortress of Bhurtpore, and maintain his hold on the Bhurtpore throne, in defiance of the Governor-General. The dangerous character of the revolution was now imminent, for Rajputs, Mahrattas, Pindharies, and Jats were flocking to Bhurtpore to rally round the venturous usurper.

Lord Amherst saw his error and hastened to retrieve it; indeed his council were unanimous for war. An army was assembled under Lord Combermere and began the siege of Bhurtpore. The British artillery failed to make any impression on the heavy mud walls. At last the fortifications were mined with ten thousand pounds of powder. A terrific explosion threw vast masses of hardened clay into the air; and the British troops rushed into the breach, and captured the fortress which had hitherto been deemed impregnable. The usurper was confined as a state prisoner, and the infant Raja was restored to the throne under the guardianship of the British government. The political ferment died away at the fall of Bhurtpore, and all danger of any disturbance of the public peace disappeared from Hindustan.

Lord Amherst embarked for England in February, 1828, leaving no mark in history beyond what is remembered of Burma and Bhurtpore. He was the first Governor-General who established a viceregal sanatorium at Simla.

CHAPTER XVII

NON-INTERVENTION—LORD WILLIAM BENTINCK

A.D. 1828 TO 1835

LORD WILLIAM BENTINCK succeeded to the post of Governor-General, and held the reins of government for seven years, namely, from 1828 to 1835. Twenty-two years had passed away since 1806, when he had been recalled from the government of Madras amid the panic which followed the mutiny at Vellore. During the interval he had protested in vain against the injustice of his recall; and his nomination to the high office was regarded as an atonement for the wrong he had suffered.[1]

The government of Lord William Bentinck covers a peaceful era. He remodelled the judicial system; introduced the village revenue settlement into the northwest provinces; reduced the allowances of civil and military officers; and employed natives in the public service far more largely than had been done by his predecessors. He promoted English education among the natives, and founded a medical college at Calcutta. He labored hard to introduce steam navigation between England and India via the Red Sea. He took active measures for suppressing the gangs of Thugs, who had strangled and plundered unsuspecting travellers in different quarters of India ever since the days of Aurangzeb. Above all he abolished the horrible rite of Sati, or burning widows with the remains of their deceased hus-

[1] Lord Amherst left India in February, 1828. Lord William Bentinck did not arrive until the following July. During the interval Mr. Butterworth Bayley, the senior member of council, was provisional Governor-General.

bands, which had been the curse of India from the earliest dawn of history. Lord William Bentinck thus established a great reputation for prudence, integrity, and active benevolence, which has endured down to our own times.

The state of affairs in Malwa and Rajputana was soon forced on the attention of Lord William Bentinck. Lord Hastings had established closer political relations with the Mahrattas and Rajputs, and his measures were beginning to bear fruit during the administration of Lord Amherst. British officers were appointed Residents at native courts for the purpose of mediating between conflicting native rulers, and otherwise keeping the peace. They were strictly prohibited from all interference in the internal administration; and each native state was left to deal with faction, rebellion, or disputed succession, after its own manner. Closer acquaintance, however, showed that such extremes of non-intervention were incompatible with the duties of the paramount power; and the subsequent history of India betrays a necessary conflict between the principle and practice, which has continued till the present day.

At first there was little difficulty as regards the Mahratta states. The policy of non-interference was preached by the British government; but the British Residents at Gwalior and Indore were occasionally driven to employ detachments of the Subsidiary Force, or other British troops, to suppress mutiny or rebellion, or to root out some dangerous outlaw. Daulat Rao Sindia was weak and impoverished, and anxious to meet the wishes of the British government. Mulhar Rao Holkar was a minor, and the provisional administration was equally as subservient to the British Resident as that of Sindia. In Nagpore the Resident, Mr. Jenkins, was virtually sovereign; and during the minority of the Raja, Mr. Jenkins conducted the administration through the agency of native officials in a highly successful fashion. Meanwhile the subjects of both Sindia and Holkar regarded the British government as the supreme authority, to whom alone they could look for redress or security against the maladministration of their rulers; and a Resident often found it necessary to use his own discretion in the way of remonstrance or expostulation, without infringing the non-intervention policy.

In Rajputana circumstances were different. Captain James Tod, one of the earliest political officers in that quarter,[1] has left a picture of the country which recalls the plots, assassinations, treacheries and superstitions revealed in Shakespeare's tragedy of "Macbeth." There was the same blind belief in witches and wise women; the same single combats, bloody murders, and flights into foreign territory. Every Raj was distracted by feuds; and the princes and chiefs of Rajputana had been impoverished by Mahrattas or Pindharies just as the old kings of Britain were harassed and plundered by the Danes. The Thakurs, or feudatory nobles, were as turbulent, lawless, and disaffected as the Thanes of Scotland, and often took the field against their sovereign, like the Thane of Cawdor, with bands of kerns and gallowglasses. Many a kinsman of a Maharaja has played the part of Macbeth; while Lady Macbeths were plentiful in every state in Rajputana. The hill tribes, including Bhils, Minas, and Mhairs, were as troublesome as the Highland clans; they made frequent raids on peaceful villages, plundered and murdered travellers, and found a sure refuge in inaccessible and malarious jungles.

Captain Tod was endowed with warm sympathies and an active imagination. He was distressed at the sight of depopulated towns, ruined villages, and pauper courts; and he could not resist the appeals for his personal interference which met him on every side. He was charmed with the relics of the feudal system which he found in Rajputana. To him they recalled a picture of Europe during the Middle Ages. One usage especially delighted him. Occasionally a princess of Rajputana sent him her bracelet as a token that she looked to him for protection. In other words she claimed

---

[1] Afterward Lieut.-Colonel Tod, and author of Annals and Antiquities of Rajasthan.

his interference as her chosen knight, on whom she might rely for succor, but whom she was never destined to see.

The condition of the three leading Rajput principalities at this period proves the necessity for the interference of British authorities. In Meywar (Udaipur), the reigning Rana, the acknowledged suzerain of Rajputana, was dependent for his subsistence on the bounty of the ruler of Kotah. In Marwar (Jodhpur), the Maharaja had for years been feigning insanity, and had abdicated the throne, out of terror of Amir Khan of Tonk; but, on the extension of British protection to the states of Rajputana, he once more ascended the throne and resumed the administration of the Raj. Subsequently he quarrelled with his ministers and feudatory nobles; treating them with savage violence, putting many to death, and seeking the help of the British government to support him in these barbarous proceedings. Indeed the endless broils between the rulers of Rajputana and their refractory Thakurs have at different intervals compelled the British government to interfere for the maintenance of the public peace; and it has often been difficult to decide whether to interfere in behalf of a tyrannical Raja or in support of oppressed Thakurs.

In Jaipur, which is much nearer British territory, matters were even worse than in Marwar. The Raja of Jaipur had died in 1818, and was succeeded by a posthumous infant son, under the regency of the mother, assisted by the minister of the deceased Raja. Then followed a series of complications not infrequent in Oriental courts. The regent-mother had a Jain banker for her paramour, as well as other worthless favorites. She squandered the revenues of the state on these parasites, and especially on a Guru, who was her religious teacher or adviser. She set the minister at defiance, quarrelled with him on all occasions, and tried to oust him from his office; and on one occasion there was a bloody conflict within the palace, which ended in the slaughter of thirty men. Next she prevailed on the Jaipur army to break out in mutiny and march to the capital; and there she distributed money among the rebel soldiery, while the minister fled for refuge to his jaghir or estate in the country.

The British government was compelled to interfere by ordering the Jaipur army to retire from the capital, and sending a British officer to effect a settlement of affairs. A great council of Thakurs was summoned to court, and after much debate and uproar decided on deposing the regent-mother, and recalling the absent minister to fill the post of regent. Such a measure would have been the best possible solution of the existing difficulty, and would consequently have been most satisfactory to the British government. But such off-hand debates and resolutions, however right in their conclusions, and however much in accordance with the unwritten traditions of Rajputs, were not in keeping with that passion for order and formality which is a deeply rooted instinct in Englishmen. Accordingly Sir Charles Metcalfe, the Resident at Delhi, proceeded to Jaipur, and convened a second and more formal council, and subjected the votes to a careful scrutiny. Then it appeared that a small majority had been won over to consider the regent-mother as the rightful ruler of Jaipur. To make matters worse, the regent-mother insisted upon appointing her paramour to be minister of Jaipur, to the scandal of the whole country; and Lord Amherst's government was so pledged to the policy of non-intervention that he declined to interfere, and thus left a legacy of difficulties to his successor.

Such was the state of affairs in Malwa and Rajputana when Lord William Bentinck assumed the post of Governor-General. Like other Anglo-Indian statesmen, before and since, he landed in India with a determination to carry out a large and liberal scheme of imperial government, which was based more on the visionary ideal of home philanthropists than on a practical acquaintance with the people and princes of India. The result was that his conduct of political relations with native states was the outcome, not of fixed political views, but of a conflict between sentiment and reality, during which his romantic authorities, died out, and he was gradually awakened to a sense of the actual wants and needs of native feudatories. The political administration of Lord William Bentinck was thus a period of probation and enlightenment; and it might be said of him, and perhaps of nearly all his successors, that he was never so well fitted for the post of Governor-General of India as when he was quitting its shores forever.

It should however be borne in mind that at this period the policy of the British government toward native states was purely experimental. Non-interference was strongly advocated by the home authorities, and strictly pursued by the new Governor-General; but at this stage of political development native rulers required counsel and discipline rather than license. Before the British government became the paramount power, native rulers were afraid lest their subjects should rebel, and were thus kept to their duties by the law of self-preservation. After the establishment of British suzerainty, native rulers found themselves deprived of their old occupation of predatory war or foreign intrigue, and sought consolation in unrestrained self-indulgences. They neglected their legitimate duties, and looked to the British government for protection from rebellion. On the death of a native ruler, disorders often reached a climax, especially if there was a disputed succession, or the heir was a minor; for then queens and ministers intrigued against each other for power, and the country was torn by faction and civil war. In the end the British government was compelled to interfere in almost every case to save the state from anarchy and ruin; whereas, if it had only interfered in the first instance, there would have been no disorders at all.

The progress of affairs in Gwalior, the most important of the Mahratta states, is a case in point. Daulat Rao Sindia, the same who had been defeated by Wellesley at Assaye, died in 1827, leaving no son to succeed him. He had been repeatedly advised by the British Resident to adopt a son, but he had persistently refused. Latterly he had been inclined to give way, but nothing was concluded; and when he was dying he sent for the Resident, and told him to settle the future government of the Gwalior principality as he might think proper. After his death, his widow, Baiza Bai, proposed to adopt a son, and carry on the government as queen regent during the minority. But Baiza Bai wanted to adopt a boy out of her own family, instead of out of Sindia's family; and as this would have been odious to the court and camp at Gwalior, and would have probably led to serious commotions, the British government refused to sanction the measure. Accordingly Baiza Bai adopted a son out of Sindia's family, known as Jankoji Rao Sindia.

In course of time it appeared that Baiza Bai was bent on becoming queen regent for life, and continuing to govern the state after the young Maharaja had attained his majority. In 1833 Lord William Bentinck proceeded to Gwalior, and both the queen regent and the young Maharaja were prepared to abide by his decision; but he declined to interfere. The result was that a civil war broke out in Gwalior and the army took different sides. The young Maharaja at the head of one body of troops besieged the queen regent in the palace at Gwalior. The queen regent escaped from the palace, placed herself at the head of another body of troops, and marched toward the British Residency. On the way the two armies met, and there would have been a deadly collision had not the British Resident hastened to the spot and prevented the conflict by his personal influence. Lord William Bentinck was then forced to interfere, and recognize the accession of the young Maharaja to the throne, while the queen regent was obliged to retire from the scene. Had the Governor-General ordered this arrangement during his visit at Gwalior all these disorders would have been averted.

In 1833 there was another complication at Indore. Mulhar Rao Holkar died, and left no son to succeed him. His widow adopted a son, and proposed, as in the case of Sindia, to carry on the administration as queen regent during the minority; and the British government recognized the arrangement. Another claimant next appeared in the person of a collateral kinsman of mature years, named Hari Rao Holkar, who was supported by the general voice of the country. Lord William Bentinck might have settled the dispute by a word, but again he declined to interfere. A civil war broke out in Indore, and at last Lord William Bentinck was forced to put an end to the anarchy by persuading the queen regent to retire from the contest with her adopted son, and sending a British force to the capital to place Hari Rao on the throne of Holkar.

Matters were even worse in the petty states of Bundelkund, to the eastward of Malwa. A Raja of Sumpthur died, leaving two queens or Ranis; the elder was childless, but the younger had an infant son. The son was placed upon the throne, and the younger Rani became regent-mother. Then followed a fierce contest as to who should be appointed manager. The minister of the deceased Raja would have been the best man for the post, but other candidates were put forward by the rival queens, and the British government declined to interfere. The ex-minister fled to his estate, but was attacked by a body of troops belonging to the regent-mother. Finding his affairs desperate, he placed his women and children on a funeral pile built over a mine of gunpowder; he then destroyed them all in a terrific explosion, and rushed out and perished with his adherents, sword in hand. Lord William Bentinck decided that the regent-mother was responsible for the catastrophe, and still declined to interfere.

In Rajputana the policy of non-intervention brought forth equally bitter fruits. Meywar and Marwar were distracted by broils between the rulers and their feudatory nobles. In 1828 the Rana of Meywar died, and seven queens and a concubine perished on his funeral pile.

In Jaipur, where the regent-mother had appointed her paramour to be minister, there was another tragedy.[1] The

[1] See ante, p. 603.

young Maharaja reached his majority, but the regent-mother, and her paramour Jhota Ram, still remained in power, and the country was in a state of anarchy. In spite of appeals from the natives, Lord William Bentinck refused to interpose the authority of the British government for the prevention of disorders. In 1832 Lord William Bentinck went on a tour to the upper provinces, and had an interview with Jhota Ram at Agra; but he was persuaded by the artful minister that it was the British authorities that were to blame, and not the Jaipur government, and accordingly he still declined to interfere.

In 1834 the regent-mother died, after keeping Jaipur in a state of turmoil for sixteen years. Shortly after her death the young Maharaja died under most suspicious circumstances, and all the leading people in Jaipur were convinced that the prince had been poisoned by Jhota Ram. Indeed Jhota Ram found the minds of the Thakurs so inflamed against him that he was forced to tender his resignation.

At this crisis Major Alves, agent for the Governor-General in Rajputana, and his assistant, Mr. Blake, proceeded to Jaipur, and were only just in time to prevent a bloody contest between Jhota Ram and the Thakurs. The ex-minister was ordered to remove to a distance from the capital; and there he concocted a scheme of revenge. In June, 1835, after a morning attendance at the durbar, the two English officers were attacked in the streets of Jaipur by assassins who had been hired by Jhota Ram. Major Alves was severely wounded, and Mr. Blake was barbarously murdered. A judicial inquiry was held, and the offenders were convicted and suitably punished. An infant son of the deceased Maharaja was placed upon the throne, and a British officer was appointed to conduct the administration; and the country was rapidly brought to a state of peace and prosperity.

But while Lord William Bentinck was so lenient toward Mahratta and Rajput states, he felt deeply the serious responsibilities incurred by the British government in perpetuating misrule in Oude. He could not shut his eyes to the growing anarchy of the Talukdars;[1] the abominable oppressions practiced on the Ryots; the lawlessness of the Oude soldiery; and the weakness and debaucheries of successive rulers, who chose to call themselves kings. He felt that so long as the British government continued to maintain a helpless and depraved king upon the throne, it was morally responsible for the evils of the maladministration. In 1831 Lord William Bentinck threatened the king of Oude that the British government would take over the management of the country unless he reformed the administration. Subsequently the Court of Directors authorized the Governor-General to assume the government of Oude; but by this time Lord William Bentinck was about to leave India, and he contented himself with giving the king a parting warning.

In two other territories, Coorg and Mysore, Lord William Bentinck was compelled to interfere; but in order to apprehend the force of his measures it will be necessary to review the history of the two countries.

Coorg is a little alpine region between Mysore and Malabar; a land of hills, forests, ravines, and heavy rains; abounding in wild elephants and different kinds of game, and enclosing valleys covered with cultivation. On three sides it is walled off from its neighbors by stupendous mountains; on the fourth side by dense and tangled jungles.

The people of Coorg are hardy, athletic, and warlike; clinging to their homes of mist and mountain with the devotion of highlanders. One-fourth of the population are Coorgs properly so-called—a warrior caste, the lords of the soil. The remaining three-fourths are low castes, who were serfs or slaves under Hindu rule, but have since become free laborers.

The Coorg Raj was founded in the sixteenth century by a holy man, who migrated from Ikkeri during the breaking up of the Hindu empire of Vijayanagar, and established a spiritual ascendency in Coorg which grew into a temporal

---

[1] See ante, p. 465, note.

sovereignty.[1] He collected shares of grain from the villages round about, and founded a dynasty known as the Vira Rajas.

For nearly two centuries nothing is known of the Vira Rajas. In the eighteenth century Hyder Ali became sovereign of Mysore, conquered Malabar, and demanded tribute from the reigning Vira Raja of Coorg. Payment was refused; Mysore troops marched into the country; mountains, ravines, and forests presented insurmountable difficulties; and the Coorgs offered a brave and bloody resistance. Hyder Ali achieved a partial success by capturing two or three fortresses; by deporting some of the inhabitants, and giving their lands to Muhammadans; and also by imprisoning and murdering several members of the reigning family.

After the death of Hyder Ali his son Tippu tried to destroy the independence of Coorg, and bring it under the Muhammadan yoke; but in every case the invaders were slaughtered or driven back; and whenever a Raja was slain, the Coorgs set up the eldest surviving prince as their Raja. The new Vira Raja was then carried away captive into Mysore; but after four years he escaped back to Coorg and renewed the old struggle. During the wars against Tippu he was the stanch ally of the English, but plundered the Mysore villages with much cruelty and barbarity. After the downfall of Seringapatam in 1799, he was relieved from tribute, but sent an elephant every year to the British authorities in acknowledgment of fealty.

For many years the British government abstained from all interference in Coorg. The country was remote, inaccessible, and uninviting. The Raja was loud in professions of loyalty and gratitude; anxious to stand well with the British authorities, and hospitable to the few officials who visited his country, entertaining them with field sports, animal fights, and other amusements of a like character.

In 1807 the Vira Raja lost his favorite wife. She left no

---

[1] A picture of Ikkeri about this period is furnished by Della Valle. See ante, p. 138. The foundation of cities and kingdoms by holy men is a common incident in Hindu tradition.

son, but several daughters; and the Vira Raja was anxious that a daughter should succeed him on the throne of Coorg, to the exclusion of his two brothers. Accordingly he begged the British authorities to sanction the arrangement. The English at Madras had no objection; they cared nothing about the Coorg succession; they supposed that the Raja might do as he liked, and that he only asked their permission out of loyal subserviency to the British government. Accordingly the Madras government acquiesced as a matter of course. Years afterward it was discovered that the succession of a daughter to the exclusion of a brother was contrary to the laws and usages of Coorg; and that the Vira Raja had requested the sanction of the British government in order that he might violate the long-established customs of his own country.

Meanwhile the Raja had fits of insanity. He was suspicious, morose and bloodthirsty. He was in constant dread of assassination, and ordered frequent executions during his furious outbreaks. He beheaded his elder brother to secure the succession of his daughter; and he would have beheaded his younger brother Lingaraja in like manner, but the latter abjured the throne, and devoted himself to a life of sanctity, and was generally regarded as stupid and imbecile.[1]

In 1809 the Vira Raja died, and was succeeded by his daughter, while her husband became minister. Subsequently his younger brother, Lingaraja, appeared upon the scene, and showed himself in his true colors. The dullwitted devotee turned out to be an extremely crafty and cruel individual. He forced the husband to retire from the post of minister, and took the government of Coorg into his hands; and he then placed his niece in prison and gave

---

[1] Sir Lewin Bowring, the late Chief Commissioner of Mysore, states that the Coorg Raja put hundreds of his subjects to death in his mad fits of passion. He expresses an opinion, in which most students in Asiatic history will concur, that a brave people, like the Coorgs, would never have submitted to the tyranny and barbarity of the Vira Rajas, but for a belief in their divine right or origin. Bowring's Eastern Experiences.

out that she had abdicated the throne. There was no one to interfere, and Lingaraja became ruler of Coorg.

But Lingaraja was in morbid fear of the British authorities. He was guilty of the most cold-blooded cruelties, but took every precaution to prevent their getting wind. He allowed none of his subjects to leave Coorg; he surrounded every British officer who visited his territories with guards and spies; and constructed stockades and defences in the passes leading into his country in order to shut out any force that might be sent to coerce or dethrone him. He died in 1820, and was succeeded by a son named Chikka Vira Raja.

For the space of fourteen years the reign of Chikka Vira Raja was a series of frightful barbarities. He murdered all who had offended him, including all his relatives, old and young, male and female. None were saved excepting his own wives and children, and a married sister who fled from his violence into British territory. Many were shot with his own hands in the courtyard of the palace. Others were dragged out of the palace at night and beheaded in the jungle. His depravity was worse than his butchery; but that was confined to the recesses of his zenana.

At last the atrocities of the Coorg Raja were noised abroad, and the Raja was told that the British government would no longer permit him to perpetrate such merciless massacres. In reply he asserted that he was an independent Raja, and demanded the surrender of his sister and her husband; and when this was refused he declared war against the British government.

In 1834 the career of Chikka Vira Raja was brought to a close. A British force was marched into Coorg. The country was difficult of access, and the Coorgs fought with all the valor of their race; but the Raja was as cowardly as he was cruel, and fled to the jungle and committed more murders. The dead body of his minister was found hanging from a tree; but whether he was hanged by the Raja, or hanged himself to escape punishment, is unknown to this day. The Raja surrendered to the British authorities, and laid all the murders at the door of his dead minister.

Lord William Bentinck, with his characteristic predilection for Hindu rulers, was anxious that the leading men of Coorg should choose a Raja for themselves. The people of Coorg, without a dissentient voice, declared their preference for the government of the East India Company; but they stipulated that the Raja should be sent away from Coorg, and never allowed to return, as otherwise they would feel bound to obey him.[1] Accordingly Chikka Vira Raja was removed to Benares, and afterward allowed to visit England; and Lord William Bentinck was reluctantly obliged to annex the territory of Coorg to the British dominions, "in consideration of the unanimous wish of the people."

Mysore was a more important country than Coorg. After the downfall of Tippu in 1799, a child of the extinct Hindu dynasty was placed on the throne of Mysore; while a Brahman named Purnea conducted the administration under the supervision of an English Resident.[2] The boy was named Krishnaraj. He was not heir to the Raj, but only a child of the family; and he owed his elevation entirely to the favor or policy of the British government. Accordingly, in

---

[1] The people of Coorg insisted on another condition, namely, that no cows should be killed in Coorg. Indeed, all Hindus, whose feelings have not been blunted by association with Muhammadans or Europeans, regard the slaughter of a cow with the same horror that they would the murder of a mother. Some authorities have cavilled at this stipulation as a concession to Hindu prejudices; and Sir John Malcolm refused to concede it to Daulat Rao Sindia after the victories of Assaye and Argaum. But the two cases were altogether different. Sindia was not in a position to demand such a concession; and setting aside all other considerations, it would have been most impolitic to have admitted it. Moreover, the people of Hindustan had been subjected for ages to Muhammadan dominion. On the other hand, the acquisition of Coorg by the English was of the nature of a compact. The concession was restricted to a little secluded territory sixty miles long and forty broad, which had never been conquered by the Muhammadans. Above all, the stipulation is no breach of morality or decency, although it may be inconvenient to Europeans. If the Hindus of Coorg had claimed the right to burn living widows, or to display obscene symbols on idol cars, the case would have been different.

[2] See ante, pp. 471, 479.

order to give him a show of right, he was formally adopted by the widows of the last two Rajas of the dynasty.

Purnea was a Brahman of experience and capacity. For years he had been the minister of Tippu, and he soon won the confidence of the English Resident at Mysore. He was courteous, dignified, industrious, and careful to keep everything unpleasant out of sight. Successive English Residents —Barry Close, Mark Wilks, and John Malcolm—were more Orientalized than political officers of the modern school, more isolated from Europeans, and more dependent on natives. They were well versed in native character, and more considerate as regards native ways. They did not expect too much from Brahman administrators; judging them by Oriental rather than by European standards; and content to let things alone so long as there were no outbreaks, no brigands, and a good surplus in the public treasury. Accordingly things went on smoothly between the Resident and the Brahman; and as Purnea accumulated large sums in the public treasury, he was lauded to the skies as a minister worthy of Akbar.

But Purnea was a Mahratta Brahman of the old Peishwa type, who considered that Brahmans should govern kingdoms while Rajas enjoyed themselves. He was willing that Krishnaraj should be a symbol of sovereignty, and show himself on state occasions to receive the homage of his subjects; but he was bent on making the Raja of Mysore a puppet like the first Maharaja of Satara, while he perpetuated his own power as minister and sole ruler.

In 1811 Krishnaraj attained his sixteenth year, and proposed to undertake the government of Mysore. The British authorities had no objection; but Purnea was exasperated at the threatened loss of power, and so far forgot himself as to use strong language. Resistance, however, was out of the question. The Raja was placed at the head of affairs, and Purnea resigned himself to his fate, retired from his post, and died shortly afterward.

The government of Mysore ought never to have been intrusted to a boy, without some controlling authority. Krishnaraj was a polished young prince of courtly manners, but he had less knowledge of the world than an English charity boy. He was imbued with a strong taste for Oriental pleasures and vices, and there was no one to say him nay. From his infancy he had been surrounded by obsequious flatterers, who were his willing slaves. The result might have been foreseen. Within three years the English Resident reported that the accumulations of Purnea, estimated at seven millions sterling, had already been squandered on priests and parasites. Later on he reported that the finances were in utter disorder. The pay of the army was in arrears, and the Raja was raising money by the sale of offices and monopolies. Worst of all, the public revenues were alienated; the lands were let to the highest bidders, and the lessees were left to extort what they could from the cultivators, while the Raja continued his wasteful expenditure on vicious indulgences and riotous living.

Had the Raja been seriously warned in time that he would be deposed from his sovereignty unless he mended his ways, he would probably have turned over a new leaf. But non-intervention proved his ruin. The English Resident advised him to reform his administration, but he used soft and conciliatory tones, which were lost upon the Raja. Matters grew worse and rebukes became louder, until at last the Raja was case-hardened. The once famous Sir Thomas Munro, the governor of Madras, solemnly pointed out the coming danger to the Raja; but he might as well have preached to the winds. Nothing was done, and the warnings became a farce. The Raja promised everything while the Resident was present; but when the Resident's back was turned, he thrust his tongue into his cheek for the amusement of his courtiers.

In 1830 the people of Mysore broke out in rebellion, and the British government was compelled to send a force to suppress it. It would be tedious to dwell on the military operations, or the political controversies that followed. In the end the administration of Mysore was transferred to English officers under the supervision of the English Resident; while the Raja was removed from the government, and pensioned off, like the Tanjore Raja, on an annual stipend of thirty-five thousand pounds, and a fifth share of the net revenues of Mysore.

But Lord William Bentinck was still anxious to perpetuate Hindu rule in Mysore. He proposed to restore the government to the Raja under a new set of restrictions; but the home authorities negatived the proposal; and indeed it would probably have ended in the same kind of explosion as that which extinguished the Mahratta Peishwa. He also contemplated a restoration of the old status of an English Resident and a Brahman minister; but Purnea's administration would not bear investigation. It had been cruel and oppressive; and the native officials under him had exacted revenue by methods which were revolting to civilized ideas.[1] Accordingly Lord William Bentinck left matters to drift on; and a few years afterward the English Resident was turned into a Commissioner, and Mysore became a British province in everything except the name. Meanwhile Mysore rose to a high pitch of prosperity; the people were contented and happy; and the yearly revenues of the province rose from four hundred thousand pounds to more than a million sterling.

In one other direction the administration of Lord William Bentinck is an epoch in the history of India. It saw the renewal of the charter of the late East India Company in 1833. Henceforth the Company withdrew from all commercial transactions; and the right of Europeans to reside in India, and acquire possession of lands, was established by law.

Lord William Bentinck retired from the post of Governor-General, and embarked for England in March, 1835, after having held the reins of government for nearly eight years. Whatever may have been his shortcomings in his

---

[1] See ante, p. 479.

dealing with native states, there can be no question as to the purity of his motives, his sincere anxiety for the welfare of the princes and people of India, and the general success of his administration of the British Indian empire. His financial and judicial reforms are forgotten now, although their results have largely contributed to the well-being of the masses; but, in other respects, the material prosperity of the empire dates from the administration of Lord William Bentinck. The acquisition of Cachar and Assam, between Bengal and Burma, during the first Burmese war, was followed by the cultivation of tea, which has already assumed proportions which would have appeared incredible in a past generation, and ought to increase the domestic comfort of every cottage throughout the British dominion. But the most memorable act in his administration was the abolition of suttee. This horrible rite, which had been practiced in India from a remote antiquity, and had been known to Europe ever since the days of Alexander, was prohibited by law throughout British territories in the teeth of dismal forebodings and prejudiced posterity; and not only has the abolition been carried out with comparative ease, but it has recommended itself to the moral sense of the whole Hindu community of India. In the present day, while the education of females is still looked upon with distrust, and the attempts to put an end to female infanticide are distasteful in many quarters, every Hindu of ordinary education and intelligence rejoices in his heart that the burning of living widows with their deceased husbands is an abomination that has passed away.

In 1835 Lord William Bentinck was succeeded by Sir Charles Metcalfe as Governor-General of India. Sir Charles, afterward Lord, Metcalfe, was one of the ablest and most experienced civil servants of the late Company; but his administration was only provisional, and, beyond repealing the regulations which fettered the liberty of the press, it occupies but a small space in history. It was brought to a close in March, 1836, by the arrival of Lord Auckland.

The present chapter brings a decade of peace to a close. It began at the end of the Burmese war in 1826, and ended in 1836, when dark clouds were beginning to gather on the northwest. The war decade begins with the outbreak of hostilities beyond the Indus in 1839, and ends with the conquest of the Sikhs and annexation of the Punjab in 1849.

The administration of Lord Auckland opens up a new era in the history of India. In the beginning of the century the Marquis of Wellesley had deemed it a peremptory duty to guard India against the approaches of France and the first Napoleon. In the second quarter of the same century Lord Auckland's government took alarm at the extension of Russian power and influence in Central Asia; and this alarm found expression in the first Afghan war. Before, however, dealing with the preliminary operations in Kandahar and Kabul, it may be as well to devote a preliminary chapter to the current of events in Central Asia and the previous history of the Afghans.

CHAPTER XVIII

CENTRAL ASIA—AFGHAN HISTORY

A.D. 1747 TO 1838

DURING the eighteenth century and first quarter of the nineteenth, Central Asia was a neutral and little known region; the homes of Usbegs and Afghans; isolated from the outer world by desert and mountain; but environed more and more closely, as time went on, by the four great Asiatic empires of Persia, Russia, China, and British India.

Roughly speaking, the country northward of the river Oxus is occupied by Usbegs; while that to the south is occupied by Afghans. The Usbegs to the northward of the Oxus may be divided into the dwellers in towns, or Usbegs proper, and the nomads of the desert, better known as Turkomans. In modern times the Usbeg dominion has been parcelled out into the three kingdoms of Khiva, Bokhara and Khokand, which may be described as three semi-civilized oases in the barbarous desert of Turkomans.

Ever since the reign of Peter the Great in the beginning of the eighteenth century, Russia has been extending her empire southward over the Kirghiz steppes which separate her from the Usbegs. These steppes are occupied by the three great tribes of nomads, known as the little horde, the middle horde, and the great horde. Gradually, by a policy of protection followed by that of incorporation, these rude hordes of nomads were brought under Russian subjection; and when Lord Auckland landed in India the tide of Russian influence appeared to be approaching the three Usbeg kingdoms of Khiva, Bokhara, and Khokand.

Meanwhile the British government had not been unmindful of the progress of affairs in Afghanistan to the southward of the Oxus. This region is distributed into four provinces, each having a city of the same name, corresponding to the four points of the compass. Kabul is on the north, Kandahar on the south, Peshawar on the east, and Herat on the west. Sometimes, but very rarely, these provinces have been formed into a single empire having its capital at Kabul. At all other times they have been parcelled out under different rulers—sons, brothers, or other kinsmen of the suzerain at Kabul, but often independent of his authority. In the centre is the ancient city of Ghazni, the halfway house between Kandahar and Kabul, and the frontier fortress to Kabul proper on the side of Kandahar.

Afghanistan is a region of rugged mountains and elevated valleys. The Hindu Kush, which forms the western end of the Himalayas, throws off toward the southwest a series of mountain ranges, which bound Kabul on the north, and then run in a westerly direction toward Herat, under the names of Koh-i-Baba and Siah Koh. Indeed, the whole region may be described as a star of valleys, radiating round the stupendous peaks of Koh-i-Baba in the centre of the Afghan country, which are clad with pines and capped with snow. The valleys and glens are watered by numberless mountain streams, and are profusely rich in vegetable productions, especially fruits and cereals.[1] The lower slopes throw out spurs which are bleak and bare, and have an outer margin of barren or desert territory.[2] The population

---

[1] Afghanistan produces wheat, barley, maize, millet and rice; also cotton, tobacco, and castor-oil. It is famous for the culture of fruits, including apples, pears, almonds, apricots, quinces, plums, cherries, pomegranates, limes, citrons, grapes, figs and mulberries. All of these fruits, both fresh and dried, are exported to Hindustan in immense quantities, and are the main staple of the country. Horses and wool are also exported to Bombay.

[2] The heights of Koh-i-Baba bear traces of a remote antiquity. They include the rock fortress of Zohak, the demon king of Arabia, who is celebrated in the Shah Namah. They also include the valley of Bamean on the north of Kabul,

of Afghanistan is about five millions, but only about half can be reckoned as Afghans.

In 1836 the Afghans were separated from British territories by the empire of Runjeet Singh in the Punjab; and also by the dominions of the Amirs of Sinde on the lower Indus. But Afghanistan had always been the highway for armies invading India; for Assyrian, Persian, and Greek in ancient times, and for Turk, Afghan, and Moghul in a later age. In the earlier years of the present century, as already related, missions were sent by the British government to form defensive alliances with the Amir of Kabul and the Shah of Persia against the supposed designs of the first Napoleon.

The Afghans are Muhammadans of the Sunni faith; they reverence the first four Khalifs, and have no particular veneration for the prophet Ali. They are split up into tribes, clans, and families, each under its own head, commander, or Sirdar; and they are often at war or feud, and often engaged in conspiracies, rebellions, and assassinations. They are tall, burly, active men, with olive complexions, dark Jewish features, black eyes, and long black hair hanging down in curls. Their countenances are calm, and they affect a frankness and bon-hommie; they will sometimes indulge in a rude jocularity; but their expression is savage, and evil passions are often raging in their hearts like hidden fires. They are bloodthirsty, deceitful, and depraved; ready to sell their country, their honor, and their very souls for lucre. They care for nothing but fighting and loot; delighting in the din of arms, the turmoil of battle, and the plunder of the killed and wounded; without any relish for home life or domestic ties; without a sting of remorse or a sense of shame. There are no people on earth that have a finer

---

with huge colossal statues and temple caves; the relics of the old Buddhist faith which was driven out of Kabul by the advance of Islam under the Khalifs of Damascus and Bagdad.

The Siah Koh includes the mountain fortress of Ghor, which gave its name to a dynasty of Afghan conquerors of Hindustan, which was founded in the twelfth century of the Christian era. The same name reappears in Gour, the ancient capital of Bengal, which is now a heap of ruins. See ante, pp. 97–102.

physique or a viler morale. They are the relics of a nation who have played out their parts in history. In bygone ages they conquered Hindustan on the one side and Persia on the other; but the conquering instinct has died away amid the incessant discord of family feuds and domestic broils.

In olden time there were fierce contentions between Abdalis and Ghilzais. The Abdalis were descended from the sons of a wife, and the Ghilzais from the sons of a concubine. Accordingly the Abdalis declared that they alone were the true Afghans, and that the Ghilzais were an illegitimate offspring. It was a later version of the old feud between Sarah and Hagar, between the children of Isaac and the children of Ishmael. Ultimately the Abdalis got the uppermost, and the Ghilzais took refuge in the mountains.

The Abdalis are pure Afghans; legitimate and orthodox. In ancient times there was a distinguished offshoot, known as the tribe of Barukzais. In modern times the Abdalis have been known as Duranis; and a distinction has grown up between the Duranis and the Barukzais. The origin of this distinction is unknown, but the rivalry between the two is the key to Afghan history. The dynasty of Ahmad Shah Abdali was known as the Durani Shahs;[1] their hereditary ministers were heads of the Barukzai tribe; and Afghan history has culminated in modern times in the transfer of the sovereignty from the Shah to the minister, from the Durani to the Barukzai.[2]

The modern history of the Afghans begins with the assassination of Nadir Shah in 1747. This catastrophe convulsed Asia like the sudden death of Alexander the Great at Babylon twenty-two centuries ago. The overgrown Persian

---

[1] Ferrier says that the name of Durani was given to the Abdalis by Ahmad Shah Abdali on his accession to the throne in 1747; but the name may have had a still earlier origin. Both Duranis and Barukzais were originally included under the name of Abdalis.

[2] There are more intricacies of clans and tribes, which would only bewilder general readers. Thus the hereditary ministers, described hereafter as Barukzais, were, properly speaking, Mohamedzais, the most distinguished branch of the Barukzais. The Mohamedzais comprised about four or five thousand families, while the Barukzais numbered fifty thousand families.

empire was broken up, and there were bloody wars for the fragments. The Afghan Sirdars and their several contingents left the Persian army, and went to Kandahar to choose a Shah for themselves, who should be a king in his own right, and owe no allegiance to the Persian or the Moghul.

The Afghans could not agree about a Shah. The Sirdars quarrelled and wrangled according to their wont. Some called out for Ahmad Khan, the chief of the Duranis; others called out for Jemal Khan, the chief of the Barukzais; but in their hearts every Sirdar wanted to be the Shah. At last a holy Dervish called out amid the uproar, "God has made Ahmad Khan the greatest man among you!" And he twisted barley stalks into a wreath and placed it on the head of Ahmad Khan. Then Jemal Khan hailed Ahmad Khan as Shah;[1] and the people carried Ahmad Khan to the great mosque at Kandahar; and the chief Mulla poured a measure of wheat upon his head, and proclaimed that he was the chosen of God and the Afghans. So Ahmad Khan Durani became Shah of Kandahar, and Jemal Khan Barukzai was the greatest man in the kingdom next the Shah.

All this while Kabul was held by certain Persian families, who were known as Kuzzilbashes, or "Red-caps"; for when Nadir Shah was alive he placed the Persian "Red-caps" in the fortress of Bala Hissar,[2] to hold the city of Kabul against the Afghans. The Kuzzilbashes are Shiahs, while the Afghans are Sunnis; nevertheless, Ahmad Shah made a league with the "Red-caps," and they opened their gates to him, and he became Shah of Kabul as well as of Kandahar. Henceforth Ahmad Khan spent the spring and summer at the city of Kabul, and the autumn and winter at the city of Kandahar.

Ahmad Shah treated his Sirdars as friends and equals, but he showed the greatest kindness to Jemal Khan. He

---

[1] Shah signifies "king," and Mirza signifies "prince," or son of the Shah.

[2] The Bala Hissar, or "palace of kings," has been the scene of many a revolution and massacre. At this moment (November, 1879) it is being destroyed by the British army.

kept the Afghans constantly at war so that no one cared to conspire against him. He conquered all Afghanistan to the banks of the Oxus; all Herat and Khorassan; all Kashmir and the Punjab as far as the Himalayas; and all Sinde and Beluchistan to the shores of the Indian Ocean. He invaded Hindustan, captured Delhi, and re-established the sovereignty of the Great Moghul.[1] He gave his Sirdars governments and commands in the countries he conquered; and they lived in great wealth and honor and were faithful to him all his days. He died in 1773, being the year after Warren Hastings was made Governor of Bengal.

Ahmad Shah left eight sons, but he set aside his first-born, and named his second son, Timur Mirza, to be his successor on the throne. The first-born was proclaimed Shah at Kandahar, but Timur marched an army against him; and all the chief men on the side of the first-born deserted his cause and went over to Timur, but Timur beheaded them on the spot lest they should prove to be spies. Then the first-born fled into exile, and Timur Shah sat on the throne of his father, Ahmad Shah.

Timur Shah gave commands and honors to his Sirdars, and heaped rewards on the head of Payendah Khan, the son of Jemal Khan, who succeeded his father as hereditary chief of the Barukzais. But the Sirdars thwarted the new Shah, and wanted to be his masters; and he abandoned himself to his pleasures and put his trust in the Kuzzilbashes.

At this time the people of Balkh to the northward of Kabul were insolent and unruly.[2] They affronted every governor that Timur Shah put over them, and refused to pay taxes; and at last no Sirdar would accept the government. So the matter became a jest among the Afghans; and monkeys were taught to howl with grief, and throw

---

[1] See ante, pp. 392, 402.

[2] Balkh is a fertile but little known territory to the northward of Kabul, between the so-called Himalayas (Koh-i-Baba) and the Oxus. It was the Baktria of Herodotus. The beautiful Roxana, whom Alexander loved and married, was a daughter of the king of Baktria.

dust upon their heads, whenever one of them was offered the government of Balkh.

Meanwhile there were troubles in the Punjab and Sinde; and Timur Shah went to Peshawar with his army of Kuzzilbashes to put them down. One afternoon the Shah was taking his siesta in the fortress at Peshawar, and the Kuzzilbashes were slumbering outside the walls, when a company of armed conspirators got in by treachery, and sought to murder him. Timur Shah heard the tumult, and ran into a tower and barred the gateway. He then hastened to the top of the tower, and shouted to the Kuzzilbashes below, and unfolded his long Kashmir turban, and waved it from the battlements. The Red-caps awoke just in time. The conspirators were breaking into the tower when they were assailed and cut to pieces. The leader of the conspiracy escaped to the mountains, but was cajoled into surrender by solemn oaths of pardon and promises of reward, and was then put to death without scruple. Timur Shah was so furious at the outbreak that he wreaked his vengeance upon the inhabitants of Peshawar, and put a third of the people to the sword.

After this massacre Timur Shah was stricken with remorse and terror, and grew melancholy mad. He died in 1793, leaving twenty-three sons to fight against each other for the throne of Afghanistan.

The princes were preparing for war when Payendah Khan, the new chief of the Barukzais, averted the bloodshed. He had resolved that the fifth son of Timur Shah, named Zeman, should succeed to the throne; but he called all the sons of Timur Shah, and all the Sirdars, together in one building in order that they might choose a Shah. After long debate Zeman quietly left the assembly followed by Payendah Khan; and all those who remained behind found that the doors and windows were locked and barred, and that the place was surrounded by soldiers. For the space of five days no one could get out, and no one could break in. Every day a small morsel of bread was given to each prisoner, which sufficed to keep him alive; and when they were all reduced to skin and bone, they yielded to their fate and swore allegiance to Zeman Shah.

After this Zeman Shah resolved to cripple the power of the Sirdars. He would not seek to conciliate them as his father and grandfather had done; but he deprived them of their commands and emoluments. He grew jealous of Payendah Khan to whom he owed his throne, and removed him from his posts and reduced him to poverty. The flames of discontent began to spread abroad among the Sirdars, but were quenched by treachery and massacre. Many were tempted to court by oaths and promises, and were then put to death. In this manner Zeman Shah established a reign of terror at Kabul.

At this time the brothers of Zeman Shah were dispersed over the provinces, and breaking out in plots and insurrections. The Sikhs were rebelling in the Punjab. Zeman Shah set out from Kabul to repress the revolt; but he was called back by the news that his eldest brother had been proclaimed Shah at Kandahar, and that another brother, named Mahmud Mirza, had rebelled at Herat. After a while his eldest brother was taken prisoner and deprived of eyesight; and Mahmud Mirza was bribed to quietness by being appointed governor of Herat.

Zeman Shah next marched to Lahore, and quieted the Sikh rebels in like manner. He cajoled the head rebel, Runjeet Singh, into a show of obedience, and appointed him Viceroy of the Punjab; but from that day the Punjab was lost to the Afghans, and passed into the hands of the Sikhs. Runjeet Singh proved himself to be a warrior of mark, who laid the foundations of a Sikh empire. His later relations with the British government have already been told in dealing with the administration of Lord Minto.

When Zeman Shah had settled Lahore, he placed his brother Shah Shuja in the government of Peshawar, which was the gate of the Punjab, and then returned to Kabul.

While Zeman Shah was at Lahore, he threatened to invade Hindustan, and invited Lord Wellesley to join him in the conquest of the Mahrattas. Had Lord Wellesley been acquainted with the surroundings of Zeman Shah, he would have scoffed at the idea of an Afghan invasion.

No sooner had Zeman Shah returned to Kabul than tidings reached him that the Barukzais were plotting against him at Kandahar, to avenge the disgrace of Payendah Khan, the chief of their tribe. Accordingly Zeman Shah hurried away to Kandahar, and thought to crush the Barukzais by confiscating their wealth, and executing all who were disaffected. The Barukzais grew desperate, and plotted to set up Shah Shuja of Peshawar in the room of Zeman Shah; but the plot was betrayed by one of the conspirators. Accordingly Payendah Khan, and every Sirdar who had leagued with him, were summoned to the fortress at Kandahar under the pretence of being consulted by the Shah on public affairs. One by one they were conducted into the presence of Zeman Shah and butchered on the spot, and their bodies were exposed in the public square. In this way Zeman Shah established his authority at Kandahar, and then returned to Kabul.

Payendah Khan, chief of the Barukzais, left nineteen sons by six different mothers, and the eldest was named Futih Khan. When the unfortunate father was murdered at Kandahar, Futih Khan fled to Herat, and began to plot with Mahmud Mirza, the governor of Herat, to dethrone Zeman Shah and set up Mahmud in his room. When their plans were all ready, Futih Khan conducted Mahmud to Kandahar, and raised an army of Barukzais, and marched toward Kabul. Zeman Shah came out against them, but was defeated utterly, and taken prisoner and deprived of sight. Mahmud thus became Shah of Afghanistan, while his blinded brother Zeman fled through many countries, and suffered many pangs and privations, and at last found an asylum at Ludhiana in British territory. Thus the once famous Afghan ruler, who threatened to conquer Hindustan, and excited the alarm of Lord Wellesley, was supported to the end of his days on a pension granted him by the East India Company.

Mahmud was Shah only in name; the real sovereign was Futih Khan, the Vizier, who had succeeded his father as chief of the Barukzais. Mahmud the Durani Shah was a puppet like the Mahratta Sahu; while Futih Khan, the Barukzai Vizier, was a Peishwa like Balaji Rao.

In 1801–2 there were risings of the Ghilzais, the children of the concubine, the Ishmaels of the Afghans; but Futih Khan attacked them in the mountains and routed them with great slaughter; and he then built up a pyramid with their heads and returned in triumph to Kabul.

After a while there was a bloody strife at Kabul between the Sunnis and the Shiahs; in other words, between the Afghans and the Red-caps. The Red-caps thought to spite the Sunnis by tormenting an Afghan boy; and the parents of the lad went to the palace for justice, and were told to go to the mosque.[1] The parents ran into the great mosque at Kabul while a Saiyid was preaching, and rent their clothes and filled the air with their cries. The Saiyid stopped the sermon to hear their story, and then issued a fatwa[2] for the slaughter of all the Shiahs in Kabul. The Sunni congregation armed themselves and rushed to the quarter of the Kuzzilbashes, slaughtered every Red-cap they met in the streets, and then broke into the houses, carried off the plunder, and set the buildings on fire. The storm raged throughout four days. At last the Barukzai Vizier interposed with a troop of horsemen, and put a stop to the riot, but not before four hundred Kuzzilbashes had been slain.

The Sunnis had been scattered by matchlock and sabre,

---

[1] The Durani Shahs had always trimmed between the Afghans and the Kuzzilbashes, or Red-caps, and stood aloof from every conflict between the two. Accordingly both the Durani Shah and the Barukzai Vizier got rid of the petition of the parents by referring the complainants to a religious tribunal.

[2] A fatwa was a religious command bearing some resemblance to a papal bull.

but their wrath was not appeased, and they swore to be revenged on the friends of the Shiahs. In 1803, when the Barukzai Vizier was putting down revolts among the mountain tribes at a distance from Kabul, Shah Shuja was persuaded to come from Peshawar, and was hailed by the Sunni multitude at Kabul with shouts and acclamations. Mahmud Shah fled in alarm to the Bala Hissar, but soon found himself a close prisoner in one of the dungeons. Shortly afterward the Barukzai Vizier returned to Kabul and became minister to Shah Shuja.[1]

In 1809 there were other plots and other explosions. Shah Shuja had grown impatient of the dictation of his Barukzai Vizier and removed him from office; and then went to Peshawar to receive Mr. Elphinstone, and make an alliance with the English against France and Napoleon. Meanwhile the deposed Vizier leagued with the Kuzzilbashes, and delivered his old master, Mahmud Shah, from his prison, and placed him on the throne at Kabul. Shah Shuja completed his negotiations with Mr. Elphinstone, and then turned back to go to Kabul, but was routed by the Barukzais and Kuzzilbashes; and he fled through the Punjab to British territory, and became a pensioner at Ludhiana like his brother Zeman Shah.

Mahmud Shah was thus restored to the throne of Afghanistan, but he was still feeble and effeminate, and a mere tool in the hands of his Barukzai Vizier, Futih Khan. He abandoned himself to his pleasures, and left the government to his Vizier. But Afghanistan prospered under the rule of the Barukzai. Futih Khan was a conqueror as well as an administrator. He reduced Sinde and Beluchistan to obedience, but he could do nothing in the Punjab, for he was constantly baffled and defeated by the Sikh ruler, Runjeet Singh.

About this time Herat became a bone of contention be-

---

[1] The Barukzai Vizier's acceptance of office under Shah Shuja, while his old master Mahmud was pining in the dungeons of the Bala Hissar, is one of those typical data which serve to bring out the real character of the Afghans.

tween the Afghans and the Persians.[1] It has already been seen that when Zeman was Shah, his brother Mahmud became governor of Herat. When Mahmud became Shah, another brother, named Firuz, became governor of Herat. Firuz coined money in the name of Mahmud Shah, and his son married a daughter of Mahmud Shah; but Firuz ruled Herat as an independent sovereign, and refused to send any tribute to Kabul.

In 1816 Firuz was between two fires. On one side Kabul demanded tribute; on the other side Persia demanded possession. At last Persia sent an army to take possession of Herat, and Firuz was forced to send for help to Kabul. The Barukzai Vizier rejoiced over the request. He marched an army to Herat before the Persians reached the place; and he entered the fortress and declared that Firuz was a rebel, and took him prisoner and sent him to Kabul. At the same time the Vizier's younger brother, Dost Muhammad Khan, broke into the zenana and robbed the ladies of their jewels, and carried away a girdle set with precious stones that was worn by the daughter of Mahmud Shah. Futih Khan was angry at this outrage, and ordered his brother to restore the girdle; but Dost Muhammad Khan refused to give it back, and fled away to Kashmir.[2]

All this while Kamran Mirza, the son of Mahmud Shah, had been very jealous of the Vizier; and when he heard that his sister at Herat had been robbed of her girdle, he complained to his father very bitterly. So Mahmud Shah was persuaded to avenge the insult by destroying the Vizier's eyesight, and Kamran hastened to Herat to carry out the

---

[1] The Shah of Persia claimed Herat on the ground that it had been conquered by Nadir Shah. The claim, however, was a mere sham. Persia might just as well have claimed Kabul and Kandahar, since both provinces had been conquered by Nadir Shah. The plain fact was that Ahmad Shah Durani had conquered Herat, but his successors could not hold it, as it was too remote from Kabul; and Herat became an independent sovereignty in the hands of any Afghan prince who obtained the government.

[2] This is the first appearance of Dost Muhammad Khan, the founder of the Barukzai dynasty, upon the page of history. At a later period he was a leading character in the Afghan war of 1839–42.

sentence. Futih Khan was surprised and bound, and his eyes were pierced with red-hot needles in the presence of Kamran.[1]

When Dost Muhammad Khan heard what had been done, he raised an army in Kashmir and marched against Kabul to avenge the atrocity committed on his eldest brother. Mahmud Shah was seized with terror at the approach of the avenging army, and fled away to Ghazni, the half-way fortress between Kabul and Kandahar. At Ghazni he was joined by his son, Kamran, and the blind Barukzai Vizier from Herat. But his kingdom had passed out of his hands, and his troops deserted him in large numbers, and went over to Dost Muhammad Khan. In his wrath he sent for the blind Vizier, and ordered his Sirdars to put him to death before his eyes. Kamran struck the first blow. All the Sirdars then began to torment the blind Vizier with their daggers; and after enduring excruciating agony, Futih Khan expired without a groan.

The plots and broils which followed are tedious and bewildering. Mahmud Shah and his son, Kamran, fled to Herat, and became independent rulers of that remote territory. The surviving sons of Payendah Shah, known as the Barukzai brothers, assumed different commands in Kabul, Kandahar, Kashmir, and Beluchistan. But Afghanistan was without a sovereign. Not one of the Barukzai brothers ventured at this period to usurp the Durani sovereignty. They were willing to set up Shah Shuja as a puppet and to rule Afghanistan in his name; but Shah Shuja refused to accept their terms, and insisted upon being absolute and uncontrolled sovereign of the Af-

---

[1] The following table of Durani Shahs and Barukzai Viziers may be found a convenient aid to the memory:

Ahmad Shah Durani . .	1747	Jemal Khan Barukzai . .	1747
Timur Shah " . .	1773	Payendah Khan " . .	1773
Zeman Shah " . .	1793	Futih Khan " . .	1800
Mahmud Shah " . .	1800	" " . .	1808
Shah Shuja " . .	1803	Dost Muhammad Khan Barukzai, Amir of Kabul .	1826
Mahmud Shah (restored) .	1809		

ghans. Under such circumstances the Barukzai brothers abandoned Shah Shuja, and he was forced to return to Ludhiana. They then tried to set up another prince of the family; but soon found that their new Durani puppet was plotting against them with Shah Shuja on one side at Ludhiana, and with Mahmud Shah on the other side at Herat. The result was that the puppet was dethroned, and the Barukzai brothers quarrelled among themselves, while Runjeet Singh occupied Peshawar and Persia threatened Herat.

At last, in 1826, Dost Muhammad Khan became master of Kabul. Subsequently he was formally elected king by an assembly of Sirdars, and proclaimed Amir by the chief Mulla, with all the ceremonies that had been observed at the coronation of Ahmad Shah. But he was environed by dangers. On the north there were revolts in Balkh; on the south one of his brothers was holding out against him at Kandahar; on the east he was harassed by Runjeet Singh at Peshawar, with Shah Shuja and the British government in the background; on the west there was Mahmud Shah and Kamran at Herat, with Persia plotting behind and Russia looming in the distance. Amid such perplexities Dost Muhammad Khan was willing and anxious to conclude an alliance with the British government, provided only he could be assured that the English were not plotting to restore Shah Shuja, and would help him to recover Peshawar from Runjeet Singh.

In the midst of these turmoils, Great Britain and Russia were at variance in Central Asia. The bone of contention was Herat. From a remote antiquity Herat has been the key to India; the first turnpike on the great highway from Persia to Hindustan.[1] In 1836 Russia was making a cat's-paw of Persia and urging the Shah to seize Herat. Great Britain was anxious to keep Persia out of Herat, lest the

---

[1] The fortified city of Herat is a quadrangle about four miles on each side. It was surrounded by a rampart of earth about ninety feet high which appeared to environ the city like a long hill. The rampart was supported on the inside by buttresses of masonry; and was surmounted by a wall thirty feet high flanked with round towers and loop-holed for musketry.

place should become a gateway through which Russia might advance toward India. But the British government did not tell Persia plainly that war would be declared if she attempted to occupy Herat. Had this been done, Persia would never have besieged Herat, and an English army would never have invaded Afghanistan.

The result of all this underplotting and hesitation was that in 1837 the Shah of Persia marched an army against Herat. By this time the government of Herat had changed hands. Mahmud Shah had been murdered in 1829, and his son Kamran was sovereign of Herat; but Kamran was a slave to opium-eating, and other enervating pleasures, and his Vizier, Yar Muhammad Khan, was the real ruler. Yar Muhammad Khan was a cruel and extortionate despot; he has been described as the most accomplished villain in Central Asia; but at this period he hated Persia with all his heart and soul. On one occasion he had been entrapped into a meeting with a Persian prince on the frontier, under pretence of settling all differences between Herat and Persia; and two of his teeth had been forcibly extracted to induce him to comply with the demands of the Shah.[1] Kamran would have submitted to the Shah of Persia at the first summons; but Yar Muhammad Khan swore that he would never surrender Herat until his teeth were restored to his gums; and that as long as he had a sabre to draw or a cartridge to fire, he would never bow his head to the Kajar Shah.

The siege of Herat was one of the most memorable events of the time. It lasted from November, 1837, to September, 1838. The Afghans fought manfully, harassing the Persian army with repeated sorties. Even the women and children

[1] The Persian prince was Abbas Mirza, eldest son of Futih Ali Shah, the second sovereign of the Kajar dynasty. Abbas Mirza died a few months afterward, and Yar Muhammad Khan escaped to Herat. Futih Ali Shah died in 1834, and was succeeded on the throne of Persia by his son, Muhammad Shah, who besieged Herat in 1837. Futih Ali Shah, sovereign of Persia, must not be confounded with Futih Khan, the Barukzai minister at Kabul, who was murdered in the year 1817.

mounted the walls and threw down bricks and stones on the Persian soldiers. But the canals which supplied the city with water were cut off by the enemy; the inhabitants were starving; and Kamran was treacherously plotting the surrender of the city to the Persians. Indeed, Herat would have been lost to the Afghans but for the heroic exertions of a young lieutenant, named Eldred Pottinger, who was present in the city during the siege. Pottinger animated the Afghan soldiery by his gallant exploits, and cheered the drooping spirits of Yar Muhammad Khan by his energy and counsel. At last the siege was brought to a close by diplomacy. The British government threatened Persia with war, and the Shah raised the siege of Herat, and returned to his own dominions.

All this while Dost Muhammad Khan was most anxious to recover Peshawar from Runjeet Singh. He implored Lord Auckland to call on Runjeet Singh to restore Peshawar. But the British government had no desire to pick a quarrel with Runjeet Singh, and declined to interfere. The result was that Dost Muhammad Khan made advances to Russia, and received a Russian mission at Kabul; and the British government in return resolved to dethrone Dost Muhammad Khan, and restore Shah Shuja to the throne of Kabul.

CHAPTER XIX

AFGHAN WAR—LORDS AUCKLAND AND ELLENBOROUGH

A.D. 1839 TO 1842

ON the 1st of October, 1838, Lord Auckland published a declaration of war at Simla; and shortly afterward the British forces were on the move for Kabul. They could not march through the Punjab, because Runjeet Singh refused permission. Accordingly they marched through Sinde to Quetta; and there the Bombay column joined the Bengal column. At Quetta Sir John Keane took the command of the united armies, and then set out for Kabul.

Kandahar was captured in April, 1839. A British force was left at Kandahar under the command of General Nott; while Major (now Sir Henry) Rawlinson was placed in political charge of the province in the name of Shah Shuja. In July Ghazni was taken by storm,[1] and Dost Muhammad Khan fled over the Oxus into Bokhara. In August the British army entered Kabul, and Shah Shuja was restored to the throne of Afghanistan. Henceforth he was supposed to govern the country under the advice and help of the English minister and envoy, Sir William Macnaghten.

In November, 1839, the Russian government sent a counter expedition from Orenberg toward Khiva, with the view of establishing Russian influence over the three Usbeg Khanates to the northward of the Oxus. The time of year, however, was most unfortunate. Winter snows and waterless

---

[1] At the storming of Ghazni the late Sir Henry Durand distinguished himself as a young subaltern in the Engineers by blowing up the Kashmir gate.

wastes forbade the Russian force to reach Khiva; and after heroically fighting against the severest privations and disasters, it was compelled to return to Orenberg.

Meanwhile the Afghans seemed perfectly satisfied with British occupation. Large subsidies were paid by the English envoy to Afghan chiefs, as well as to the mountain tribes who guarded the passes; while the presence of the English troops was a godsend to all the shopkeepers and provision-dealers in the bazars. The British army remained at Kabul during 1840. Toward the end of the year, Dost Muhammad Khan surrendered to the English envoy, and was sent to Calcutta, where he was detained as a prisoner, but treated as a guest. The old Barukzai warrior was indeed often entertained at Government House, where he is said to have played at chess with Miss Eden, the sister of the Governor-General.

Meanwhile there were complications at Herat. After the retreat of the Shah of Persia in 1838, the revenues of Herat were exhausted, the troops were without pay, the inhabitants were starving, and the Vizier, Yar Muhammad Khan, was trying to raise money and get rid of the surplus population, by selling the people as slaves to the Usbegs. The British government averted these evils by advancing large sums of money for the payment of the troops, the repair of the fortifications, and the relief of Kamran and his Vizier; no doubt with the view of establishing a permanent influence at Herat.

Kamran and his Vizier were in no way grateful for these subsidies. They suspected that the British government had sinister designs on Herat, and accordingly opened up a treacherous correspondence with the Shah of Persia. Major D'Arcy Todd, who had been appointed English envoy at Herat, withheld the money payments on his own authority, unless the Vizier agreed to receive a contingent of British troops into Herat. The result was that the Vizier grew furious at the stoppage of the subsidies, and called on Major Todd either to pay up the money or to leave Herat. Major Todd was so disgusted with the perfidy and greediness of the Herat rulers that he threw up his post and returned to British territory. Lord Auckland was naturally exasperated at the abandonment of Herat. Matters had been squared with Persia, and the continued presence of Major Todd would have sufficed to maintain British influence at Herat. Major Todd was dismissed from political employ, but found a soldier's death four years afterward on the field of Ferozeshahar.

The British occupation of Afghanistan continued through the year 1841, for it was not deemed safe to leave Shah Shuja unprotected at Kabul. Meanwhile, the double government satisfied no one. Shah Shuja was smarting under the dictation of Sir William Macnaghten. The English envoy and minister was in his turn impatient of Afghan ways and prejudices. The Afghan officials were disgusted with the order and regularity of English administration, which was introduced under the new regime. The Mullas refused to offer up public prayers for Shah Shuja, declaring that he was not an independent sovereign. Even the rise of prices, which filled the pockets of the bazar dealers, lessened the value of money and excited the discontent of the masses.

So long, however, as subsidies and money allowances were lavished among turbulent Sirdars and refractory mountain tribes, there was no lack of loyalty toward Shah Shuja and his English allies. But the flow of gold could not last forever. The revenues of Afghanistan had been overrated. The British authorities had put their trust in the estimates of Shah Shuja when at Ludhiana; forgetting the Machiavellian maxim that it is dangerous to rely upon the representations and hopes of exiles. The expenses of the British occupation were so enormous that economy was imperative. Accordingly Sir William Macnaghten began to cut down the subsidies and money allowances. From that moment the loyalty which had sprung up in a single night like the prophet's gourd began to sicken and die away. The Afghans grew weary of the English and their puppet ruler, Shah Shuja. Conspiracies were formed; petty outbreaks became frequent; while the Ghilzais, and other mountain tribes at the passes, being no longer bribed into acquiescence, became most troublesome and disorderly.

At this period there were no alarms for the safety of the British army in Kabul. On the contrary, English officers had been induced to bring up their wives and families from the depressing heats of Bengal to the cool climate of Kabul; and no precautions were taken against a possible rising of the whole people. The British cantonment was three miles from the city, with only a mud wall round it that could be easily ridden over. Sir William Macnaghten and his family lived in a house close by the cantonments; he had been appointed Governor of Bombay, and was about to be succeeded by Sir Alexander Burnes as envoy and minister at Kabul. Burnes himself was as much at home at Kabul as at Calcutta; he occupied a house near the centre of the city, surrounded by bazars, and above all by a turbulent population of Afghans and Kuzzilbashes, who were ever and anon endeavoring to settle the knotty disputes between Sunnis and Shiahs by force of arms.

Meantime there had been some changes in the command of the British army of occupation. General Elphinstone, an aged and infirm officer, unfit for the post, had taken the place of Sir John Keane. Next to General Elphinstone were Sir Robert Sale and Brigadier Shelton.

The British army of occupation was exposed to danger from another cause. It had been originally quartered in the fortress known as the Bala Hissar, which commanded the whole city and suburbs of Kabul. So long as the British kept possession of the Bala Hissar, they could hold out against any insurrection. But Shah Shuja quartered his harem in the Bala Hissar, and objected to the presence of the English soldiers; and Sir William Macnaghten was weak enough to remove the troops from the fortress, and quarter them in an unprotected cantonment about three miles from the city.

The catastrophe that followed may be told in a few

words. In October, 1841, Sir Robert Sale left Kabul with a brigade to reopen communications between Kabul and Jellalabad, which had been closed by the disaffected mountaineers. Sale effected his task after a long struggle and considerable loss. His subsequent defence of Jellalabad against the repeated assaults of a large Afghan army is one of the heroic events in the war.

On the 2d of November, 1841, an insurrection broke out in the streets of Kabul. Sir Alexander Burnes thought of escaping to the English cantonment in the disguise of an Afghan; but he changed his mind, and resolved to hold out to the last in his English uniform. He barricaded his house, and sent to Macnaghten for a battalion of infantry and two field-pieces. Such a force at the beginning of the outbreak would have saved the life of Burnes. Its appearance in the streets of Kabul would have led the Kuzzilbashes to rally round Burnes, and raise the war-cry against the Sunnis. But Macnaghten was doubtful, and General Elphinstone was afraid that Shah Shuja might object, and the two together agreed to wait for further information. Meanwhile the mob of Kabul, the most dangerous in Central Asia, was surging round the house of the Englishman. Burnes held out with thirty-two others from eight o'clock in the morning until two in the afternoon, when the mob burned down the gate, and rushed in, and all was over. Burnes and twenty-three others were killed; the remaining nine escaped by a miracle.

At three o'clock that same afternoon, Brigadier Shelton made a lame attempt to enter the city with a couple of battalions of infantry; but by this time the suburban population had joined the rioters. It was impossible to cut a way through the narrow streets and crowded bazars, and Shelton was compelled to return to the cantonment. Meanwhile the uproar was increasing in the city. Thousands of Afghans flocked to Kabul in hopes of plunder; and it soon appeared that the whole Afghan nation had risen against the rule of the foreigner.

At this crisis the British commanders appear to have been paralyzed. General Elphinstone and Sir William Macnaghten were planning a retreat to Jellalabad, the half-way house between Kabul and Peshawar. Provisions were running short; the people of Kabul kept back all supplies from the British cantonment, and the army of occupation was becoming demoralized.

At last Macnaghten began to negotiate with the leaders of the insurrection, and especially with Akbar Khan, the eldest son of Dost Muhammad Khan. This man had fled from Kabul about the same time that his father had made his way to Bokhara; but, on hearing of the revolt, he had hastened back to Kabul, and was bent on seizing the government of the country. Shah Shuja was shut up in the Bala Hissar, but could do nothing; he was already ignored, and his end was drawing nigh.

Akbar Khan and other Afghan Sirdars solemnly engaged to supply the British army with carriage and provisions. In return they received from Macnaghten promises of large sums of money and hostages for the payment. But instead of keeping to their engagement, the Afghans demanded more money and more hostages. Winter had set in, and snow was falling; and it was even proposed that the British army should remain at Kabul till the spring. At length, after many delays and evasions, there was a final meeting between Macnaghten and the Afghan chiefs on the 23d of December, 1841. But the English envoy had given mortal offence to the Afghans, and when he appeared at the meeting he was suddenly attacked and murdered by Akbar Khan.

Subsequently the Afghan chiefs tried to explain away the murder. Akbar Khan vowed that he had acted on the mad impulse of the moment, and not with any deliberate intention of committing murder. Negotiations were renewed, and in January, 1842, the British forces began their retreat from Kabul, followed by Akbar Khan and a large army of Afghans. Then followed a horrible series of treacheries and massacres. Akbar Khan demanded more hostages, including English ladies and children. The Ghilzai mountaineers covered the heights on either side of the Khaiber Pass, and poured a murderous fire on the retreating force. Akbar Khan declared that he could not restrain the Ghilzais, but at the same time he permitted his own forces to share in the massacre and plunder. Thousands of British troops and camp-followers were carried off by successive volleys, or died of hunger and privations, or fell down in the snow from wounds or fatigue and were butchered by the Afghans. Thus perished a force which left Kabul with four thousand fighting men, and twelve thousand followers. Out of all this number, only a solitary individual, an English surgeon named Brydon, managed to escape to Jellalabad. He was brought in by Sale's garrison half dead from hunger and wounds; but he lived to tell the tale for more than thirty years afterward.

Such was the state of affairs in February, 1842, when Lord Ellenborough landed at Calcutta and succeeded Lord Auckland as Governor-General. Men's hearts were bursting with shame and indignation as they heard of the murder of the British envoy, and the destruction of sixteen thousand men. Englishmen in India were burning to retrieve the disgrace which had befallen British arms, and to avenge the slaughter which cast a gloom over the whole country. But Lord Auckland had been too much oppressed by the disaster to respond to the call; while Lord Ellenborough, who succeeded him, was too much alarmed at the danger to which the British garrisons were exposed at Jellalabad and Kandahar to plan such a scheme of vengeance as should vindicate the honor of England, and restore the prestige of British arms.

A force was assembled under General Pollock to march through the Punjab, and relieve Sale's garrison at Jellalabad. Runjeet Singh died in June, 1839, and the Sikh rulers who came after him did not resist the passage of British troops. In due course Pollock marched his army through the Punjab and reached Peshawar, but halted there for some weeks to reassure the sepoys who were reluctant to enter the Khaiber Pass.

In April, 1842, Pollock crowned the heights of the Khaiber with British infantry, and engaged hotly with the mountaineers; and within a short space of time the white dresses of the Ghilzais were to be seen flying off in all directions. He then pursued his victorious march through the Khaiber to Jellalabad, and reached the place at a critical moment. Sale had been closely beleaguered by a large army of Afghans under the command of Akbar Khan; and he had just inflicted a heavy defeat on the enemy, and compelled Akbar Khan to raise the siege and return to Kabul.

Meanwhile the city of Kabul was distracted by the struggle between the factions of Barukzais and Duranis. A Barukzai chief, named Zeman Khan, had taken possession of the city;[1] while the Durani sovereign, Shah Shuja, shut himself up in the Bala Hissar. Indeed Shah Shuja was in sore peril and perplexity. He sent letters to Jellalabad, swearing eternal devotion to the British government; and he sent messages to the Barukzai leaders, swearing to drive the British out of Afghanistan. At last the Barukzais called upon him to lead the Afghan army against the British garrison at Jellalabad, and bound themselves by solemn oaths to protect him from all harm. The old Durani left the fortress of the Bala Hissar decked out in all his robes and jewels; and was then shot dead by an ambush of matchlock men, and rifled of all his precious things.

The Barukzais, however, failed for the moment to get the mastery. The Bala Hissar was still in the hands of the Duranis, and a son of Shah Shuja was proclaimed sovereign within the walls of the fortress. The civil war continued to rage between the two parties. There was fighting in the streets from house to house, while the guns of the Bala Hissar were playing upon the city.

At this juncture Akbar Khan returned from his defeat

---

[1] Zeman Khan was a nephew of Dost Muhammad Khan. He had been elected king by the Barukzais in the absence of Akbar Khan.

at Jellalabad. Both Barukzais and Duranis were dreading the return of the English; and Akbar Khan commanded the respect of all parties of Afghans by declaring that he was negotiating with General Sale. But Akbar Khan had his own game to play. He joined the Barukzais and captured the Bala Hissar. Then he went over to the Duranis, paid his homage to the son of Shah Shuja, and began to rule as minister. The boy sovereign, however, was in mortal fear of being murdered by his self-constituted minister; and he at last escaped to the British camp, and placed himself under the protection of General Pollock.

Akbar Khan thus became ruler of Kabul, and the fate of the prisoners and hostages was in his hands. He had not treated them unkindly, but he was determined to use them for his own purposes. He wrote to General Pollock offering to deliver them up, provided the English departed from Jellalabad and Kandahar without advancing to Kabul. Pollock rejected the proposals. Akbar Khan then sent the captives to a hill fortress far away to the northward; and marched out of Kabul with a large army to prevent Pollock from advancing on the Afghan capital.

Meanwhile Lord Ellenborough was hesitating whether to withdraw the garrisons from Jellalabad and Kandahar, or permit them to march to Kabul. Secret instructions were sent to the two generals to withdraw; but the secret got wind and raised a storm of indignation, as it was imagined that the captives were to be abandoned to the tender mercies of the Afghans. Accordingly Lord Ellenborough modified his instructions, and ordered the two generals to use their own discretion as regards an advance to Kabul.

General Nott was a hot-tempered officer, and when he received the orders to withdraw he was furious with rage. Both Nott and Rawlinson knew that a retreat from Kandahar would raise the whole country against them, and end in disaster like the retreat from Kabul. Rawlinson had already tried to stir up the neighboring Durani chiefs to rally round Shah Shuja, but found that they were as bitterly opposed to the British occupation as the Barukzais. Accordingly there was no alternative but to wait for reinforcements; and for months the force at Kandahar was exposed to desperate assaults, which were met by still more desperate repulses; while Nott and Rawlinson continued to hope for a change of orders.

General Pollock was the mildest of men, but even he was moved with shame and anger at the order to withdraw. He wrote to Nott begging him not to leave Kandahar until he heard more; and reported to headquarters that he could not leave Jellalabad for want of transport. Subsequently, he received the modified instructions; and in August, 1842, he heard that Nott had set his face toward Kabul. Accordingly he left Jellalabad accompanied by Sale, and entered the Tezeen valley.

At Tezeen the British soldiers beheld a sight which could never be forgotten. The valley was the scene of one of the bloodiest massacres during the ill-starred retreat from Kabul. The remains of their murdered comrades were still lying on the ground, and the sight exasperated the avenging army. At that moment the army of Akbar Khan appeared upon the scene; and the heights around bristled with matchlock men from Kabul. Pollock's force advanced in the face of a murderous fire, and gave no quarter. The enemy was utterly routed; indeed the victory at Tezeen was the crowning event of the war. Akbar Khan fled to the northern mountains, never to return until the English left Afghanistan; and in September, 1842, the British flag was floating over the Bala Hissar.

Nott soon arrived at Kabul bringing with him the sandalwood gates of Somnath, which Mahmud of Ghazni had brought away from Guzerat in the eleventh century, and had since then adorned his tomb at Ghazni. This was a whim of Lord Ellenborough's, who had ordered the gates to be brought away as trophies of the war.[1]

[1] Sir Henry Rawlinson was of opinion that the gates were not genuine, but fac-similes of the originals, which must have perished long ago. The author has seen the gates at Agra, and has no doubt of the correctness of Sir Henry Rawlinson's conclusions.

All this while the probable fate of the prisoners and hostages caused the utmost anxiety. Suddenly all fears were allayed. The captives managed to bribe their keepers, and were brought into the British camp at Kabul amid general acclamation.

The glory of the avenging army was marred by acts of barbarity. The great bazar at Kabul was blown up by gunpowder. It was one of the finest stone buildings in Central Asia, but it was the place where Macnaghten's remains had been exposed, and it was destroyed as a fitting punishment for the crime. Amid the confusion, the two armies broke into the city and perpetrated deeds in revenge for the slaughter of their comrades in the Khaiber, over which history would fain draw a veil.

The proceedings of Lord Ellenborough at the close of the Afghan war were much condemned by his contemporaries. He issued a bombastic proclamation respecting the gates of Somnath which exposed him to much ridicule. The gates had been carried away from an idol temple by a follower of the prophet; consequently their recovery could not delight the Muhammadan princes of India. Again the gates had adorned the tomb of Mahmud of Ghazni; consequently they were impure in the eyes of Hindus. Lord Ellenborough also received the avenging army, on its return from Kabul, with a show of painted elephants, and other displays of Oriental pomp, which jarred against English tastes. But these eccentricities are forgotten by the present generation, and can hardly be treated as history.

One episode in the history of the Afghan war conveys a useful lesson. In the heyday of success, when Afghanistan was first occupied by a British army, it was proposed to establish British influence in the Usbeg Khanates to the northward of the Oxus. Colonel Stoddart was sent to Bokhara to form friendly relations with the Amir; and Captain Conolly, who had been sent on a like mission to the ruler of Khokand, joined Colonel Stoddart at Bokhara. The Amir of Bokhara regarded both officers with suspicion, and kept them under close surveillance; but he hesitated to proceed to extremities; for aught he knew, the British army at Kabul might be moved across Balkh and the Oxus into Bokhara. But successive disasters in Kabul sealed the doom of the two officers. When the news of the insurrection at Kabul and murder of Sir Alexander Burnes reached Bokhara, both officers were imprisoned in loathsome dungeons; but when it was known that the British army had perished in the Khaiber Pass they were taken out of their dungeons and publicly beheaded in the market-place of Bokhara.

CHAPTER XX

SINDE AND GWALIOR—LORD ELLENBOROUGH

A.D. 1843 TO 1844

THE first act of Lord Ellenborough after the Kabul war was the conquest of Sinde. This territory occupied the lower valley of the Indus. In the middle of the eighteenth century it formed a province of the Afghan empire of Ahmad Shah Abdali. Subsequently the Amirs or rulers of Sinde established a certain kind of independence, or only paid tribute to Kabul when compelled by force of arms.

During the early part of the British occupation of Afghanistan, the Sinde Amirs had rendered good service to the British government; but after the disastrous retreat from Kabul some of the Amirs swerved from their treaty obligations. The result was a war which was triumphantly carried to a close by Sir Charles Napier. In February, 1843, Napier won the battle of Meanee; and in the following March he won the battle of Hyderabad in the neighborhood of the Sinde capital of that name. The war was brought to an end by the annexation of Sinde to the British empire.

It would be useless, in the present day, to attempt to review the Sinde question. Sir Charles Napier, who commanded the army, considered that the Amirs were guilty of disaffection and deception; while Major Outram, who was political agent in Sinde, considered that their guilt was not sufficiently proved. One Amir, who professed the utmost loyalty to the British government, and who convinced Sir

Charles Napier of the guilt of the others, was subsequently convicted of perjury and forgery, which was punished at the time, but since then has been more or less condoned. The difficulty of proof among a people who cannot be bound by oaths, and who have always been accustomed to the forgery of seals and fabrication of documents, has often enabled the guilty to escape, and may sometimes have led to the punishment of the innocent. The question, however, of whether the Sinde Amirs were guilty or otherwise of treacherous designs against the British government has long since died out of political controversy.

During the administration of Lord Ellenborough there was a change of policy in dealing with the Mahratta states of Sindia and Holkar. Lord Ellenborough remodelled the government of Gwalior, and contemplated the annexation of Indore. Such strong proceedings were direct violations of the non-intervention policy of Lord William Bentinck; but in order to decide how far they were expedient, it will be necessary to bring the following facts under review.

The condition of Gwalior under Daulat Rao Sindia has already been indicated.[1] It will be remembered that, at his death in 1827, his widow Baiza Bai became queen regent and adopted a boy to succeed her deceased husband as Maharaja. In 1833 the boy attained his majority, but disputes arose which ended in civil war. At last Lord William Bentinck was forced to interfere against his will, and the war was at an end. Baiza Bai retired from Gwalior, and Maharaja Jankoji Rao ascended the throne of Sindia.

Justice was satisfied by the elevation of the young Maharaja, but the queen regent was revenged. Baiza Bai had proved herself to be an able administrator; and as long as she was sole ruler, the government of Gwalior worked smoothly. On the other hand, Jankoji Rao Sindia was a do-nothing Maharaja. He was content with the pride and

---

[1] See ante, pp. 606–7.

pomp of power; he was assured of the protection of the British government; and he cared nothing for his country or people. Accordingly the government was weak and distracted. The administration was carried on by a council of ministers, but there was a rankling rivalry for the post of premier between an uncle of the Maharaja, named Mama Sahib, and the hereditary keeper of the crown jewels, named Dada Khasji. In the end the uncle of the Maharaja got the better of the jewel-keeper, and Mama Sahib became chief minister.

Meanwhile the army of Gwalior had grown turbulent and disaffected. It numbered thirty thousand infantry, ten thousand cavalry, and two hundred guns. It was not required for defence, as Gwalior was protected against foreign invasion by the subsidiary alliance with the British government; but it absorbed two-thirds of the revenues of Gwalior, and resisted all attempts at disbandment or reduction.

The British government had no concern with the army of Gwalior so long as it kept within Sindia's territories. But the Punjab had become a political volcano. Ever since the death of Runjeet Singh, in 1839, the Sikh army of the Khalsa, numbering seventy thousand soldiers and three hundred guns, had been a menace to Hindustan. Lord Ellenborough foresaw that sooner or later the Sikh army would cross the Sutlej into British territory. A spark would have kindled a flame in the army of Gwalior; and if its movements were combined with those of the Sikh army, they would have raised such a storm in Hindustan as had not been witnessed since the days of Nadir Shah.[1]

Jankoji Rao Sindia died in February, 1843, leaving no children real or adopted. His widow, named Tara Bai, was a girl of twelve years of age. This girl adopted a boy, who

---

[1] It was this consideration which induced Lord Ellenborough to pause before sending the avenging army under General Pollock into Kabul. Meanwhile any attempt at explanation would have precipitated a Sikh invasion. Consequently Lord Ellenborough, while proving himself a statesman of forecast, was for some time one of the best abused Governors-General that ever landed in India.

was a distant relative of her husband's family. The boy was only eight years of age, but he was enthroned as Maharaja under the name of Jyaji Rao Sindia.[1] The adoption was approved by the durbar and the army, and was recognized by the British government.

The next question was the appointment of a regent. The Gwalior durbar wished the administration to be carried on as before by a council of ministers; but Lord Ellenborough urged the appointment of one individual as regent. The girl queen was anxious that the Dada should be regent; but Lord Ellenborough was in favor of Mama Sahib. Accordingly the Gwalior durbar was told that the Governor-General preferred Mama Sahib, and Mama Sahib was appointed regent of Gwalior.

Then followed a feminine intrigue. Tara Bai, in spite of her youth, set to work with the other palace ladies to thwart and harass Mama Sahib. The vexed and baffled regent sought to strengthen himself against this female confederacy, by betrothing the boy Maharaja to his own niece; but this step proved his ruin. Tara Bai feared that the marriage would ultimately destroy her own influence over the Maharaja; and in spite of the remonstrances of the British Resident, this young girl dismissed Mama Sahib on her own authority, and assumed the name of regent, leaving all real power in the hands of the Dada.

Lord Ellenborough was excessively angry at this movement, and well he might be. He had interfered in behalf of a minister whom he would not support; and he had been defied by a Mahratta girl of twelve. The restoration of Mama Sahib was out of the question; the Governor-General could not reinstate a regent minister who had been outwitted by a girl. He could, however, insist on the removal of Dada Khasji; and accordingly he ordered the British Resident to withdraw from Gwalior, and not to return until the Dada had been dismissed from office. The Gwalior durbar was

---

[1] In the present year (1880) Jyaji Rao Sindia is still Maharaja of Gwalior.

greatly alarmed, and entreated the Resident to return, but he was immovable.

Meanwhile the Dada had gained over the army of Gwalior by his largesses, and disturbances broke out in which fifty or sixty persons were killed. Accordingly Lord Ellenborough determined to take active measures for restoring tranquillity to Gwalior, and disbanding the army. In December, 1843, he arrived at Agra, but there were no signs of submission at Gwalior. He ordered the British army to advance to Gwalior under Sir Hugh Gough. The Dada now made his submission, but Lord Ellenborough was bent on the disbandment of the dangerous army.

The chiefs and soldiers of Sindia saw that the independence of the state, and the existence of the army, were threatened by the British government. Accordingly they made common cause against the Governor-General, and were defeated in the battles of Maharajpore and Punniar, both of which were fought on the 29th of December, 1843.

In January, 1844, a treaty was concluded at Gwalior which placed the future relations of the British government with that state on an improved footing. The administration was intrusted to a council of six nobles, which was called the council of regency, and was required to act implicitly on the advice of the Resident whenever he might think fit to offer it. The new government was required to cede enough territory to maintain a contingent trained and disciplined by British officers, henceforth known as the Gwalior Contingent. At the same time the overgrown army of Gwalior was reduced to six thousand cavalry, three thousand infantry, and thirty-two guns.

In February, 1844, there was a crisis in Holkar's state of Indore. Hari Rao Holkar died in 1843, and was succeeded by an adopted son, who died in 1844, leaving no son, real or adopted. There was not only no heir, but no person having the right to adopt an heir. The Indore state was of modern origin; it owed its existence to predatory conquest; and it was maintained for the sole benefit of the followers of the court. Lord Ellenborough ordered steps to be taken to ascertain the national feeling on the subject.

Meanwhile the government of Indore was left under the regency of the mother of Hari Rao Holkar, who died in 1843; and this lady proposed to nominate a fitting successor to the boy who died in 1844. Before, however, Lord Ellenborough could decide the question, the British Resident at Indore declared, on his own authority, that the British government would perpetuate the state of Holkar; and he enthroned the nominee of the queen mother, with all the formality of a hereditary chieftain, under the name of Tukaji Rao Holkar.[1] Lord Ellenborough was exceedingly wroth at this unauthorized proceeding, and severely censured the Resident, but, under the circumstances, he declined to interfere with the succession of Tukaji Rao Holkar.

In June, 1844, Lord Ellenborough was recalled from the post of Governor-General. This arbitrary measure took India by surprise. There had, however, been angry controversies between Lord Ellenborough and the Court of Directors, and the former had not been always discreet; but the ability, industry, and energy of the noble earl had deeply impressed the public mind, and there were many who regretted his recall.

Lord Ellenborough was succeeded by Sir Henry Hardinge in the post of Governor-General. During the remainder of 1844, and nearly the whole of 1845, the new Governor-General was chiefly occupied in watching the progress of events in the Punjab until the breaking out of the first Sikh war. Before, however, treating of those important transactions, it will be necessary to glance at the current of affairs in other quarters.

---

[1] In the present year (1880) Tukaji Rao Holkar is still Maharaja of Indore.

CHAPTER XXI

WAR DECADE—BURMA AND NIPAL

A.D. 1839 TO 1849

DURING the administration of Lords Auckland and Ellenborough, there were strange troubles in Burma, Nipal, and the Punjab. The native courts at Ava, Khatmandu, and Lahore, were in a state of ferment, more or less excited by the Kabul war; and the political workings are all the more important from the pictures which they present of Oriental life outside the area of British suzerainty.

This ferment was not visible within the British pale. The Mahratta governments of Sindia and Holkar were too weak and distracted to indulge in hopes or fears as regards the possible downfall of the British empire. The Rajput states were a prey to the maladministration of their rulers and the disaffection of their respective feudatories. In Marwar especially, the growing anarchy and disorder compelled the British government to send a force to keep the peace between the Maharaja and his Thakurs during the very year that the columns from Bengal and Bombay were advancing on Kabul. Neither Rajput nor Mahratta troubled about disasters in Central Asia, or imagined the possibility of a renewal of the old wars in Hindustan.

But public feeling was different in the three courts outside the frontier. Rumors were rife that the Governor-General had sent the flower of the British army into the remote regions of Central Asia to fight against the Amir, the Shah, and the Czar; and the air was clouded with predictions that British power would be shattered in the coming storm, and that Brahma and Muhammad, Gotama Buddha and Guru Govind would be avenged on the followers of the Nazarene.

In Burma and Nipal there was marked hostility toward the British government. Indeed in 1840 it seemed likely that while one *corps d'armée* was occupying Kabul, and a second was keeping the peace in Rajputana, a third would be threading the valley of the Irawadi, while a fourth would be climbing the slopes and shelves of the Himalayas. At Lahore there was less hostile display, but the war spirit was burning beneath the surface like the hidden fires of a volcano, and was destined at no distant period to burst into flames.

Burma was essentially a weak government, and its army was beneath contempt; but the heavy cost of the Burmese war of 1824–26, and the terrible loss of life from fever and malaria, had rendered the British government most anxious to keep on friendly terms with the Court of Ava. In 1830 Colonel Burney was sent as a permanent Resident to Ava, in accordance with the treaty of Yandabo; but he was treated by the barbarous court more as a spy to be watched and guarded, than as an envoy anxious only for the maintenance of friendly relations.

In 1837 there was a revolution in the palace at Ava. The king, Phagyi-dau, had become hypochondriacal and insane, and was dethroned by his brother Tharawadi, and placed in confinement. Then followed the inevitable massacre. The sorceress queen, the heir-apparent, and the ministers of the deposed sovereign, were all put to death, together with their dependents. Tharawadi became king of Burma, and sought to blot out the memory of his predecessor by removing his capital from Ava to Amarapura.

Colonel Burney was alarmed at this revolution. He knew that Tharawadi was a bitter enemy of the English, and had heard him express contempt for the British government. Accordingly he deemed it prudent to retire from

DEATH OF TIPPU SAHIB AT SERINGAPATAM

India, vol. two.

the scene, and thus escape an insult which might provoke a rupture.

Lord Auckland was angry at the withdrawal of Colonel Burney, and sent another Resident to take his place. But Tharawadi was intolerable; he was not only cruel and depraved, but arrogant and insolent to the last degree. No English officer would remain long in the depressing climate of Upper Burma, to be treated with scorn and contumely by an ignorant barbarian. One Resident after another retired to Rangoon on the plea of ill-health. At last in 1840 Tharawadi drove the Residency out of the capital, in violation of the treaty of Yandabo. Lord Auckland's government ignored the outrage rather than resent it, and abstained from all further attempts to maintain a Resident at Amarapura.

Tharawadi was puffed up beyond measure at the success of his efforts to throw off the English alliance. In 1841 he marched a large army to Rangoon, threatening to drive the English out of Arakan and Tenasserim. But his warlike ardor cooled down as he approached Rangoon, for he remembered how the Burmese fled from before the English in 1824. Accordingly he put aside all thoughts of war, and amused his subjects by casting a great bell for the golden pagoda at Rangoon. After a few months he returned to his remote capital in the upper valley of the Irawadi with all the barbaric pomp of gilded barges, while nothing more was heard of war.

In 1845 the reign of Tharawadi was brought to a close. He had degenerated into a tyrant of the worst type; drinking himself into such paroxysms of fury that it was dangerous to approach him. In these mad fits he would shoot a minister or stab a queen; and courtiers and ladies plotted together for their own protection. Suddenly Tharawadi passed away from the palace, and was never seen again. Whether strangled, smothered, or poisoned, is a palace mystery, like the suicide with scissors in the palace at Stamboul. It is sufficient to know that in 1845 Tharawadi ceased to reign, and his eldest son ascended the throne of Burma.

Pagan Meng, the new sovereign, was of a different stamp to his father. Tharawadi, with all his faults, had a majestic presence, and spoke and looked like a king. Pagan Meng, on the contrary, was a man of low tastes and vulgar pleasures. He moved his capital from Amarapura to Ava, and there he devoted himself to cock-fighting, ram-fighting, gambling, and other mean pursuits. Meanwhile, like Macbeth, he was in constant terror. He would not trust his own Burmese courtiers, but preferred a Muhammadan for his minister. He condemned all suspected persons to the most horrible deaths; and stifled all complaints by throwing the blame upon the minister. Two of his own brothers were butchered in this horrid fashion, together with their wives, children, servants, and dependents of every kind.

At last the people of Ava rose in revolt against such detestable cruelty. The minister was given up to the populace to secure the safety of the king. For three days this unfortunate Muhammadan was tortured by the mob, and was then beheaded at the place of execution with numbers of his creatures.

All this while there was no British Resident at Ava to act as a check upon the king or his people. Rangoon was near the sea, and was consequently free from such atrocities; but petty acts of tyranny were practiced by the local governor toward European and American strangers, who were fined, imprisoned, or put in the stocks on the most frivolous charges. No civilized man will endure such barbaric insolence without appealing to his government for redress; and no government can ignore such appeals without loss of prestige and national honor. It was not, however, until the Punjab had been brought under British administration that Lord Dalhousie saw the necessity for remonstrating with the king of Burma. The sequel will be told hereafter in dealing with Lord Dalhousie's administration.

The progress of affairs in Nipal during the war decade was more serious than in Burma. There was some bond of common interest between the Ghorka and British governments; while the court of Khatmandu was more respectable and intelligent than the court of Ava, and had a much better army at its command.

Here it should be explained that from a remote period in history the sacred city of Benares has been the resort, not only of pilgrims and devotees, but of Hindu political refugees of every class and kind. Dethroned sovereigns, childless queens, disgraced ministers, and forlorn princes and princesses have taken up their abode at Benares, and generally to intrigue and plot, as well as to sacrifice and pray.

Ever since the rise of the Ghorka dynasty in Nipal, revolutions have been frequent in the court of Khatmandu. Sometimes an able minister of the stamp of Bhim Sein Thapa and Jung Bahadur has kept the peace for a number of years; but such intervals of tranquillity are always sooner or later brought to a close by revolutions. Such revolutions were common enough in every Hindu court in India before the British government became the paramount power; and one and all have been accompanied by a massacre, together with a stampede to Benares of all the survivors of a fallen dynasty or ministry. Consequently throughout the present century Benares has been a hot-bed of intrigues and plots for restoring some royal exile to Nipal.

From 1804 to 1837 Bhim Sein Thapa was the sole ruler of Nipal; not only as prime minister, but for a long period as the paramour of the regent-mother; and for thirty-three years he filled up all superior posts and commands at the annual Panjani with members of the Thapa clan; and rigidly excluded all others, whether Bharadars or Brahmans, from office or power.

The Nipal war of 1814–16 did not weaken the authority of Bhim Sein Thapa. The young Maharaja attained his majority in 1816, but died shortly afterward, and was succeeded in his turn by an infant son. In 1832 the old regent-mother died, but Bhim Sein Thapa was still supreme. The infant attained his majority, and was placed upon the throne;

but he proved a weak and vacillating prince, and for a long time was a mere puppet in the hands of Bhim Sein Thapa.

But Bhim Sein Thapa was thwarted by an unexpected enemy. He had selected the daughter of a Hindu farmer in British territory to be the bride of the young Maharaja.[1] The girl grew into an ambitious and scheming woman, and was constantly stirring up her husband to throw off the yoke of the minister. Bhim Sein Thapa thought to neutralize or divide her influence by introducing a second bride into the palace. The step, however, proved fatal to his power. The elder queen became more bitter than ever; she soon behaved like a female fiend bent on the destruction of Bhim Sein Thapa and his family.

The restless activity of this extraordinary woman is a remarkable feature in Nipal history. She formed a close intimacy with Runjung Pandey, the son of the prime minister who had been disgraced and ruined in 1803. She persuaded the Maharaja to restore the estates of the Pandey family, which had been confiscated on that occasion. She won over the Guru, or spiritual teacher of the Maharaja, known as the Misr Guru;[2] and this religious intriguer soon proved a most formidable opponent to the British government as well as to the Thapa ministry.

Mr. Hodgson, the British Resident at Khatmandu, was in danger of being entangled in this web of intrigue. Ever since the war of 1814–16, Bhim Sein Thapa had been as friendly toward the English as a Ghorka nobleman of those times could allow himself to be. At the conclusion of the war the enemies of the prime minister wanted the British government to deliver the young Maharaja out of his hands; but the predecessor of Mr. Hodgson had declared emphatically that the British government would not interfere in the

---

[1] The duty of the minister to choose a bride for the boy Maharaja is as old as the Maha Bharata. It will be remembered that Bhishma provided wives for his half-brother and nephews.

[2] If a Brahman is addressed as a learned man he is called Pundit; if otherwise he is called Misr, or Mitter; *i.e.*, Mithra, or the sun.

affairs of Nipal. This very refusal to interfere led the whole court to regard that British Resident as the friend of Bhim Sein Thapa; and Mr. Hodgson was thus hated by all the enemies of the prime minister; by the elder queen, the Pandeys, and the Misr Guru.

In 1837 there was an explosion. The youngest son of the elder queen died suddenly. It was widely rumored that the infant had taken poison intended for the mother; and Bhim Sein Thapa was charged with having instigated the court physicians to administer poison to the elder queen. Amid the commotion, Runjung Pandey, the head of the Pandey clan, was appointed prime minister by the Maharaja. Bhim Sein Thapa was arrested, put in irons, and thrown into prison, together with a nephew named Matabar Singh. The family of Bhim Sein Thapa was placed under a guard, and all the family property was confiscated. The physician who attended the child was put to the torture until he implicated Bhim Sein Thapa, and then he was put to death.

This revolution, however, only went half way, and was then met by a reaction. There was a moderate party at Khatmandu, represented by a Brahman named Rughonath Pundit,[1] and a Bharadar named Futteh Jung Chountria. This moderate party was willing that Bhim Sein should be brought under some control, but was opposed to the destruction of the Thapas and elevation of the Pandeys. Again the younger queen was a stanch friend of Bhim Sein Thapa: she had been given in marriage to the Maharaja in order that she might act as a counterpoise to the elder queen; and she perpetually urged the Maharaja to restore Bhim Sein Thapa to the post of prime minister.

The working of these jarring influences ended in a political compromise. The Pandeys were removed from the ministry. Rughonath Pundit, the leader of the moderate party, was made premier, and moderate councils prevailed. The Thapas were not restored to power, but Bhim Sein and his

---

[1] See last note on previous page.

nephew, Matabar Singh, were released, pardoned, and received by the Maharaja in public durbar. They were then each presented with a dress of honor and a caparisoned horse, and returned to their respective homes amid the cheers and acclamations of soldiers and citizens. The family estates were still under confiscation, but a garden house was restored to Bhim Sein Thapa, and a yearly pension was assigned for his support. Thus for a brief space matters seemed to quiet down at Khatmandu.

These moderate measures would not satisfy either of the two queens. In 1838 there were violent dissensions in the palace. The elder queen insisted on the restoration of the Pandeys to the ministry, while the younger queen insisted on the restoration of the Thapas. Suddenly the elder queen left the palace in a fury, and proceeded to the temple of Pusput Nath, accompanied by Runjung Pandey, declaring that she would never return to the palace until the Maharaja appointed her favorite to be prime minister.

The temple of Pusput Nath is about three miles from Khatmandu. It is well worthy of description, for it is the most celebrated fane in all Nipal. It is approached by a road through the suburbs of the city, beautifully paved with brick and granite. Hard by the temple precinct are the houses of priests, three or four stories high, built of bricks, which are hidden by woodwork curiously carved; with wooden balconies supported by carved rafters, and railed in by wood carvings. Intricate tracery hangs down from the balconies in broad wooden fringes; while other tracery surrounds the grotesque windows. The temple precinct is enclosed by a wall. Massive folding doors open into a handsome courtyard, filled with images, shrines, a kneeling figure of Siva, a huge bell, and other sacred objects in picturesque confusion. The temple building stands in the centre of the court facing the folding doors. It is a quaint structure roofed with lead, with silver doors, carved windows, and large eaves covered with gilding. It is ascended by a double flight of steps, guarded by four sculptured lions, and a large copper figure of a bull kneeling, superbly covered with gilding.

In this sacred place the elder queen took up her abode; and during her stay there the Maharaja attended on her daily with all his court. This flight to Pusput Nath was the first of a series of vagaries by which the elder queen tormented the whole court and forced the Maharaja to do her bidding. In the present case she was appeased by the retirement of Rughonath Pundit, and the appointment of Runjung Pandey to the post of premier.

In 1839 the elder queen succeeded in wreaking her vengeance on the Thapa family. The charge of poisoning was revived. The execution of the physician who attended her infant son would not satisfy her thirst for vengeance. The other court physicians were thrown into prison, and only escaped torture by committing suicide. The brother of Bhim Sein, named Runbir Singh, turned fakir. Bhim Sein saw that he was doomed, and appealed to the Resident for protection; but the Resident could do nothing, for he had been strictly forbidden to interfere in the affairs of Nipal.

At last Bhim Sein Thapa was brought before the durbar, and the so-called confessions of the dead physicians were produced against him, charging him with wholesale poisonings at intervals during a long series of years. He manfully defended himself, denounced the confessions as forgeries, and demanded to be confronted with his accusers. Not a single chieftain, however, dared to say a word in his behalf. The Maharaja gave way to a burst of indignation, real or feigned, and ordered him to be chained and imprisoned as a traitor.

The fate of Bhim Sein Thapa has many parallels in Oriental history. He was threatened with torture, with dishonor in his zenana, with torment and shame unknown to Europe, until he killed himself in despair. His remains were dismembered and thrown to the dogs and vultures. His family was reduced to penury, and banished to the snows of the Himalayas; and a decree was issued declaring that the Thapas were outcasts, and that no one of the Thapa clan should be employed in the public service for the space of seven generations.

All this while the elder queen and the Pandey ministry had been intriguing against the British government. Matabar Singh had been sent to the court of Runjeet Singh at Lahore, and thus escaped the doom which had befallen his uncle. A second emissary was sent to Burma to report on the growing rupture between the Burmese court and the British government. A third had gone to Lhassa to persuade the Chinese authorities that some recent conquests of the Sikhs in Ladakh had been made at the instigation of the British government. A fourth had been sent to Herat to report on the prospects of a war between the English and Persia. Meanwhile prophecies were disseminated through British provinces predicting the speedy downfall of the British supremacy, and preparations were being made for war throughout Nipal. It was thus evident that the Ghorka court was only waiting for some disaster to the British arms to declare war against the British government.

In 1840 Lord Auckland addressed a letter of remonstrance to the Maharaja, and moved a corps of observation to the frontier. This measure had a wholesome effect upon the Maharaja. He dismissed the Pandey ministry in a panic, and appointed Futteh Jung Chountria to be premier. This latter chieftain belonged to the moderate party, and was well disposed toward the British government. In 1841 the Maharaja dismissed the Misr Guru, and the latter was forced to go on pilgrimage to Benares.

The elder queen was driven frantic by this reversal of her designs. She was not content with leaving the palace and going to Pusput Nath; she separated herself altogether from the Maharaja, assumed the dress of a female ascetic, and threatened to go on pilgrimage to Benares. She tried to terrify the Maharaja into abdicating the throne in favor of her eldest son, the heir-apparent. On one occasion she induced the soldiery at Khatmandu to break out in mutiny.

She encouraged the heir-apparent to commit the most extravagant and cruel acts in order to alarm the Maharaja. All this while she was constantly urging the Maharaja to reinstate the Pandeys, dismiss the British Resident, and declare war against the British government.

The weak and vacillating Maharaja was moved to and fro like a pendulum by alternate hopes and fears. At one time he expatiated in durbar on the rumored disasters of the English in Burma and China. At another time he was assuring the Resident of his friendship toward the British government, and offering to send his forces in support of the British army in Afghanistan.

In 1841 the elder queen was indisposed, and the Maharaja was anxious for a reconciliation. She became softened by her sickness, and threw off her ascetic dress, and talked of restoring the Thapas to their caste and estates. Toward the end of the year she died suddenly, not without suspicions of poison. After her death there was no more talk of hostility with the British government, and the corps of observation was soon withdrawn from the frontier. All difficulties in the relations between the two states were thus removed; and all signs of secret agents from other native states passed away from Khatmandu.

In 1842 a curious incident occurred which reveals something of the working of English journalism on Oriental minds. A report appeared in a Calcutta newspaper that the elder queen had been poisoned. The Maharaja was wild with rage, and called on the British Resident to surrender the editor. He was determined, he said, to flay the journalist alive, and rub him to death with salt and lemon-juice; and he threatened to declare war if the Governor-General refused to accede to his demand. After a suitable explanation of British law and usage, the Maharaja cooled down, and subsequently sent an apology to the Resident for the warmth of his language.

At this period the mad freaks of the heir-apparent caused great excitement in Nipal. He engaged elephants to fight in the streets of Khatmandu, and caused the death of several persons. He wounded Bharadars and their sons with a sword or knife. He was only a boy of twelve, but he would often beat his wives, who were girls of nine or ten. Sometimes he threw them into the river; and he kept one poor girl so long in a tank that she died in consequence. A female attendant interfered and he set her clothes on fire. He was brutally jealous of his stepmother, the younger queen and her two sons, and they ultimately fled from his cruelty into the plains.[1] In these acts of insane violence he had been originally encouraged by his deceased mother in the hope of terrifying his father into abdication; and after her death they became more frequent than ever.

When the news of the destruction of the British army in the Khaiber Pass reached Khatmandu, the heir-apparent indulged in still more dangerous freaks. He threatened to murder the British Resident, or drive him out of the country. He displayed a special spite against Jung Bahadur, the same chief who afterward became celebrated in Europe. He commanded Jung Bahadur and other chiefs at court to jump down wells at the hazard of their lives; and no one seems to have ventured to disobey him.[2] Many of the common soldiers were maimed for life by being compelled at his orders to jump down wells or off the roofs of houses. Strange to say, the Maharaja made no attempt to restrain his son in these eccentric cruelties, because the astrologers had declared that the young prince was an incarnation of deity, and foretold that at no distant period he would extirpate the English foreigners. The consequence was that on more than one occasion the prince assaulted his own father, and once inflicted severe wounds.

---

[1] Major, afterward Sir Henry, Lawrence succeeded Hodgson as Resident at Khatmandu. He refers to these strange scenes, and gives the leading actors the names of Mr. Nipal, Mrs. Nipal, and Master Nipal. See Memoirs of Lawrence, by Edwardes and Merivale.

[2] In after years Jung Bahadur boasted that he had practiced the art of jumping down wells as the best means of saving his life on these occasions. See Oliphant's Journey to Khatmandu.

Meanwhile the disasters in Kabul induced the Maharaja to recall the Pandeys to court, and the Misr Guru from Benares. One of the Pandeys, named Kubraj, amused the heir-apparent by getting up mock fights between Ghorkas and English. The English were represented by natives of low caste painted white, and dressed in British uniforms; and they were of course defeated, and dragged about the streets in most ignominious fashion.

At this juncture, however, the Pandeys made a false step. A number of libels, reviving the old scandal that the elder queen had died from poison, were traced to Kubraj Pandey, and he and other Pandeys were arrested and put in irons. A State trial was held by the Bharada Sobah, or council of chieftains, at which the Maharaja sat as President. The trial lasted several days, during which there was a general stoppage of business. At last Kubraj Pandey was convicted; his right hand was cut off, his property was confiscated, and he was sent into banishment.

Toward the close of 1842 the cruelties and insults of the heir-apparent toward all classes, and the cowardly apathy of the Maharaja, brought Nipal to the brink of a revolution. The chiefs and people complained that they did not know who was the Maharaja, the son or the father. The ferment spread through the whole valley; public meetings were held on the parade ground at Khatmandu; and at one large meeting, said to number eight thousand people, a committee was appointed for drawing up a petition of advice and remonstrance to the Maharaja. Finally the soldiery made common cause with the chiefs and people. They demanded that the Misr Guru should be sent back to Benares, and that the surviving queen should be recalled from her voluntary exile in the plains, and appointed regent of Nipal.

On the 2d of December, 1842, there was a meeting of the chiefs and officers, at which the Maharaja unexpectedly made his appearance. His presence prevented any allusion to the regency of the queen. He sought by arguments, entreaties, and threats, to induce the assembly to let things remain as they were. In reply, he was told that the people could not obey two masters; that he must either keep his son under control, or abdicate the throne in his son's favor. Many instances were quoted in which the soldiers had been punished by the heir-apparent for obeying the commands of the Maharaja. The Maharaja promised to abdicate by and by, and begged that during the interval his son might be addressed by his title; but the assembly raised a groan of dissent. The Maharaja ordered the officers of the army to leave the meeting, but they refused. Next he ordered the Bharadars to leave, but they also refused. He then retired, and the assembly broke up, convinced that the Maharaja and his son were infatuated beyond redemption.

There was evidently something behind the scenes. It was said that the Maharaja had solemnly promised the deceased queen that he would abdicate the throne in favor of her son, and that he was equally afraid of breaking his oath and retiring from the sovereignty. The Chountria ministry vacillated between father and son. They were anxious to know who was to be Maharaja, but they were jealous of the movement for the regency of the surviving queen.

On the 5th of December the draft petition was submitted by the committee to a vast assembly of all the Bharadars, municipal authorities, merchants, and officers and soldiers of every grade. It was unanimously approved and ordered for presentation on the 7th, as the intermediate day was unlucky. The Maharaja was present with the heir-apparent, and tried to browbeat the assembly, but all his wrath was expended in vain.

On the night of the intermediate day there was an outbreak in the city of Khatmandu. The bugles were sounded, and three hundred soldiers tried to arrest the Bharadars under the orders of the Maharaja. The attempt failed, and kindled the popular indignation to the highest pitch. Next day the Maharaja yielded to the petition, and a deputation was despatched to bring in the young queen.

Next day the queen was conducted into Khatmandu, and invested with the authority of regent. The Bharadars and officers presented their honorary gifts and congratulations. But the ferment soon died out, and her authority ebbed away. The Chountrias vacillated between the Maharaja, the heir-apparent, and the regent queen; and the counsels and commands of the queen were unheeded by the durbar.

In 1843 the Chountria ministers were again in trouble. They implored the queen to stand forth as the head of the country, to insist on the December pact, or to retire to the plains; and they promised to accompany her with all the leaders of her party. But she said that they had let the occasion slip, and the country was not ripe for another revolution. In reality she was plotting to set aside the heir-apparent on the plea of insanity, and to set up the elder of her two sons in his room; and she suspected that the Chountrias were secret supporters of the heir-apparent.

About this time all parties at Khatmandu were inviting Matabar Singh to return to Nipal. This man was as able and brave as his famous uncle Bhim Sein Thapa. He spent some time feeling his way, but at last entered Khatmandu, and had an interview with the Maharaja.

A few days afterward there was a council of Bharadars at the palace. The written confessions of the Pandeys were produced, admitting that the charges of poisoning originally brought against the Thapas were all false. Five Pandeys were then beheaded. Kubraj Pandey was dragged to the place of execution with a hook through his breast. Others were flogged and their noses cut off. Runjung Pandey, the head of the family, was on his death-bed, and was mercifully permitted to die in peace. In this way Matabar Singh wreaked his vengeance on the murderers of Bhim Sein Thapa.

Before the end of 1843, the decree against the Thapas was annulled, and Matabar Singh was appointed premier in the room of Futteh Jung Chountria; but he soon found that it was impossible to please the conflicting parties. He tried to support the heir-apparent in the hope of procuring the restoration of the confiscated estates of his family; but by so doing he excited the bitter resentment of the queen; and from this time she was apparently bent upon working his destruction.

In 1844 Nipal seemed to be again on the eve of a revolution. The violent acts of the heir-apparent, the vacillations of the Maharaja, the rash and overbearing conduct of Matabar Singh, and the absurd and contradictory orders which daily issued from the palace, were exhausting the patience of the Bharadars. These chiefs were anxious that there should be but one ruler in Nipal, but they were unwilling that Matabar Singh should be that ruler. Matabar Singh would probably have cut his way to supreme power by a wholesale massacre of Bharadars, as his uncle Bhim Sein had done at the beginning of the century; but he was restrained by the wholesome counsels of Major, afterward Sir Henry Lawrence, who about this time succeeded Mr. Hodgson as British Resident at Khatmandu.

All this while Matabar Singh was plotting to drive the Maharaja to abdicate the throne in favor of the heir-apparent; while the Maharaja and the queen were secretly plotting to destroy Matabar Singh. The Maharaja, however, continued to heap honors on the head of the minister he had resolved to destroy. In the beginning of 1845, Matabar Singh was appointed premier for life. Later on, the Maharaja bestowed other marks of favor on the premier. At last, on the night of the 18th of May, 1845, Matabar Singh was murdered in the palace.

The story was horrible. Late at night the minister had been summoned to the palace, under the pretence that the queen had seriously hurt herself. He hurried off unarmed to obey the summons, accompanied by two kinsmen. The kinsmen were stopped at the foot of the palace stairs, and Matabar Singh was conducted alone to a room next the queen's where the Maharaja was standing. As he advanced toward the Maharaja a rapid fire was opened upon him from behind the trellised screen. He begged for mercy for his wife and children, and then expired. His mangled remains were lowered into the street, and carried off for cremation to the temple of Pusput Nath; and the paved road to the sanctuary was trickled with his blood. Many chiefs were suspected of being implicated in the murder. Jung Bahadur boasted that he had fired the fatal shot; but the prime mover in the plot is said to have been Guggun Singh, the paramour of the relentless queen.

The murder of Matabar Singh was followed by a ministerial crisis which lasted many months. Meanwhile all India was watching the Sikh war on the northwest. The war was brought to a close early in 1846, and the year was approaching its fourth quarter when Khatmandu was aroused by a story of a massacre which sent a thrill of horror through Hindustan.

Ever since the murder of Matabar Singh, there had been bitter quarrels in the palace. A ministry had been formed by Futteh Jung Chountria; and the queen had procured the appointment of her favorite Guggun Singh, as a member of the ministry.[1] At this period the queen exercised a commanding influence in the government of Nipal, and plotted to secure the succession of her elder son to the throne in the room of the heir-apparent.

The heir-apparent was filled with wrath at the aspect of affairs. He swore to be revenged on the murderers of Matabar Singh, and he publicly threatened Guggun Singh. He abused his father for not abdicating the throne in his favor, and declared that he would seize the government; while the Maharaja vacillated as usual, or played one party against another to suit his own purposes.

On the night of the 14th of September, 1846, Guggun Singh was murdered in his own house. The queen heard of the catastrophe, and hastened to the place on foot, and filled the air with her lamentations. She despatched a mes-

[1] The ministry comprised Futteh Jung Chountria as premier, three other members as his colleagues and deputies, and Jung Bahadur as military member.

senger to tell the Maharaja of the murder; and she summoned all the civil and military officers to the spot. The council assembled in such hot haste that many appeared without arms. The queen demanded the immediate execution of one of the Pandeys, whom she charged with the murder; but the Maharaja refused to have the man put to death unless it was proved that he was guilty. Altercations arose; shots were fired; and the premier and others fell dead. A party of soldiers, armed with double-barrelled rifles, poured in a murderous fire, and more than thirty chiefs were slaughtered.[1] Jung Bahadur was appointed premier on the spot, and undertook the sole management of affairs.

The queen next called on Jung Bahadur to destroy the heir-apparent and his brother; but the new premier declared for the heir-apparent, and carried out more executions. Subsequently, the Maharaja proceeded on pilgrimage to Benares, accompanied by the queen, leaving the heir-apparent to carry on the government until his return to Khatmandu.

In 1847 the Maharaja left Benares to return to his capital, but he loitered so long on the way, and displayed so many aberrations of mind, that the Bharadars installed the heir-apparent on the throne, and declared that the Maharaja had abdicated the sovereignty.

Meanwhile, Jung Bahadur was appointed prime minister for life, and tranquillity returned to the court of Nipal. In 1850 Jung Bahadur paid a visit to England, and after his return in 1851 an abortive plot was formed to destroy him. Since then the Ghorkas have engaged in wars on the side of Thibet, but nothing of permanent interest has transpired in Nipal. Jung Bahadur died early in 1877.

---

[1] It is impossible to say how many persons fell in this horrible butchery. Reports vary from thirty to a hundred and twenty.

CHAPTER XXII

SIKH HISTORY—RUNJEET SINGH, ETC.

Ante 1845

THE history of the Punjab is one of the most important episodes in Indian history. The Sikh government was a theocratic commonwealth like that of the Hebrews under the Judges; but they were a sect rather than a nationality, animated with a stern military enthusiasm like Cromwell's Ironsides. Nanuk Guru founded the Sikh community in the fifteenth century, but great reforms were carried out in the seventeenth century by Guru Govind. The essence of the Sikh faith was that there was only one God; that the Guru for the time being was his prophet; that all Sikhs were equal in the eyes of God and the Guru; and that all were bound together in a holy brotherhood known as the Khalsa. Guru Govind abolished all social distinctions among the Khalsa. He sprinkled holy water upon five faithful disciples, namely, a Brahman, a Kshatriya, and three Sudras. He hailed them as Singhs or lion warriors; he declared that they were the Khalsa,[1] or brotherhood of faith in God and the Guru;[2] and he promised that whenever five Sikhs were gathered together he would be in the midst of them. This idea of five Sikhs forming a Khalsa will be found to have a strange meaning in the later history.

Henceforth a representative of Nanuk Guru and Guru Govind was the spiritual teacher of the Sikhs. He was em-

---

[1] According to Cunningham, the Khalsa signifies "the saved or liberated."

[2] God, as taught by Guru Govind, was a spirit invisible to ordinary eyes, and only to be seen by the eye of faith in the general body of the Khalsa.

phatically known as the Guru, and the watchword of the Sikhs was "Hail, Guru!"[1] He combined the functions of a prince with those of a prophet. The city of Umritsir, the "pool of immortality," became the religious centre of the Sikhs; and every year there was a grand gathering at the sacred city, like the Hebrew gatherings at Shiloh.

The Sikhs originally had no nationality. They were a close religious community formed out of Hindus, Muhammadans, and others. They were all soldiers of the Khalsa. They were divided into twelve fraternities, known as Misls, or "equals." The Misls were not tribes in the Hebrew sense of the word. They were not descended from the twelve sons of a common ancestor; there was no division of the land among the twelve Misls as there was among the twelve tribes. The Misls were fraternities, increasing and diminishing according to circumstances. Indeed, the number "twelve" was more traditional than real; some gave birth to other Misls, while some died out altogether.

The leader of a Misl was known as the Sirdar; he was the arbiter in time of peace, and the leader in time of war. The Sirdar might be fervent in his devotion to God and the Guru, and at the same time he might be nothing more than a freebooter. Irrespective of the Misls, any Sikh warrior who gained distinction by killing a tiger, or shooting an arrow through a tree, would soon be joined by a band of lawless followers, and call himself a Sirdar. There was no question of pay. Every man provided himself with a horse and matchlock, and perhaps other weapons, and then fought and plundered under the banner of his chosen Sirdar, in the name of God and the Guru.

The Sirdars were warriors and judges, like Joshua or Jephthah, and they differed just as widely. There were Sirdars of the Puritan type, who took the field at the head of their sons and vassals; tall wiry men, with eagle eye, soldier-like bearing, unshorn locks, and flowing beards; armed to the teeth with matchlock, pistol, blunderbuss, sword, and

[1] The cry "Hail, Guru!" implies "Hail to the state or church of the Guru!"

spear; and attended with all the showy accompaniments of stately camels, prancing steeds, and tinkling bells. There were also Sirdars of the Pindhâri type, whose followers were low caste men, turned into Sikhs by twisting up the hair, combing out the beard, assuming a tall turban and yellow girdle, and mounting a strong bony horse with a sword at their side and a spear in their hand.

Besides these regular and irregular Sikhs, there was a set of fierce fanatics known as Akalis. They were a stern and sombre brotherhood of military devotees—soldiers of God—instituted by Guru Govind, and distinguished by steel bracelets and blue dresses and turbans. The Akalis were not lazy drones like Fakirs, for when not engaged in arms they would find other work to do for the good of the community at large.[1]

Toward the close of the eighteenth century, the Sikh Misls were dying out. The fraternities had been broken up by assaults from Afghan and Moghul, by internal feuds, and by the freebooting habits of irregular Sirdars. The old religious fervor was still burning in the breasts of the Khalsa, but there was no one to direct it or control it.

About 1800 the young warrior Runjeet Singh came to the front. Born in 1780, he was appointed viceroy of Lahore by the Afghan sovereign at Kabul before he was twenty. His career was now before him. He stirred up the enthusiasm of the Khalsa to throw off the yoke of the Afghans. He engaged in conquests on all sides, and brought new countries and peoples under the dominion of the Khalsa. He never suffered the Khalsa to be at rest; and he thus prevented the Sirdars from revolting against his authority, or fighting one another. His ambition was boundless except

---

[1] The late Captain Cunningham states in his History of the Sikhs that he once found an Akali repairing, or rather making, a road among precipitous ravines. On the other hand, a Sikh fakir has been lying on a large stone outside Allahabad for the last thirty or forty years, absorbed in religious contemplations, and supported by voluntary subscriptions. He is said to have lain there during the mutiny, regardless of shot or shell. The author saw him in 1878, when he appeared to be a robust devotee of seventy, or perhaps older.

on the side of the Sutlej. Had he flourished a generation earlier he might have conquered Hindustan; but while he was still a young man, the British empire in India was an established fact; and the victories of Lord Lake had inspired him with a wholesome respect for the British power. He refused to protect Jaswant Rao Holkar in 1805; and he yielded to the demands of the British government in 1809 as regards the Cis-Sutlej states. Henceforth he proved as faithful to his alliance with the British government as Herod, king of the Jews, was faithful to his alliance with Rome.

Meanwhile Runjeet Singh knew how to deal with the Khalsa. The Sikh army was drilled by successive French adventurers, named Allard, Ventura, Avitable and Court; but Runjeet Singh would not needlessly excite the jealousy of the Sirdars by treating the Europeans as trusted advisers. Again, Runjeet Singh was known as the Maharaja of the Punjab, but he only styled himself the commander of the army of the Khalsa, and he ascribed all the glory of his victories to God and the Guru Govind.

Runjeet Singh was short in stature, and disfigured with smallpox which had deprived him of his left eye. He could neither read nor write. Yet this stunted and illiterate being was gifted with a genius, tact, and audacity, which enabled him to keep both the Punjab and army of the Khalsa under perfect control. He shrank from inflicting capital punishments, but he was remorseless in cutting off noses, ears, and hands; and for years after his death there were many poor wretches at Lahore who complained of the mutilations they had suffered under the iron rule of Runjeet Singh.

The religion of Guru Govind may have purified the forms of public worship, and reformed the morals of the lower classes, but many abominations lingered in the land down to the end of the Sikh government. Widows were burned alive with their deceased husbands. Murders were frequent in the provinces. The court of Lahore was a sink of iniquity; rampant with all the vices that brought down fire and brimstone on the cities of the plain.

Runjeet Singh died in 1839, and five favorite queens and seven female slaves were burned alive with his remains. Then began a series of revolutions which shook the Sikh dominion to its foundations, and left it prostrate at the feet of the British power.

At this period the court of Lahore was split into two factions, the Sikhs and the Rajputs. The Sikhs had been jealous of the rapid rise of two Rajput brothers in the favor of Runjeet Singh. The brothers were originally common soldiers, but had been raised to the rank of Rajas, and were known as the Jamu Rajas. Gholab Singh, the elder, was appointed viceroy of Jamu, between Lahore and Kashmir. Dhian Singh, the younger, was prime minister at Lahore.

In 1839, Kharak Singh, eldest son of Runjeet Singh, succeeded to the throne of Lahore. He was an imbecile, but he had a son of great promise, named Nao Nihal Singh. Both father and son were bent on the destruction of the Jamu Rajas. They began by the removal of Dhian Singh, the younger of the two Rajas, from his post as head of the administration at Lahore; and they appointed a wretched parasite in his room, who was regarded with contempt by the whole court. But the Rajput blood of Dhian Singh boiled at the indignity, and he cut his successor to pieces in the presence of his royal master. Kharak Singh took fright at the murder, and shut himself up in his palace, where he perished within a year of his accession.

In 1840, Nao Nihal Singh became Maharaja, but was killed at his father's funeral by the fall of an archway.[1] This sudden and tragic event led to the general belief that both father and son were murdered by the exasperated ex-minister.

Dhian Singh was an intriguer of the common Asiatic

---

[1] Strange to say, there is a plot in an ancient Hindu drama for the destruction of Chandra-gupta, the Sandrokottos of the Greeks, by the very same artifice of a falling archway. The drama is known as "Mudra Rakshasa," or the "Signet of the Minister." An English translation will be found in Wilson's Theatre of the Hindus. For the story of Chandra-gupta, see ante, p. 67.

type. He thought to set up a son of Runjeet Singh as a puppet Maharaja, and to rule in his name under the title of minister. But he was checkmated for a while by the old dowager queen, the widow of Kharak Singh. This lady declared that the widowed queen of the young Nao Nihal Singh was about to become a mother; and on the strength of this assertion she assumed the post of queen regent in behalf of the unborn infant. The story was a farce, for the alleged mother was a girl of eight; but the Sikh court at Lahore held Dhian Singh in such hatred that all the chief Sirdars affected to believe the story, and recognized the regency of the dowager queen.

In 1841, the Sirdars were disgusted with the queen regent. Her private life was detestable; and she was compelled to resign the regency and retire into the country. Subsequently, she was beaten to death at the instigation of Dhian Singh, by four of her own slave girls, who dashed out her brains with a heavy stone while engaged in dressing her hair.

Meanwhile Dhian Singh was triumphant. He placed Sher Singh, a reputed son of Runjeet Singh, on the throne at Lahore, and ruled the kingdom as minister. But a new power had risen in the body politic, which within a few short years was destined to work the ruin of the dynasty.

Ever since the death of Runjeet Singh in 1839, the army of the Khalsa had grown more and more turbulent and unruly. They rose against their French generals, and compelled them to fly for their lives.[1] They clamored for increase of pay, and committed the most frightful excesses and outrages. Sher Singh and his minister were compelled to yield to the demands of the troops; and henceforth the army of the Khalsa was absolute master of the state. The soldiers continued to obey their own officers, but the officers themselves were subject to the dictation of punchayets, or committees of five, which were elected from the ranks. Guru Govind had promised that whenever five Sikhs were

[1] At this period there were only two French generals in the Sikh army, Avitable and Court.

assembled in his name, he would be in the midst of them. Accordingly, punchayets were formed in every regiment, and were supposed to be under the guidance of the unseen Guru; and their united action controlled the whole army. Sher Singh and his minister saw that no power, save that of the English, could deliver the Sikh government from the dictation of the Khalsa. In 1841, they opened the Punjab to troops passing between British territory and Kabul, and they begged the British government to interfere and suppress the growing disorders of the Khalsa.

In 1843 there was an explosion at Lahore. Maharaja Sher Singh had been plotting the murder of the minister, and the minister had been plotting the murder of the Maharaja. Both plots were successful, and recoiled on the heads of the authors. One morning Sher Singh was shot dead on parade, and his son was assassinated, while Dhian Singh was murdered about the same hour.

Amid these commotions, a son of Dhian Singh, named Hira Singh, appealed to the army of the Khalsa, and promised large money rewards. With the aid of these Pretorian bands, he placed an infant son of Runjeet Singh upon the throne, under the name of Maharaja Dhulip Singh. The mother of the boy was then appointed queen regent, and Hira Singh succeeded his murdered father in the post of minister. It was at this crisis that Lord Ellenborough foresaw that the army of the Khalsa would one day threaten Hindustan; and he marched a British force toward Gwalior with the view of disbanding Sindia's unruly army as described in a previous chapter.

During 1844 affairs at Lahore reached a crisis. The new minister tried in vain to break up the army of the Khalsa; the punchayets were all-powerful, and would not allow a company to be disbanded, or even removed from Lahore, without their consent. The result was that Hira Singh was murdered, and the government of Lahore was left in the hands of a boy Maharaja, a regent-mother, and a disaffected army.

The regent-mother was as depraved as the widow of Kharak Singh, who was deposed in 1841. She appointed two ministers; one was her own brother, and the other was a paramour, named Lal Singh. The army of the Khalsa grew more and more clamorous for largesses and increase of pay; and were only prevented from plundering Lahore by being moved away under the sanction of the punchayets to exact money contributions from the viceroys of outlying provinces, such as Kashmir and Multan. At the same time the two ministers, the brother and the paramour, were intriguing against each other. The brother gave mortal offence to the army of the Khalsa, and was tried and condemned by the punchayets as a traitor to the commonwealth, and was finally shot dead by a party of soldiers outside Lahore.

The regent-mother and her paramour were now in sore peril. The paramour, Lal Singh, became sole minister, but another Sirdar, named Tej Singh, was appointed to the nominal command of the army of the Khalsa. But Tej Singh was the slave as well as the commander-in-chief of the army of the Khalsa; and was compelled to act according to the dictation of the punchayets. In a word, the new government was at the mercy of the army, and saw no way of saving themselves, except by launching the Sikh battalions on British territories, and no way of averting the sack of Lahore, except by sending the Sikh soldiery to sack Delhi and Benares.

CHAPTER XXIII

TWO SIKH WARS—LORDS HARDINGE AND DALHOUSIE

A.D. 1845 TO 1849

IN November, 1845, the Sikh army of the Khalsa crossed the Sutlej, to the number of sixty thousand soldiers, forty thousand armed followers, and one hundred and fifty large guns. The Sikh army had been strangely underrated by the British government. It was as superior to all other native armies, excepting perhaps the Ghorkas, as Cromwell's Ironsides were to the rabble following of the other parliamentary leaders. Its marked strength, however, was neutralized by the duplicity of its leaders—Lal Singh, the paramour, and Tej Singh, the nominal commander-in-chief. Both men were traitors of the deepest dye; both at heart were willing to see the Sikh battalions mowed down by British artillery in order that they might secure their own personal safety and the continuance of their own government at Lahore. All this crafty and unscrupulous villany was conspicuous throughout the subsequent war.

The British government, under Sir Henry Hardinge, the new Governor-General, was scarcely prepared for the storm that was gathering on the line of the Sutlej. Sir John Littler held the fortress of Ferozepore with ten thousand troops and thirty-one guns; but if the Sikh generals had only been true to the Khalsa, they might have environed Ferozepore, overwhelmed Littler's force, and pushed on to the heart of Hindustan. As it was, Littler marched out of Ferozepore and offered the enemy battle; but the Sikh generals declined it, and divided their forces. Lal Singh moved with one *corps d'armée* toward Ferozeshahar, about ten miles off, and began to build formidable intrenchments, leaving Tej Singh to watch Littler at Ferozepore.

Meanwhile Sir Hugh Gough, Commander-in-Chief, and Sir Henry Hardinge, the new Governor-General, were hurrying toward the frontier with a large force to relieve Littler. On the 18th of December they met the army of Lal Singh at Moodkee, and gained a doubtful victory. The British sepoys reeled before the Khalsa battalions, and even a European regiment was staggered for a few moments by the rapidity and precision of the Sikh fire. But Lal Singh fled at the beginning of the action, and thus brought about the defeat of the Sikh army.

Two days after the battle of Moodkee, the British army advanced against the Sikh intrenchments at Ferozeshahar, and was joined there by the force under Littler. The assault was made on the 21st of December, but the Sikhs defended their position with the obstinacy and desperation of fanatics. Such resistance was terrific and unexpected. Gough charged up to the muzzle of the Sikh guns, and carried the batteries by cold steel; but it was in the face of an overwhelming fire. British cannon were dismounted and the ammunition blown into the air. Squadrons were checked in mid career; battalion after battalion was hurled back with shattered ranks; and it was not until after sunset that portions of the enemy's positions were finally carried by the British army.[1]

After a night of horrors the battle was renewed, but meanwhile there had been mutiny and desertion in the enemy's camp. The treasury of Lal Singh had been plundered by his own soldiers. The British troops met with feeble opposition; and it was soon discovered that, owing to the cowardice or treachery of Lal Singh, the Sikh army was in full flight to the Sutlej. Tej Singh marched up at

---

[1] Cunningham's History of the Sikhs.

this crisis, and found the intrenchments at Ferozeshahar in the hands of the British. Accordingly, after a brief cannonade, he fled precipitately to the Sutlej, leaving his forces without orders, to fight or follow at their pleasure.

In January, 1846, both sides were reinforced; the Sikhs recrossed the Sutlej into British territory, and hostilities were renewed. On the 26th of the month, Sir Harry Smith defeated a Sikh force at Aliwal.

At this time Gholab Singh of Jamu had arrived at Lahore, and offered to make terms with the Governor-General. Sir Henry Hardinge replied that he was ready to acknowledge a Sikh sovereignty at Lahore, but not until the army of the Khalsa had been disbanded. The Sikh generals were utterly unable to fulfil such a condition; they were literally at the mercy of the Khalsa army. It is said, however, that they offered to abandon the Khalsa army to its fate, and to leave the road open to the march of the British army to Lahore, provided the Governor-General acknowledged the sovereignty of Maharaja Dhulip Singh, and accepted the government of the regency.

Meanwhile the main body of the Khalsa army had thrown up a formidable series of intrenchments at Sobraon. Early in February, 1846, the British army advanced to the attack under Gough and Hardinge. Sobraon proved to be the hardest fought battle in the history of British India. The Sikh soldiers, unlike their treacherous commander Tej Singh, were prepared to conquer or die for the glory of the Khalsa. The British brought up their heavy guns, and prepared to pour in a continuous storm of shot and shell, and then to carry the intrenchments by storm.

Shortly after midnight on the 10th of February, the British planted their guns in the desired positions. At early morning, amid darkness and fog, the English batteries opened upon the enemy. At seven o'clock the fog rolled up like a curtain, and the soldiers of the Khalsa, nothing daunted, returned flash for flash, and fire for fire. As the sun rose higher, two British divisions of infantry in close order prepared for the assault. The left division advanced in line instead of column, and the greater part was driven back by the deadly fire of muskets and swivels and enfilading artillery. The right division formed instinctively into wedges and masses, and rushed forward in wrath, leaped the ditch with a shout, and then mounted the rampart and stood victorious amid captured cannon. Tej Singh fled to the Sutlej at the first assault, and broke the bridge over the river; but whether this was done by accident or treachery is a problem to this day. Meanwhile the soldiers of the Khalsa fought with the valor of heroes, the enthusiasm of crusaders, and the desperation of zealots sworn to conquer the enemy or die sword in hand. At last they gave way; they were driven by the fire of batteries and battalions into the waters of the Sutlej, and the battle of Sobraon was won. But the victory was dearly purchased. More than two thousand British troops were killed or wounded before the day was brought to a close; but the Sikhs are said to have lost eight thousand men.

Thus ended the first Sikh war. The British army crossed the Sutlej in a bridge of boats, and pushed on to Lahore, and dictated their own terms at the old capital of Runjeet Singh. The reduction of the Sikh army of the Khalsa was carried out without further parley, and its numbers were limited for the future to twenty thousand infantry and twelve thousand cavalry. The Jullunder Doab was taken over by the British government, and the British frontier was extended from the Sutlej to the Ravi. Meanwhile Sir Henry Hardinge was raised to the peerage.

Lord Hardinge called on the Lahore government to pay one million and a half sterling toward the expenses of the war. But the treasures of Runjeet Singh, estimated at the time of his death at twelve millions sterling, had been squandered during the anarchy which followed his decease, and only half a million remained to meet the demands of the British government at this crisis. Gholab Singh, viceroy of Kashmir and Jamu, offered to pay the million to the

British government, provided he was recognized as Maharaja of those territories. The bargain was concluded, and henceforth Gholab Singh was an ally of the British government, and independent of the Sikh government of Lahore.

Lord Hardinge was next called upon to decide on the future settlement of the Punjab. He would not annex the country, or take over the internal administration. He preferred accepting the existing government of the infant Maharaja, Dhulip Singh, and the regency of the queen mother and her paramour. But he would not create a subsidiary army for the protection of the native government, as had been done in the case of the Nizam of Hyderabad and the Mahrattas. On the contrary he was resolved to withdraw the British troops from the Punjab at the earliest possible opportunity; for experience had taught the bitter lesson that a subsidiary force only demoralized native rulers, and rendered the British government responsible for the maintenance of oppression and misrule.

But Lord Hardinge was thwarted by circumstances. The Lahore durbar loudly declared that unless a British force remained to keep the peace in the Punjab, the army of the Khalsa would recover its strength and overturn the regency. Accordingly, much against his inclination, Lord Hardinge deferred withdrawing the British force until the close of the year; but he solemnly assured the Lahore durbar that at the end of 1846 every British soldier and sepoy must return to British territory. The Sirdars bent to their fate, but many declared that annexation had become a necessity; and that so long as a Sikh government was maintained at Lahore, with or without British troops, so long the disbanded army of the Khalsa would cherish hopes of a return to independent power.

Major Henry Lawrence was appointed British Resident at Lahore, and Lal Singh, the paramour of the queen mother, filled the post of prime minister.[1] Shortly afterward a fla-

[1] In dealing with the modern history of British India, the distinction between the three Lawrence brothers must always be borne in mind. George was one

grant act of treachery was proved against Lal Singh. A rebellion broke out in Kashmir and Jamu against the sovereign authority of Maharaja Gholab Singh. Major Lawrence hastened to the spot with a body of Sikh troops, and effectually suppressed it; and the leader of the rebellion then produced the written orders of Lal Singh, urging him to resist Gholab Singh by every means in his power. Such a breach of faith was unpardonable. Lal Singh was removed from his office, and deported to British territory, where he passed the remainder of his days in confinement.

The year 1846 drew to a close. Again the Lahore durbar assured Lord Hardinge that the Khalsa army would regain its old ascendency if the British force was withdrawn. Accordingly a compromise was effected. Eight leading Sirdars were formed into a council of regency under the express stipulation that the entire control and guidance of affairs should be vested in the British Resident. Having thus guarded against oppression or misrule, Lord Hardinge decided that the British force should remain in the Punjab for a period of eight years, by which time Maharaja Dhulip Singh would attain his majority, and might be intrusted with the supreme authority.

This settlement of the Punjab continued, without material change, until the departure of Lord Hardinge from India in 1848. During the interval many useful measures were carried out. The British army in India was reorganized; the finances were restored; and efforts were made to induce the native states to follow the example of the British government, in forbidding widow burning, female infanticide, slavery, and other abominations, throughout their respective territories. In 1848 Lord Hardinge returned to England with the pleasant conviction that he had secured the peace of India for some years to come.

---

of the hostages in the first Afghan war, and had a narrow escape with his life at the time when Macnaghten was murdered. Henry had been Resident in Nipal, and was now transferred to Lahore. John was Commissioner of the Jullunder Doab, and afterward became successively Chief Commissioner and Lieutenant-Governor of the Punjab, and finally Governor-General and Viceroy of India.

Lord Dalhousie, the new Governor-General, landed at Calcutta in January, 1848. The history of his administration will be told in the next chapter, but it may be as well in the present place to review the current of Punjab affairs, which ended in the second Sikh war, and permanent annexation of the kingdom of Runjeet Singh.

Major Henry Lawrence, the Resident at Lahore, was an officer in the Bengal artillery, of large political experience. About this time he was obliged to proceed to England on account of his health, and was succeeded by Sir Frederic Currie, a Bengal civilian. New systems of finance and revenue were subsequently introduced into the Punjab, which guarded against undue exactions, and secured a greater regularity in the collection of revenue, but gave great umbrage to Sikh Sirdars. Discontent and disaffection began to seethe beneath the surface, and it was soon evident that the spirit of the Khalsa was still burning in the breasts of the disbanded soldiery.

A spark sufficed to set the Punjab in a conflagration. Mulraj, viceroy of Multan, had succeeded his father in the government of the province as far back as 1844; but the Lahore durbar had required him to pay a million sterling as a fine on succession. He took advantage of the struggles between the regency and the soldiery to delay payment. He then managed to get his claim reduced to less than one-fifth, and finally refused to pay the fraction. When, however, the Sikh war was over, and a British Resident was posted to Lahore, Mulraj found that further resistance was useless, and that he must pay up. But he was irritated at the new order of things. He complained that the new system of finance and revenue about to be introduced by the British Resident would diminish his income. Finally he resigned the government of Multan on the plea that there were dissensions in his family.

Sir Frederic Currie and the council of regency took Mulraj at his word. A succesor, named Khan Singh, was appointed to the government of Multan. Mr. Vans Agnew, a Bengal civilian, was appointed to accompany Khan Singh, and introduce the new fiscal system into Multan. In April, 1848, Khan Singh, Mr. Vans Agnew, and Lieutenant Anderson, arrived at Multan with an escort of three hundred and fifty Sikh troops and a few guns, and encamped at a fortified mosque in the suburbs, known as the Edgah.

Mulraj paid a visit to Mr. Vans Agnew at the Edgah, and declared himself ready to deliver up the town and citadel. He then produced the accounts of the previous year, and asked for a deed of acquittance. Mr. Vans Agnew, however, called for the accounts of the previous six years. Mulraj was affronted at the demand, but nevertheless agreed to furnish the documents. Mr. Vans Agnew and Lieutenant Anderson next proceeded with Mulraj to inspect the establishments in the citadel, and at his request they dismissed a portion of their escort. On leaving the citadel the two Englishmen were felled from their horses and dangerously wounded. Mulraj was riding by the side of Mr. Vans Agnew, but at once galloped off to his country residence. The wounded officers were carried off by their attendants to the Edgah, but the guns of the citadel began to open fire upon the mosque. In spite, however, of their wounds the two officers made a manful resistance, and returned the fire with the guns of the Sikh escort; but the escort proved treacherous, and went over to the enemy; and a mob of savages rushed into the mosque, and cut the two Englishmen to pieces. Immediately afterward Mulraj removed his family and treasure into the citadel, and issued a proclamation calling upon the people of every creed to rise against the English.

These atrocious murders were committed after the setting in of the hot weather. Lord Gough was anxious to postpone military operations for some months until the beginning of the cold weather; and there was consequently much delay in putting down the revolt. A young lieutenant, named Herbert Edwardes, who was employed in the revenue settlement of Bunnu, beyond the Indus, marched a force to Multan on his own responsibility; and being joined by other levies, he defeated Mulraj on the 18th of June, and ultimately shut him up in the citadel at Multan.

Meanwhile there was treachery in the Sikh government at Lahore. The queen mother of Dhulip Singh was exasperated at the loss of her paramour, and was secretly corrupting the troops. At the same time she was organizing a confederacy of Sirdars against the British government, and carrying on intrigues with the Amir of Kabul, the Maharaja of Kashmir, and the princes of Rajputana. Fortunately these proceedings were discovered in time, and the dangerous lady was removed from Lahore to the sacred city of Benares, and provided with a suitable pension.

Subsequently, an influential Sirdar, named Sher Singh, was sent at the head of a Sikh force to co-operate with Lieutenant Edwardes against Mulraj. But Sher Singh played a double game. While swearing eternal fidelity to the British government he was secretly corresponding with the rebels. A force of seven thousand British troops under General Whish was sent against Multan, and it was confidently expected that the town and fortress would be speedily taken, and that Mulraj would then receive the just punishment of his crimes. The guns had already begun to open on Multan, when Sher Singh ordered the drums of religion to be beaten, and went over to the enemy with five thousand Sikhs, and proclaimed a religious war against the English. General Whish was obliged to retire from Multan and throw up intrenchments. It was soon evident that the whole of the Punjab was in a state of revolt; and that the veterans of Runjeet Singh's army were assembling to renew the contest with the British government, retrieve their lost honor, and revive the glory and supremacy of the army of the Khalsa. In a word, the delay in crushing the paltry outbreak of Mulraj had aroused the military enthusiasm of the Sikhs throughout the Punjab, and necessitated a second Sikh war.

Lord Dalhousie rose to the occasion. Being new to India

he had deferred to the opinion of the Commander-in-Chief as regards the postponement of military operations, but he soon apprehended the dangerous significance of the revolt. He saw that the work of his predecessor had to be done over again; and he was resolved that this time there should be no half measures; no bolstering up of an effete and treacherous government, but a restoration of order and law under British administration. In October, 1848, he proceeded from Bengal to the Punjab. Before he went he made a declaration in a public speech, which is at once characteristic and historical —"Unwarned by precedent, uninfluenced by example, the Sikh nation has called for war, and on my word, sirs, they shall have it with a vengeance."

All this while Sher Singh had been coldly and suspiciously received by Mulraj. Both had revolted against a common enemy, but each one was jealous of the other, and had his own ends to pursue. Accordingly, Sher Singh left Multan, and marched boldly toward Lahore. About the same time his father, Chutter Singh, had been tempting Dost Muhammad Khan, Amir of Kabul, to join in the general rising against the British government, by promising to make over the coveted province of Peshawar. Major George Lawrence, a brother of Henry, was in charge of Peshawar, which was held by a garrison of eight thousand Sikhs; but the Sikh garrison went over to the Afghans and attacked the Residency, and George Lawrence and others were carried off prisoners. Captain Herbert held out for a while in the fort of Attock, near the junction of the Kabul river and the Indus to the eastward of Peshawar, but was forced in like manner to succumb to the Afghans.

In October, 1848, the British army under Lord Gough was assembled at Ferozepore. In November it crossed the Ravi, and engaged Sher Singh in an indecisive action at Ramnuggur. On the 13th of January, 1849, Lord Gough approached Sher Singh's intrenchments at Chilianwallah, which were held by thirty thousand Sikhs and sixty guns. Nothing was known of the disposition of the Sikhs, for their camp was covered by a thick jungle, and Lord Gough resolved to defer the attack till the following morning. At that moment the Sikhs opened fire with some guns in advance. The indignation of Lord Gough was kindled at the challenge, and he rashly ordered a general charge. Then followed the most sanguinary encounter in the history of British India, which ended in a doubtful victory on the part of the English. The Sikhs were driven from their position, but they took up another three miles off. Both sides fired salutes in honor of victory, but the English had lost more than two thousand four hundred officers and men.

The fatal field of Chilianwallah is already half forgotten, but the tidings of the disaster were received in England with an outburst of alarm and indignation. Sir Charles Napier was hastily sent to India to supersede Lord Gough as Commander-in-Chief. Meanwhile General Whish captured the town of Multan, and opened a terrible cannonade on the citadel. Mulraj offered a desperate resistance, but was at last compelled to surrender the fortress, and gave himself up to the English. General Whish then left Multan in charge of Lieutenant Edwardes, and proceeded to join Lord Gough in a final struggle with Sher Singh.

The crowning victory at Guzerat was gained by Lord Gough on the 22d of February, 1849. It was essentially an artillery action, and is known as the battle of the guns. The Sikhs opened a cannonade with sixty guns and fired with singular rapidity, but their resistance was in vain. For two hours and a half they were exposed to a storm of shot and shell, which was eventually followed by a charge of bayonets, and rush of cavalry. The Sikh army became literally a wreck; its camp, its standards, and nearly all its cannon, fell into the hands of the conquerors. The battle of Guzerat decided the fate of the Punjab, and the hopes of the Khalsa were quenched forever.

Lord Dalhousie was fully prepared for this result. He had resolved on the annexation of the Punjab, and had already drawn up a programme for the civil administration of the province, and the appointment of British officials to the several grades. All old errors in former settlements were rectified in dealing with the Punjab; all known abuses were guarded against; and the government of the Punjab, instead of struggling into existence like the government of Bengal, seemed to spring, like another Minerva, full armed from the brain of Zeus. To this day the administration of the Punjab is one of the greatest triumphs of British rule, and a model for Asiatic statesmen throughout all time.

The minor details connected with the conclusion of the war may be dismissed in a few words. Dost Muhammad Khan and his Afghans were driven out of Peshawar, and narrowly escaped to Kabul. Mulraj was imprisoned for life on account of the part he played in the murder of the two Englishmen. The young Maharaja Dhulip Singh was provided with a yearly annuity of fifty thousand pounds, and ultimately settled in England. Within a few short years the memory of Runjeet Singh died away from the land. The soldiers of the Khalsa enlisted under British banners, and during the sepoy revolt of 1857 were the foremost among those who wrested Delhi from the sepoy mutineers, and avenged the insulted sovereignty of British rule.

CHAPTER XXIV

MATERIAL PROGRESS—LORD DALHOUSIE

A.D. 1848 TO 1856

LORD DALHOUSIE was a man of energy and power. Short in stature, like the once famous Marquis of Wellesley, there was a fire and determination in his eye which revealed a genius for command.[1] So long as he held the reins of government his administrative ability and intellectual vigor commanded general respect and admiration; but his imperious temper, impatience of opposition, and alleged lack of sympathy for native rulers, stirred up an antagonism to his policy which is only slowly fading away.

Lord Dalhousie was Governor-General of India at the age of thirty-six. He was a stanch believer in moral and material progress, and he had already served an apprenticeship to the work as President of the Board of Trade under the premiership of Sir Robert Peel. Within two years of his arrival in India he had perfected his knowledge of the country and people. The Sikh uprising of 1848 familiarized him with those convulsions on the frontier to which Hindustan has always been exposed; while the newly conquered territory of the Punjab opened out a virgin field to his administrative energies.

The Punjab is nearly as large as England. It covers fifty thousand square miles, and contains a population of four millions. One-fourth of the people are Sikhs; the re-

[1] De Quincey talks of the foppery of the eye, and quotes the cases of Lord Wellesley, Dr. Parr, and Augustus Cæsar; but there was no foppery about the eye of Lord Dalhousie.

mainder are Hindus and Muhammadans. The Sikh government and the army of the Khalsa had been scattered to the winds. Accordingly Lord Dalhousie was called upon to create a new administration out of chaos, which should adapt itself to a mixed population who knew nothing of order or law; and he brought to bear upon his task the experiences which had been gained during a century of British rule in India, and which enabled him to avoid the mistakes which had been committed by his predecessors in Bengal and elsewhere.

The new province was divided by Lord Dalhousie into seven divisions, and each division into as many districts as were necessary. Each division was placed under a commissioner and each district under a deputy-commissioner. Fifty-six officers were employed in these two grades; one-half being selected from the civil service, and the other half from the army. Below these were the subordinate grades of assistant and extra-assistant commissioners, who were selected from what is known as the uncovenanted service, and comprised Europeans, East Indians, and natives.

The management of the new administration was intrusted to a Board of Administration, consisting of three members, namely, Henry Lawrence, John Lawrence, and Robert Montgomery.[1] Henry Lawrence presided at the Board, and carried on the political work, namely, the disarming of the country, the negotiations with Sikh Sirdars, and the organization of new Punjabi regiments. John Lawrence took charge of the civil administration, especially the settlement of the land revenue. Robert Montgomery superintended the administration of justice throughout the province, and compiled a short manual for the guidance of the officials and people, which contained all that was necessary in a few pages.

---

[1] Colonel, afterward Sir Henry, Lawrence, belonged to the Bengal Artillery. John Lawrence, afterward Viceroy of India and a peer of the realm, belonged to the Civil Service. Mr. Charles Grenville Mansel was originally third member of the Board, but he was subsequently succeeded by Sir Robert Montgomery. Both Mansel and Montgomery belonged to the Civil Service.

The working of the Board of Administration was not satisfactory. The sympathies of Henry Lawrence were all on the side of the Sikh Sirdars, who were regarded with disfavor by Lord Dalhousie, and whose antecedents were certainly as bad as they well could be. The result was that in 1853 the Board of Administration was broken up, and John Lawrence was placed in the sole charge of the government as Chief Commissioner.

The British administration of the Punjab was in every way a new creation. The government of Runjeet Singh had been the rude work of an unlettered warrior, without constitutional forms of any sort or kind, and without any law except the will of the one great despot at the head. The only officers of state were soldiers and tax-collectors; the only punishments were fines and mutilations; and there was not a single civil court in the Punjab excepting at Lahore. The local authorities were little despots who oppressed the people and defrauded the state, like the underlings of Tippu Sultan in Mysore; but sooner or later the majority were compelled to disgorge their ill-gotten wealth, and were often condemned to poverty and mutilation at the arbitrary will of Runjeet Singh.

The officers of the new Punjab commission were required to fulfil every kind of administrative duty. They were magistrates and judges, revenue collectors and head policemen, diplomatists and conservancy officers. For many months of the year their homes were in camp, with their tents open to all comers, from the lowest class of petitioners to the wealthiest Sirdars.[1]

One of the first measures of Lord Dalhousie was to provide for the military defence of the province. The British frontier had been advanced from the Sutlej westward to the

---

[1] The general confidence of the natives of the Punjab in British officers was sometimes carried to an amusing excess. On one occasion, when the late Lord Lawrence was Viceroy of India, a number of Punjab people travelled to Calcutta, a distance of some fifteen hundred miles, to speak to "Jan Larrens Sahib" about a cow. The writer saw the men himself. Unfortunately "Jan Larrens Sahib" was at Simla.

range of mountains beyond the Indus. The mountains were inhabited by brave and lawless tribes, who numbered a hundred thousand men at arms, and had been the pest of the plains ever since the days of Akbar. Lord Dalhousie tried to bar out these barbarians by a series of fortifications, connected by a line of roads, along the whole frontier; and he organized a special force of five regiments of infantry and four of cavalry for the protection of the marches.[1] Meanwhile he disarmed the whole of the population of the Punjab, excepting the inhabitants on the British side of the border. A hundred and twenty thousand weapons were surrendered to British officers; and the manufacture, sale, or possession of arms was strictly prohibited.

The land revenue was settled on easy terms. Runjeet Singh had collected half the produce. Lord Dalhousie reduced it to an average of one-fourth, and ordered a further reduction of ten per cent, to reconcile the renters to the payment of coin instead of kind. The consequence was that cultivation largely increased, and thirty thousand of the old Khalsa soldiery exchanged the sword for the plow.

Transit duties were abolished altogether. Runjeet Singh had covered the Punjab with a network of custom-houses for the collection of these duties on goods and merchandise; but all were swept away by a stroke of the pen from Lord Dalhousie.

Meanwhile slavery and thuggee were rooted out of the Punjab; and infanticide, that bane of Oriental life, was suppressed as far as might be. Bands of outlaws and dacoits, who had been accustomed under Sikh rule to plunder villages and travellers with impunity, were attacked, captured and punished by sheer force of arms. The Punjab was intersected with roads as if it had been a Roman province.[2] In

[1] This is the line of frontier which has recently been abandoned (1880). Further particulars respecting it will be found in the story of the Sitana campaign of 1863, which is told in the concluding chapter of the present volumes.

[2] The most important road constructed in the Punjab was that which united Lahore with Peshawar. It extended very nearly 300 miles, passed over 100 great bridges and 450 smaller ones, penetrated six mountain chains, and was

a word, within seven years of the battle of Guzerat, the Punjab presented more traces of British civilization and dominion than any other province in British India.

Three years after the conquest of the Punjab the British government was drawn into a second war with the king of Burma. Never was a war begun with greater reluctance. To all appearance there was nothing to gain; for the territories of Arakan and Tenasserim, which had been acquired after the first war, had never paid their expenses. But Lord Dalhousie had no alternative. By the treaty of Yandabo both the British and Burmese governments were pledged to afford protection and security to all merchants trading at their respective ports or residing within their respective territories. This treaty, however, had been repeatedly broken; and Englishmen trading at Rangoon were oppressed and maltreated by the Burmese officials, while every effort to obtain redress was treated with contempt and scorn.

In 1851 the European merchants at Rangoon laid their complaints before the British government at Calcutta. English sea-captains had been condemned on false charges to pay heavy fines, and were then subjected to imprisonment and insult. British merchants, who had been living at Rangoon under the provisions of the treaty of Yandabo, were driven to declare that unless they were protected by their own government they must abandon their property and leave Burmese territory.

Ever since 1840 the British government had ceased to maintain an accredited agent at Ava. Accordingly Lord Dalhousie sent Commodore Lambert to Rangoon in Her Majesty's ship the Fox, to investigate the complaints; and

---

carried by embankments over the marshes of two great rivers. Every obstacle was overcome by Colonel Robert Napier of the Bengal Engineers, whose work in the Punjab would have won him the highest honors in Europe, and who has become famous in later days as Lord Napier of Magdala. Canals and irrigation works were not forgotten. Among others the great canal of the Bari Doab was constructed between the Ravi and the Chenab, under the direction of Colonel Napier. It was equal to the noblest canal in Europe, and extended with its three branches to the length of 465 miles.

also intrusted him with a letter of remonstrance to the king of Burma, which he was to forward to Ava or withhold as might seem expedient. When the Fox reached Rangoon, the Burmese governor threatened to put any one to death who dared to communicate with the ship. Some Europeans, however, escaped to the frigate, and the Commodore sent on the letter from Lord Dalhousie to the king at Ava. After some weeks a reply was received to the effect that the offending governor would be removed from Rangoon, and that strict inquiries would be made into the complaints brought against him.

Commodore Lambert was delighted with the letter from Ava. He thought everything was settled, but he was soon undeceived. The governor was certainly recalled from Rangoon, but he went away in triumph, with all the pomp of music and war boats. A new governor arrived, but he was bent on treating the English with the same contempt and arrogance as had been displayed by his predecessor. He took no notice whatever of the Commodore. At last he was asked to fix a day for receiving a deputation of English officers, and he replied that any day would do. Accordingly early one morning he was told that a deputation would wait upon him at noon. At the time appointed the English officers reached the governor's house, but were not allowed to enter. They were kept out in the sun by the menial servants, and told that the governor was asleep; while the governor himself was looking insolently out of the window, and seeing them exposed to the insults and jeers of the mob. At last the patience of the officers was exhausted, and they returned to the frigate.

Commodore Lambert then took possession of one of the king's ships lying in the river, but promised to restore it, and to salute the Burmese flag, on receipt of ten thousand rupees, as compensation for the injured merchants, and a suitable apology from the governor of Rangoon. In reply, the Burmese opened fire on the Fox from some stockades on both sides of the river; but the guns of the Fox soon demolished the stockades, and the Burmese ports were declared in a state of blockade.

Lord Dalhousie made another appeal to the king of Burma, and meanwhile prepared for war. A land force of five thousand eight hundred men was sent to Rangoon under General Godwin, together with nineteen steamers manned with two thousand three hundred sailors and marines. A steamer was sent up the river Irawadi with a flag of truce to receive a reply from the king, but it was fired upon by the Burmese. Accordingly the troops were landed; Rangoon was captured in the face of a heavy cannonade, the three terraces of the great Shive Dagon pagoda were carried by storm, and the British ensign was fixed on the golden dome.

The capture of Rangoon was followed by that of Bassein and Prome.[1] The Burmese soldiery fled to Upper Burma, and the people flocked to Rangoon and hailed the British as their deliverers. Meanwhile there had been a revolution in Ava. The Pagan Meng had been deposed, and his half-brother, the Meng-don Meng, was taken from a Buddhist monastery and placed upon the throne. The new sovereign was anxious for peace, but refused to conclude any treaty. Lord Dalhousie steamed to Rangoon the following September and decided on annexing Pegu to the British empire, and leaving the king in possession of Upper Burma.

The same administrative changes were carried out at Pegu as had been begun in the Punjab, but with limited resources and on a less brilliant scale. Major, the present Sir Arthur Phayre, was appointed Commissioner of Pegu, and introduced British administration with a strong substratum of Burmese officials. With the assistance of Captain, now General Fytche, and other distinguished officers, Major Phayre succeeded in clearing the new province of

---

[1] There are two places named Bassein. There is Bassein, near Bombay, where the Peishwa concluded a treaty with Lord Wellesley; and the Bassein named in the text, which is situated on the southwest corner of the delta of the Irawadi.

robbers and outlaws and establishing order and law. Ultimately in 1862 the three territories of Arakan, Pegu, and Tenasserim were formed into the province of British Burma, with Major Phayre as Chief Commissioner. The consequence has been that British Burma not only pays the whole expense of the local administration, but contributes a large yearly surplus to the imperial treasury. Since 1852 the population of Rangoon alone has increased tenfold, and promises to become another Calcutta; and when the population of Pegu has increased in a like ratio, the province will prove as productive as Bengal. Already the Irawadi is beginning to pour down as much wealth to the sea as the Ganges and Jumna before the introduction of the railways; and within another generation, when existing obstructions are removed, new fields of commerce will be opened out in Western China, and restore the fabled glories of the Golden Chersonese to the Malacca peninsula.[1]

The Punjab and Pegu were the favorite, but not the only fields of Lord Dalhousie's labors. His influence was felt in every province of the empire, every department of government, and every native state under British protection. His reforms extended to every branch of the administration—army, public works, education, revenue, finance, justice, and general legislation. He promoted canals and steam navigation, and he introduced railways and cheap postage. He constructed four thousand miles of electric telegraph wires, and two thousand miles of road, bridged and metalled. He opened the Ganges canal, the longest in the world. In a word, Lord Dalhousie was emphatically the pioneer of western civilization in India; the first of that modern dynasty of rulers, under whom India has ceased to be a remote and outlying region, and has become part and parcel of the British empire, sharing in all the blessings of European science and culture.

[1] Should the frontier of British India ever be conterminous with Persia, Russia, and China, new markets will be opened to British manufactures of which the present generation can form no conception, while the resources of the new countries, which at present are undeveloped, will serve to enrich half Asia.

The administrative successes of Lord Dalhousie naturally impressed him with a strong sense of the vast superiority of British administration over Oriental rule. He would not interfere with the treaty rights of native allies, but he was resolute in putting down widow burning, witch torturing, self-immolation, mutilation, and other barbarous usages, in the territories of native princes, as much as in those under British administration. Any prince, Rajput or Mahratta, who hesitated to punish such atrocities within his own territories to the entire satisfaction of the British government, was visited with the marked displeasure of Lord Dalhousie, threatened with the loss of his salute, refused admittance to the Governor-General's durbar, or deprived of one or other of those tokens of the consideration of the British government which are valued by the princes and nobles of India. At the same time Lord Dalhousie was never wanting in paternal regard for native states during a minority. He duly provided for the education and administrative training of Sindia and Holkar; and was anxious that they should be fitted for the duties of government before they attained their majority and were placed in charge of their respective territories.

The administration of native states was no doubt wretched in the extreme. Indeed it is only of late years that native officials have received an English education, and profited by the example set in British territories, to carry out some measures of reform. Both Lord Dalhousie, and his predecessor, Lord Hardinge, were deeply impressed with the responsibility incurred by the British government in perpetuating native misrule. Both agreed that no rightful opportunity should be lost of acquiring territory and revenue; in other words, of bringing native territory under British administration. The motives of both rulers were unquestionably pure; neither Hardinge nor Dalhousie could have any personal object in adding to the territories of the late East India Company, beyond the promotion of the moral and material welfare of the native populations. But their sentiments were open to misconstruction, and might be interpreted to mean that the appropriation of native territory would be always justifiable, provided a decent excuse could be found for the transfer.

No one seems to have doubted that the British government was bound to maintain the integrity of native states so long as a native ruler did not forfeit his rights by some public crime. Again, no one doubted the right of a son, or other male heir, to inherit a Raj. But a question was raised as to the rights of an adopted son; and as this question has been much distorted by controversy, it may be as well to explain it from a Hindu point of view. Practically, the law of adoption has ceased to have any political importance. The British government has conceded the right of adopting an heir to the Raj to native princes in general. But a right understanding of the law of adoption is absolutely necessary to a right understanding of the policy of Lord Dalhousie.

Among all orthodox Hindus a son is regarded as a religious necessity. A son is required to offer cakes and water to the soul of a deceased father, and indeed to the souls of all deceased ancestors up to a certain generation. Moreover, in the belief of modern Hindus, the world of shades is a kind of temporary hell or purgatory, where the soul of the father is supposed to dwell until all its sins have been wiped away by the sacrifices and other good works of the son. When this end has been attained, the soul either returns to earth to resume its existence through successive transmigrations, or it ascends to eternal life in some superior heaven, or is absorbed in the Supreme Spirit—Vishnu, Siva, or Brahma.

It is this religious necessity which has brought about the early marriage of Hindu boys. Should, however, the husband fail to become the father of a son, he may either marry a second wife, or he may adopt a son; and a son in either case, whether natural or adopted, inherits the property at the father's death, and becomes the head of the household.

The question of adoption in the case of a Hindu principality stands on a different footing. The adopted son may succeed to the property of his nominal father, and perform all his religious duties; but the question of inheriting a Raj is of a political character, and depends on the will of the paramount power. In either case, whether the inheritance to a Raj is granted or refused, the adopted son is still expected to perform all the religious duties necessary for the well-being of the deceased father.[1]

The question of the right of adoption in the case of a Hindu principality was never raised in India before the rise of British power. There was no public law in the matter; the question of might alone made the right. If a Hindu principality was conveniently near, it was brought under Moghul rule by treachery, chicanery, or force of arms, without the slightest regard to the rights of a reigning Raja, or the rights of his heirs or representatives.[2] If a principality was remote and strong, every effort was made to seduce or threaten the native ruler into paying tribute; or at any rate into rendering homage and presenting nuzzers, or honorary gifts, as an acknowledgment of the suzerainty of the Moghul. Whatever, however, might be the circumstances of the case, no succession was deemed valid unless it received the formal approval and sanction of the paramount power; and this end could only be obtained by a Hindu prince in the same way that a Muhammadan officer obtained the government of a province, namely, by sending presents and tribute to the Moghul court, and receiving letters and insignia of investiture in return.

The British government, however, professed from the very first to adhere to the policy of non-intervention, and

---

[1] The present Maharaja Holkar has more than once taken over the estate of a feudatory on the ground that he had left no natural heirs, and that the adopted son had no claim to inherit landed property.

[2] Akbar was anxious to maintain the Rajput principalities as a counterpoise against Afghans and Moghuls, and his policy was to give a daughter in marriage to a Rajput prince, and insist upon her son being the heir to the principality. But Aurangzeb was only anxious to convert the Hindus to Islam, and a Rajput prince who turned Muhammadan would have been recognized as heir to the principality in the same way that an Irishman of a Roman Catholic family secured the family estate in the last century by becoming a Protestant. Neither Akbar nor Aurangzeb were likely to trouble themselves about the law of adoption.

cared not who succeeded to the throne so long as there were no civil wars.[1] Accordingly in the case of Sindia, as already seen, the dying ruler was advised by the British government to adopt a son in order to prevent any broils as regards a successor. At the same time the queen or minister was generally anxious for an adoption, as if it could be established it might set aside the claim of a brother or other collateral heir, and would enable the queen or minister to exercise sovereign authority during the minority. It thus became customary for a native prince to apply for the consent of the British government before adopting a son who should be heir to the Raj; and at every succession, whether the son was natural or adopted, the recognition of the British government was deemed necessary to its validity. The youthful heir was formally invested with a dress of honor by the British representative, and in return he publicly acknowledged his fealty to the British government.

The policy of Lord Dalhousie will be rendered intelligible by dealing with matters of fact. The first native principality brought to his notice was that of Satara. The story of Satara has already been told. The representative of Sivaji reigned as a puppet Raja in a state prison at Satara, while successive Peishwas, or ministers, reigned as real sovereigns at Poona. After the extinction of the Peishwas in 1818, Lord Hastings resuscitated the Raja of Satara for reasons of state; took him out of a prison, and invested him with a small principality. He thought by so doing to reconcile Sindia and Holkar to the extinction of the Peishwas. But the generosity, whether real or apparent, was thrown away. The Mahrattas had long forgotten to care for the Raja of Satara, and they soon forgot the ex-Peishwa.

But the elevation of the Raja of Satara from a prison to a principality turned the young man's head. Instead of being grateful for his change of fortune, he was incensed with his benefactors for not restoring him to the throne and

---

[1] See ante, p. 601.

empire of Sivaji. He fondly imagined that if he could only get rid of the British government he might recover the old Mahratta sovereignty which had been usurped by the Peishwas for more than seventy years, and which, as far as Satara was concerned, had never been anything more than a shadow and a sham. Accordingly, in spite of his treaty obligations to abstain from all correspondence with states or individuals outside his jurisdiction, the Raja of Satara opened up communications with the Portuguese authorities at Goa, and even with the exiled Appa Sahib of Nagpore; and to crown his misdoings, he employed certain Brahmans to tamper with some sepoy officers in the Bombay army.

It was impossible to overlook these proceedings, and there was some talk of punishing the Raja; but Sir James Carnac, the Governor of Bombay, took a lenient view of the case, and told the Raja that all would be forgiven if he would only promise to keep the treaty more faithfully for the future. But by this time the Raja was too far gone to listen to reason. He spurned all interference, asserted his sovereignty, and was accordingly deposed and sent to Benares, and his brother was enthroned in his room.

The new Raja of Satara took warning by the fate of his predecessor, and gave no trouble to the British authorities. But he had no son or male heir, and he repeatedly requested the British government to permit him to adopt a son who should inherit the Raj. Every application, however, was refused. Under such circumstances he might possibly have adopted a son who would have inherited his private property, and performed all the religious ceremonies necessary for delivering his soul from a Hindu purgatory. But he appears to have hoped on to the last; and in 1848, two hours before his death, he adopted an heir on his own responsibility, and left the result in the hands of the British government.

Lord Dalhousie decided that the adopted son might inherit the private property of the deceased Raja, but that the principality of Satara had lapsed to the British government. This decision was confirmed by the Court of Directors. The result was that the Raj of Satara was incorporated with the Bombay Presidency, and brought under British administration.

Shortly afterward, the Kerauli succession was taken into consideration. Kerauli was a Rajput principality, which had paid a yearly tribute to the Peishwa; but it was taken under British protection in 1818, and relieved from the further payment of tribute. The Raja showed his gratitude by joining in the outbreak of Durjan Sal of Bhurtpore in 1826; but he subsequently expressed his attachment to the British government, and his offence was condoned.

The Raja of Kerauli died in 1848 without a natural heir, but, like the Satara Raja, he adopted a son just before his death. Lord Dalhousie was inclined to think that Kerauli, like Satara, had lapsed to the British government; but the Court of Directors decided that Kerauli was a "protected ally," and not a "dependent principality," and accordingly the government of Lord Dalhousie recognized the adopted son as the heir to the Raj.

In 1853 the Nagpore succession was brought under discussion. The fortunes of this Raj are of peculiar interest. The story begins with Lord Hastings and ends with Lord Dalhousie; but it may be told in the present place as an episode.

In 1818 the territory of the Bhonsla Rajas was placed at the disposal of the British government. The treacherous Appa Sahib had fled into exile, leaving no son, real or adopted, to succeed him on the throne of Nagpore. Accordingly the ladies of the family were permitted to adopt a boy, who assumed the name of Bhonsla, and was accepted as an infant Raja; and Mr. Richard Jenkins, the Resident at Nagpore, was intrusted with the management of affairs during the minority, and exercised something like uncontrolled powers.

The management of Mr. Jenkins was denounced in England as a departure from the ruling doctrine of non-intervention; but nevertheless it was attended with singular success. Mr. Jenkins organized a native administration under British management, and did not commit the fatal error of expecting too much.[1] The consequence was that in Nagpore, and in Nagpore alone, outside British territory, disorders were repressed, vexatious taxes abolished, debts liquidated, and expenditure reduced; while crime diminished, revenue improved, and a large surplus accumulated in the public treasury.[2]

In 1826 the young Raja attained his majority, and the British management was withdrawn from Nagpore. In 1837 the Raja had grown utterly demoralized; he cared nothing for his people, but spent his whole time, like a little Sardanapalus, in the female apartments of his palace. In spite of this adverse circumstance, the people of Nagpore were less oppressed than those of any other native state in India. The system organized by Mr. Jenkins was much

---

[1] There is a well-known couplet by Mat Prior, which English officials in high position would do well to bear in mind in dealing with native subordinates:

"Be to their virtues very kind,
Be to their faults a little blind."

[2] The exponents of the policy of non-intervention had much to say in its favor. The subsidiary system which secured native princes on their thrones was supposed to have aggravated the evils of native rule by stripping the state of all responsibility, and thus stifling all desire for the improvement of the country and people. The princes of India lost their accustomed stimulants of war and plunder, and sank into apathy, or sought consolation in vicious self-indulgence. Under such circumstances there were grounds for hoping that non-intervention would revive the sense of responsibility, and enable every native principality to recover its lost vitality.

But this lost vitality is a myth. It may have existed in some remote era, some golden age of Rajput romance; but it is as unknown to history as the exploits of King Arthur and the Knights of the Round Table. It was the dream of the Brahmanical compilers of the Hindu epics, and is as unreal as the fabled stories in the Arabian Nights of the golden reign of Haroun Alraschid. Ever since Europeans became acquainted with India the vitality of native rule has only found expression in predatory wars and administrative extortions; and when at last the princes of India were bound over by the subsidiary alliances to keep the peace, the native states were moribund, and nothing but new blood would impart life or energy to native administrations.

What was really wanted was a guiding influence to open the eyes of native rulers to their duties toward their subjects, and to inspire them with that spirit of emulation which is necessary to awaken them to a higher ambition and loftier aims. After the wars of 1817–18 the princes of India were peculiarly amenable to such influences, and hence the administrative successes of Mr. Jenkins in Nagpore.

deteriorated, especially in the administration of justice. But the people spoke of "Dunkin Sahib" with affection, and all the middle and lower classes were heartily desirous of British rule.

In 1853 the Raja of Nagpore died, leaving no son or heir, natural or adopted. Nagpore had been a "dependent principality" ever since 1818, and Lord Dalhousie had to determine whether to permit the widows to adopt a son, and thus make over Nagpore to a Mahratta lad who might have turned out no better than his successor;[1] or to bring Nagpore under a similar administration to that which had proved so successful in the Punjab. Lord Dalhousie decided on the latter course, and his view was accepted by the Court of Directors. Accordingly Nagpore was incorporated with British territory, and now forms a part of the Central Provinces.

Besides the annexation of territories, Lord Dalhousie abolished certain expensive pageants, which had long ceased to exercise any authority or influence, and only proved a dead weight on the public treasury. In 1853 the titular Nawab of the Carnatic died without an heir; and Lord Dalhousie declared the dignity extinct, and withdrew the heavy share of the revenue which had been made over by Lord Wellesley for the maintenance of the pageantry. At the same time pensions were assigned to the different members of the Carnatic family. Shortly afterward the titular Raja of Tanjore died without heirs, and the family were treated in like fashion. Since then the home government have placed the different pensions on a more liberal footing.[2]

In 1853, Baji Rao, the ex-Peishwa, was gathered to his fathers. He was the last relic of the old Mahratta empire. He was born in 1775, when Warren Hastings was being

---

[1] The widows of the deceased Raja are said to have adopted a son immediately after his demise, but this was a religious ceremony having nothing to do with the Raj. Indeed the widows were aware at the time that such an adoption was invalid as regards the Raj without the previous sanction of the British government.

[2] Besides the foregoing annexations the little principality of Jhansi, in Bundelkund, lapsed to the British government in like manner from want of natural heirs. The matter is only of moment from the terrible revenge exacted by the ex-queen during the sepoy revolt of 1857.

dragged into the first Mahratta war. In 1795, at the age of twenty, he became Peishwa of Poona. In 1802 he ran away from Jaswant Rao Holkar, and threw himself into the arms of the English at Bassein, near Bombay. He was restored to Poona by the British army, but forfeited his throne in 1817 by his treacherous outbreak against the British government. From 1818 to 1853, from the age of forty-three to that of seventy-seven, he dreamed away his life in Oriental indulgences at Bithoor, on the liberal pension of eighty thousand pounds a year.

Baji Rao left no natural heir. He had adopted a son, who was afterward known as Nana Sahib. He must have saved a large sum out of his yearly allowance. Nana Sahib acknowledged that the accumulations amounted to nearly three hundred thousand pounds sterling; but it was subsequently discovered that they aggregated half a million. Nevertheless, Nana Sahib prayed for the continuation of the pension, and pretended that it had been granted, not by way of grace or favor, but as compensation to the ex-Peishwa for his loss of territory. Such a preposterous claim was beneath discussion; but it was taken into consideration by Lord Dalhousie and the Court of Directors, and was only rejected after the fullest inquiry.

The dealings of Lord Dalhousie with the Nizam of Hyderabad demand a passing notice. By the treaty of 1801 the Nizam was bound to furnish a military contingent in time of war of six thousand infantry and nine thousand horse. But the rabble soldiery which he supplied during the subsequent wars proved to be worse than useless in the field. Accordingly it was agreed by mutual consent that a permanent force should be maintained by the Nizam, reduced to half the number of native troops, but to be disciplined and commanded by British officers. This new body of troops was known as the Nizam's Contingent, as distinguished from the Hyderabad Subsidiary Force.[1]

---

[1] The Nizam's Contingent on the new footing consisted of 5,000 infantry, 2,000 cavalry, and four field batteries.

From a very early period the Nizam had failed to provide the necessary funds for the maintenance of the Contingent. From time to time large advances were made by the British government to meet the current expenditure, until a debt accumulated of half a million sterling. The Nizam might have escaped this obligation by disbanding the Contingent; but this he repeatedly and obstinately refused to do, and indeed the force was necessary for the maintenance of peace and order in his own territories. Again, he might have disbanded the hordes of foreign mercenaries, Arabs and Rohillas, which he kept up under the name of an army, and which were a burden upon his treasury, a terror to his subjects, and useless for all military purposes. But he was as obstinate upon this point as upon the other. At last, in 1843, he was told by Lord Ellenborough that unless the debt was liquidated and the necessary funds were provided regularly for the future, the British government would take over territory and revenue as security for the payment.

This threat seems to have created some alarm in Hyderabad. Chandu Lal resigned the post of minister, and the Nizam attempted to carry on the administration alone, but his efforts were fitful and desultory. Meanwhile mere dribblets of the debt were paid off, and the Resident was amused with excuses and promises; and in this fashion matters drifted on.

At last Lord Dalhousie insisted on a cession of sufficient territory to provide for the maintenance of the Nizam's Contingent. He would not touch the hereditary dominions of the Nizam; he merely took over the territory of Berar, which Lord Wellesley had given to the Nizam in 1803, after the conquest of the Raja of Nagpore. Accordingly Berar was brought under British administration; and since then all surplus revenue accruing from the improvements in the revenue system has been made over to the Nizam's treasury.

The last important measure in the career of Lord Dalhousie was the annexation of Oude. The story of Oude is an unpleasant episode in the history of British India. In

1764 the English conquered Oude, but Lord Clive gave it back to the Nawab Vizier. In 1801 Lord Wellesley took over one-half of the territory to provide for the defence of Hindustan against Afghans, French, and Mahrattas. From the days of Lord Wellesley to those of Lord Dalhousie Oude was a millstone round the neck of the British government. Every Governor-General in turn condemned the administration of Oude as tyrannical, extortionate, and corrupt to the last degree; each in turn denounced the reigning Nawab Vizier, and yet shrank from the distasteful task of taking the necessary steps for carrying out a radical reform. Lord Hastings tried polite remonstrance; he wished, he said, to treat the Nawab Vizier like a gentleman; and the result was that the Nawab Vizier assumed the title of "king," in order to place himself on a par with the so-called king of Delhi. In 1831 Lord William Bentinck, the friend of native princes, threatened to assume the direct administration of Oude, but ultimately left India without doing it. From the day of his departure the introduction of British rule in Oude was a mere question of time. It was one of those painful operations which no Governor-General liked to perform; but it was absolutely necessary to the well-being, not only of the people of Oude, but of the British empire in India. In 1847 Lord Hardinge, who had labored to save the Sikh government in the Punjab, was so aghast at the desolation of Oude that he solemnly warned the king that the British government would assume the management of his country within two years unless he employed the interval in carrying out a complete reform in his administration.

In 1851 Colonel Sleeman, the British Resident at Lukhnow, made a tour through Oude, and reported on the state of the country. The people were at the mercy of the soldiery and landholders. While Oude was protected by British troops from every possible foe, a standing army of seventy thousand men was kept up by the king; and as the pay of the troops was very small, and nearly always in arrears, they were driven to prey upon the helpless villagers. It is needless to dwell on the plunder, outrage and crime that were the natural consequence. The wretched inhabitants complained that brigands and outlaws were sometimes merciful, but that the king's troops never knew how to pity or how to spare. The Talukdars, or landholders, built forts throughout the country, and levied revenue and blackmail, like the Afghan chiefs who preyed on Hindustan before the days of Akbar. All this while the king was shut up in his palace; he was seen by no one except women, musicians, and buffoons. The government was a monstrous system of corruption, under which every office was bought with money, and every official was left to reimburse himself as fast as he could by oppression and extortion. Reform was out of the question; every evil had been festering in the body politic for the greater part of a century, and nothing but new blood could save the country from destruction.

Lord Dalhousie was anxious to deal gently with the king of Oude. The family had always been loyal to the British government, and had always done their best to help it in the hour of need. Lord Dalhousie would have left the king in the possession of the sovereignty while taking over the direct management of his territories. But the patience of the Court of Directors was worn out; they were determined to annex the country and abolish the throne; and in 1856, being the last year of Lord Dalhousie's administration, the sovereignty of the kings of Oude was brought to a close.

During the administration of Lord Dalhousie the hill tribes of Bengal forced themselves on the attention of the British government. As far back as 1832 there had been a strange rising of the Koles, an aboriginal tribe of Western Bengal, who at some remote period had been driven into the hills by the Hindu settlers, and there maintained their primitive language, habits, and superstitions, down to modern times. The Koles had been troubled by British laws and exasperated by encroaching Zemindars. Accordingly they broke out in rebellion, and committed many outrages before they were repressed. Lord William Bentinck withdrew the

Koles from the operation of the ordinary laws, and placed their country in charge of a special commissioner. Since then the Koles had advanced in civilization and prosperity, and large numbers had been converted to Christianity. In 1855 there was an insurrection of another aboriginal tribe, known as the Santals, who inhabit the hill ranges of Rajmahal on the northwest frontier of Bengal proper. They had been harassed by the civil suits of Bengali money-lenders, and they advanced into the plains, to the number of thirty thousand men, to make war upon the British government with pickaxes and poisoned arrows. The British authorities were taken by surprise. The Santals began the work of pillage and murder, and spread abroad a wild alarm before a British force could be marched against them. The outbreak, however, was soon suppressed, and Lord Dalhousie dealt with the Santals in the same way that Lord William Bentinck had dealt with the Koles, namely, by placing them in charge of a special commissioner.

CHAPTER XXV

SEPOY MUTINIES—LORD CANNING

A.D. 1856 TO 1858

LORD CANNING was forty-four years of age when he succeeded Lord Dalhousie as Governor-General of India. He had seen something of official life; he had been Under-Secretary for Foreign Affairs under Sir Robert Peel, and Postmaster-General under Lord Aberdeen and Lord Palmerston. He was a good administrator—moderate, cautious, conscientious, and "safe"; and as such he was well fitted to carry on, slowly but surely, the great work of moral and material progress begun by Lord Dalhousie.

In 1856 the political atmosphere of India was without a cloud. A few events occurred, but they were of small historical interest, and cannot be regarded as in any way foreshadowing the storm which was about to burst upon the plains of Hindustan.

The annexation of Oude had been carried out with more harshness than Lord Dalhousie had intended. The king removed from Lukhnow to Calcutta, and settled down with his women and dependents in the suburbs at Garden Reach, while the queen-mother and heir-apparent went on a bootless mission to England. Meanwhile an administration, like that which had proved so successful in the Punjab, was introduced into Oude; but it did not work smoothly. The new rulers forgot that Oude was not a conquered country like the Punjab; and that the Oude Talukdars, bad as they may have been, were not rebels and traitors against the British government. Consequently the leading officers disputed among themselves; and there were many complaints of severity toward native officials and landholders. At last, early in 1857, Sir Henry Lawrence was appointed Chief Commissioner of Oude, and it was believed that all would soon be well.

The status of the so-called kings of Delhi was placed upon a new footing. Ever since 1803, when Shah Alam was taken under British protection by Lord Wellesley, the kings had been without a history. The family dwelt in the old Moghul palace at Delhi, and multiplied in Muhammadan fashion. Palace life was made up of vain attempts to revive the dignity and pomp of a bygone age, or to obtain an increase of pension from the British government. All political vitality had died out of the family. Deaths, marriages, and births followed in dreary monotony, varied by quarrels and intrigues, which had little meaning or interest outside the palace walls.

The continued residence of the Moghul family at Delhi infected the whole capital. The Muhammadan population was more disaffected toward the British rule than in any other city in India. Lord Wellesley would have removed the family to Bengal at the beginning of the century; but the poor old pageant of that day clung to Delhi with the pertinacity of second childhood, and it seemed cruel to remove him in his old age. Since then two generations had passed away; the Moghul court had become an antiquated nuisance, and Lord Dalhousie determined to banish it forever.

The reigning king at Delhi was an infirm old man named Bahadur Shah. The heir-apparent was his grandson; and Lord Dalhousie agreed to recognize the grandson as the successor to the pageant throne, and to make some addition to his pension, on the condition that he should clear out of Delhi on the death of his grandfather, and take up his abode at the Kutub—an old royal residence near Delhi which had been founded in the thirteenth century.[1] But Bahadur Shah

[1] See ante, p. 100.

married a young wife in his old age, and she gave birth to a son; and henceforth the young queen strained every nerve to secure the pageant throne for her boy, after the manner of younger wives since patriarchal times.

In July, 1856, the heir-apparent died suddenly in the palace. There is no moral doubt that he was poisoned, and that the young queen was implicated in the crime. The catastrophe was suspiciously followed by applications from old Bahadur Shah that the son of his favorite wife might be recognized by the Governor-General as the heir and successor to the throne. But the request was refused. An elder brother stood in the way, and Lord Canning recognized this elder brother as heir-apparent, but without any bargaining or agreement. When Bahadur Shah died the new king was to remove to the Kutub by the simple decree of the British government.

The wrath of the favorite queen may be left to the imagination. She is said to have been a daughter of the house of Nadir Shah, and the hereditary ambition of the family was burning in her brain. She intrigued in all directions against the British government; possibly with the Shah of Persia, with whom Great Britain was at war; possibly with Kuzzilbash chiefs at Kabul; but the extent and character of her plots must be left to conjecture. No one dreamed that the mortified princess could in any way work mischief to the British government; and to this day it is difficult to believe that she was in any way the originator of the sepoy mutiny.

Meantime there were more difficulties with Persia respecting Herat. The death of Yar Muhammad Khan, in 1852, was followed by troubles in Herat; and the province became a bone of contention between the Shah of Persia and old Dost Muhammad Khan, of Kabul. At last the Shah moved an army to Herat and captured the fortress, contrary to his treaty with the British government. Accordingly England declared war against Persia. An expedition was sent from Bombay to the Persian Gulf under the command of Sir James Outram. The alliance with Kabul was strengthened;[1] four thousand stand of arms were presented to Dost Muhammad Khan, and he was promised a subsidy of ten thousand pounds a month so long as the Persian war lasted. The capture of Bushire by the English and the victory at Mohamrah brought the Shah to his senses. He withdrew from Afghanistan, and renounced all pretensions to Herat; and in March, 1857, peace was concluded between Great Britain and Persia.

About this time there is said to have been rumors of a coming danger to British rule in India. In some parts of the country chupaties, or cakes, were circulated in a mysterious manner from village to village. Prophecies were also rife that in 1857 the Company's Raj would come to an end. Lord Canning has been blamed for not taking alarm at these proceedings; but something of the kind has always been going on in India.[2] Cakes or cocoanuts are given away in solemn fashion; and as the villagers are afraid to keep them or eat them, the circulation goes on to the end of the chapter. Then again holy men and prophets have always been common in India. They foretell pestilence and famine, the downfall of British rule, or the destruction of the whole world. They are often supposed to be endowed with supernatural powers, and to be impervious to bullets; but these phenomena invariably disappear whenever they

---

[1] The hostility of Dost Muhammad Khan during the second Sikh war had been condoned; and a treaty of friendship was concluded by Lord Dalhousie with the Kabul ruler in 1855.

[2] A great deal of alarm has been written and spoken as regards native intrigues. As a matter of fact, plots and intrigues of one sort or another are the daily life of the natives of India. There are more plots and intrigues in a single establishment of native servants than in a hundred English households. An Englishman in India, who chooses to study the character of his servants, will know more in a few months of native thoughts and ways than he can learn in books from the study of a lifetime. A still better insight into native character may be obtained in government schools. The author is conscious that during the three or four years that he held the post of Professor of Moral Philosophy and Logic in the Madras Presidency College, he gained a larger knowledge of Hindu life, and a greater respect for Hindu character, than during the many years he has since spent in official and literary duties. The warm friendships among young Hindus, their devotion to the wishes of their parents, and the unreserved trust which they place in their English instructors who take the trouble to win their confidence, have never perhaps been sufficiently appreciated.

come in contact with Europeans, especially as all such characters are liable to be treated as vagrants without visible means of subsistence.[1]

One dangerous story, however, got abroad in the early part of 1857, which ought to have been stopped at once, and for which the military authorities were wholly and solely to blame. The Enfield rifle was being introduced; it required new cartridges, which in England were greased with the fat of beef or pork. The military authorities in India, with strange indifference to the prejudices of sepoys, ordered the cartridges to be prepared at Calcutta in like manner; forgetting that the fat of pigs was hateful to the Muhammadans, while the fat of cows was still more horrible in the eyes of the Hindus.

The excitement began at Barrackpore, sixteen miles from Calcutta. At this station there were four regiments of sepoys, and no Europeans except the regimental officers.[2] One

---

[1] There are few human beings so helpless or so ignorant that they cannot prophesy the end of all things. Prophecies, however, are not confined to Orientals. The great German traveller, Carsten Niebuhr, who visited Bombay in 1763, two years after the battle of Paniput, was guilty of the following oracular utterance, which reads somewhat strangely by the light of later history: "The power of the Muhammadans indeed becomes daily less; and there are at present some Hindu princes who may restore the nation to its ancient splendor. The Mahrattas have successfully begun a project which has this aspect. It is the exorbitant power of the English that at present retards the progressive improvement of the Hindus. But when this colossal statue, whose feet are of clay, and which has been raised by conquering merchants, shall be broken in pieces, an event which may fall out sooner than is supposed, then shall Hindustan become again a flourishing country." The learned German must have been utterly ignorant of Mahratta rule, and seems to have formed an idea out of his moral consciousness.

[2] A sepoy regiment of infantry in the Bengal army was at this time composed of 1,000 privates, 120 non-commissioned officers, and 20 commissioned officers, all natives. It was divided into ten companies, each containing 100 privates, 12 non-commissioned officers, and 2 commissioned officers. The non-commissioned officers were known as naiks and havildars, corresponding to corporals and sergeants. The commissioned officers were known as jemadars and subahdars, corresponding to lieutenants and captains. The European officers corresponded to those in English regiments.

The sepoy regiment was never quartered in barracks, but in lines. Every regiment occupied ten rows of thatched huts, a company to each row. In front of each row was a small circular building for storing arms and accoutrements after they had been cleaned.

The European officers lived in bungalows, or thatched houses near the lines,

day a low caste native, known as a Laskar, asked a Brahman sepoy for a drink of water from his brass pot. The Brahman refused, as it would defile his pot. The Laskar retorted that the Brahman was already defiled by biting cartridges which had been greased with cow's fat. This vindictive taunt was based on truth. Laskars had been employed at Calcutta in preparing the new cartridges, and the man was possibly one of them. The taunt created a wild panic at Barrackpore. Strange, however, to say, none of the new cartridges had been issued to the sepoys; and had this been promptly explained to the men, and the sepoys left to grease their own cartridges, the alarm might have died out. But the explanation was delayed until the whole of the Bengal army was smitten with the groundless fear; and then, when it was too late, the authorities protested too much, and the terror-stricken sepoys refused to believe them.[1]

The sepoys have proved themselves brave under fire, and loyal to their salt in sharp extremities; but they are the most credulous and excitable soldiery in the world. They regarded steam and electricity as so much magic;[2] and they fondly believed that the British government was binding India with chains, when it was only laying down railway lines and telegraph wires. The Enfield rifle was a new mystery; and the busy brains of the sepoys were soon at work

---

but too far off to control the movements of the men during the heat of the day. In order, however, to maintain continuous European supervision, two European sergeants were allowed to every regiment to live within the lines, and report day by day all that was going on to the European adjutant.

[1] There is, however, some excuse for the military authorities even in the matter of greased cartridges. Bazar rumors are often flying about in India, and causing the utmost alarm, while any attempt at authoritative contradiction on the part of government only gives further currency to the fable, and increases the panic. If a bridge is about to be built, it is noised abroad that children's heads are wanted for the foundations, and then not a child is to be seen in the streets for weeks. This has been of common occurrence, even within the last twenty years. Again, in Lord Auckland's time, a rumor got abroad that the blood of hill-men was required to restore the Governor-General to pristine youth; and all the coolies and hill-men at Simla suddenly ran away. Contradiction would have been useless in such extreme cases; but still, if undertaken in time, it might have quieted the minds of the sepoys.

[2] To this day the Asiatic Museum at Calcutta is only known to natives as the "magic house."

to divine the motive of the English in greasing cartridge's with cow's fat. They had always taken to themselves the sole credit of having conquered India for the Company; and they now imagined that the English wanted them to conquer Persia and China. Accordingly, they suspected that Lord Canning was going to make them as strong as Europeans by destroying caste, forcing them to become Christians, and making them eat beef and drink beer.

The story of the greased cartridges, with all its absurd embellishments, ran up the Ganges and Jumna to Benares, Allahabad, Agra, Delhi, and the great cantonment at Meerut; while another current of lies ran back again from Meerut to Barrackpore. It was noised abroad that the bones of cows and pigs had been ground into powder, and thrown into wells and mingled with flour and butter, in order to destroy the caste of the masses and convert them to Christianity.[1]

The stories of sinister designs on the part of the English were sharpened by sepoy grievances. Very much had been done for the well-being of the native army; the sepoys had become puffed up and unmanageable; and they complained of wrongs, or what appeared in their eyes to be wrongs, which Englishmen cannot easily understand. When quartered in foreign countries, such as Sinde and the Punjab, they had been granted an extra allowance, known as batta; but when Sinde and the Punjab became British territory the batta was withdrawn. Numbers, again, had been recruited in Oude, and they had another secret grievance. So long as Oude was under Muhammadan rule, every complaint from an Oude sepoy, that his family or kindred were oppressed, was forwarded to the British Resident at Lukhnow, and promptly redressed. When, however, the country was brought under British administration the complainants were referred to the

---

[1] There was some excuse for this credulity. Forced conversions had been common enough under Muhammadan rule. Aurangzeb destroyed pagodas and idols, and compelled all servants of government to become Muhammadans. Tippu Sultan converted crowds of Brahmans to Islam by compelling them to swallow cow's flesh. The Hindu sepoys, who had been taken prisoners by the Afghans during the Kabul war, were forced to become Muhammadans.

civil courts. This was resented by the sepoy as a grave indignity. He was no longer the great man of the family or village; he could no longer demand the special interference of the British Resident in their behalf. Accordingly he was exasperated at the introduction of British rule in Oude; at the same time he never manifested the slightest desire for the restoration of the ex-king.

In January, 1857, there were incendiary fires at Barrackpore. In February, General Hearsey, who commanded the Presidency division, expostulated with the sepoys on the absurdity of their fears as regarded their religion; but his words were without authority, and no one heeded them.

Toward the end of February a detachment of the Thirty-fourth Native Infantry at Barrackpore arrived at Berhampore, a hundred and twenty miles up country, near Murshedabad. Accordingly the sepoys from Barrackpore told the story of the cartridges to their comrades of the Nineteenth Native Infantry, which was stationed at Berhampore. A day or two afterward the sepoys of the Nineteenth refused to receive the cartridges that were served out to them; and at night-time they seized their arms, shouted defiance, and created a disturbance. Unfortunately there were no European soldiers at Berhampore; indeed there was only one European regiment in the whole line of country from Barrackpore to Patna, a distance of four hundred miles; and half of that was quartered at Fort William at Calcutta, and the other half at Dumdum, six miles from Calcutta.[1] Colonel Mitchell, the officer in command at Berhampore, had no force to bring to bear upon the mutinous infantry except a detachment of native cavalry and a battery of native artillery; and it was exceedingly doubtful whether they would act against their fellow-countrymen. However, the Nineteenth was not ripe

[1] There was also one European regiment at Dinapore, near Patna, and another at Agra. Beyond these there was nothing but a handful of European artillerymen and a few invalided soldiers of the Company's European army. The largest European force in Hindustan was stationed at Meerut, forty miles from Delhi.

for revolt; and after some remonstrances the sepoys laid down their arms and returned to the lines.

In March, the Eighty-fourth Europeans was brought away from Rangoon to the river Hughli. With this additional strength, Lord Canning resolved to take action. Accordingly the Nineteenth was marched from Berhampore to Barrackpore to be disbanded. Before it reached its destination there was much excitement in the lines of the Thirty-fourth, which probably originated in the sympathies of the sepoys for their comrades who were coming from Berhampore. A sepoy, named Mungal Pandy, walked about the lines with a loaded pistol, calling upon his comrades to rise, and threatening to shoot the first European that appeared. Lieutenant Baugh, the adjutant of the regiment, rode to the parade-ground, followed by the European sergeant and a Muhammadan orderly. Mungal Pandy fired at him, wounded his horse, and brought Lieutenant Baugh to the ground. A scuffle ensued; Baugh received a severe blow from a sword; while a guard of sepoys under a jemadar stood by and did nothing. The sergeant came up breathless, called on the jemadar for help, and tried to seize Mungal Pandy; but he too was struck down. To crown all, the jemadar came up with his twenty sepoys and began to beat the heads of the two Europeans with the butt-ends of their muskets. At this moment Mungal Pandy was arrested by the Muhammadan orderly; and General Hearsey galloped up, pistol in hand, and ordered the sepoy guard back to their posts, threatening to shoot the first man who disobeyed orders. The sepoys were overawed by the general, and the disaffection was stayed. Mungal Pandy saw that his game was up, and tried to shoot himself, but failed. A day or two afterward the European regiment from Rangoon was marched to Barrackpore; and the Nineteenth Native Infantry arrived from Berhampore, and was disbanded without further trouble. In the following April Mungal Pandy and the mutinous jemadar were brought to trial, convicted, and hanged.

For a brief interval it was hoped that the disaffection

was suppressed. Excitement manifested itself in various ways at different stations throughout the length of Hindustan and the Punjab—at Benares, Lukhnow, Agra, Umballa, and Sealkote. In some stations there were incendiary fires; in others the sepoys were wanting in their usual respect to their European officers. But it was believed that the storm was spending itself, and that the dark clouds were passing away.

Suddenly, on the 3d of May, there was an explosion at Lukhnow. A regiment of Oude Irregular Infantry, previously in the service of the king, broke out in mutiny and began to threaten their European officers. Sir Henry Lawrence, the new Chief Commissioner, had a European regiment at his disposal, namely, the Thirty-second Foot. That same evening he ordered out the regiment, and a battery of eight guns manned by Europeans, together with four sepoy regiments, three of infantry and one of cavalry. With this force he proceeded to the lines of the mutineers, about seven miles off. The Oude Irregulars were taken by surprise; they saw infantry and cavalry on either side, and the European guns in front. They were ordered to lay down their arms, and they obeyed. At this moment the artillery lighted their port fires. The mutineers were seized with a panic, and rushed away in the darkness; but the ringleaders and most of their followers were pursued and arrested by the native infantry and cavalry, and confined pending trial. Subsequently it transpired that the native regiments sympathized with the mutineers, and would have shown it but for their dread of Henry Lawrence and the Europeans. The energetic action of Lawrence sufficed to maintain order for another month in Oude. Meanwhile the Thirty-fourth Native Infantry was disbanded at Barrackpore, and again it was hoped that the disaffection was stayed.

The demon of mutiny was only scotched. Within a week of the outbreak at Lukhnow, the great military station of Meerut was in a blaze. Meerut was only forty miles from Delhi, and the largest cantonment in India. There were three regiments of sepoys—two of infantry and one of cavalry; but there were enough Europeans to scatter four times the number; namely, a battalion of the Sixtieth Rifles, a regiment of Dragoon Guards known as the Carabineers, two troops of horse artillery, and a light field battery.

In spite of the presence of Europeans there were more indications of excitement at Meerut than at any other station in the northwest. At Meerut the story of the greased cartridges had been capped by the story of the bone-dust; and there were the same kind of incendiary fires, the same lack of respect toward European officers, and the same whispered resolve not to touch the cartridges, as at Barrackpore. The station was commanded by General Hewitt, whose advancing years unfitted him to cope with the storm which was bursting upon Hindustan.

The regiment of sepoy cavalry at Meerut was strongly suspected of disaffection; accordingly it was resolved to put the men to the test. On the 6th of May it was paraded in the presence of the European force, and cartridges were served out; not the greased abominations from Calcutta, but the old ones which had been used times innumerable by the sepoys and their fathers. But the men were terrified and obstinate, and eighty-five stood out and refused to take the cartridges. The offenders were at once arrested, and tried by a court-martial of native officers; they were found guilty, and sentenced to various periods of imprisonment, but recommended for mercy. General Hewitt saw no grounds for mercy, excepting in the case of eleven young troopers; and on Saturday, the 9th of May, the sentences were carried out. The men were brought on parade, stripped of their uniforms, and loaded with irons. They implored the general for mercy, and finding it hopeless, began to reproach their comrades; but no one dared to strike a blow in the presence of loaded cannon and rifles. At last the prisoners were carried off and placed in a jail, not in charge of European soldiers, but under a native guard.

The military authorities at Meerut seem to have been

under a spell. The next day was Sunday, the 10th of May, and the hot sun rose with its usual glare in the Indian sky. The European barracks were at a considerable distance from the native lines, and the intervening space was covered with shops and houses surrounded by trees and gardens. Consequently the Europeans in the barracks knew nothing of what was going on in the native quarter. Meanwhile there were commotions in the sepoy lines and neighboring bazars. The sepoys were taunted by the loose women of the place with permitting their comrades to be imprisoned and fettered. At the same time they were smitten with a mad fear that the European soldiers were to be let loose upon them. The Europeans at Meerut saw nothing and heard nothing. Nothing was noted on that Sunday morning, excepting the absence of native servants from many of the houses, and that was supposed to be accidental. Morning service was followed by the midday heats, and at five o'clock in the afternoon the Europeans were again preparing for church. Suddenly there was an alarm of fire, followed by a volley of musketry, discordant yells, the clattering of cavalry, and the bugle sounding an alarm. The sepoys had worked themselves up to a frenzy of excitement; the prisoners were released with a host of jail birds; the native infantry joined the native cavalry, and the colonel of one of the regiments was shot by the sepoys of the other. Inspired by a wild fear and fury, the sepoys ran about murdering or wounding every European they met, and setting houses on fire, amid deafening shouts and uproar.

Meanwhile there were fatal delays in turning out the Europeans. The Rifles were paraded for church, and time was lost in getting arms and serving out ball cartridges. The Carabineers were absurdly put through a roll call, and then lost their way among the shops and gardens. Meanwhile European officers were being butchered by the infuriated sepoys. Gentlemen and ladies were fired at or sabred while hurrying back in a panic from church. Flaming houses and crashing timbers were filling all hearts with terror, and the shades of evening were falling upon the general havoc and turmoil, when the Europeans reached the native lines and found that the sepoys had gone, no one knew whither.

The truth was soon told. The mutiny had become a revolt; the sepoys were on the way to Delhi to proclaim the old Moghul as sovereign of Hindustan; and there was no Gillespie to gallop after them and crush the revolt at its outset, as had been done at Vellore half a century before. One thing, however, was done. There were no European regiments at Delhi; nothing but three regiments of sepoy infantry, and a battery of native artillery. The station was commanded by Brigadier Graves; and there were no Europeans under his orders excepting the officers and sergeants attached to the three native corps. Accordingly telegrams were sent to Brigadier Graves to tell him that the mutineers were on their way to Delhi.

Monday at Delhi was worse than the Sunday at Meerut. The British cantonment was situated on a rising ground about two miles from the city, which was known as the Ridge. The great magazine, containing immense stores of ammunition, was situated in the heart of the city. One of the three sepoy regiments was on duty in the city; the other two remained in the cantonment on the Ridge.

The approach to Delhi from Meerut was defended by the little river Hindun, which was traversed by a small bridge. It was proposed to procure a couple of cannon from the magazine and place them on the bridge; but before this could be done the rebel cavalry from Meerut were seen crossing the river, and were subsequently followed by the rebel infantry. The magazine remained in charge of Lieutenant Willoughby of the Bengal Artillery. He was associated with two other officers, and six conductors and sergeants; the rest of the establishment was composed entirely of natives.

Brigadier Graves did his best to protect the city and cantonment until the arrival of the expected Europeans from Meerut. Indeed, throughout the morning and greater part of the afternoon every one in Delhi was expecting the arrival of the Europeans. Brigadier Graves ordered all the non-military residents, including ladies and children, to repair to Flagstaff Tower—a round building of solid brickwork at some distance from the city. Large detachments of sepoys were sent from the Ridge to the Kashmir gate, under the command of their European officers, to help the sepoy regiment on duty to maintain order in the city.

Presently the rebel troops from Meerut came up, accompanied by the insurgent rabble of Delhi. The English officers prepared to charge them, and gave the order to fire, but some of the sepoys refused to obey, or only fired into the air. The English officers held on, expecting the European soldiers from Meerut. The sepoys hesitated to join the rebels, out of dread of the coming Europeans. At last the Delhi sepoys threw in their lot with the rebels, and shot down their own officers. The revolt spread throughout the whole city; and the suspense of the English on the Ridge, and at Flagstaff Tower, began to give way to the agony of despair.

Suddenly, at four o'clock in the afternoon, a column of white smoke arose from the city, and an explosion was heard far and wide. Willoughby and his eight associates had held out to the last, waiting and hoping for the coming of the Europeans. They had closed and barricaded the gates of the magazine; and they had posted six-pounders at the gates, loaded with double charges of grape, and laid a train to the powder magazine. Messengers came in the name of Bahadur Shah to demand the surrender of the magazine, but no answer was returned. The enemy approached and raised ladders against the walls; while the native establishment escaped over some sheds and joined the rebels. At this crisis the guns opened fire. Round after round of grape made fearful havoc on the mass of humanity that was heaving and surging round the gates. At last the ammunition was exhausted. No one could leave the guns to bring up more shot. The mutineers were pouring in on all sides. Lieutenant Willoughby gave the signal; Conductor Scully fired the train; and with one tremendous upheaval the magazine was blown into the air, together with fifteen hundred rebels. Not one of the gallant nine had expected to escape. Willoughby and three others got away, scorched, maimed, bruised, and nearly insensible; but Scully and his comrades were never seen again. Willoughby died of his injuries six weeks afterward, while India and Europe were ringing with his name.

All this while bloody tragedies were taking place within the palace at Delhi. The rebels from Meerut were quartering themselves in the royal precincts, and murdering every European they could find. Mr. Fraser the commissioner, Mr. Hutchinson the collector, and Captain Douglas, who commanded the palace guards, were all slaughtered within the palace walls. So was an English chaplain, with his wife, daughter, and another young lady, all of whom had been residing as guests with Captain Douglas. Fifty Christian people—men, women, and children—who had been captured by the rebels and thrown as prisoners in the palace dungeons, were butchered in cold blood by the order of the king.[1]

On the evening of that terrible Monday all was lost. The city of Delhi was in the hands of the rebels. The so-called royal family, which had been maintained by the generosity of the British government for more than half a century, had joined the rebel sepoys. Brigadier Graves and the surviving officers on the Ridge, and all the anxious fugitives in Flagstaff Tower, were compelled to fly for their lives. Their subsequent trials and sufferings were among the most touching episodes in the story of the great convulsion. Meanwhile the European regiments which might have saved them, and saved Delhi, were kept at Meerut to guard the barracks and treasury. The greased cartridges had created the panic and brought about the mutiny; but it was the

---

[1] The old king, Bahadur Shah, has been held responsible for these murders, but his vindictive queen was probably more to blame. Her son, a mere lad at the time, was appointed vizier to his father.

SEPOY REBELS BEING SHOT FROM THE MOUTHS OF THE CANNON

India. vol. two.

incapacity of the military authorities at Meerut that raised the revolt in Hindustan.

The revolution at Delhi opened the eyes of Lord Canning to the gravity of the crisis. Hitherto his sympathies had been with the sepoys. An ignorant and credulous soldiery had been thrown into a panic, and had been worked into a state of perilous excitement by intriguing Brahmans and fanatical Mullas, as well as by secret agents and alarmists of all kinds. But now the excitement had culminated in intoxication and madness; the sepoys were thirsting for the blood of Europeans; and pity was changed to indignation and horror. Accordingly Lord Canning telegraphed for European regiments from every quarter—from Bombay and Burma, from Madras and Ceylon—to crush a rebellion which was establishing a reign of terror in Hindustan.

The sepoy mutiny at Barrackpore might possibly have been crushed at the outset by physical force. In 1824, at the beginning of the Burmese war, there was a similar mutiny at the same cantonment. Three sepoy regiments had been ordered to Chittagong, but refused to march. They had been frightened by rumors of the bad climate of Burma, and the magical arts which were said to be practiced by the Burmese. There had also been some difficulties about transport, and they demanded an extra allowance, known as double batta. Sir Edward Paget was Commander-in-chief in Bengal. He marched to Barrackpore with two regiments of Europeans and a detachment of artillery. He paraded the disaffected regiments in the presence of the Europeans, and loaded his guns with grape. The sepoys were told that they must either begin the march or ground their arms. They replied with defiant shouts. Then the fatal order was given, and the guns opened fire on the disaffected soldiery. Eleven sepoys only were killed, but the remainder broke up and fled in a panic of terror. Sir Edward Paget was much censured, but a generation passed away before there was another mutiny.

Whether Paget was right or wrong, it would have been

a blunder and a crime to have taken such an extreme measure at the outset of the disaffection in 1857. Indeed, Lord Canning indignantly refused to contemplate such measures; and by so doing he saved the reputation of the British nation. But when the sepoy rebels set up the Moghul at Delhi as their nominal sovereign, the security of the population of India was at stake. In other words, the establishment of the supremacy of the British government at the earliest possible date was necessary, not only for the safety of the British empire in India, but for the salvation of the masses.

The progress of the revolt throws no further light on its origin or character. Station after station followed the example of Meerut. The sepoys seem to have all been infected by the same delirious fever; they rose in mutiny, shot down their officers in most cases, set the buildings on fire, plundered the treasury, and then rushed off to Delhi. Wherever, however, the Europeans were in any force, and were brought directly to bear upon the mutineers regardless of red tape and routine, the station was either saved from destruction, or the mischief was reduced to a minimum.

It would be tedious and needless to tell the story of the sepoy revolt so far as it was a mere military mutiny, with Delhi for its headquarters. But at three stations the mutiny was more or less of a political character, which imparts an individuality to the history; namely, at Lukhnow, at Jhansi, and at Cawnpore.

The city of Lukhnow, the capital of Oude, extends four miles along the right bank of the river Goomti. All the principal buildings, including the British Residency, were situated between the city and the river. The Residency was a large walled enclosure, comprising not only the mansion of the Chief Commissioner, but several houses and underground buildings on a large scale. Near it was a strong turreted, castellated structure known as the Muchi Bawun.

Ever since the explosion at Lukhnow on the 3d of May, Sir Henry Lawrence had been incessantly occupied in taking precautionary measures against an outbreak which he knew to be inevitable. On one side of the Residency was a disaffected city, the homes of palace parasites, who had been deprived of their means of subsistence by the breaking up of the native court and departure of the royal family to Calcutta. On the opposite bank of the river Goomti was the native cantonment, occupied by British sepoys as evilly disposed toward the English as the disaffected rabble of Lukhnow. Accordingly Sir Henry Lawrence saw that the work before him was to prevent mutiny in the cantonment and rebellion in the city; and to make every preparation for a successful defence in the event of a general insurrection.

The native force at Lukhnow consisted of the three sepoy regiments of infantry, and one of cavalry; there was also a native battery of artillery. The whole numbered thirty-five hundred men. The European force consisted of the Thirty-second Foot, numbering five hundred and seventy strong, and sixty artillerymen.

The communication between the cantonment and the city was by two bridges; one near the Residency, and the other at the Muchi Bawun. Sir Henry Lawrence brought all the European non-combatants with their families within the Residency walls; and took steps to prevent any combined movements on the part of the cantonment and city. He disposed his troops, European and native, in such a way as to bear directly on the sepoys in the event of a rising; and he established a strong post between the Residency and the Muchi Bawun to command the two bridges leading to cantonments.

At nine o'clock on the night of the 30th of May, the outbreak began at the native cantonment. Shots were fired as a signal, and parties of sepoys began to burn down the bungalows and shoot their European officers. Presently the insurgents rushed to the bridges, infuriated with bhang and excitement, but were received with such a volley of grape that they retreated toward their lines hotly pursued by Sir Henry Lawrence and his Europeans. They attempted to return to the cantonment, but found it hopeless, and made off to Delhi. Sir Henry Lawrence dared not pursue them with a disaffected city in his rear, which was already surging with excitement. Accordingly, he left a detachment of Europeans to guard the cantonment, and then returned to Lukhnow. Of all the thirty-five hundred sepoys, scarcely a fourth remained true to their colors, and these gradually dropped off during the progress of the rebellion.

On the 4th of June there was a mutiny at Jhansi—a little chiefship of Bundelkund, which had lapsed to the British government in 1853 from want of natural heirs. The town was situated about a hundred and forty miles to the south of Agra. It was garrisoned entirely by sepoys, and the mutiny was of the usual type. The sepoys went about burning and murdering; while the Europeans, including women and children, and numbering fifty-five in all, took refuge in the fort.

At this moment, the Rani of Jhansi, the widow of the deceased chief, sent guns and elephants to help the mutineers. She was a vindictive woman, inflamed with the blind ferocity of an Oriental, and burning to be revenged on the English for not having been intrusted with the adoption of a son, and the management of the little principality.

The fugitives in the fort were short of provisions; they could not have held out for twenty-four hours longer. The Rani solemnly swore that if they surrendered the fort without further fighting their lives should be spared and they should be conducted in safety to some other station. The rebel sepoys took the same oath, and the little garrison were tempted to accept the terms and leave the fort two by two. With fiendish treachery the whole fifty-five—men, women, and children—were seized and bound, and butchered in cold blood, by the orders of the Rani.

Still more terrible and treacherous were the tragedies enacted at Cawnpore, a city situated on the Ganges about fifty-five miles to the southwest of Lukhnow. Cawnpore had been in the possession of the English ever since the beginning of the century, and for many years was one of the most important military stations in India; but the extension of the British empire over the Punjab had diminished the importance of Cawnpore; and the last European regiment quartered there had been removed to the northwest at the close of the previous year.

In May, 1857, there were four native regiments at Cawnpore, numbering thirty-five hundred sepoys. There were no Europeans whatever, excepting the regimental officers, and sixty-one artillerymen. To these were added small detachments of European soldiers, which had been sent in the hour of peril from Lukhnow and Benares during the month of May.

The station of Cawnpore was commanded by Sir Hugh Wheeler, a distinguished general in the Company's service, who was verging on his seventieth year. He had spent fifty-four years in India, and had served only with native troops. He must have known the sepoys better than any other European in India. He had led them against their own countrymen under Lord Lake; against foreigners during the Afghan war; and against Sikhs during both campaigns in the Punjab.

The news of the revolt at Meerut threw the sepoys into a ferment at every military station in Hindustan. Rumors of mutiny, or coming mutiny, formed almost the only topic of conversation; yet in nearly every sepoy regiment the European officers put faith in their men, and fondly believed that though the rest of the army might revolt yet their own corps would prove faithful. Such was eminently the case at Cawnpore, yet General Wheeler seems to have known better. While the European officers continued to sleep every night in the sepoy lines, the old veteran made his preparations for meeting the coming storm.

European combatants were very few at Cawnpore, but European impedimenta were very heavy. Besides the wives and families of the regimental officers of the sepoy regiments there was a large European mercantile community. Moreover, while the Thirty-second Foot was quartered at Lukhnow, the wives, families, and invalids of the regiment were residing at Cawnpore. It was thus necessary to secure a place of refuge for this miscellaneous multitude of Europeans in the event of a rising of the sepoys. Accordingly General Wheeler pitched upon some old barracks which had once belonged to a European regiment; and he ordered earthworks to be thrown up, and supplies of all kinds to be stored up, in order to stand a siege. Unfortunately there was fatal neglect somewhere; for when the crisis came the defences were found to be worthless, while the supplies were insufficient for the besieged.

All this while the adopted son of the ex-Peishwa was residing at Bithoor, about six miles from Cawnpore. His real name was Dhundu Punt, but he is better known as Nana Sahib. The British government had refused to award him the absurd life pension of eighty thousand pounds sterling which had been granted to his nominal father; but he had inherited at least half a million from the ex-Peishwa; and he was allowed to keep six guns, to entertain as many followers as he pleased, and to live in half royal state in a castellated palace at Bithoor. He continued to nurse his grievance with all the pertinacity of a Mahratta; but at the same time he professed a great love for European society, and was profuse in his hospitalities to English officers, and was popularly known as the Raja of Bithoor.

When the news arrived of the revolt at Meerut on the 10th of May, the Nana was loud in his professions of attachment to the English. He engaged to organize fifteen hundred fighting men to act against the sepoys in the event of an outbreak. On May 21st there was an alarm. European ladies and families, with all European non-combatants, were removed into the barracks; and General Wheeler actually accepted from the Nana the help of two hundred Mahrattas and a couple of guns to guard the treasury. The alarm, however, soon blew over, and the Nana took up his abode at the civil station at Cawnpore, as a proof of the sincerity of his professions.

At last, on the night of the 4th of June, the sepoy regiments at Cawnpore broke out in mutiny. They were driven to action by the same mad terror which had been manifested elsewhere. They cared nothing for the Moghul, nothing for the pageant king at Delhi; but they had been panic-stricken by extravagant stories of coming destruction. It was whispered among them that the parade ground was undermined with powder, and that Hindus and Muhammadans were to be assembled on a given day and blown into the air. Intoxicated with fear and bhang, they rushed out in the darkness —yelling, shooting, and burning according to their wont; and when their excitement was somewhat spent, they marched off toward Delhi. Sir Hugh Wheeler could do nothing. He might have retreated with the whole body of Europeans from Cawnpore to Allahabad; but there had been a mutiny at Allahabad, and moreover he had no means of transport. Subsequently he heard that the mutineers had reached the first stage on the road to Delhi, and consequently he saw no ground for alarm.

Meanwhile the brain of Nana Sahib had been turned by wild dreams of vengeance and sovereignty. He thought not only to wreak his malice upon the English, but to restore the extinct Mahratta empire, and reign over Hindustan as the representative of the forgotten Peishwas. The stampede of the sepoys to Delhi was fatal to his mad ambition. He overtook the mutineers, dazzled them with fables of the treasures in Wheeler's intrenchment, and brought them back to Cawnpore to carry out his vindictive and visionary schemes.

At early morning on Saturday, the 6th of June, General Wheeler received a letter from the Nana, announcing that he was about to attack the intrenchment. The veteran was taken by surprise, but at once ordered all the European officers to join the party in the barracks, and prepare for the defence. But the mutineers were in no hurry for the advance. They preferred booty to battle, and turned aside to plunder the cantonment and city, murdering every Christian that came in their way, and not sparing the houses of their own countrymen. They appropriated all the cannon and ammunition in the magazine by way of preparation for the siege; but some were wise enough to desert the rebel army, and steal away to their homes with their ill-gotten spoil.

About noon the main body of the mutineers, swelled by the numerous retainers of the Nana, got their guns into position, and opened fire on the intrenchment. For nineteen days—from the 6th to the 25th of June—the garrison struggled manfully against a raking fire and fearful odds, amid scenes of suffering and bloodshed which cannot be recalled without a shudder. It was the height of the hot weather in Hindustan. A blazing sun was burning over the heads of the besieged; and to add to their misery, one of the barracks containing the sick and wounded was destroyed by fire. The besiegers, however, in spite of their overwhelming numbers, were utterly unable to carry the intrenchment by storm, but continued to pour in a raking fire. Meanwhile the garrison was starving from want of provisions, and hampered by a multitude of helpless women and children. Indeed, but for the latter contingency, the gallant band would have rushed out of the intrenchment, and cut a way through the mob of sepoys, or perished in the attempt. As it was, they could only fight on, waiting for reinforcements that never came, until fever, sunstroke, hunger, madness, or the enemy's fire, delivered them from their suffering and despair.

On the 25th of June a woman brought a slip of writing from the Nana, promising to give a safe passage to Allahabad to all who were willing to lay down their arms.[1] Had there been no women or children the European garrison would never have dreamed of surrender. The massacre at Patna a century before had taught a lesson to Englishmen which ought never to have been forgotten. As it was, there were some who wanted to fight on till the bitter end. But

---

[1] Nana Sahib pretended to grant this boon only to those who were not connected with the acts of Lord Dalhousie. Subsequent events prove that this was sheer hypocrisy.

the majority saw that there was no hope for the women or the children, the sick or the wounded, except by accepting the proffered terms. Accordingly the pride of Englishmen gave way, and an armistice was proclaimed.

Next morning the terms were negotiated. The English garrison were to surrender their position, their guns, and their treasure, but to march out with their arms, and with sixty rounds of ammunition in the pouch of every man. Nana Sahib on his part was to afford a safe conduct to the river bank, about a mile off; to provide carriage for the conveyance of the women and children, the sick and the wounded; and to furnish boats for carrying the whole party, numbering some four hundred and fifty individuals, down the river Ganges to Allahabad. The Nana accepted the terms, but demanded the evacuation of the intrenchment that very night. General Wheeler protested against this proviso. The Nana began to bully, and to threaten that he would open fire. He was told that he might carry the intrenchment if he could, but that the English had enough powder left to blow both armies into the air. Accordingly the Nana agreed to wait till the morrow.

At early morning on the 27th of June the garrison began to move from the intrenchment to the place of embarkation. The men marched on foot; the women and children were carried on elephants and bullock-carts, while the wounded were mostly conveyed in palanquins. Forty boats with thatched roofs, known as budgerows, were moored in shallow water at a little distance from the bank; and the crowd of fugitives were forced to wade through the river to the boats. By nine o'clock the whole four hundred and fifty were huddled on board, and the boats prepared to leave Cawnpore.

Suddenly a bugle was sounded, and a murderous fire of grape shot and musketry was opened upon the wretched passengers from both sides of the river. At the same time the thatching of many of the budgerows was found to be on fire, and the flames began to spread from boat to boat. Numbers were murdered in the river, but at last the firing ceased. A few escaped down the river, but only four men survived to tell the story of the massacre.[1] A mass of fugitives were dragged ashore; the women and children, to the number of a hundred and twenty-five, were carried off and lodged in a house near the headquarters of the Nana. The men were ordered to immediate execution. One of them had preserved a Prayer-book, and was permitted to read a few sentences of the liturgy to his doomed companions. Then the fatal order was given; the sepoys poured in a volley of musketry, and all was over.

On the 1st of July Nana Sahib went off to his palace at Bithoor, and was proclaimed Peishwa. He took his seat upon the throne, and was installed with all the ceremonies of sovereignty, while the cannon roared out a salute in his honor. At night the whole place was illuminated, and the hours of darkness were whiled away with feasting and fireworks. But his triumph was short-lived. The Muhammadans were plotting against him at Cawnpore. The people were leaving the city to escape the coming storm, and were taking refuge in the villages. English reinforcements were at last coming up from Allahabad, while the greedy sepoys were clamoring for money and gold bangles. Accordingly the Nana hastened back to Cawnpore, and scattered wealth with a lavish hand; and sought to hide his fears by boastful proclamations, and to drown his anxieties in drink and debauchery.

Within a few days more the number of helpless prisoners was increased to two hundred. There had been a mutiny at Futtehgurh, higher up the river, and the fugitives had fled in boats to Cawnpore, a distance of eighty miles. They knew nothing of what had transpired, and were all taken prisoners by the rebels, and brought on shore. The men

---

[1] The survivors were Lieutenants Mowbray-Thomson and Delafosse, and Privates Murphy and Sullivan.

were all butchered in presence of the Nana; the women and children, eighty in number, were sent to join the wretched sufferers in the house near the Nana.

Meanwhile Colonel Neill, commanding the Madras Fusiliers,[1] was pushing up from Calcutta. He was bent on the relief of Cawnpore and Lukhnow, but was delayed on the way by the mutinies at Benares and Allahabad. In July he was joined at Allahabad by a column under General Havelock, who was destined within a few short weeks to win a lasting name in history.

General Havelock was a Queens officer of forty years' standing; but he had seen more service in India than perhaps any other officer in her Majesty's army. He had fought in the first Burma war, the Kabul war, the Gwalior campaign of 1843, and the Punjab campaign of 1845–6. He was a pale, thin, thoughtful man; small in stature, but burning with the aspirations of a puritan hero. Religion was the ruling principle of his life, and military glory was his master passion. He had just returned to India after commanding a division in the Persian war. Abstemious to a fault, he was able, in spite of his advancing years, to bear up against the heat and rain of Hindustan during the deadliest season of the year.

On the 7th of July General Havelock left Allahabad for Cawnpore. The force at his disposal did not exceed two thousand men, Europeans and Sikhs. He had heard of the massacre at Cawnpore on the 27th of June, and burned to avenge it. On the 12th of July he defeated a large force of mutineers and Mahrattas at Futtehpore. On the 15th he inflicted two more defeats on the enemy. Havelock was now within twenty-two miles of Cawnpore, and he halted his men to rest for the night. But news arrived that the women and children were still alive at Cawnpore, and that

---

[1] The Madras Fusiliers was a European regiment which had been raised by the East India Company for local service. It fought under Clive at Arcot and Plassy. At the amalgamation of the army of the Company with that of the Queen it became the One Hundred and Second Foot.

the Nana had taken the field with a large force to oppose his advance. Accordingly Havelock marched fourteen miles that same night, and on the following morning, within eight miles of Cawnpore, the troops bivouacked beneath some trees.

On that same night, the 15th of July, the crowning atrocity was committed at Cawnpore. The rebels, who had been defeated by Havelock, returned to the Nana with the tidings of their disaster. In revenge the Nana ordered the slaughter of the two hundred women and children. The poor victims were literally hacked to death, or almost to death, with swords, bayonets, knives, and axes. Next morning the bleeding remains of dead and dying were dragged to a neighboring well and thrown in.

At two o'clock in the afternoon after the massacre, the force under Havelock was again upon the march for Cawnpore. The heat was fearful; many of the troops were struck down by the sun, and the cries for water were continuous. But for two miles the column toiled on, and then came in sight of the enemy. Havelock had only one thousand Europeans and three hundred Sikhs; he had no cavalry, and his artillery was inferior. The enemy numbered five thousand men, armed and trained by British officers, strongly intrenched, with two batteries of guns of heavy calibre. Havelock's artillery failed to silence the batteries, and he ordered the Europeans to charge with the bayonet. On they went in the face of a shower of grape, but the bayonet charge was as irresistible at Cawnpore as at Assaye. The enemy fought for a while like men in a death struggle. Nana Sahib was with them, but nothing is known of his exploits. At last they broke and fled, and there was no cavalry to pursue them.

As yet nothing was known of the butchery of the women and children. Havelock halted for the night, and next morning marched his force into the station at Cawnpore. The men beheld the scene of the massacre, and saw the bleeding remains in the well. But the murderers had vanished, no one knew whither. Havelock advanced to Bithoor, and destroyed the palace of the Mahratta. Subsequently he was joined by General Neill, with reinforcements from Allahabad; and on the 20th of July he set out for the relief of Lukhnow, leaving Cawnpore in charge of General Neill.

The defence of Lukhnow against fifty thousand rebels was, next to the siege of Delhi, the greatest event in the mutiny. The whole province of Oude was in a blaze of insurrection. The Talukdars were exasperated at the hard measure dealt out to them before the appointment of Sir Henry Lawrence as Chief Commissioner. Disbanded sepoys, returning to their homes in Oude, swelled the tide of disaffection. Bandits that had been suppressed under British administration returned to their old work of robbery and brigandage. All classes took advantage of the anarchy to murder the money-lenders.[1] Meanwhile the country was bristling with the fortresses of the Talukdars; and the cultivators, deprived of the protection of the English, naturally flocked for refuge to the strongholds of their old masters.

The English, who had been lords of Hindustan ever since the beginning of the century, had been closely besieged in the Residency at Lukhnow ever since the final outbreak of the 30th of May. For nearly two months the garrison

---

[1] Money-lenders in India are a special institution. The masses are in a normal state of debt. They are compelled by custom to incur large expenses at every marriage and festival, and in consequence are driven to borrow of money-lenders. An enormous rate of interest is charged, and a son becomes responsible for the debts of his father.

Under native rule loans were regarded as debts of honor, or rather of piety. They might possibly be recovered in a civil tribunal, but native courts were hopelessly corrupt, and the judge always appropriated a fourth of the claim as his rightful fee. Accordingly the payment was regarded not so much a legal obligation as an act of piety, except in cases of forgery or cheating.

The introduction of British administration put all such debts on a new footing. A money-lender could enforce the payment of a decree in the civil court; and lands and personal property were alike treated as available assets. Accordingly soon after the annexation of Oude the people became very bitter against the English courts. When the courts were closed in consequence of the mutiny, the people wreaked their vengeance upon the money-lenders.

A law against usury would scarcely remedy the evil. The people have been so long accustomed to high rates of interest that they would continue to pay them in spite of the law, from a sense of religious obligation.

had held out with a dauntless intrepidity, while confidently waiting for reinforcements that seemed never to come. "Never surrender" had been from the first the passionate conviction of Sir Henry Lawrence; and the massacre at Cawnpore on the 27th of June impressed every soldier in the garrison with a like resolution. On the 2d of July the Muchi Bawun was abandoned, and the garrison and stores removed to the Residency. On the 4th of July Sir Henry Lawrence was killed by the bursting of a shell in a room where he lay wounded; and his dying counsel to those around him was "Never surrender!"

On the 20th of July the rebel force round Lukhnow heard of the advance of General Havelock to Cawnpore, and attacked the Residency in overwhelming force. They kept up a continual fire of musketry while pounding away with their heavy guns; but the garrison held their ground against shot and shell, and before the day was over the dense masses of assailants were forced to retire from the walls.

Between the 20th and 25th of July General Havelock began to cross the Ganges, and make his way into Oude territory; but he was unable to relieve Lukhnow. His small force was weakened by heat and fever, and reduced by cholera and dysentery; while the enemy occupied strong positions on both flanks. In the middle of August he fell back upon Cawnpore. Meanwhile General Neill was threatened on his right by the Nana, who reoccupied Bithoor in great strength; and on his left by a large force of rebel sepoys; and he could not attack either without leaving his intrenchment exposed to the other.

On the 16th of August Havelock left a detachment at Cawnpore, and advanced toward Bithoor with fifteen hundred men. He found the enemy drawn up in a position which revealed the handiwork of a born general. The infantry were posted in front of an intrenched battery, which was nearly masked with sugar canes, and defended with thick ramparts of mud. This position was flanked on both sides by intrenched quadrangles filled with sepoys, and sheltered by plantations of sugar cane.[1] Havelock brought up his guns and opened fire; but the infantry had only been posted in front of the enemy's intrenchment to draw the English on. The moment Havelock's guns began to fire, the infantry retreated into their defences, while the batteries poured a storm of shot and shell upon the advancing line of the British army. After twenty minutes Havelock saw that his guns made no impression on the enemy's fire, and ordered a charge with the bayonet. Again the English bayonets prevailed against native batteries, and the enemy fled in all directions. Havelock, however, had no cavalry for the pursuit, and was compelled once more to fall back on Cawnpore. Thus ended Havelock's first campaign for the relief of Lukhnow.

All this while the Mahratta and Rajput princes remained loyal to the British government. They had nothing to do with the sepoy mutiny, for they were evidently taken by surprise and could not understand it; and if some held aloof, and appeared to await events, there were others who made common cause with the British government at the outset. But the sepoys in the subsidiary armies, who were commanded by British officers, were as much terrified and troubled by the greased cartridges as those in the Bengal regiments; and the revolt at Delhi on the 11th of May acted upon them in the same way as it acted upon the sepoys in British territories. The Gwalior Contingent, which was largely composed of Oude soldiery, was more than once inclined to mutiny; but Maharaja Sindia managed to temporize with them; and they did not finally break away from Gwalior until the following October. At Indore the army of Holkar broke out in mutiny and attacked the British Residency, and then went off through Gwalior territory to join the rebels near Agra; but at that time the Gwalior

---

[1] The only rebel leader who showed a real genius for war throughout the mutinies was a Mahratta Brahman, in the service of the Nana, known as Tantia Topi. No doubt it was Tantia Topi who drew up the rebel army at Bithoor.

soldiery were tolerably stanch, and refused to accompany them.[1]

During the four months that followed the revolt at Delhi on the 11th of May, all political interest was centred at the ancient capital of the sovereigns of Hindustan. The public mind was occasionally distracted by the current of events at Cawnpore and Lukhnow, as well as at other stations which need not be particularized; but so long as Delhi remained in the hands of the rebels, the native princes were bewildered and alarmed; and its prompt recapture was deemed of vital importance to the prestige of the British government, and the re-establishment of British sovereignty in Hindustan. The Great Moghul had been little better than a mummy for more than half a century; and Bahadur Shah was a mere tool and puppet in the hands of rebel sepoys; but nevertheless the British government had to deal with the astounding fact that the rebels were fighting under his name and standard, just as Afghans and Mahrattas had done in the days of Ahmad Shah Durani and Mahadaji Sindia. To make matters worse, the roads to Delhi were open from the south and east; and nearly every outbreak in Hindustan was followed by a stampede of mutineers to the old capital of the Moghuls.

Meanwhile, in the absence of railways, there were unfortunate delays in bringing up troops and guns to stamp out the fires of rebellion at the head centre.[2] The highway from

---

[1] Major, afterward General, Sir Henry Durand, who had served for eight years as political agent at Bhopal, was residing at Indore at this crisis, as agent to the Governor-General in Central India. The Residency at Indore held out until the safety of the ladies and their families was secured; and the subsequent hospitable reception of the refugees by the late Begum of Bhopal is a touching illustration of the loyalty of a native princess toward the British government.

Sir John Kaye, in the first edition of his history of the sepoy revolt, was unfortunately led to give currency to an untrue statement about Major Durand's conduct at Indore. It is gratifying to know that before he died he publicly retracted the insinuation.

[2] The deaths of successive Commanders-in-chief led to other delays. The news of the revolt at Delhi brought General Anson down from Simla to undertake the siege of Delhi; but he died at Kurnal on the 27th of May. Sir Henry Barnard, who succeeded him as Commander-in-chief, died on the 5th July.

Calcutta to Delhi was blocked up by mutiny and insurrection; and every European soldier sent up from Calcutta was stopped for the relief of Benares, Allahabad, Cawnpore, or Lukhnow. But the possession of the Punjab at this crisis proved to be the salvation of the empire. Sir John Lawrence, the Chief Commissioner, was called upon to perform almost superhuman work—to maintain order in a newly conquered province; to suppress mutiny and disaffection among the very sepoy regiments from Bengal who were supposed to garrison the country; and to send reinforcements of troops and guns, and supplies of all descriptions, to the siege of Delhi. Fortunately the Sikhs had been only a few short years under British administration; they had not forgotten the miseries that prevailed under the native government, and could appreciate the many blessings they enjoyed under British rule. They were stanch to the British government, and eager to be led against the rebels. In some cases terrible punishment was meted out to mutinous Bengal sepoys within the Punjab;[1] but the imperial interests at stake were sufficient to justify every severity, although all must regret the painful necessity that called for such extreme measures.

On the 8th of June, about a month after the revolt at Delhi, Sir Henry Barnard took the field at Alipore, about ten miles from the rebel capital. He defeated an advance division of the enemy; and then marched to the Ridge, and reoccupied the old cantonment which had been abandoned on the 11th of May. So far it was clear that the rebels were unable to do anything in the open field, although they might fight bravely under cover. They numbered about thirty thousand strong; they had a very powerful artillery, and ample stores of ammunition; while there was an abundance of provisions within the city throughout the siege.

General Reed succeeded Barnard, but was compelled by ill health to resign the appointment on the 17th July. General Wilson of the Bengal artillery then took the command, while Colonel Baird Smith was chief engineer.

[1] The wholesale executions in the Twenty-sixth Regiment of native infantry, which were carried out by the late Mr. Cooper, can only be justified by stern necessity.

The defences of Delhi covered an area of three square miles. The walls consisted of a series of bastions, about sixteen feet high, connected by long curtains, with occasional martello towers to aid the flanking fire. Every bastion was mounted with eleven guns; namely, one on the salient, three on each face, and two on each flank. Both bastions and curtains were built of masonry about twelve feet thick. Running round the base of these bastions and curtains was a berm or terrace varying in width from fifteen to thirty feet, having on its exterior edge a wall loop-holed for musketry. The whole was surrounded by a ditch twenty feet deep and twenty-five feet wide.[1] On the eastern side of the city the river Jumna ran past the palace of the king and the old state prison of Selimgurh. The bridge of boats leading to Meerut was in front of Selimgurh.

There were seven gates to the city, namely, Lahore gate, Ajmir gate, Turkoman gate, Delhi gate, Mori gate, Kabul gate, and Kashmir gate. The principal street was the Chandni Chouk, which ran in a direct line from the Delhi gate to the palace of the Moghuls. The great mosque, known as the Juma Musjid, stands on a rocky eminence at the back of the Chandni Chouk.

The British camp on the Ridge presented a picture at once varied and striking; long lines of European tents, thatched hovels of the native servants, rows of horses, parks of artillery, English soldiers in their gray linen coats and trousers, Sikhs with their red and blue turbans, Afghans with their gay headdresses and colored saddle-cloths, and the Ghorkas in Kilmarnock hats and woollen coats. There were but few Hindu sepoys in the British ranks, but the native servants were very numerous. In the rear were the booths of the native bazars; and further out in the plain were thousands of camels, bullocks and baggage horses. Still further to

---

[1] Meeting of the Bengal Army, London, 1858. Bacon's First Impressions of Hindustan, London, 1837. The loop-holed wall was a continuation of the escarp or inner wall of the ditch. The counterscarp, or outer wall of the ditch, was not of masonry, but was a mere earthen slope of easy incline.

the rear was a small river crossed by two bridges; but the bridges were subsequently blown up. On the extreme right of the camp, on a spot nearest the city walls, was a battery on an eminence, known as the Mound battery, which faced the Mori gate. Hard by was Hindu Rao's[1] house, the head-quarters of the army during the siege. From the summit of the Ridge was to be seen the river Jumna winding along to the left of the city: the bridge of boats, the towers of the palace, the minarets of the great mosque of the Juma Musjid, the house roofs and gardens of the doomed city, and the picturesque walls, with batteries here and there sending forth white clouds of smoke among the green foliage that clustered round the ramparts.

To the right of the Mound battery was the old suburb known as the Subzi Mundi. It was the vegetable bazar which figures in the scandalous stories of the later Moghul princes as the scene of their frolics and debaucheries. It was occupied by old houses, gardens with high walls, and narrow streets and lanes; and thus it furnished the very cover which makes Asiatics brave.[2] Similar suburbs intervened between the actual defences of Delhi and the whole line of the English position.

For many weeks the British army on the Ridge was unable to attempt siege operations. It was, in fact, the besieged rather than the besiegers; for although the bridges in the rear were blown up, the camp was exposed to continual assaults from all the other sides.

On the 23d of June, the hundredth anniversary of the battle of Plassy, the enemy made a greater effort than ever to carry the British position. The attack began on the right

---

[1] Hindu Rao is one of the forgotten celebrities who flourished about fifty years ago. He was a brother of Baiza Bai, the ambitious widow of Daulat Rao Sindia, who worried Lord William Bentinck. Hindu Rao had a claim to the throne of Gwalior, but was outwitted by his strong-minded sister, and sent to live at Delhi on a lakh of rupees per annum; *i.e.*, ten thousand pounds a year. Like the great Jaswant Rao Holkar, he was a victim to cherry brandy.

[2] The Subzi Mundi was subsequently cleared from all the rubbish and débris. At the Imperial Assemblage at Delhi, on the 1st of January, 1877, it formed the site of part of the Viceregal encampment.

from the Subzi Mundi, its object being to capture the Mound battery. Finding it impossible to carry the battery, the rebels confined themselves to a hand to hand conflict in the Subzi Mundi. The deadly struggle continued for many hours; and as the rebels came up in overwhelming numbers, it was fortunate that the two bridges in the rear had been blown up the night before, or the assault might have had a different termination. It was not until after sunset that the enemy was compelled to retire with the loss of a thousand men. Similar actions were frequent during the month of August; but meanwhile reinforcements were coming up, and the end was drawing nigh.

In the middle of August, Brigadier John Nicholson, one of the most distinguished officers of the time, came up from the Punjab with a brigade and siege train. On the 4th of September a heavy train of artillery was brought in from Ferozepore. The British force on the Ridge now exceeded eight thousand men. Hitherto the artillery had been too weak to attempt to breach the city walls; but now fifty-four heavy guns were brought into position and the siege began in earnest. From the 8th to the 12th of September four batteries poured in a constant storm of shot and shell; number one was directed against the Kashmir bastion, number two against the right flank of the Kashmir bastion, number three against the Water bastion, and number four against the Kashmir and Water gates and bastions. On the 13th of September the breaches were declared to be practicable, and the following morning was fixed for the final assault upon the doomed city.

At three o'clock in the morning of the 14th September, three assaulting columns were formed in the trenches, while a fourth was kept in reserve. The first column was led by Brigadier Nicholson; the second by Brigadier Jones; the third by Colonel Campbell; and the fourth, or reserve, by Brigadier Longfield.

The powder bags were laid at the Kashmir gate by Lieutenants Home and Salkeld. The explosion followed, and the third column rushed in, and pushed toward the Juma Musjid. Meanwhile the first column under Nicholson escaladed the breaches near the Kashmir gate, and pushed along the ramparts toward the Kabul gate, carrying the several bastions in the way. Here it was met by the second column under Brigadier Jones, who had escaladed the breach at the Water bastion. The advancing columns were met by a ceaseless fire from terraced houses, mosques, and other buildings; and John Nicholson, the hero of the day, while attempting to storm a narrow street near the Kabul gate, was struck down by a shot and mortally wounded. Then followed six days of desperate warfare. No quarter was given to men with arms in their hands; but women and children were spared, and only a few of the peaceable inhabitants were sacrificed during the storm.

On the 20th of September the gates of the old fortified palace of the Moghuls were broken open, but the royal inmates had fled. No one was left but a few wounded sepoys and fugitive fanatics. The old king, Bahadur Shah, had gone off to the great mausoleum without the city, known as the tomb of Humayun. It was a vast quadrangle raised on terraces and enclosed with walls. It contained towers, buildings, and monumental marbles, in memory of different members of the once distinguished family; as well as extensive gardens, surrounded with cloistered cells for the accommodation of pilgrims.

On the 21st of September Captain Hodson rode to the tomb, arrested the king, and brought him back to Delhi with other members of the family, and lodged them in the palace. The next day he went again with a hundred horsemen, and arrested two sons of the king in the midst of a crowd of armed retainers, and brought them away in a native carriage. Near the city the carriage was surrounded by a tumultuous crowd; and Hodson, who was afraid of a rescue, shot both princes with his pistol, and placed their bodies in a public place on the walls for all men to see.

Thus fell the imperial city; captured by the army under

Brigadier Wilson before the arrival of any of the reinforcements from England. The losses were heavy. From the beginning of the siege to the close the British army at Delhi had nearly four thousand killed and wounded. The casualties on the side of the rebels were never estimated. Two bodies of sepoys broke away from the city, and fled down the valleys of the Jumna and Ganges, followed by two flying columns under Brigadiers Greathed and Showers. But the great mutiny and revolt at Delhi had been stamped out; and the flag of England waved triumphantly over the capital of Hindustan.

The capture of Delhi, in September, 1857, was the turning-point in the sepoy mutinies. The revolt was crushed beyond redemption; the rebels were deprived of their head centre; and the Moghul king was a prisoner at the mercy of the power whom he had defied. But there were still troubles in India. Lukhnow was still beleaguered by a rebel army, and insurrection still ran riot in Oude and Rohilkund.

In the middle of August General Havelock had fallen back on Cawnpore, after the failure of his first campaign for the relief of Lukhnow. Five weeks afterward Havelock made a second attempt under better auspices. Sir Colin Campbell had arrived at Calcutta as Commander-in-chief. Sir James Outram had come up to Allahabad. On the 16th of September, while the British troops were storming the streets of Delhi, Outram joined Havelock and Neill at Cawnpore with one thousand four hundred men. As senior officer he might have assumed the command; but with generous chivalry, the "Bayard of India" waived his rank in honor of Havelock.

On the 20th of September General Havelock crossed the Ganges into Oude at the head of two thousand five hundred men. The next day he defeated a rebel army, and put it to flight, while four of the enemy's guns were captured by Outram at the head of a body of volunteer cavalry. On the 23d Havelock routed a still larger rebel force which was strongly posted at a garden in the suburbs of Lukhnow, known as the Alumbagh. He then halted to give his soldiers a day's rest. On the 25th he was cutting his way through the streets and lanes of the city of Lukhnow; running the gantlet of a deadly and unremitting fire from the houses on both sides of the streets, and also from guns which commanded them. On the evening of the same day he entered the British intrenchments; but in the moment of victory a chance shot carried off the gallant Neill.

The defence of the British Residency at Lukhnow is a glorious episode in the national annals. The fortitude of the beleaguered garrison was the admiration of the world. The ladies nursed the wounded, and performed every womanly duty, with self-sacrificing heroism; and when the fight was over they received the well-merited thanks of Her Majesty Queen Victoria.

During four long months the garrison had known nothing of what was going on in the outer world. They were aware of the advance and retreat of Havelock, and that was all. At last, on the 23d of September, they heard the booming of the guns at the Alumbagh. On the morning of the 25th they could see something of the growing excitement in the city; the people abandoning their houses and flying across the river. Still the guns of the rebels kept up a heavy cannonade upon the Residency, and volleys of musketry continued to pour upon the besieged from the loopholes of the besiegers. But soon the firing was heard from the city; the welcome sounds came nearer and nearer. The excitement of the garrison grew beyond control. Presently the relieving force was seen fighting its way toward the Residency. Then the pent-up feelings of the garrison burst forth in deafening cheers; and wounded men in hospital crawled out to join in the chorus of welcome. Then followed personal greetings as officers and men came pouring in. Hands were frantically shaken on all sides. Rough bearded soldiers took the children from their mothers' arms, kissed them with tears rolling down their cheeks, and thanked

God that they had come in time to save them from the fate that had befallen the sufferers at Cawnpore.

Thus after a siege of nearly four months Havelock succeeded in relieving Lukhnow. But it was a reinforcement rather than a relief, and was confined to the British Residency. The siege was not raised; and the city of Lukhnow remained two months longer in the hands of the rebels. Sir James Outram assumed the command, but was compelled to keep on the defensive. Meanwhile reinforcements were arriving from England. In November Sir Colin Campbell reached Cawnpore at the head of a considerable army. He left General Windham with two thousand men to take charge of the intrenchment at Cawnpore; and then advanced against Lukhnow with five thousand men and thirty guns. He carried several of the enemy's positions, cut his way to the Residency, and at last brought away the beleaguered garrison, with all the ladies and children. But not even then could he disperse the rebels and reoccupy the city. Accordingly he left Outram at the head of four thousand men in the neighborhood of Lukhnow, and then returned to Cawnpore.

On the 24th of November, the day after leaving Lukhnow, General Havelock was carried off by dysentery and buried in the Alumbagh. His death spread a gloom over India, but by this time his name had become a household word wherever the English language was spoken. In the hour of surprise and panic, as successive stories of mutiny and rebellion reached England, and culminated in the revolt at Delhi and massacre at Cawnpore, the victories of Havelock revived the drooping spirits of the British nation, and stirred up all hearts to glorify the hero who had stemmed the tide of disaffection and disaster. The death of Havelock, following the story of the capture of Delhi, and told with the same breath that proclaimed the deliverance at Lukhnow, was received in England with a universal sorrow that will never be forgotten, so long as men are living who can recall the memory of the mutinies of Fifty-seven.

Sir Colin Campbell was approaching Cawnpore, when he heard the roll of a distant cannonade. There was another surprise, and unfortunately another disaster. Tantia Topi had come once more to the front. That wonderful Mahratta Brahman had made his way from the side of Nana Sahib to the capital of Sindia; and had persuaded the Gwalior Contingent to break out in open revolt and march against Cawnpore. General Windham was an officer of distinction. He had earned his laurels in the Crimean campaign, but he was unfamiliar with Asiatic warfare. He went out to meet the rebels, and routed the advanced body; but he was outwitted by the consummate genius of Tantia Topi. He found himself outflanked, and took alarm, and fell back upon the intrenchment; leaving not only his camp equipage and stores, but the whole city of Cawnpore in the hands of the rebel sepoys.[1] To crown all, the bridge of boats over the Ganges, by which Sir Colin Campbell was expected to cross the river on his way to Cawnpore, was in imminent danger of being destroyed by the rebels.

Fortunately the bridge escaped the vigilance of Tantia Topi, and Sir Colin Campbell reached the intrenchment in safety. His first act was to despatch the garrison from Lukhnow, together with his sick and wounded, down the river to Allahabad. He then took the field and routed the Gwalior rebels that repulsed General Windham, and drove them out of Cawnpore. The naval brigade under Sir William Peel gained great renown during these operations, handling their 24-pounders like playthings; while Generals Little and Mansfield and Brigadier Hope Grant distinguished themselves in the pursuit of the rebels.

In January, 1858, the ex-king Bahadur Shah was tried

---

[1] Major Adye of the Royal Artillery was present at the engagement and lost two of his guns. In sheer desperation he went out at night with a small party, and succeeded in finding his guns and bringing them back in triumph. It thus appeared that not even Tantia Topi could persuade Asiatics to keep on guard against a night attack; and had Windham beaten up the enemy's quarters at midnight he might possibly have retrieved his disaster. Major Adye is now General Sir John Adye, Governor of the Royal Military Academy at Woolwich.

by a military commission at Delhi, and found guilty of ordering the massacre of Christians, and of waging war against the British government. Sentence of death was recorded against him; but ultimately he was sent to Rangoon, with his favorite wife and her son, and kept under surveillance as a state prisoner until his death five years afterward.

The subsequent history of the sepoy revolt is little more than a detail of the military operations of British troops for the dispersion of the rebels and restoration of order and law. Sir Colin Campbell, now Lord Clyde, undertook a general campaign against the rebels in Oude and Rohilkund, and restored order and law throughout those disaffected provinces; while Sir James Outram drove the rebels out of Lukhnow, and re-established British sovereignty in the capital of Oude.

At the same time a column from Bombay under Sir Hugh Rose, and another from Madras under General Whitlock, carried out a similar work in Central India and Bundelkund. History has scarcely done justice to the brilliant campaign of Sir Hugh Rose in Central India from the borders of the Bombay Presidency to the banks of the Jumna. The military operations of Lord Clyde were on a far larger scale, but they were conducted in an open and well-peopled country. The campaign of Sir Hugh Rose was carried out amid the jungles, ravines, and broken ground of the Vindhya mountains, and the equally secluded region of Bundelkund, which for centuries had set the Muhammadan power at defiance. With a small but well-appointed force, a tithe of that under Lord Clyde's command, Sir Hugh Rose captured fortresses and walled towns, fought battles against enormous odds, and never for a moment gave the enemy time to breathe. He besieged and captured the rebel fortress of Jhansi, where Tantia Topi had come to the help of the Rani. The bloody-minded Rani fled to the jungles; and Tantia Topi escaped to the northeast, and concentrated a rebel army of twenty thousand men near Kalpi on the Jumna. After some desperate actions, Sir Hugh Rose utterly routed Tantia Topi, and scattered his forces in all directions. Sir Hugh Rose considered that he had now brought his campaign in Central India to a glorious close; and he congratulated the troops under his command at having marched a thousand miles and captured a hundred guns.

But Sir Hugh Rose had reckoned without his host. At this very time the irrepressible Mahratta Brahman, Tantia Topi, had secretly proceeded to Gwalior, the capital of Maharaja Sindia. He had made Gwalior the rallying-point for all the scattered troops of the rebel army; and organized a conspiracy against Sindia to be supported by the rebels as fast as they arrived. The plot was discovered in time by the Maharaja and his minister, Dinkur Rao; and it was plain that neither the one nor the other could have felt the slightest sympathy in a movement for upsetting the British government and restoring a dynasty of Peishwas.

Dinkur Rao counselled the Maharaja to adopt a defensive policy until a British force arrived from Agra. But Sindia was young and enthusiastic, and anxious to show his loyalty to the British government. Accordingly he marched out with eight thousand men and twenty-five guns to attack the rebel army. The result was one of those surprises and disasters which characterized different epochs of the mutiny. Sindia's army deserted him, and either joined the rebels or returned to Gwalior. His own bodyguard remained with him, and fought against the rebels with the old Mahratta spirit, but they suffered heavily in the action. Sindia was thus compelled to fly to Dholepore on the road to Agra, where he was joined by Dinkur Rao.

The city of Gwalior, with all its guns, stores, and treasure, was thus abandoned to the rebels. Nana Sahib was proclaimed Peishwa; and a revolution was beginning of which no one at Gwalior could see the ending. In the beginning of June, 1858, in the height of the hot weather, a new rebel army, numbering eighteen thousand men, had sprung into existence in Central India under the command of Tantia Topi, with all the famous artillery of Sindia at his disposal.

This astounding state of affairs soon called Sir Hugh Rose to the front. On the 16th of June he defeated a rebel force which was posted in the cantonment at Morar. The next day he was joined by a column under Brigadier Smith; and on the 18th all the rebel intrenchments and positions were stormed and captured. During these operations the Rani of Jhansi fought on the side of the rebels in male attire. She was killed by a trooper before her sex was discovered; and is said to have courted her fate to escape the punishment of her crimes.

Tantia Topi, however, was a born general, and his genius never deserted him. He made good his retreat from Gwalior with six thousand men, and carried away thirty field-pieces. But his case was hopeless. Two days afterward, Brigadier Robert Napier, the present Lord Napier of Magdala, dashed among the retreating force with six hundred horsemen and six field-guns, and put them to flight, while recovering nearly all the artillery they had carried away. This successful action was regarded as one of the most brilliant exploits in the campaign.

In spite of these crushing defeats, Tantia Topi evaded all pursuit for ten months longer. Different columns strove to hem him in; but the active Mahratta, with all the spirit and pertinacity of his race, made his way to the banks of the Nerbudda with a large body of fugitives, mounted on the small hardy ponies of India. With all the pertinacity of a Mahratta, he still clung to the wild hope of reaching the western Dekhan, and creating a new Mahratta empire in the dominions of the ex-Peishwa, which had been British territory for more than forty years. Whether it was possible for him to have raised a Mahratta insurrection is a problem he was never destined to solve.

Tantia Topi was driven back by the Bombay troops, and never crossed the Nerbudda. From that time Tantia Topi and the British troops appeared to be playing at hunting the hare all over Central India. He and his men rode incredible distances, and often appeared to be in several places at once. At last a cordon of hunters surrounded him. He was driven into the western deserts of Rajputana, but compelled, from want of supplies, to double back on Bundelkund. In April, 1859, his hiding-place in the jungles was betrayed by one of his own rebel generals; and he was arrested by Major Meade, and tried, convicted, and hanged, to the general satisfaction of all concerned.

Tantia Topi was a cruel and crafty villain, with a cleverness that calls to mind the genius and audacity of the old Mahratta Peishwas. He was no doubt the originator of the rebellion of the Nana Sahib, and the prime mover in the massacres at Cawnpore; while the Nana was a mere tool and puppet in his hands, like Maharaja Sahu in the hands of the Peishwas. Could the Nana have succeeded in gaining a throne, he would most probably have been imprisoned or murdered by Tantia Topi; and Tantia Topi would have founded one of those dynasties of ministerial sovereigns which so often sprung into existence in the palmy days of Brahmanical rule.[1]

[1] The death of Tantia Topi has carried the reader beyond the mutinies into the year 1859. In the next chapter it will be necessary to revert to the close of the mutinies in 1858.

CHAPTER XXVI

IMPERIAL RULE: CANNING, ELGIN, LAWRENCE, MAYO, NORTHBROOK AND LYTTON

A.D. 1858 TO 1880

ON the 1st of November, 1858, the proclamation of her Majesty Queen Victoria brought the sepoy revolt to a close. It was the Magna Charta of India, and was translated into all the languages of the country. It announced the transfer of the direct government of India from the Company to the Crown. It confirmed all existing dignities, rights, usages, and treaties.[1] It assured the people of India that the British government had neither the right nor the desire to tamper with their religion or caste. It granted a general amnesty to all mutineers and rebels, excepting only those who had been directly implicated in the murders.

In January, 1859, Lord Canning published a despatch from Lord Clyde, declaring that rebellion no longer existed in Oude.[2] The campaign was at an end, for no organized armies of rebels remained in the field; but hordes of armed men, of whom Tantia Topi was a type, were still fighting

[1] The administrative results of the transfer of the government of India from the East India Company to the Crown may be summed up in a few words. The Governor-General became a Viceroy. Non-officials, natives and Europeans, were introduced into the so-called legislative councils at the different Presidencies, and into the legislative council of the Viceroy. The Company's army was amalgamated with the Queen's army. The Company's Courts of Appeal at the different Presidencies, known as the Suddar Courts, in which the judges were selected from the Civil Service, were amalgamated with the Supreme Courts, in which the judges were sent out from England under the nomination of the Crown. The new Courts are now known as High Courts.

[2] Oude was disarmed after the rebellion, just as the Punjab had been disarmed after the annexation. The number of arms collected was very large; there were 684 cannon, 186,000 firearms, 560,000 swords, 50,000 spears, and more than 600,000 weapons of other descriptions; while more than 1,500 fortresses, great and small, were demolished or dismantled.

as it were with halters round their necks. But brigades and detachments were in motion from the Nerbudda river to the northeast frontier of Oude; and the work of trampling out the last embers of the great conflagration was gradually brought to a close.

During the cold weather of 1859 Lord Canning left Calcutta for a tour in the upper provinces. In November he held a grand durbar at Agra, at which his dignified presence created an impression among the native princes which was never forgotten. He acknowledged the services rendered to the British government during the mutinies by Maharaja Sindia, the Raja of Jaipur, and others. At the same time, as the representative of her Majesty, he publicly announced the concession to native rulers of the right of adopting a son, who should succeed to the government of their several principalities in the event of a failure of natural heirs.

In March, 1862, Lord Canning left India forever. The leading event of his administration was the sepoy revolt; but it was followed by measures of economy and reform which proved him to be one of the most conscientious and hard-working statesmen that ever governed India. Unfortunately his career was rapidly brought to a close. He died the following June, and was buried in Westminster Abbey.

Lord Elgin succeeded Lord Canning as Viceroy of India. His administration was short, but was marked by two events which will always find a place in history; namely, a little mountain expedition on the northwest frontier which led to an expensive campaign, and a mission to Bhutan which led to a still more disastrous war.

The frontier of British India westward of the river Indus was formed in 1849 by a chain of mountains which ran southward from the Hindu Kush into Sinde, and served as a natural wall between the Punjab and Afghanistan.[1] These moun-

[1] The wall is not continuous. It is pierced by the Khaiber Pass which leads to Kabul, and the Bolan Pass which leads to Quetta and Kandahar. Other passes were discovered during the campaigns of 1878–79.

tains are known as the Sulaiman range. They are inhabited by tribes who are closely akin to the Afghans; equally bloodthirsty and treacherous, and still more ignorant and barbarous. They have no government, but each tribe has its own council of elders, known as the Jirgah. They are Muhammadans of the worst type; intolerant and priest-ridden. They always carry arms, such as matchlocks and short swords, whether grazing cattle, tilling the soil, or driving beasts of burden; for every tribe has its internecine war, every family its hereditary blood feud, and every man his personal enemy. At the same time, whenever they are exposed to the assaults of an invader, they forget all their feuds and quarrels, and make common cause against the foreigner.[1]

In the old days of Runjeet Singh and his successors, the mountain tribes were always ready to carry fire and sword into the bordering villages of Sikhs and Hindus, on the side of the Punjab. They plundered homesteads, slaughtered all who opposed them, and carried off women, children, and cattle. Since the British conquest of the Punjab there has been a vast improvement in the state of affairs on the frontier; and the mountain tribes have been kept out of the plains by the Punjab Irregular Force organized by Lord Dalhousie.

The most important British district on the line of frontier is that of Peshawar. It is the key of the whole position. It extends from the fort of Attock, at the junction of the Kabul and Indus rivers, westward as far as the mouth of the Khaiber Pass, which leads to Kabul. Accordingly the British cantonment at Peshawar has always been held by a large force of the regular army.

Forty miles to the north of Attock is a village, or group of villages, called Sitana. The settlement is situated outside the frontier, on the eastern face of a square mass of rock,

---

[1] The data respecting the population of the Sulaiman range is condensed from a Report on the independent tribes of the northwest frontier, drawn up many years ago by Sir Richard Temple. The original extract will be found in page 27 of the Blue Book on Afghanistan, published in 1878.

eight thousand feet high, known as the Mahabun mountain.[1] It had been occupied ever since 1831, or thereabout, by a colony of Hindustani fanatics from Bengal. These men are a sect of Muhammadan puritans, known as Wahabis, who affect a strict and ascetic way of life, such as prevailed in the time of the Prophet, and denounce all commentaries on the Koran, and all such modern innovations as the worship of relics. The Hindustani fanatics at Sitana were dangerous neighbors. They were brigands as well as bigots, like the zealots described by Josephus. They committed frequent raids on British territory, being inspired by religious hatred as well as love of plunder; and, strange to say, they were recruited from time to time with men and money from disaffected Muhammadans in Patna and other localities in Bengal, at least twelve hundred miles off. In 1858 they were driven out of Sitana by General Sir Sydney Cotton, who commanded at Peshawar; but they only retired to Mulka, on the further slope of the Mahabun mountain; and in 1862 they returned to Sitana and renewed their depredations.

In 1863 a British force of five thousand men, under General Sir Neville Chamberlain, was sent to root out the Hindustani fanatics from Mulka as well as Sitana. It would, however, have proved a difficult operation to march a column up the side of a steep mountain in the face of swarms of mountaineers and fanatics; and then, after capturing Sitana, to march over a crest eight thousand feet high, in order to attack a strong force at Mulka on the further slope. Accordingly it was resolved to reach the slope in question by a narrow gorge that ran along the western face of the Mahabun mountain, and was known as the Umbeyla pass; and thus to take Mulka, as it were, in the rear.[2]

---

[1] The whole region is classic ground, the scene of Alexander's invasion of India. The Mahabun mountain has been identified with the natural fortress of Aornos, which was captured by the Macedonians. Attock has been identified with Taxila, the first city entered by the great conqueror after the passage of the Indus.

[2] See Sitana; a Mountain Campaign on the Borders of Afghanistan, by Colonel John Adye, R.A. The author is largely indebted to this valuable con-

While, however, one side of the Umbeyla pass was formed by the Mahabun mountain, the other side was formed by another steep height, known as the Guru mountain; and beyond the Guru mountain were many strong tribes, known as Bonairs and Swatis; and above all there was a certain warrior priest, known as the Akhoond of Swat, who exercised a powerful influence as prince and pontiff over many of the tribes far and wide. Then again the Umbeyla pass was outside the British frontier, and really belonged to the Bonairs. It was, however, imagined that the Afghan mountaineers could have no sympathy with the Hindustani fanatics; especially as the Akhoond of Swat had fulminated his spiritual thunder against the Hindustani fanatics at Mulka and Sitana in a way which betokened a deadly sectarian hostility. Moreover, as the Umbeyla pass was only nine miles long, it was possible to reach Mulka and destroy the village before Bonairs or Swatis could know what was going on.

Unfortunately the Hindustani fanatics were too sharp for the British authorities. They got an inkling of the coming expedition, and sent out letters to all the neighboring tribes. They declared that the English infidels were coming to devastate the mountains and subvert the religion of the tribes. It was cunningly added that in the first instance the infidels would say that they only came to destroy the Hindustanis; but if once they got into the mountain, every one of the tribes would share the fate of the Hindustanis.

Unconsciously General Chamberlain played into the hands of the Hindustanis. He told the neighboring tribes that he was going to destroy Mulka, but that he had no intention whatever of interfering with any one but the Hindustanis. He entered the Umbeyla pass before he could receive any

---

tribution to military history. Colonel, now General, Sir John Adye, maintains that the Hindu Kush and not the Sulaiman range is the true frontier of our British Indian empire. The author would add that if we accept the Hindu Kush as our mountain fortress, then, to use a technical phrase, Afghan-Turkistan is our berm and the Oxus our ditch. Russia already holds the glacis as represented by Bokhara and Khiva.

reply; but, on getting three parts of the way, he was compelled to halt for the baggage. He sent on a party to reconnoitre the Chumla valley, which intervened between the pass and Mulka, and then it was found that the Guru mountain was swarming with armed men. Accordingly the reconnoitring party had much difficulty in returning to the camp; and it was soon evident that the British force had been drawn into a defile; and that it would be impossible to advance without reinforcements, and almost equally impossible to return to British territory.

The movements of the British force had excited the suspicions of the tribes by confirming all that the Hindustanis had said. The Bonairs were exasperated at the violation of their territory, without any previous reference to their council of elders. Fear and alarm spread far and wide, and the tribes flocked to the Guru mountain from all quarters. The Akhoond of Swat came in person with fifteen thousand men. The mountain tribes on the Mahabun made common cause with the Hindustanis in resisting the invaders. In a word, General Chamberlain was threatened by swarms of matchlock men on his two flanks, while his rear was blocked up by mules, camels, and other impedimenta. Under such circumstances he was compelled to keep off the enemy as he best could, and wait for reinforcements, or for orders to retire. To make matters worse, he himself was wounded; while Lord Elgin was dying at Dhurmsala in the Himalayas.

At this crisis Sir Hugh Rose, who had succeeded Lord Clyde as Commander-in-chief, solved the difficulty. He protested against any retirement, as it would only necessitate an expensive campaign in the following spring; and he ordered up reinforcements with all speed from Lahore.

Lord Elgin died in November, 1863. Sir William Denison, Governor of Madras, came up to Calcutta to act as his successor until a Viceroy could be appointed by the home government; and he at once sanctioned the steps taken by Sir Hugh Rose. General Garvock assumed the command in the room of General Chamberlain, and found himself at the head of nearly nine thousand men all eager for the fray. The mountain tribes were soon brought to reason; and a brilliant campaign ended in a political triumph. The Bonairs were so satisfied of the good faith of the British authorities that they went themselves to Mulka and burned down the village; and for a while nothing more was heard of the Hindustanis.[1]

The idea of a Muhammadan conspiracy, running along a line of one thousand two hundred miles between Patna and Sitana, created undue alarm in England. The result was that Sir John Lawrence, whose administration of the Punjab during the sepoy mutinies had excited general admiration, was appointed to succeed Lord Elgin as Viceroy of India. The appointment was contrary to established usage, for it had been ruled in the case of Sir Charles Metcalfe that no servant of the Company could fill the substantive post of Governor-General. The elevation of Sir John Lawrence, however, was regarded with universal satisfaction. He arrived at Calcutta in January, 1864; but by this time the Sitana campaign had been brought to a close.

Shortly after Sir John Lawrence had taken over the government of India, a mission which had been sent to Bhutan by Lord Elgin was brought to an unfortunate close. Before, however, describing the progress of events, it will be necessary to glance at the country and people of Bhutan, and review the circumstances which led to the despatch of the mission.

Bhutan is a mountain region in the Himalayas, having Thibet on the north and Bengal and Assam on the south. It also lies between Nipal on the west and another portion of Thibet on the east.[2] Like Nipal, it forms a fringe of

[1] In 1868 an expedition under the command of General Wylde was sent against the Afghan tribes on the Black Mountain, immediately to the north of the Mahabun. The military operations were successful, and sufficed for the suppression of disturbances and restoration of peace.

[2] Bhutan is separated from Nipal by the little principality of Sikhim and the hill station of Darjeeling.

mountain territory to the south of the great Thibetan tableland. Originally it belonged to Thibet, but became independent from the inability of the Thibetan government to keep the mountaineers in subjection.

The people of Bhutan are rude, robust, and dirty; with flat faces of the Tartar type, and high cheekbones narrowing down to the chin. They have ruddy brown complexions; black hair cut close to the head; small black almond-shaped eyes; very thin eyelashes; and little or no eyebrows or beards. They are coarse and filthy in their manners, and leave all the field work to the women, who are as coarse as the men.

This repulsive barbarism is the outcome of a corrupt form of Buddhism. Thousands of Buddhist monks lead lives of religion and laziness in their secluded monasteries; leaving the laity to grovel away their existence in gross and undisguised debaucheries.

The government of Bhutan is half clerical and half secular; including a pontiff as well as a prince. The pontiff is known as the Dharma Raja; he is supposed to be an incarnation, not of deity, but of that exalted virtue and goodness which are summed up by Buddhists in the single term—Dharma;[1] and the Bhutanese believe that the Dharma Raja has the power of raising evil spirits, or demons, for the destruction of their enemies. The temporal prince is known as the Deb or Deva Raja, and is subordinate to the Dharma Raja. He represents the hero Rajas—the Devas or Devatas of Hindu traditions—who figured as heroes and were worshipped as gods until the old mythology was submerged in the metaphysical atheism of Buddhism.[2]

Bhutan is separated into three provinces, each of which is in charge of a governor known as a Penlow. The governor of western Bhutan is called the Paro Penlow; that of

---

[1] Dharma was the religion of the edicts of Asoka. See ante, p. 70.

[2] In the ancient Sanskrit religion, Indra was the hero of the Aryan race and the Vaidik god of the firmament; as such he was worshipped as the king of the Devas or Devatas. See ante, p. 81.

central Bhutan is the Daka Penlow; and that of eastern Bhutan is the Tongso Penlow. Subordinate to the three Penlows are the commandants of fortresses, known as Jungpens. Below these is an inferior class of officials, who serve as messengers, and are known as Zingaffs.

There is, however, a constitutional element in the Bhutan government. The Dharma and Deva Rajas are assisted by a council composed of the chief secretary to the Dharma Raja, the prime minister, the chief justice, the three Penlows when present at the capital, and three of the principal Jungpens.

The disputes between the British government and the tribes and states beyond the border are of the same mixed character along the whole line of frontier from Afghanistan to Arakan. Sometimes British villages are harried by mountain tribes; sometimes they have been silently and systematically annexed, as in the case of Nipal. Bhutan was guilty of both offences. Abortive attempts were made by the British government to keep the peace by paying yearly rent for disputed tracts; but nothing would stop the raids and kidnapping; and at last Lord Elgin sanctioned a proposition of the Bengal government to send an English mission to Punakha, the capital of Bhutan, to lay the complaints of the British authorities before the Bhutanese government.

The story of the mission to Bhutan is only historical so far as it brings out the national characteristics of the Bhutanese. In the first instance a native messenger was sent to the Deva Raja to announce the coming of the mission. The Deva Raja replied that the complaints were too trivial to be referred to the Dharma Raja, and that the British government ought not to have listened to them; but he promised to send some of the lowest officials, known as Zingaffs, to settle all disputes. The Zingaffs never came, and at last the English mission left Darjeeling for Punakha.

At this very moment there was a revolution in Bhutan. The Deva Raja lost his throne and retired to a monastery; but civil war was still at work in western Bhutan, the very country through which the mission was about to pass on its way to Punakha. The Paro Penlow was stanch to the ex-Deva Raja; but his subordinate, the Jungpen of the frontier fortress of Dhalimkote, had joined the revolutionary party. The troops of the Paro Penlow were besieging the fortress of Dhalimkote, but retired on the approach of the English mission.

Under such circumstances the Jungpen of Dhalimkote welcomed the approach of the English mission with warm professions of attachment to the British government. But the selfish craft of the Bhutanese barbarian was soon manifest. He sent musicians and ponies to conduct the Envoy to Dhalimkote; but he charged exorbitant prices for every article he supplied; and paid long complimentary visits to the different members of the mission, during which he drank spirits until he was permitted to retire, or, properly speaking, was turned out. Meanwhile the Envoy received a letter from the new Deva Raja, telling him to acquaint the Jungpen with the object of his mission. The Envoy replied that he could only negotiate with the head of the Bhutanese government. Accordingly, after many delays, he at last set out for Punakha.

It was obviously unwise to send a mission into a barbarous country like Bhutan without some knowledge of the state of parties. It was still more unwise for the British government to appear to side with either party. Yet Sir William Denison, the provisional Governor-General from Madras, ordered the mission to proceed on the ground that as the revolutionary party had got the uppermost, it would be politic to secure the help of the Jungpen who had espoused its cause. Thus a mission was sent to a new ruler, whose predecessor had only just been ousted from the throne, not with a formal recognition of his usurpation, but to complain of cattle lifting and kidnapping, and to settle all disputes respecting the border territory.

In reality the Bhutanese authorities did not want to receive a mission at all; or to conclude a treaty which would only tie their hands. Accordingly they threw every obstacle in the way of the Envoy, and exhausted every possible means of inducing him to return short of main force. Of course it would have been more dignified to retire; but the Envoy was naturally anxious to carry out the instructions of his own government, and to lose no opportunity which would enable him to realize the object of his mission; and he would probably have been open to as much blame for a premature return to British territory as for a rash advance to the capital of Bhutan.

After leaving Dhalimkote, an incident occurred which brings out the peculiar temper of the Bhutanese. Some messengers appeared carrying two letters to the Jungpen of Dhalimkote. They took upon themselves to tell the Envoy that the letters contained the orders of the new Deva Raja for the return of the mission; and then, as the Envoy was the party concerned, they made over to him the letters which were intended for the Jungpen. Accordingly the letters were opened and read. In one the new Deva Raja expressed a warm attachment to the British government, and directed the Jungpen to satisfy the Envoy on every point, and to settle every dispute. The other letter ought certainly to have been marked "private." It threatened the Jungpen with death for having permitted the mission to cross the frontier, and ordered him to make every effort to induce the Envoy to go back. Should, however, the Envoy still persist in going to Punakha, he was to be sent by another road, and to be furnished with all necessary supplies.

Such were the unpromising circumstances under which the Envoy pushed on to the capital. At Punakha the barbarian government gave vent to its coarseness. The Envoy was treated with rudeness and insult, and forced to sign a treaty "under compulsion," engaging to restore the territory in dispute to Bhutan.[1] No redress was offered for the out-

---

[1] The real offender on this occasion was the Tongso Penlow, the governor of eastern Bhutan, and prime head of the revolutionary party, who was trying

rages committed on British subjects, and none of the kidnapped persons were surrendered. On the contrary, the Bhutanese authorities set the British government at defiance; and the great Dharma Raja, the living incarnation of goodness, threatened to raise a score of demons of enormous magnitude for the destruction of the British empire, unless the territories signed away by the Envoy were promptly made over.

Under these circumstances the treaty was nullified by a declaration of war. A campaign was begun in a difficult country of passes and precipices, reeking with a deadly malaria, and defended by a contemptible enemy, armed with matchlocks and poisoned arrows. It is needless to dwell upon military operations which reflect no glory on British arms or diplomacy. In the end the Bhutanese were brought to their senses, and compelled to restore the British subjects that had been carried away into slavery, and to make other restitutions which were necessary to satisfy the insulted honor of the British government. Arrangements were subsequently concluded as regards the disputed territory, and the payment of a yearly rent, which have proved satisfactory. Since then the Bhutanese authorities have profited by the lessons of 1864–65, and have proved better neighbors than at any previous period.

Meanwhile the progress of events in Central Asia was forced upon the attention of the British government. Russia had reached the Jaxartes, and was supposed to be threatening the Usbeg states between the Jaxartes and the Oxus. Great Britain still maintained the Sulaiman range as her frontier against Afghanistan; but could not shut her eyes to the approaches of Russia toward the Oxus. At this crisis Dost Muhammad Khan was gathered to his fathers, and Afghanistan was distracted by a war between his sons for the succession to the throne. Dost Muhammad Khan died in

---

to usurp the government. The Deva Raja, and other members of the council, attempted to apologize for the rudeness of the Tongso Penlow, by pretending that it was all done in the way of friendly jocularity.

June, 1863. Ever since the treaties of 1855 and 1857 he had proved stanch to the English alliance. His anxiety to recover Peshawar was as strong as in the days of Runjeet Singh; but he held out against the temptations offered by the sepoy mutinies of 1857–58, and continued to respect the British frontier. Meanwhile, however, he established his suzerainty over Afghan-Turkistan,[1] as well as over Kabul and Kandahar; and shortly before his death he wrested Herat from the government of a disaffected son-in-law, and thus became the undisputed sovereign of a united Afghan empire.

Dost Muhammad Khan had fallen into the patriarchal error of nominating Sher Ali Khan, a younger son by a favorite wife, to be his successor to the throne, to the exclusion of Muhammad Afzal Khan, his eldest son by a more elderly partner. Accordingly a fratricidal war seemed inevitable. Afzal Khan was governor of Afghan-Turkistan; a post which he had held for many years during the lifetime of his father; and he began to prepare for a deadly struggle with his younger brother. Under such circumstances Sher Ali Khan was anxious for the recognition of the British government to his succession to the throne; and after some delay this was formally granted in December, 1863, by Sir William Denison, the provisional Viceroy.

The bare recognition of Sher Ali Khan by the British government could not avert the fratricidal war. In June, 1864, there was an indecisive battle between Sher Ali Khan and his elder brother, which was followed by a sham reconciliation. Each in turn swore on the Koran to abandon all designs against the other; and then, with the customary faithlessness of an Afghan, Sher Ali Khan suddenly ordered the arrest of Muhammad Afzal Khan, bound him with chains, and kept him in close confinement until the iron entered his soul.

This act of treachery was followed by a fearful retribu-

[1] Afghan-Turkistan is the geographical term for the region northward of Kabul, lying between the Hindu Kush and the river Oxus. It comprises the districts of Maemana, Andkui, Saripul, Shibrghan, Balkh, Khulm, Kunduz and Badakhshan.

tion in the Amir's own family. Sher Ali Khan was warmly attached to his eldest son, and had appointed him heir-apparent. The son was killed by an uncle in a fit of jealousy; and the uncle was in his turn cut to pieces by the soldiery. The murder of his eldest son drove Sher Ali Khan into a state of temporary insanity; and to the end of his days he was often morose, melancholy and mad, like another Saul.

All this while Afzal Khan was in prison at Kabul; but his brother, Azim Khan, and his son, Abdul Rahman Khan, remained in possession of Afghan-Turkistan, and prepared for a renewal of the war. In May, 1866, the uncle and nephew marched an army toward Kabul. A battle was fought in Afghan fashion. There was a brisk cannonade which did no execution, and then the bulk of Sher Ali Khan's troops suddenly deserted him and went over to the rebel army. The result was that Sher Ali Khan fled with a few horsemen to Kandahar, while Muhammad Afzal Khan was released from prison and proclaimed Amir amid general illuminations and a salute of a hundred guns.

In June, 1866, Afghanistan was distributed as follows: Kabul and Afghan-Turkistan were in the possession of Muhammad Afzal Khan. Kandahar remained in the hands of Sher Ali Khan; while his son Yakub Khan held the government of Herat, and retained it throughout the war.

The British government was in a dilemma. It had recognized Sher Ali as Amir of Afghanistan, on the plea that he was *de facto* Amir; but it was not prepared to give the Amir material help in the contest with his eldest brother. The fortunes of war, however, had placed Muhammad Afzal Khan in the position of *de facto* Amir. Sir John Lawrence tried to solve the problem by recognizing Afzal Khan as ruler of Kabul and Afghan-Turkistan, and Sher Ali Khan as ruler of Kandahar.

Imprisonment, however, had exercised an evil influence on Afzal Khan, and he was no longer fitted to rule. He left the administration of affairs in the hands of his brother Azim Khan, and took to hard drinking. The government of Azim Khan was fearfully oppressive, owing to the pressing want of money. Caravans were stopped and plundered until all trade was at a standstill. Loans and contributions were mercilessly exacted from the people. Every sign of disaffection was stamped out by murder and confiscation; while the women and children of the offenders were condemned to beggary or starvation.

In January, 1867, Sher Ali Khan made an effort for the recovery of his throne. He raised an army at Kandahar and then marched toward Kabul. Azim Khan tempted him to a premature advance by feigning to retreat; and then suddenly opened a fire from his guns, which cut up the army from Kandahar. Sher Ali Khan managed to escape with a small body of horsemen to his son, Yakub Khan, at Herat; but by so doing he left Kandahar in the hands of his brothers. To all appearance he had been deprived of his kingdom forever, and was condemned to pass the remainder of his days in exile.

In October, 1867, Muhammad Afzal Khan perished of intemperance and disease. His death was followed by a fierce contest between his brother Azim Khan and his son, Abdul Rahman Khan. But the widow of Afzal Khan forced Abdul Rahman Khan to submit to his uncle, by pointing out that any rivalry between them would only serve to strengthen the hands of Sher Ali Khan.

Azim Khan reigned as Amir of Afghanistan from October, 1867, until August, 1868, when another revolution drove him from the throne. Yakub Khan marched an army from Herat to Kandahar, and began an unexpected career of victory which ended in the restoration of his father, Sher Ali Khan, to the throne of Afghanistan. Azim Khan and his nephew, Abdul Rahman Khan, flew away to the northward, into Afghan-Turkistan; but were driven out the following year, and compelled to seek a refuge in Persian territory.[1]

During the fratricidal war in Afghanistan, the advances

[1] The writer was of opinion at the time, and freely ventilated it in an Indian journal, that the progress of the fratricidal war ought to have been stopped by

of Russia toward the Usbeg states of Khokand and Bokhara continued to excite attention. Sir John Lawrence, however, was of opinion that all difficulties might be removed by a friendly understanding with Russia. He was averse to any change of frontier, or to any interference whatever in the affairs of Afghanistan. But Sher Ali Khan was complaining, and with some show of reason, that while he had shown his attachment to the British government in a variety of ways, he had received but few tokens of friendship or kindness in return. Accordingly it was proposed to strengthen the friendship between Great Britain and Afghanistan by a free gift of money and arms to the restored Amir.[1]

Early in 1869 Sir John Lawrence was succeeded by Lord Mayo as Viceroy of India. He returned to England, and was raised to the peerage; and lived ten years longer, doing all the good work that fell in his way. He died in 1879 and was buried in Westminster Abbey. Few men of modern times have approached him in energy and capacity, and none has rendered greater services to the empire of British India.

Lord Mayo was a Viceroy of a different stamp from the famous Indian civilian. He was naturally wanting in a thorough familiarity with the details of Indian administration, but he had a wider knowledge of humanity, and a larger experience in European statesmanship. Courtly as well as dignified and imposing, there was a charm in his manner which insured him a larger share of personal pop-

---

the partition of Afghanistan between two or more chiefs; while the British government assumed the paramount power, and threatened to interfere unless the rival parties kept the peace. Later events have not induced him to change that opinion.

[1] The policy of recognizing a *de facto* ruler, and refusing to help him in times of difficulty and danger, may appear to be wise and prudent from an English point of view, but must seem cold and selfish to Oriental eyes. When Sher Ali Khan was in danger of his throne and life, the English not only refused to help him, but recognized Muhammad Afzal Khan as Amir of Kabul and Afghan-Turkistan. When, however, Sher Ali Khan recovered his territory and throne, the British government was willing to help him with money and arms. Such friendship, so easily transferred from one prince to another (with perhaps for decency's sake an expression of pity for the prince who has been worsted), may be the outcome of masterly inactivity, but it has the disadvantage of appearing hollow and insincere.

ularity than often falls to the lot of a Governor-General of India.

Shortly after the arrival of Lord Mayo at Calcutta, preparations were made for a meeting between the new Viceroy and Sher Ali Khan. In March, 1869, the conference took place at Umballa, about a hundred and twenty miles to the northwest of Delhi. It was attended with the best possible results. Sher Ali Khan had been chilled by the icy friendship of Sir John Lawrence, but he threw off all reserve and suspicion in the presence of Lord Mayo. The English nobleman won the heart of the Afghan, and established a personal influence which brightened for a while the political relations between the British government and the Amir.

But difficulties always crop up between a civilized power like Great Britain and a semi-barbarous government like that of Afghanistan, whenever attempts are made on either side to place political relations on a footing of equality. Sher Ali Khan naturally scrutinized the existing treaty with a jealous and jaundiced eye. It had been negotiated in 1855 by Sir John Lawrence with Dost Muhammad Khan.[1] It bound the Amir to consider the friends and enemies of the British government as his friends and enemies; but it did not bind the British government to like conditions as regards the friends and enemies of the Amir. Sher Ali Khan declared that this was a one-sided arrangement, and so in truth it was; but the British government was the protecting power, and had the right to insist on its conditions; and this was still more emphatically the case when it appeared as the giver of arms and money. Moreover, if the British government committed itself to the obligations proposed, it might have found itself compelled to interfere in civil broils, or take a part in foreign wars, in which it had no concern, and in which Sher Ali Khan might have been obviously in the wrong.

Accordingly Lord Mayo tried to reassure the Amir by

[1] The subsequent treaty of 1857 was also concluded by Sir John Lawrence, but was confined to arrangements consequent on the war which had broken out between Great Britain and Persia, and in no way superseded the treaty of 1855.

telling him that the British government regarded him as the rightful as well as the *de facto* ruler of Afghanistan; and would view with severe displeasure any attempt on the part of his rivals to oust him from his throne. He added that the British government would not interfere with the internal affairs of Afghanistan, and would not, under any circumstances, employ its troops beyond the frontier to quell civil dissensions or family broils. The home government subsequently directed that Sher Ali Khan should be further informed that the British government would still be free to withhold the promised help should his government become notoriously cruel and oppressive. This, however, never seems to have been done.[1]

Lord Mayo was the first Indian Viceroy since Lord Dalhousie who took a special interest in the affairs of British Burma. In 1862 Sir Arthur Phayre had been appointed Chief Commissioner of the united provinces of Arakan, Pegu and Tenasserim; and had proceeded to Mandalay the same year, and concluded a friendly treaty with the king of Burma. In 1867 his successor, General Fytche, proceeded in like manner to Mandalay, and concluded a second treaty, which led to a large extension of trade with Upper Burma, and the establishment of a line of steamers to Mandalay and Bhamo. No Viceroy, however, had landed at Burma since the visit of Lord Dalhousie in 1852. Accordingly, when it was known in 1871 that Lord Mayo proposed making a trip to the province, the susceptible Burmese population were thrown into excitement by his expected arrival.

The career of Lord Mayo was, however, destined to end in a tragedy. He landed at Rangoon in February, 1872, with his personal staff and a brilliant party of guests, and

[1] All conditions as regards cruelty and oppression should be understood rather than expressed in dealing with foreign states. No diplomatic language can prevent its being regarded as a direct insult by any ruler, European or Asiatic. Moreover, it is wholly unnecessary. It is always competent for a state to threaten to break off all political relations in the case of notorious cruelty and oppression, or to carry its threats into execution in the event of a persistence in such a line of conduct. Similar conditions are understood in all societies, whenever a gross outrage is committed by any one of its members.

was welcomed with the acclamations of thousands. Crowds of native ladies, a sight unknown in India, were present at the wharf to welcome Lord and Lady Mayo with offerings of flowers. Nearly an entire week was spent by Lord Mayo in receiving deputations from all classes of the community, and in surveying the vast strides which western civilization had made in that remote territory during the brief period of twenty years. From Rangoon he paid a flying visit to Maulmain, and then steamed to the Andaman Islands to inspect the penal settlement at Port Blair. There in the dusk of the evening he was suddenly stabbed to death by an Afghan, who had been condemned to penal servitude for life on account of a murder he had committed on the British side of the northwest frontier, and who had taken the opportunity of wreaking his blind vengeance on the most popular of modern Viceroys.

With the death of Lord Mayo in 1872 the modern history of India is brought to a natural close. Lord Northbrook succeeded Lord Mayo as Viceroy, but resigned the post in 1876, and was succeeded in his turn by Lord Lytton. The details of their respective administrations are as yet too recent to be brought under review as matters of history. Two events, however, have occurred since 1872 which may be mentioned in the present place as likely to become landmarks in Indian annals.

On the 1st of January, 1877, her Majesty Queen Victoria was proclaimed Empress of India in the old imperial capital at Delhi. The visit of His Royal Highness the Duke of Edinburgh to India in 1869, and the subsequent visit of His Royal Highness the Prince of Wales in 1875–76, had prepared the way for a closer association of the princes and people of India with the British Crown; and the celebration of an Imperial Assemblage at Delhi for the proclamation of the Empress will prove to all future ages an epoch in the annals of British India. It swept away the memory of the sepoy revolt of 1857, and associated Delhi with the might and majesty of the sovereign of the British empire. At the same time it brought all the princes and chiefs of India into personal intercourse in the same camp under the shadow of the British sovereignty. Old feuds were forgotten; new friendships were formed; and for the first time in history the Queen of the British Isles was publicly and formally installed in the presence of the princes and people as the Empress of India.

Meanwhile, at the very moment that Delhi was the scene of festivity and rejoicing, black clouds were gathering beyond the northwestern frontier. Sher Ali Khan had become estranged from the British government. He had placed his eldest son, Yakub Khan, in close confinement on charges of disloyalty and rebellion; and he resented an attempt made by the British government to bring about a reconciliation. He considered himself ill-used in the settlement of his frontier on the side of Seistan with the Persian government. He was also mortified at the refusal of the British government to conclude a defensive alliance on equal terms, which had proved so disastrous in our dealings with Hyder Ali a century before.[1] In an evil hour he refused to receive a British mission at Kabul; while he made overtures to Russia, and received a Russian mission at his capital, at a time when British relations with Russia were known to be unsatisfactory.

Under such circumstances Sher Ali Khan was doomed to share the fate which befell his father, Dost Muhammad Khan, in 1839–40. In 1878 the British government made a final effort to save him by sending a mission to his court; but it was driven back with threats and contumely. Accordingly the British government declared war, and a British force entered Afghanistan. Sher Ali Khan made a futile attempt at resistance, and then fled northward into Russian territory, where he died shortly afterward.

Yakub Khan came to terms with the British government. He was accepted as successor to his deceased father on the throne of Afghanistan; and he agreed to receive a British

[1] See ante, p. 399.

Resident, who should permanently remain at his capital. The treacherous attack on the Residency in September, 1879, and massacre of Sir Louis Cavagnari and other officers, has led to the abdication of Yakub Khan and British occupation of Afghanistan. What the result will be is one of the political problems of the day.[1]

[1] The probable destiny of the Afghan people may possibly be gathered from a historical parallel in Jewish history, which the controverted question of Afghan ethnology renders none the less striking. The parallel is helped out by the fact which is beyond controversy; namely, that in physical characteristics and national instincts the Afghans closely resemble, if they are not akin to, the Jews (see ante, p. 149). The old Assyrian kings tried hard to maintain Palestine as a buffer against Egypt; but they were ultimately compelled to transplant the Ten Tribes of Israel to the cities of the Medes; while the only king of Judah who was actively loyal to the Crown of Assyria was the unfortunate Josiah, who was slain by Pharaoh Necho in the battle of Megiddo. Four centuries later the Greek kings of Syria endeavored to convert Palestine into a similar buffer; but after trying in vain to crush out the spirit of the nation by military despotism and massacre, they were compelled to succumb to the revolt of the Maccabees. Two centuries later the Romans made every effort to maintain order and law among the turbulent populations of Palestine; but after the death of Herod the Great—a Dost Muhammad in his way—the princes of his family dared not govern mildly lest their subjects should rebel, nor severely lest they should be deposed by Cæsar. Their régime proved a failure. No rulers, except Roman procurators of the stamp of Pilate and Festus, could succeed in keeping the peace. In the end, the grinding tyranny and rapacity of procurators of the stamp of Florus drove the nation frantic; and the struggle ended in the destruction of Jerusalem by Titus and final scattering of the Jewish nation.

From the sixteenth century to the nineteenth the political situation of Afghanistan has tallied with that of Palestine. The Moghuls tried to make Kabul a buffer against Persia, and Persia tried to make Kandahar a buffer against the Moghul. In the eighteenth century the Afghans rose against their conquerors; those of Kandahar overran Persia, and those of Kabul and Kandahar overran Hindustan. A new Afghan empire was subsequently founded by Ahmad Shah Durani, who bears a strange resemblance to King David; for in spite of his predatory wars and conquests, he gave utterance to strains of psalmody of which the following lines are a specimen:

"I cry unto thee, O God! for I am of my sins and wickedness ashamed;
But hopeless of thy mercy, no one hath ever from thy threshold departed.
Thy goodness and mercy are boundless, and I am of my evil acts ashamed;
'Tis hopeless that any good deeds of mine will avail, but thy name I'll every refuge make.
O Ahmad! seek thou help from the Almighty, but not from pomp and grandeur's aid."

It will also be seen that the reign of his grandson Zeman Shah bears some resemblances to that of Rehoboam; while the revolt of the Barukzais, the viziers of the Duranis, is not unlike the revolt of Jeroboam, the minister of Solomon. How far Afghanistan is likely to prove a buffer between British India and Russia, with or without British procurators, remains to be seen.

SUPPLEMENTARY CHAPTER

LORD RIPON—AFGHANISTAN—THE MARCH FROM KABUL TO KANDAHAR—LORD DUFFERIN AND KING THEEBAW—THE ANNEXATION OF UPPER BURMA—THE MARCH OF EMPIRE—LORD CURZON INSTALLED

A.D. 1879 TO 1899

IN 1880 Lord Lytton retired from India and Lord Ripon was appointed Viceroy. Meanwhile Lord Beaconsfield had resigned office and Gladstone had returned to power. This was the first time in history that a change of Ministers in England was followed in India by a change of Viceroys and a change of policy. Lord Ripon was bent on peace. But Roberts had yet to march from Kabul to Kandahar. The Afghan war had not been fought.

Afghanistan is India's natural barrier, consisting mainly of bleak and rugged tablelands that are girdled by stupendous mountain ranges and intersected by precipitous ravines, it is the only road by which an invading army can reach the banks of the Indus. The people, fanatical Muhammadans, are as turbulent as the country, and so averse to any kind of control that a chief once cried to a traveller: "We are content with discord, we are content with blood, but we will never be content with a master."

With reference to their fighting qualities an able officer wrote: "An Afghan never thinks of asking quarter, but fights with the ferocity of a tiger, and clings to life till his eyes glaze and his hands refuse to pull a pistol trigger, or use a knife in a dying effort to kill or maim his enemy. The stern realities of war were more pronounced on the battlefields of Afghanistan than perhaps they have ever been in India, if we except the retribution days of the Mutiny. To spare a wounded man for a minute was probably to cause the death of the next soldier who unsuspectingly walked past him. . . . One thing our men certainly learned in Afghanistan, and that was to keep their wits about them when pursuing an enemy or passing over a hard-won field. There might be danger lurking in each seemingly inanimate form studding the ground, and unless care and caution were exercised, the wounded Afghan would steep his soul in bliss by killing a Kafir just when life was at its last ebb. This stubborn love of fighting *in extremis* is promoted, doubtless, by fanaticism, and we saw so much of it that our men at close quarters always drove their bayonets well home, so that there should be no mistake as to the deadliness of the wound. The physical courage which distinguished the untrained mobs who fought so resolutely against us was worthy of all admiration; the temerity with which men, badly armed, and lacking skilled leaders, clung to their positions, was remarkable, to say nothing of the sullen doggedness they so often showed when retiring. But when the tide of the fight set in fully against them, and they saw that further resistance would involve them more deeply, there was so sudden a change always apparent that one could scarcely believe that the fugitives hurrying over the hills were the same men who had resisted so desperately but a few minutes before. They acted wisely; they knew their powers in scaling steep hills, or making their escape by fleetness of foot; and the host generally dissolved with a rapidity which no one but an eye-witness can appreciate. If cavalry overtook them, they turned like wolves, and fought with desperation, selling their lives as dearly as ever men sold them; but there was no rally in the true sense of the word, and but faint attempts at aiding each other. Their regular troops were but little amenable to discipline, by reason of deficient training, and they resorted to the tactics they had pursued as tribesmen when once they were forced to retire."

In 1877 the Amir, Sher Ali, refused to receive a British Resident at his court. His reasons were threefold: First, the persons of British subjects would not be safe—as the event proved; secondly, they might make demands that would occasion quarrels; thirdly, if British agents were admitted, Russia would demand the same privilege.

Prior to all this, in 1872, an arrangement had been entered into between Lord Granville and Prince Gortschakoff, by which Afghanistan was declared to be "outside the sphere within which Russia should be called upon to exercise her influence." The Oxus was laid down as the boundary of the territories of the Amirs of Bokhara and Afghanistan, and of the legitimate influence of Russia and Great Britain. But this did not prevent Russia in 1878—the period when the two empires were "diplomatically at war"—from sending the fatal Stoletoff Mission to Kabul. "We have thus," says Geddie, "to thank Russia for the cost and trouble of the Afghan war; and the unfortunate Sher Ali, who died near the Oxus while fleeing for refuge to his faithful 'friend,'" also owed to her the loss of his kingdom.

It was in the summer of 1878 that Russia sent an embassy on a grand scale, accompanied by a military escort, from Samarcand, a city of Bokhara which Russia had seized about ten years before, and thus thought she had opened the avenue that would eventually lead to British India!

A little later the Amir instructed the commandant of the fort in the Khaiber Pass to refuse permission to the British Special Mission to proceed to Kabul. Now, in view of the fact already noted that the Amir had received a Russian envoy in his capital, and had treated him with marked consideration, Lord Lytton, as we saw in the last chapter, issued a formal declaration of war and four columns were formed for invasion.

Of these columns one was placed under the command of Major-General Frederick Roberts, V. C.—now Lord Roberts of Kandahar—another under Sir Samuel Browne, the third under Lieutenant-General Donald Stewart, and the fourth, known as the Thal-Chotiali Field Force, under Major-General Sir Michael Biddulph.

The chief laurels of the Afghan war were, however, carried off by Roberts, who, little known at its beginning, earned a world-wide fame at its end. His first object was to dislodge the enemy from the strong position which it had assumed in the Peiwar Kotul, an almost impregnable pass. In this he was brilliantly successful, but meanwhile the government having decided to defer further advance till the spring, and subsequently a treaty having been signed, hostilities were apparently terminated. But in the East nothing is so certain as the unforeseen. In accordance with the terms of the treaty, Yakub Khan, the son and successor of Sher Ali—who in the interim had died—agreed to receive a British officer as Resident at Kabul. Sir Louis Cavagnari was appointed to the post and was welcomed there with every appearance of cordiality. Within two months the Residency was environed by an army of Afghans and, as related in the last chapter, Cavagnari and his officers were massacred.

Roberts was at Simla when this occurred. On the morrow, at the head of about six thousand men, he started for Ali Kheyl. Pushing on thence to Kabul, he encountered the Afghan army, strongly intrenched at Charasia.

"Their position," as he has described it, "was so strong, and could only have been carried with such loss, that I determined the real attack should be made by an outflanking movement upon the right of the enemy, while their left continued to be occupied by a feint from our right." Dividing his force into two parts, he intrusted to Brigadier-General Baker the difficult task of dislodging the enemy from the heights above the Chardeh valley, which formed their extreme right, placing at his disposal a force of about two thousand men, while a second column, under Major White, of the Ninety-second Highlanders, was directed to proceed toward the Sang-i-Nawishta defile, where the enemy had concentrated all their guns in the belief that the main British attack would be on that point.

According to Mr. C. R. Low,[1] from whose account of the

[1] Battles of the British Army.

expedition the following details are derived, Roberts, owing to his numerical weakness, could only retain in camp a small force, and as Macpherson's brigade was advancing from the rear, he determined to incur the risk of an attack on his camp, and left for its defence only seven hundred infantry and four hundred and fifty cavalry.

Having secured his base in the wooded enclosures of Charasia, a collection of detached villages, Baker advanced over some bare, undulating hills—forming a position easily defensible, and flanked by steep, rocky crags, varying in height from one thousand to one thousand eight hundred feet above the sloping plains which the troops had to cross—against the main position of the enemy, about four hundred feet higher, which commanded his entire front, and was only accessible in a few places. A portion of the Ninety-second Highlanders and Fifth Ghorkas advanced to crown the heights on the left, while the remainder of these regiments and two hundred men of the Fifth Punjaubees made the direct attack, and, after some spirited fighting, about two o'clock the British troops succeeded in seizing the ridge on the left of the position, when the general advance was sounded. The Afghans retreated to a position about six hundred yards in the rear, but from this they were driven by the troops advancing in rushes, supported by the fire of the mountain guns. By a quarter to four the entire ridge was gained, thus exposing the enemy's line of defence to being taken in reverse, which caused them to retire precipitately from their position on the Sang-i-Nawishta, in which quarter the operations were conducted by Major White with a judgment and skill that fully justified the trust reposed in him by Roberts. When the enemy, perceiving that the real attack was on the right of their position, weakened their left resting on the defile, Major White attacked with spirit, himself leading his men with characteristic gallantry. The Afghans gave way, leaving some guns in his hands, on which he pursued them through the pass and effected a junction with General Baker in the rear of the enemy's position.

The Afghan loss in killed was estimated at upward of three hundred, and all their guns, twenty in number, brought out from Kabul to assist in defence of the position, were captured. Roberts calculated that thirteen regiments of regular infantry were opposed to him, and the enemy were aided by contingents from the city and neighboring villages, and by a large number of tribesmen, chiefly Ghilzais, from the hills which lay to the east and west of the camp. Macpherson's advance from Zahidabad was opposed, but he easily drove off his assailants, and, after his arrival in camp, all anxiety on the score of its safety ceased. The British loss in the action of Charasia was sixteen killed, and three officers and fifty-nine men wounded.

Roberts marched early on the following morning through the Sang-i-Nawishta defile to Beni Hissar, on the Kabul road, and on October 8 the great cantonment of Sherpur was occupied by the cavalry brigade, under Brigadier-General Massy, who captured seventy-three guns. Some troops occupied the Bala Hissar, or citadel-palace of Kabul, through the streets of which the British army marched, and those concerned in the massacre of the mission were brought to justice and executed. Meanwhile the Ghilzais and other tribes had attacked the troops left at the Shutargardan pass, under Colonel Money, but Roberts sent Brigadier-General Hugh Gough with a force to his assistance, and the tribesmen were defeated with considerable loss. As the winter season forbade the pass from being used as a line of communication with India, which in future would have to be carried on by the Khaiber route, General Gough and Colonel Money evacuated the Shutargardan and arrived at Sherpur on November 4 with their troops.

On October 16 there were terrific explosions of gunpowder, cartridges, and shells in the Bala Hissar, and Captain Shafto, R.A., and some soldiers and many natives were killed, and the British troops were all marched into the Sherpur cantonments, where was ample barrack accommodation. The general had learned the wisdom of concentrating his troops by the sad lessons taught by the events of the first Afghan war, in which his father, Sir Abraham Roberts, had been employed. With a people so fierce and independent as the Afghans, nothing was more probable than an attempt to repeat the scenes of that terrible winter, when the infuriated Kabulees besieged the small British army in the cantonment partially situated on the site of that occupied thirty-eight years later by another British force. But the commander of 1879 was of a different mold from General Elphinstone, and the troops also were animated by a sense of superiority and not cowed by repeated defeats, the result of incapacity and vacillation. The events that happened throughout the first Afghan war, including the massacre of a British Envoy, and the destruction of a British force, were faithfully repeated in 1879, even to the investment of the British cantonment; but as the disasters of 1842 were wiped out by British triumphs, so the leaguer of Sherpur ended, not in disgrace, but in a crushing defeat for the besiegers.

It was in December, some two months after his arrival at Kabul, that the people and tribes of this portion of Afghanistan—instigated by an aged fanatic Moollah, Mooskh-i-Alum (literally "scent of the world"), Sultan Jan, from the Maidan and Ghuznee districts, Meer Butcha, from the mountainous Kohistan country to the north of the city, and other rebel leaders—rose to the number of about one hundred thousand combatants to expel the invaders from the soil of their country. Roberts was at first unaware of the strength of the coalition, but took immediate steps to disperse the large bodies of tribesmen before they could effect a junction, and, on December 8, sent Macpherson with a brigade toward the west, *viâ* Urghandeh, in order to engage the enemy coming from Maidan, and Baker with a column, *viâ* Charasia, also toward Maidan, with the object of placing himself across the line by which the enemy would retire. The troops at Sherpur were thus reduced to a point of dangerous weakness, notwithstanding that they were reinforced by the arrival of the Guides Corps from Jugdulluck; and had it not been for Roberts' promptitude and military skill, after the check received on December 11 by the cavalry, it is certain that a great disaster must have ensued. This was the only miscalculation Roberts made throughout the war, and we know, from the dictum of the great Napoleon, who was himself guilty of strategic mistakes, that the greatest general is he who makes the fewest blunders, hence implying that the military commander must not be expected to be exempt from the failures that await the action of all human agency.

Acting under orders, Macpherson changed his line of advance, and marched to disperse the Kohistanees; and, in order to cut the enemy's line of retreat, the cavalry and horse artillery, under Brigadier-General Massy, were despatched from Sherpur to his assistance. Without waiting for orders from Macpherson, Massy attacked a force of about ten thousand infantry, in a position in which his cavalry could not act with advantage, and the result was that he lost two guns, and the cavalry were forced to retreat after delivering two charges, in which they lost twenty-seven killed, including four officers, and twenty-five wounded, the Ninth Lancers being the chief sufferers. Roberts immediately proceeded from Sherpur with the Seventy-second Highlanders to secure the Deh Mazung defile, barring the road to the city of Kabul, and was barely in time to prevent its falling into the hands of the enemy. Here he was joined by Macpherson, and on the following morning recalled Baker's brigade, the guns lost having been recovered by Colonel C. Macgregor, chief of the staff. On the morning of the 12th, Macpherson, advancing from the Bala Hissar and Deh Mazung, sent Colonel Money with a portion of his force to attack the enemy on the crest of the Takt-i-Shah. The fighting lasted all day without result, and on the following morning Baker, who had returned to Sherpur, acted in concert with Macpherson's brigade, and after some desperate fighting, the Ninety-second and Guides, led by Major

White, reached the summit, where the Seventy-second, Third Sikhs and Fifth Ghorkas, under Major Sym, had arrived a few minutes before. Meanwhile large bodies of the enemy, issuing from the city, collected on the Siah Sung heights and the villages toward Beni Hissar. From the latter they were driven out by Baker's brigade, when returning from Takt-i-Shah, and the masses collected at Siah Sung were dispersed by dashing cavalry charges made by the Guides, Fifth Punjab Cavalry and Ninth Lancers, which lost Captain Butson and four men killed, and two officers and eight men wounded. The Afghans, nothing daunted by their reverses, and reinforced by great masses of men, now occupied the Asmai heights. Baker was sent to dislodge them from this position and cut off their communications with the north. Colonel Jenkins, of the Guides, was successful in driving them from a conical hill, and the Asmai heights were gained; but the enemy were largely reinforced, and after a stubborn defence of the conical hill, Jenkins's column was compelled to retreat with the loss of two guns. At this time, a dashing cavalry charge was made by twelve men of the Fifth Punjab Cavalry, led by Captain Vousden, who killed five Afghans with his own hand, for which he received the V.C.

As it was evident that the enemy were in overwhelming force, General Roberts abandoned the Bala Hissar and Asmai heights, which were occupied by the enemy, and by the night of December 14 concentrated his troops in Sherpur, where, with considerable foresight, he had collected some months' stores in preparation for all eventualities. While waiting for the reinforcements for which he had applied to the government of India, he employed his troops in strengthening the defences of Sherpur.

The losses during the operations between December 10 and 14 were eight officers and seventy-five men killed, and twelve officers and one hundred and eighty-five wounded. Two of the officers, Colonel Cleland, Ninth Lancers, and Major Cook, Fifth Ghorkas, who had gained the V.C. for gallantry at the Peiwar Kotul, died of their wounds.

There was desultory fighting with the enemy between December 14 and 21, and on the 23d, the anniversary of the murder of Sir William Macnaghten at this spot in 1841, they delivered their long-prepared attack, but were repulsed with great slaughter. The fighting lasted between daybreak and nightfall, and the Afghans brought scaling-ladders to enter the works; but they were never able to plant them, and so rapidly did they disperse that by night not a trace of them could be seen by the cavalry, which sallied out in pursuit during a heavy snowstorm. The casualties during the investment of Sherpur were two officers and eight men killed, and five officers, including Brigadier-General Hugh Gough, and forty-one rank and file wounded. On the 24th reinforcements arrived, under Colonel Hudson, from Lutterbund, and from Gundamuck under Brigadier-General Charles Gough, who now occupied the Bala Hissar, while a column was despatched, under General Baker, to punish the Kohistanees.

Some months later Roberts sent a force under Major-General John Ross to Shekabad, in the neighborhood of which they had successful encounters with the enemy on April 25, 1880, and two succeeding days. A severe action was fought on the 25th, on the old battlefield of Charasia, by a small force of eight hundred and eighty-three officers and men, under Colonel Jenkins, who was reinforced from Sherpur during the action by General Macpherson's brigade. The enemy, about four thousand or five thousand strong, attacked Jenkins, who remained on the defensive until the arrival of Macpherson, when the gallant officers made a combined movement in advance, and the enemy were defeated with great loss, after which the whole force returned to Sherpur. The loss incurred during the day was four killed and thirty-four wounded.

On May 2, General Donald Stewart arrived from Kandahar with a strong column, including the Fifty-ninth Regiment and Second Battalion Sixtieth Rifles, with three batteries of artillery. He left at Kandahar a division of his troops, under General Primrose, the object of his march being to break up any hostile combination at Ghuznee, and open communications with Kabul. As Stewart was senior to Roberts, he assumed the chief command. His march was remarkable for a severe action fought at Ahmed Khel. The route from Kandahar was through a country deserted by its inhabitants, where supplies were scarce; and though the advance was not so striking in its rapidity and results as the famous march made a few months later by Roberts, it deserves greater commendation than it has received. For several days previous to the approach of the troops to Ghuznee, a hostile gathering marched about eight miles on the right flank, and, on April 19, the enemy were observed in position at Ahmed Khel, three miles in advance of the head of the column, which covered in the order of march no less than six miles. When the leading brigades, under Generals Palliser and Hughes, were about two thousand five hundred yards from the enemy's line, the guns came into action, but scarcely had they opened fire, and before the intended attack of the position was developed, the crest of the range occupied by the enemy was observed to be swarming with men along a front of nearly two miles, a body of horsemen on the right outflanking the left of the British line. In an incredibly short space of time, an enormous mass of men, with standards, formed on the hilltop, a considerable number of horsemen riding along the ridge, with the intention of sweeping to the rear of the British line to attack the baggage. From the central mass out rushed successive waves of swordsmen on foot, stretching out right and left, and seeming to envelop the position. The horsemen turned the British left, forcing back the native cavalry, and the right of the line of infantry, then hotly pressed, gave way. The onslaught of between three thousand and four thousand fanatic swordsmen was at this time so rapid, and was pushed with such desperation, that it became necessary to place every man of the reserve in the firing line. The enemy, however, continued to push on, and approached within a few yards of the guns, when, the whole of their case-shot being expended, both batteries were withdrawn a distance of two hundred yards, and the infantry of the right also took up a fresh position. But the attack had spent itself, and time being given for the guns to check the forward movement of the enemy's horsemen round the left flank, General Barter came up with the rearguard and reinforced the right centre. The action was over at ten o'clock, within one hour of its commencement, and the enemy, who numbered between twelve thousand and fifteen thousand infantry and one thousand horsemen, broke up and dispersed over the country, their loss being estimated at from two thousand to three thousand, while that of the victors was seventeen killed and one hundred and twenty-four wounded, including nine officers. After a halt of two hours, the army continued its march, with the baggage in close formation, over the enemy's position, completing a distance of seventeen miles.

On the following day Ghuznee was entered, and as the Afghans had taken up a position at some villages about sixteen miles from camp, on the 23d General Stewart marched to dislodge them, and the enemy were driven off with the loss of four hundred men.

No important military operations were undertaken by the large army now assembled at and near Kabul, amounting to some eighteen thousand men, under these two distinguished Indian generals. On July 1, the cavalry brigade of General Hills' division, numbering five hundred and seventy-seven sabres, under Brigadier-General Palliser, encountered and routed, in the Logar valley, a body of one thousand five hundred tribesmen belonging to Zermut, of whom two hundred were killed during the pursuit, the British loss being only three killed and twenty-nine wounded.

Everything now portended a speedy return of the Expeditionary force to India. Since March, Roberts and (on his arrival at Kabul) Sir Donald Stewart, and Mr. Lepel Griffin, the political officer sent from India by the Viceroy, had been negotiating with Abdurrahman Khan—son of Afzul Khan, elder brother of Sher Ali, and grandson of Dost Muhammad Khan, the great Amir of Afghanistan during the former war—who, for ten years, had been resident in Russian Turkestan as a pensioner of the Czar. Incensed at his exclusion, Ayub Khan, a younger brother of Yakub Khan, now a prisoner in India, quitted Herat on June 27, resolved to strike a blow for power, and moved upon Kandahar, with the intention of seizing the southern capital of Afghanistan. At this time an Afghan force was stationed at Giriskh, on the Helmund, under the Wali, or governor of Kandahar; and to check the advance of Ayub Khan, who was known to have left Herat with a force of six thousand men and thirty guns, a British brigade left Kandahar, on July 3, under Brigadier-General Burrows, and joined the Wali at Giriskh.

On the 14th the Wali's troops mutinied and deserted to Ayub Khan, and as this increased the difficulties of his position, and the river Helmund was fordable, Burrows, on the following day, marched from Giriskh to Khuski-Nakud. The strength of his column was one thousand seven hundred and eighty-eight bayonets, including five hundred and sixteen of the Sixty-sixth Foot, five hundred and fifty-six sabres (Sinde Horse and Bombay Cavalry), a detachment of forty-four sappers, and a battery of horse artillery, manned by one hundred and forty-six officers and men. In addition, there was a battery of six-pounders taken from the mutinous troops and manned by forty-two men of the Sixty-sixth Foot. On the 26th, Burrows, who had received imperative instructions that Ayub was to be intercepted if he attempted to slip past Kandahar toward Ghuznee, learned that two thousand of the enemy's cavalry and a large number of Ghazis had arrived near Maiwand, and that Ayub was about to follow with the main body of his army.

Accordingly, at half-past six on the morning of July 27, Burrows marched with his brigade for Maiwand, twelve miles distant, encumbered by an enormous train of stores and baggage, which, owing to the hostile state of the country, he could not leave behind without weakening his already small force. After proceeding about eight miles, large masses of the enemy, estimated at twenty-five thousand men, were discovered about four miles distant, moving in a diagonal direction across his right front. As it was evident that a collision with Ayub Khan must take place before he reached his destination, Burrows placed his baggage in the village under a guard, and on the higher ground beyond deployed his infantry into line, with guns in the centre, and the cavalry on the left, covering the movement with two horse artillery guns, escorted by a troop of cavalry.

About noon the engagement commenced by the advanced guns coming into action on the left, followed shortly by two more guns and the smooth-bore battery in the centre. The remaining two nine-pounders were soon after brought up from the rearguard. In about half an hour the enemy began to reply from their right, gradually extending along their front, and concentrating their fire on the British position. The infantry were ordered to lie down, and the wing of the Thirtieth N. I., which had been in reserve, was brought up on the flanks, which were threatened on the right by Ghazis and on the left by the enemy's regular cavalry. Thus the brigade remained for nearly three hours, the artillery making excellent practice, the cavalry holding the enemy's cavalry in check, but losing heavily in horses under the accurate artillery fire, and the infantry keeping up a steady fusillade on the Ghazis on the right. A large body of the enemy's regular infantry were on the British left front, and about the middle of the day they advanced in line, but were checked by well-directed volleys.

Between two and three o'clock the fire of the enemy's guns slackened, and swarms of Ghazis advanced rapidly toward the British centre. "Up to this time," says General Burrows, "the casualties among the infantry had not been heavy, and as the men were firing steadily and the guns were sweeping the ground with case-shot, full confidence was felt by the little army as to the result." But a rapid change came over the scene. The chief lesson inculcated by our Indian military history is that a British force should act on the offensive. It has ever been so—at Plassy, Assaye, Meanee, and in all the battles where a determined charge, even by a handful of British infantry, has turned the day. Encouraged by their foe remaining on the defensive for so many hours—a tacit acknowledgment of weakness—the Ghazis, regardless of the British fire, came on in overwhelming numbers, and, making good their rush, seized the two advanced horse artillery guns. With the exception of two companies of the Thirtieth N. I., which had displayed unsteadiness early in the day, the conduct of the troops had been splendid up to this point; but now, at a critical moment, when a firm resistance might have achieved a victory, these companies, which had lost their European officers, gave way, and soon the remainder of the Native Infantry fell back on the Sixty-sixth, which maintained a steady front. General Burrows in vain used every effort, assisted by his staff, to rally the troops, who, he says, "commencing from the left, rolled up like a wave to the right." As a last resort, he called upon his cavalry to charge across the front, and thus give the infantry a chance of re-forming; but the terrible artillery fire to which they had been exposed, and from which they had suffered severely, had so demoralized them that only the officers and a few men responded to General Nuttall's order.

All was now over, and the gallant Sixty-sixth Regiment, and a portion of the First Bombay N. I., retreating across the nullah and the gardens near the village, reached a small walled enclosure, where about one hundred and fifty men with several officers made a stand and checked the enemy for a time. Seeing, however, that they were rapidly being outflanked, and that their line of retreat would presently be cut off, the general gave the order to retire. A scene of disorder ensued, but a remnant of the infantry succeeded in joining the guns and cavalry in rear of the baggage, which was by this time stretching for miles over the country toward Kandahar, over forty miles distant. Fortunately, no vigorous pursuit was made by the enemy, though after daylight the fugitives were fired on from every village they passed, until they met a small force under Brigadier-General Brooke, which cleared the way for them into Kandahar. Of the horse artillery and smooth-bore guns taken into action, four of the former and one of the latter were brought safely into Kandahar, the five other smooth-bore guns had, one by one, to be abandoned during the retreat, the horses being unable to bring them on. Nothing could exceed the determined valor of the European portion of the force, the soldiers of the Sixty-sixth, who died fighting, like the Twenty-fourth at Isandhlwana, and the gunners of the artillery. "Exposed," says Burrows, "to a heavy fire, the artillerymen served their guns coolly and steadily as on parade, and when the guns were rushed, they fought the Ghazis with handspikes and sponge-rods. There fell at Maiwand twenty-six officers (including Colonel Galbraith of the Sixty-sixth, and Major Blackwood, commanding the artillery), two hundred and ninety-seven European soldiers and seven hundred and one sepoys, and three hundred and thirty-one camp followers. Fourteen officers, forty-two European and one hundred and thirty-nine native soldiers were wounded. As soon as the shattered remnants of General Burrows' force arrived at Kandahar, General Primrose hastily evacuated the cantonment outside the city, and concentrated his force—consisting of two batteries of artillery, the Seventh Fusiliers, and two regiments and a wing of N. I.—in the citadel, in expectation of an attack by Ayub Khan, who, advancing leisurely, took up a position for beleaguering the British garrison. General Primrose made a sortie, but it was mismanaged, and Brigadier-General Brooke and a large number of officers and men of the Seventh Fusiliers and Native Infantry were killed and wounded. After this the garrison remained inactive until relieved.

It was on July 29, as Sir Donald Stewart and Roberts were engaged concerting measures for withdrawing the army from Kabul to India by way of the Khaiber pass and Kurram valley, that the startling news of the disaster at Maiwand, like "a bolt out of the blue," was received at the British headquarters. Roberts immediately offered to assume command of a force of ten thousand men to relieve Kandahar and rehabilitate British honor, and the offer was accepted by the Indian government. An arrangement having been already concluded with Abdurrahman Khan for taking over the government of the country, on August 8 the troops selected marched out of Sherpur into camp, and Roberts issued a characteristic order before commencing one of the most famous marches recorded in British history.

The strength of the Kabul-Kandahar Field Force—which included three batteries of artillery, the Ninth Lancers, the Seventy-second and Ninety-second Highlanders, and the Second Battalion Sixtieth Rifles—was ten thousand one hundred and forty-eight combatants, two hundred and twenty-three medical staff, and eight thousand one hundred and thirty-four camp followers. As wheeled artillery was unsuitable for the country to be traversed, a battery of seven-pounders (jointed guns) was carried on mules.

The army set out on its adventurous march of nearly three hundred miles on August 9. On the 15th, Ghuznee, ninety-seven and a half miles distant, was reached, and on the following day the army passed over the battlefield of Ahmed Khel. The strong fort of Khelat-i-Ghilzye, held by a small column, under Colonel Tanner, was reached on August 23, the distance traversed in eight days being one hundred and thirty-six miles, or sixteen and three-quarter miles per day. The division halted here on August 24, and on the following day, accompanied by the garrison of that fortress, continued the march to Kandahar, eighty-eight miles distant, by the Turnuk valley route. Communication was opened with General Primrose by the cavalry on August 27 at Robat, and the Field Force moved to Momund on August 31, and on the following day arrived before Kandahar.

Though suffering from fever, Roberts quitted his doolie, and, mounting his horse, reconnoitred the enemy's position, when he determined to turn the Baba Wali pass, where they had posted heavy guns, instead of carry it by direct assault, which would entail heavy loss. A reconnoissance in force was made the same day by the cavalry under General Hugh Gough, and on the following morning, September 1, the two brigades of the Kabul Field Force, with the Third in reserve, advanced against the enemy's position at Gundigan and Pir Paimal, while the cavalry brigade was posted so as to cut off the enemy's line of retreat to Giriskh, and the Kandahar garrison were directed to hold the city and precincts, and make a feint on the Baba Wali pass.

The village of Gundi Mulla Sahibdad was stormed by the Ninety-second Highlanders and Second Ghorkas, supported by the Second Brigade, and it was while engaged clearing some enclosures that the gallant Colonel Brownlow, commanding the Seventy-second Highlanders, who had faced death so often since the capture of the Peiwar Kotul, met his end. Soon after noon the village of Pir Paimal was carried at the point of the bayonet, and, pushing on, the First and Second Brigades, at 1 P.M., entered the enemy's camp. In this advance, Major White, of the Ninety-second Highlanders, "gallant and ever foremost," as Roberts said of him in his despatch, greatly distinguished himself.

The rout of Ayub Khan was complete, among the trophies being thirty-two pieces of ordnance, including five in position at Baba Wali Kotul, abandoned by the enemy, and the two horse artillery guns captured at Maiwand. Leaving one thousand dead on the field, he fled toward Herat with a handful of infantry and cavalry, the remnants of a force of thirteen thousand men. The British loss was three officers and forty men killed, and two hundred and twenty-eight wounded, including eleven officers. Not another shot was fired during the remainder of the stay of the British force at Kandahar, which was evacuated in accordance with the promise of the British government and the advice of many officers of distinction, including Lord Wolseley and General Gordon, though others equally qualified to give an opinion, as Sir Donald Stewart and Roberts, were opposed to the measure. As a result of the war, the districts of Pishin, Sibi and Thal Chotiali were annexed, and more recently the Kakar country and Khetrai valley became subject to British administration. But the sacrifice in lives and treasure was immeasurably greater than the value of the results attained, and for the second time in history Afghanistan was a synonym for disaster. The time may not be far distant when this difficult country will again be the theatre of military operations. When the Russian and the English soldier, the Cossack and the Sepoy, are locked in deadly struggle on the banks of the Oxus and the Helmund, let us hope the name of Afghanistan may be an augury for victory, and the warlike races within its borders, oblivious of the memories of the invasions of 1839 and 1879, may be rallied under our banners as allies, and not assembled under those of our enemies, eager to pay off old scores.

The British army returned from Afghanistan in 1881, and thenceforth the administration of Lord Ripon was one of peace. During the interval he abolished the import duties, especially those on cotton goods, enlarged the principle of local self-government, extended the criminal jurisdiction of native civil servants, and initiated other domestic measures which raised grave questions of policy, and of which the value is undetermined still.

Lord Ripon was in 1884 succeeded by Lord Dufferin, under whose Viceroyalty the annexation of Upper Burma and the final expansion of British India occurred.

Burma is situated in the region beyond the mountains which form the eastern frontier of Bengal, and until Lord Dufferin's administration had been divided into independent Burma, of which Mandalay is the capital, and British Burma, of which the capital is Rangoon. The latter is on the coast, the former in the interior.

Rangoon has existed as a town for over two thousand years, but it was long known only as a stopping place for pilgrims on their way to the great Shway Dagohn pagoda, which is the Mecca of the Indu-Chinese Buddhists. Later it was the residence of the regent of Pegu, as being the guard station on the most accessible mouth of the Irawadi, on which Mandalay is situated. At the beginning of the present century the town stretched along the bank for about a mile, and did not extend more than five hundred yards from the river. The official town was surrounded by a log stockade, fortified by an indifferent kind of fosse, spanned by a wooden bridge. Swine and dogs roamed at will over the town, as they were allowed to do in Mandalay, and acted as efficient scavengers. The principal building was the custom house, and this was just tottering into ruins, and there was a rickety erection known as the King's Wharf. Jungle grew close up to the palisading on the north, and southward the rice-fields extended from the doors of the suburban houses right away to the mouth of the river.

The town came into the hands of the English in 1852. The morasses were filled up with earth from the higher ground inland, the stockade was pulled down, and at the present time it is impossible to realize the old dismal descriptions of the place. Now there are broad smooth roads, well laid out public gardens and parks, abundant street lamps, spacious mercantile offices, schools, mills, hospitals, jails, law courts, halls, and club-houses. Railways connect it with the interior, and large sea-going steamers visit it in ever-increasing numbers. The population, from a paltry ten thousand, has grown to two hundred thousand, and the central town threatens soon to swallow up the neighboring villages of Poozoondoung and Kemmendine and Kokhine, just as London has engulfed the Highgates and Kensingtons and Chelseas of last century. Rangoon claims the title of

Queen of the East, and, with the new openings for trade offered by the annexation of Upper Burma, there is little doubt that she will justify the claim and outstrip Calcutta. Hitherto the progress made will compare with the most vaunted of American city successes.

Three hundred miles to the north is Mandalay. Like all Indu-Chinese official towns it is divided into two, the walled city and the suburbs. The latter extend two miles down to the river, and straggle for about the same distance in all directions over the level plain. The city proper is a huge walled square, each face a mile and an eighth long. The mud-mortar built walls are twenty-six feet high, machicolated at the top; they are three feet thick, backed with a heavy mass of earth, and along the ramparts are wooden lookout towers of an ornate style of architecture suggestive of China. There are twelve gates to the city, three on each side, but only one bridge over the moat to each three, except on the west, where there are two. The moat is about sixty feet from the walls, and considerably more than that wide, covered in many places with the lotus-plant that the Buddhist loves. Here and there upon it float royal craft, state barges, and despatch-boats, gilt from stem to stern and manned by sometimes as many as sixty paddlers. The city is well and regularly laid out. From the gates roughly macadamized roads a hundred feet wide run parallel to the walls. They are lined with young trees (Mandalay only exists since 1857), and down the sides of most of them run little streams of water. Between these main streets, and parallel to them, are others, narrower, but still very orderly. There is no attempt at a drainage system, but the town is essentially clean and airy, thanks to the unmolested, or, rather, cherished pigs and dogs that act as highly efficient scavengers, and the constant open spaces insuring ventilation.

Forming a species of redoubt in the centre of the city is the palace, which has two successive enclosures—the outer, a log stockade, with elaborate turreted gateways; the inner, a brick wall, with a broad esplanade between the two. In the exact centre of the palace and of the city rises the seven-roofed spire, emblematic of royalty and religion, which the Burmese look upon as the centre of Burma, and, therefore, of creation. Apart from the supreme court and hall of audience, the royal dwelling consists mainly of a rambling succession of gardens, and pleasure or residential houses. The higher officials live within the palace stockade, and there also are the mint, arsenal, treasury, powder-magazines, and other public buildings.

In the walled city live the lower officials and the soldiery, and in the suburbs outside the traders and general population. This is estimated all around at something over a hundred thousand. There was a good deal of wealth in the commercial town, but it was in the hands of Chinese and Moghuls, with whom the king was afraid to meddle. No Burman could get rich with safety.

Scattered about over the outer town are great numbers of pagodas and monasteries and religious buildings. The monastic population is especially great. It has been estimated as high as thirty thousand. Chief among them is the royal monastery. This is a mass of gilding from the roof to the side-posts, inside and out. The eaves and the top of the side walls are covered with the bold open carving in which the Burmese show so much artistic skill, and this is as richly gilt as everything else. The boxes in which the palm-leaf manuscripts are kept are as elaborate in decoration as the commentaries themselves, and are valuable to students of Buddhist literature. Among the pagodas the most interesting is the so-called "Incomparable Pagoda." Round about the main shrine, which in itself is a marvel of decoration, there are many rows of other smaller ones, each sheltering a series of marble slabs in shape and appearance not unlike large gravestones. On these are engraved the "Tripitaka" the "Three Baskets of the Law," the Buddhist scriptures.

In figure the people are short and thickset, with high

cheek-bones and slightly projecting jaw, and the flat face which is undoubtedly Mongolian. There is but very little of the Chinese tilt of the eye. In color they vary from the tint of a wax-candle to that of a dead oak-leaf, according as they belong to the leisured town-classes or the workers in the rice-fields. Both men and women have long black hair, not unseldom three or four feet in length, and they are very proud of it. The men wear it in a knot on the top of the head, encircled by a turban; the women, in a chignon at the back. Both sexes are fond of bulking out this knot with false tresses. The men tattoo breeches on themselves from the waist to below the knee with sessamum-seed, sool. The figures traced are ogres, tigers, monkeys, spirits; and each is surrounded by a border of mysterious cabalistic letters, while magic squares and lucky marks are also commonly introduced. Vermilion figures are also tattooed on the chest and arms and back.

The streets are a curious study. There is an extraordinary variety of nationalities to be seen constantly in Mandalay. Every here and there one comes across a band of Shans; tall, stalwart men, very Chinese in feature, wearing usually nothing but baggy blue trousers and tattooed from the waist down to the ankles. Occasionally, too, though much more rarely of late years, one comes across a Kachyen hill-chieftain, with his train of ragged followers, slight, but wiry in figure, with aquiline noses, and shifty, fierce eyes, as different as possible from the thickset, open-faced Burman. Then there are parties of Arakanese, come over the hills to worship at the most holy "Arakian Pagoda," with its famous brass Gantama, said to have been cast from a model of the great Master himself, and to have been inspired with life by him for a day in response to ardent prayers.

Some one with a taste for comparisons has called the Burmese "the Irish of the East." In their love of fun and rollicking they certainly resemble "the finest peasantry in the world," and they are quite as ready to break one another's heads for the mere joke of the thing; but they are much too easy-going to bother themselves with demands for home rule, or the organization of land or any other leagues. A Burman is always ready to welcome a joke, and not unseldom is ready to cap it, while nothing is so remarkable about the natives of India as their utter incapacity to recognize wit.

During Lord Lytton's administration the king of these people was a mild and gentle prince. So long as he lived there was little or no bloodshed, and peaceful relations between the British government and Upper Burma were secured by the presence of a Resident at Mandalay.

Theebaw, his successor, was a monster of cruelty. His reign opened with a horrible massacre which included women and children, the remains being carried off in cartloads from the palace and thrown into the river. There was no one to restrain or control, no one with a shadow of power, save officials dependent on his will and who trembled for their lives. Some fugitives escaped to British territory, and their surrender was demanded by Theebaw. The British government refused to give up the refugees to certain death and torture, and then he manifested a spite which no consideration could mitigate. He treated the British Resident with such contumely that the latter was obliged to retire to Rangoon.

Theebaw then sent envoys to France and other European powers to secure their support. The British government tried to bring him to reason, but without success. He proposed to levy an exorbitant tax on all British ships entering the Upper Irawadi, and he called on the government to grant a free passage through its territory to all arms and ammunition that he might import from Europe. At last, as a State necessity, he was told that for the future he must admit a British Resident at Mandalay, and be guided by his advice in all dealings with foreign powers. By way of reply he issued proclamations calling on his subjects to prepare for war. The result added to the British dominions a country larger than any European state except Russia, and made its boundaries conterminous with those of China and Siam.

General Prendergast, V.C., of the Royal (Madras) Engineers, who served with distinction in the mutiny under Sir Hugh Rose, and in Abyssinia, under Lord Napier, commanded the expedition, which, in consequence of Theebaw's proclamations, then proceeded up the Irawadi, and no opposition was experienced until the troops arrived near Pagan. It was on November 24, 1885, that, after the Naval Brigade had dispersed a body of the enemy, the Second Hampshire Regiment (Sixty-seventh Foot) and Madras Sappers were landed and scaled the works of Pagan. King Theebaw's soldiers fled to the jungle without firing a shot, and on the same day the Naval Brigade and flotilla shelled the enemy out of their earthworks at the important town of Myingyan. Mandalay was occupied on the 28th, and the deposition was decreed of the "Golden-footed Monarch, Lord of the Sea and Land," as he arrogantly styled himself, who had treated the demands of the British government for justice to its subjects with an insolent defiance that could only have been justified by his power to brave their resentment. Theebaw quitted Mandalay on November 29 for India, and was at first detained at Arcot, near Madras, the scene of Clive's historic defence. Significantly enough, the so-called "White Elephant" died on the same day the kingdom ceased to exist, but whether from poison or natural causes is unknown. Like the Emperor Caligula's horse, the royal beast lived in great pomp, and ate and drank out of huge silver buckets.

But no sooner was the conquest of the ancient kingdom of Burma achieved, with an ease almost unexampled, than the British were compelled to undertake, as in Pegu, in 1853, the difficult task of pacifying the country and extirpating dacoity. A general disarmament took place, and troops were poured into Upper Burma, until, in November of the following year, besides eight thousand military police, there were no less than thirty-two thousand soldiers in the country—including ten battalions and nine batteries of Europeans—under Roberts, who was engaged in succession to Sir Herbert Macpherson, until his departure on the following February 6th, in carrying into execution a plan for crushing the dacoits, who were led by Boshway and other noted chiefs. An expedition took possession of Bhamo, on the extreme northern frontier, bordering on the possessions of China, and the district containing the famous ruby mines was occupied by a column under General Stewart. The Shan country, extending from Bhamo to the southward of Mandalay and as far east as the Chinese and Siamese frontiers, comprising one-third of Theebaw's dominions, was reduced to subjection, and the Looshai-Chin Expeditionary Force in 1889–90 had an arduous task in traversing the intermediate countries, when the eastern column suffered heavily from fever. Under General Symons it advanced from Burma, and the second, or Looshai column, under General Tregear, pushed on from the Chittagong frontier, in the west, and joined hands, when the country was pacified and a route for a trunk road between Upper Burma and Lower Bengal was explored.

In the task of reducing Upper Burma to subjection and putting down dacoity, Sir Frederick Roberts was assisted by his Afghan associates, Sir George White and Sir Robert Low; and on his return to India, his successors, Generals White and Gordon, carried through the task indicated by him, though many valuable lives were lost in the effort. These able commanders, besides reducing the Shan states and the wild Chin tribes inhabiting the Yau country, subjugated the large district of Chindwin, extending from the Irawadi to Munipore, on the frontier of Assam, the Sagaing division to the northward, and the Montsobo district (the birthplace of Alompra, founder of the Burmese dynasty), further to the north, whence extends to Bhamo the Kachyen country.

Meanwhile Lord Dufferin had in 1888 been succeeded by Lord Lansdowne, and a peaceful settlement of misunderstandings with Russia in connection with differences occurring beyond the northwest frontier was attained. At this juncture, for the first time in the history of British rule, native princes stepped forward with offers of money, of jewels even, of transport and men, to repulse what was feared might be the prelude to a Cossack invasion. The invasion did not occur and the offers were declined, but it was recommended that the character of the forces at the disposal of these princes be raised and fitted to combine with the British for purposes of national defence.

The administration of Lord Lansdowne was further marked by the annexation of the districts now known as British Beluchistan, the occupation in 1890 of the Zhob valley, and the opening up for traffic of the Guinal pass.

In 1893 Lord Lansdowne was succeeded by Lord Elgin, who, this year (1899), was replaced by Lord Curzon. The chief events which occurred during Lord Elgin's tenure of office were, apart from an appalling famine and plague, the international arrangements whereby the northwest and southeast frontiers of India have been brought almost in touch with the advancing soldiers of Russia and France.

Thus has the empire been built. The imagination is stimulated by the mere contemplation of the extent and potentialities of this vast realm which in little more than a century has been consolidated by the enterprise and valor of the English race. To it nothing in ancient or modern history offers a parallel, for the empire of Alexander broke to pieces on his death, as did the conquests of Genghis Khan and Tamerlane, while ancient Rome, whose dominion extended from Hadrian's Wall to the "pillars of Hercules." held sway over semi-civilized or barbarous states, and the modern empire of Russia in Asia is composed of countries which, though once the seats of opulent dynasties, are now poor and backward in civilization.

Of Lord Curzon's administration it is yet too early to speak. But in view of the fact that Lady Curzon (formerly Miss Leiter of Chicago) is an American lady, an account of the installation may without impropriety be appended.

There are, an eye-witness of it noted, few spectacles more interesting than the reception of a new Viceroy at the magnificent flight of steps that lead to the palace which the great Marquis, who first attempted to carry out the daring policy of Hastings, built for the rulers of the realm. He told his mercantile masters that India should be governed not from a counting house, but from a palace, not with the ideas of a shopkeeper, but with those of a prince.

The palace which resulted cost one hundred and fifty thousand pounds, and the furniture fifty thousand pounds. The merchants of the East India Company expressed their strong disapproval, but it was built. The Hon. Emily Eden, who first revealed to an incredulous world that India was not hopelessly dull, describes it "as an enormous building looking more like a real palace, a palace in the 'Arabian Nights,' than anything I have been able to dream on the subject. It is something like I expected, and yet not the least, at present as far as externals go; it seems to me that we are acting a long opera." The spectacle on January 3, 1899, might well have been a scene in an opera. At the top of the steps stands Lord Elgin, and on it are clustered high officials in blue and gold, soldiers in scarlet uniforms, naval officers, and native chiefs one blaze of diamonds. Facing the steps on the green turf is drawn up a red line of British soldiers; and flitting to and fro in the grounds are turbaned attendants in their scarlet dresses. Beyond the girdle of palms, plantains, and feathery bamboo that encircles the grounds of Government House rises the lofty row of houses which the Italian architects built in the days of old. They are gay with flags and bunting, and the spacious verandas are enlivened by the costumes of the fair dames who have come to see the procession. The roofs are a mass of color, for they are crowded with natives draped in their clothes of dark red, bright orange, and rich green. A boom is heard—it is the first gun of the salute; then a hum of voices; then a loud English cheer. A clatter of hoofs, and through the lofty gateway come at a fair trot the troopers of the bodyguard in scarlet uniforms—magnificent men on splendid horses; a carriage, with four horses and Eastern postilions in dresses of red, black, and gold, containing the future Viceroy and Vice-Queen, follows. Then, as she alights amid the saluting of the troops, there comes across the memory Burke's most famous purple patch. The Lieutenant-Governor of Bengal meets Lord Curzon at the lowest step and leads him up the tall flight. Lord Elgin advances to the edge of the landing to receive him, and as soon as the introduction to the members of Council is over, the Viceregal party enters the Marble Hall.

In the old days it was the custom for all to proceed at once to the Council Chamber, where the commission was read and the new Viceroy took the oaths and was invested with the charge of the government. "George (Lord Auckland) was sworn in ten minutes after he arrived," writes Miss Eden. But of late years it has become the habit to postpone the act of demission to the morning of the departure of the reigning Viceroy. On Friday, January 6, Lord Curzon received charge of the Indian Empire. The Council Chamber is bright with suits of blue and gold, scarlet uniforms, and the rich apparel of native chiefs. Sindia, a short, stout typical Mahratta, is dressed in a pink silk surtout with a row of priceless pearls round his neck. Pattiala is attired in a silken white suit, and diamonds cover his breast. Near him stands a chief from whose turban gleams a magnificent diamond star. There is the Maharajah of Cashmere in the uniform of an English general. Nobles and chiefs from all parts of the vast empire are present to do homage to the new representative of her Imperial Majesty the Empress of India.

May Lord Curzon's future career enable him to take his place among the wisest and best of her great rulers, whose silent faces look down at the scene from the walls! There is Warren Hastings, whose far sight first saw, and whose brave and confident genius realized, the remarkable idea of England founding an empire in the East. By his individual energy he raised the Company from being a body of merchants and adventurers into the most powerful State in the politics of India. There is the great Marquis, who by magnificent military triumphs enforced peace throughout India, and provided for the permanent security of the British possessions by impressing upon every native State the authoritative security of the British government. There is Lord Hastings, who, by the disarmament and pacification of the military chiefships, completed the work of the Marquis Wellesley, the extension of British supremacy and protectorate over every native State in the interior of India. There is Viscount Hardinge, who first broke the power of the last of its formidable enemies, the Sikhs, and who, "trained in war, sought by the arts of peace to elevate and improve the various nations committed to his charge." Dalhousie, the greatest of the great Indian proconsuls, was only thirty-six when he entered that Council Room and assumed the reins of office. After eight years of splendid rule he left it, having completed the fabric of British rule in India. Now, at the appointed hour, preceded by his staff, there enters once more a young statesman to whom the great and perilous task of governing an empire is about to be assigned. Dressed in plain black, the future ruler takes his position on the dais, and his councillors, in uniforms rich with gold, stand in a semi-circle around him. The Home Secretary reads the Royal Warrant appointing "you the said George Nathaniel Baron Curzon to be Governor-General of India and of all or singular our forts, factories, settlements, lands, territories, countries, places, and provinces, which now are or shall from time to time be subject to or under our government in the East Indies." After the Royal Warrant is read, Lord Curzon bows, the troops outside present arms, and a royal salute announces that the millions of India have passed under the sway of a new ruler.

THE END

CHRONOLOGICAL TABLES OF INDIAN HISTORY

CHRONOLOGICAL TABLES OF INDIAN HISTORY

I. HINDU INDIA.

1500 B.C.—1400 B.C.	Probable period of the Maha Bharata.
1000 "	Probable period of the Ramayana.
500 "	Probable period of Sakya Muni, or Gotama Buddha.
327 "	Alexander invades the Punjab.
	Passage of the Jhelum.
	Defeat of Porus the Elder.
	Alexander's retreat.
320 "	Empire of Magadha (Behar).
	Chandra-gupta (Sandrokottos).
	Asoka: Edicts of Asoka.
280 "	Græko-Baktrian supremacy.
100 "	Indo-Scythian supremacy.
56 "	Kanishka (Kanerke).
78 A.D.—	Battle of Kahror.
	Gupta supremacy.
319 "	Vallabhi Rajas.
	Kingdoms of Andhra and Pandya.
400 "	Pilgrimage of Fah-Hian.
640 "	Travels of Hiouen-Thsang.
	Empire of Kanouj: Maharaja Siladitya.
	Buddhist-Brahman controversies.
1001 "	Muhammadan invasion.

II. MUHAMMADAN INDIA.

997 A.D.—	Mahmud of Ghazni.
1001 "	Mahmud at Peshawar.
	Turkish conquest of the Punjab.
	Twelve Turkish invasions of Hindustan.
	Battle of Somnath.
1030 "	Death of Mahmud.
1180 "	Afghan supremacy at Delhi: Muhammad Ghori (d. 1206).
1194 "	Mussulman advance to Benares.
	Foundation of principalities in Rajputana.
1206 "	Dynasty of Afghan Slave-kings: Kutub-ud-din, Sultan of Delhi (d. 1210).
1290 "	Death of Jelal-ud-din, the last of the Slave-kings.
	Ala-ud-din, Sultan of Delhi (d. 1316).
	Conquest of Guzerat.
	Siege of Chitor.
1316 "	Tughlak, founder of the Tughlak Sultans of Delhi.
1325 "	Muhammad Tughlak (d. 1350).
1350 "	Firuz Shah (d. 1388).
	Bahmani Sultans in the Dekhan.
1398 "	Timur the Tartar invades Hindustan.
1400 "	Deva Rai, Maharaja of Narsinga.

1450 A.D.—Lodi dynasty of Afghan Sultans at Delhi.
1498 " Portuguese arrival in Malabar.
1500 " Five Muhammadan kingdoms in the Dekhan.
Nanuk Guru founds the Sikh brotherhood in the Punjab.
1509 " Albuquerque, Viceroy of Portuguese India (d. 1519).
1526 " Afghan Sultans at Delhi overthrown by Baber the Moghul (d. 1530).
Foundation of the Moghul empire.
1530 " Baber succeeded by Humayun (d. 1556).
1538 " Portuguese mission to Bengal.
Turkish attack on the Portuguese at Diu.
1540 " Humayun defeated by Sher Khan.
Afghan rule in Hindustan.
1555 " Return of Humayun.
1556 " Akbar, Padishah (d. 1605).
Akbar defeats the Afghans.
1565 " Battle of Talikota.
1567 " Destruction of Chitor.
Moghul conquest of Ahmadnagar and Berar.
1575 " Rise of Abul Fazl.
Rebellion of Selim (Jehangir).
1599 " Formation of the East India Company.
1605 " Jehangir, Padishah (d. 1627).
1608 " Mission of Captain Hawkins to Agra.
1615 " Embassy of Sir Thomas Roe.
1623 " Travels of Pietro della Valle.
1625 " Venk-tapa Naik, Raja of Kanara.
1627 " Shah Jehan, Padishah (d. 1665).
1632 A.D.—Moghul capture of the Portuguese settlement at Hughli.
1639 " English settlement at Madras.
1640 " English settlements in Bengal at Hughli, Patna, and Dacca.
1658 " Aurangzeb, Padishah (d. 1707).
1664 " Sivaji the Mahratta captures Surat.
1666 " War between Mahrattas and Moghuls.
Aurangzeb threatened by Persia.
Afghan massacre of Moghuls in the Khaiber Pass.
1673 " Travels of Dr. Fryer.
1674 " Sivaji, Maharaja of the Mahrattas (d. 1680).
1677 " Mahratta conquest in the Lower Carnatic.
1682 " Moghul rebuffs in Rajputana.
1685 " War between the English and Moghuls.
1687 " Moghul conquest of Bijapur and Golkonda.
1689 " Foundation of Calcutta.
1701 " Daud Khan besieges Madras.
1707 " Bahadur Shah, Padishah (d. 1712).
Sahu Rao, Maharaja of the Mahrattas (d. 1748).
Balaji Visvanath, first Peishwa (d. 1720).
1712 " Jehandar Shah, Padishah.
1713 " Farrukh Siyar, Padishah (d. 1719).
1715 " English mission from Calcutta to Delhi.
1719 " Muhammad Shah, Padishah (d. 1748).
1720 " Baji Rao, second Peishwa (d. 1740).
1736 " Mahratta advance on Agra and Delhi.
Nizam-ul-mulk, Nizam of the Dekhan; defeated by Baji Rao.

1738 A.D.—Invasion of Nadir Shah.
1739 " Battle of Kurnal.
Nadir Shah enters Delhi.
1740 " Balaji Rao, third Peishwa (d. 1761).
1743 " Raja Ram, the puppet Maharaja of the Mahrattas, a state prisoner at Satara.
Afghan invasion of India under Ahmad Shah Abdali.

III. BRITISH INDIA.

1736 A.D.—Civil war in Trichinopoly.
1739 " Sarfaraz Khan, Nawab of Bengal (d. 1742).
1740 " Mahrattas invade the Carnatic.
1742 " Alivardi Khan, Nawab of Bengal.
Mahratta invasions of Bengal.
1743 " English mission to Nizam-ul-mulk at Trichinopoly.
1745 " War between England and France.
1746 " Labourdonnais captures Madras.
1747 " Rise of Ahmad Shah Durani, founder of the Afghan empire (d. 1773); Jemal Khan Barukzai.
1748 " Stringer Lawrence fails to take Pondicherry.
Death of Muhammad Shah: Ahmad Shah, Padishah.
Death of Nizam-ul-mulk.
Death of Maharaja Sahu.
Peishwa sovereignty begins.
First appearance of Clive.
1749 " English aggressions on Tanjore.
1750 " Nasir Jung at Arcot; appoints Muhammad Ali Nawab.
Victories of Dupleix.
1750 A.D.—Bussy captures Jingi.
French capture of Masulipatam.
Peace between Alivardi Khan and the Mahrattas.
Alom Phra the hunter founds a dynasty in Burma.
1751 " Ascendency of Dupleix.
Clive's expedition to Arcot.
Siege of Arcot.
1752 " Clive's victories in the Carnatic.
The French surrender Trichinopoly.
1753 " Clive goes to England.
1754 " Janoji Bhonsla succeeds Rughoji Bhonsla as Raja of Berar.
1755 " Anglo-French treaty at Pondicherry.
Removal of Dupleix.
Return of Clive.
1756 " Destruction of Gheria by Watson and Clive.
Suraj-ud-daula, Nawab of Bengal.
Suraj-ud-daula captures Calcutta.
The Black Hole.
1757 " Clive and Watson recapture Calcutta.
English capture of Chandernagore.
Battle of Plassy.
Mir Jafir, Nawab of Bengal.
Mahrattas claim chout for Bengal and Behar.
Ahmad Shah Abdali at Delhi; drives out Ghazi-ud-din.
Bussy's war against the Hindu Poligars; self-sacrifice of Bobili Rajputs.
Bussy captures Vizagapatam.
1758 " Advance of the Shahzada, eldest son of Ahmad Shah Padishah, toward Behar: defeated by Clive.
Lally at Pondicherry.

1758 A.D.—Lally captures Fort St. David.
Forde's successes in the Northern Circars.
Siege of Madras by Lally.
Clive governor of the English settlements in Bengal.

1759 " Alamghir, Padishah, murdered at Delhi by Ghazi-ud-din.
Second invasion of Ahmad Shah Abdali.
Lally raises the siege of Madras.
Battle of Wandiwash.

1760 " Coote besieges Pondicherry.
Clive departs for England; succeeded by Holwell.

1761 " Madhu Rao, fourth Mahratta Peishwa (d. 1772).
Nizam Ali, Nizam of the Dekhan.
Coote captures Pondicherry.
Battle of Paniput.
Ahmad Shah Abdali appoints Jewan Bakh (son of the Shahzada) deputy Padishah.
Regency of Najib-ud-daula (d. 1770).
Return of the Shahzada to Behar: proclaimed Padishah under the name of Shah Alam.
Shuja-ud-daula, Nawab of Oude (d. 1775), appointed Vizier to Shah Alam.
Vansittart, governor at Calcutta.
Deposition of Mir Jafir.
Mir Kasim, Nawab of Bengal; defeats the Nawab Vizier of Oude.
Installation of the Great Moghul at Patna.

1762 " Disputes about private trade.

1762 A.D.—Warren Hastings in the Calcutta council.

1763 " General abolition of duties by Mir Kasim.
Patna captured by the English, and recaptured by the Nawab's troops.
Capture of Cossimbazar by the Nawab's troops.
Mir Jafir proclaimed Nawab.
The English capture Monghyr.
Massacre of English at Patna.
English storm Patna.
Delhi threatened by the Jats.

1764 " The Nawab Vizier repulsed by the English at Patna.
Hector Munro stops a sepoy mutiny.
Battle of Buxar.
Rise of Shitab Rai.
Surrender of the Nawab Vizier.
Suraj Mal, the Jat hero, slain at Delhi.

1765 " Death of Mir Jafir.
Governor Spencer sells Bengal and Behar to Muhammad Reza Khan.
Return of Clive to India; foundation of the double government.

1766 " English treaty with Nizam Ali.

1767 " Final departure of Clive.
Verelst, governor of Bengal.
Rise of Hyder Ali of Mysore.
Hyder Ali and Nizam Ali invade the Carnatic.
Death of Mulhar Rao Holkar: accession of Ailah Bai (d. 1795), and Tukaji Holkar (d. 1797).
Last invasion of Ahmad Shah Abdali.

1767 A.D.—Ghorka conquest of Nipal: Prithi Narain, the Ghorka hero (d. 1771).

1768 " Second English treaty with Nizam Ali.

Hostile advance of Hyder Ali against the English.

1769 " English treaty with Hyder Ali at Madras.

Cartier, governor of Bengal.

Mahratta aggressions in Hindustan.

1770 " Famine in Bengal.

1771 " Mahadaji Sindia restores Shah Alam to the throne of Delhi.

1772 " Warren Hastings, governor of Bengal.

Narain Rao, fifth Peishwa.

1773 " Warren Hastings holds a secret conference with Shuja-ud-daula at Benares.

Narain Rao murdered.

Rughonath Rao, sixth Peishwa.

Rughjio Bhonsla, Raja of Berar.

Tanjore made over to Muhammad Ali.

Timur Shah on the throne of Kandahar (d. 1793); Payendah Khan Barukzai.

1774 " Rohilla war.

Warren Hastings, first Governor-General.

The Calcutta Council; Francis, Clavering, Monson, and Barwell.

Creation of a Supreme Court of Judicature at Calcutta.

Revolution at Poona.

1775 " Asof-ud-daula, Nawab Vizier of Oude (d. 1797).

Charge of corruption against Warren Hastings.

Execution of Nundkomar.

1775 A.D.—Treaty between the English at Bombay and Rughonath Rao.

Rebellion of Cheit Singh, Raja of Benares.

Run Bahadur, Maharaja of Nipal.

1776 " Treaty of Purundhur.

Tanjore restored to the Raja by Lord Pigot.

1778 " Rumbold, governor of Madras.

English capture of Pondicherry.

Bombay expedition to Poona.

1779 " Convention of Wurgaum.

First Mahratta war.

Bhodau Phra, King of Burma (d. 1819).

1780 " English capture of Gwalior.

Whitehill, governor of Madras.

Hyder Ali invades the Carnatic.

Battle of Porto Novo.

Runjeet Singh, Viceroy of Lahore.

1781 " Lord Macartney, governor of Madras.

War between English and Dutch; capture of Pulicat and Sadras.

1782 " Close of the first Mahratta war.

Nana Farnavese ratifies the Treaty of Salbai.

Mahdu Rao II., seventh Peishwa (d. 1795).

Death of Hyder Ali.

1784 " Treaty of Mangalore.

Mr. Pitt's Bill; the Board of Control.

1785 " Warren Hastings leaves India.

Macpherson, Mr., provisional Governor-General.

1786 " Lord Cornwallis, Governor-General.

1787 " Tippu Sultan attacks Travancore.

1788 " Gholam Kadir at Delhi.

1790 A.D.—Mysore war.
1792 " Submission of Tippu Sultan.
Mahadaji Sindia at Poona.
Chinese invasion of Nipal.
Ghorka treaty with the English.
Permanent land settlement in Bengal.
1793 " Sir John Shore (Lord Teignmouth), Governor-General.
Zeman Shah succeeds Timur Shah at Kandahar.
1794 " Mahadaji Sindia succeeded by Daulat Rao Sindia.
1795 " Battle of Kurdla.
Umdut-ul-Umra, Nawab of Arcot (d. 1801).
Baji Rao II., eighth Peishwa (d. 1853).
Revolution at Khatmandu.
Threatened invasion of Zeman Shah.
1797 " Saadut Ali, Nawab Vizier of Oude.
Rise of Jaswant Rao Holkar.
1798 " Lord Mornington (Marquis of Wellesley), Governor-General.
English alliance with Nizam Ali against Tippu.
1799 " Last Mysore war.
Storming of Seringapatam.
Death of Tippu.
Purnea, minister at Mysore (d. 1811).
1800 " Buchanan's travels in Mysore.
Malcolm's mission to Persia.
Death of Nana Farnavese.
Pandey conspiracy at Khatmandu: flight of Run Bahadur.
Mahmud, Shah of Afghanistan (died 1829).

1801 A.D.—Assumption of the government of the Carnatic.
Risings of the Ghilzais in Kabul, suppressed by Futih Khan.
1802 " Baji Rao and Sindia defeated by Jaswant Rao Holkar.
Treaty of Bassein.
Mission of Captain Knox to Khatmandu.
1803 " Baji Rao restored to Poona.
Second Mahratta war.
Battles of Assaye and Argaum.
Battles of Alighur and Delhi.
Revolution of Khatmandu.
Moghul kings of Delhi become the pensioners of the British government.
Shah Shuja, Shah of Afghanistan.
1804 " War between the English and Jaswant Rao Holkar.
Col. Monson's retreat.
Return of Run Bahadur to Khatmandu.
Downfall of the Pandeys.
Murder of Run Bahadur.
Massacre at Khatmandu of the enemies of the Thapas.
Ascendency of Bhim Sein Thapa.
1805 " Lake defeats Holkar and besieges Bhurtpore.
Lord Cornwallis, Governor-General a second time.
Sir George Barlow, Governor-General.
Submission of Jaswant Rao Holkar.
1806 " Mutiny at Vellore.
1807 " Lord Minto, Governor-General.

1807 A.D.—Runjeet Singh's aggressions on the Cis-Sutlej states.

1808 " Metcalf's mission to Runjeet Singh.

1809 " Restoration of Mahmud Shah to the throne of Kabul by the Barukzais.

1810 " British occupation of the Mauritius and Java.

1811 " Mulhar Rao Holkar succeeds to the throne of Indore.

Depredations of Amir Khan and of the Pindharies.

Lingaraja, ruler of Coorg (d. 1820).

Krishnaraj assumes the government of Mysore.

1813 " Lord Moira (Marquis of Hastings), Governor-General.

Ghorka aggressions on British territory.

Nipalese occupation of British districts.

Ghorka slaughter of British police.

1814 " Nipal war.

1815 " The Gaekwar of Baroda sends Gungadhur Shastri to Poona.

Murder of Gungadhur Shastri.

Imprisonment of Trimbukji Dainglia.

1816 " Treaty of Segowlie.

Pindhari raids on British territories.

Quarrels between Persia and Afghanistan respecting Herat.

Escape of Trimbukji Dainglia.

1817 " Treaty of Poona.

Pindhari war.

Baji Rao repulsed by the English at Khirki.

Flight of the Peishwa from Poona.

Battle of Sitabuldi.

Battle of Mehidpore.

1818 A.D.—Defence of Korygaum.

Extinction of the Pieshwa.

Settlement of the Holkar state.

Resuscitation of the Raj of Satara.

Early Burmese history.

Portuguese adventurers.

Byeen-noung conquers Pegu.

Siege and capture of Martaban by Byeen-noung.

1820 " Metcalfe, Resident at Hyderabad, condemns the bank of Palmer & Co.

Chikka Vira Raja succeeds Lingaraja at Coorg.

1823 " Mr. Adam, provisional Governor-General.

Lord Amherst, Governor-General.

1824 " First Burmese war: British expedition to Rangoon.

Phagyi-dau, King of Burma.

1825 " British advance to Prome.

Outbreak at Bhurtpore.

1826 " Treaty of Yandabo.

Crawfurd's mission to Ava.

Capture of Bhurtpore.

Dost Muhammad Khan, Amir of Kabul.

1827 " Daulat Rao Sindia succeeded by Jankoji Rao Sindia (d. 1843).

1828 " Lord William Bentinck, Governor-General.

1830 " Rebellion in Mysore: deposition of Krishnaraj by the British government.

1832 " Disturbances in Jaipur.

1833 " Civil wars stopped at Gwalior and Indore by British intervention.

Hari Rao Holkar on the throne of Indore.

1833 A.D.—Renewal of the East India Company's charter.

1834 " The Maharaja of Jaipur poisoned.
British campaign in Coorg.
Annexation of Coorg.

1835 " Murder of Mr. Blake in Jaipur.
Sir Charles Metcalfe, provisional Governor-General.

1836 " Lord Auckland, Governor-General.

1837 " The Shah of Persia marches against Herat.
Siege of Herat.
Revolution at Ava.
Tharawadi, king of Burma.
The fall of Bhim Sein Thapa at Khatmandu.

1838 " The Shah of Persia raises the siege of Herat.
Lord Auckland declares war against Afghanistan.
British advance to Quetta.

1839 " British capture of Kandahar, Ghazni and Kabul.
Russian expedition to Khiva.
Death of Runjeet Singh.
Tragedies at Khatmandu.
Death of Bhim Sein Thapa.
Kharak, Maharaja of Lahore (d. 1840).
Dethronement of the Raja of Satara.

1840 " British occupation of Kabul.
The British Residency expelled from Ava.
Lord Auckland remonstrates with the Maharaja of Nipal.
Nao Nihal Singh, Maharaja of Lahore.

1841 A.D.—Withdrawal of Major Todd, the British Resident, from Herat.
Insurrection at Kabul: murder of Sir Alexander Burnes.
General reconciliation at Khatmandu.
Dhian Singh places Sher Singh on the throne of Lahore.

1842 " Destruction of the British army in the Khaiber Pass.
Sale's defence of Jellalabad.
Lord Ellenborough, Governor-General.
Pollock's advance to Jellalabad.
British advance to Kabul.
Battle of Tazeen.
Murder of Stoddart and Conolly at Bokhara.
Disturbances at Khatmandu.

1843 " Jyaji Rao Sindia, Maharaja of Gwalior.
Disturbances at Gwalior.
Battles of Maharajpore and Punniar.
Matabar Singh overthrows the Pandeys at Khatmandu.
Assassination of Dhian and Sher Singh at Lahore: Dhulip Singh, Maharaja.

1844 " Settlement of Gwalior affairs.
Irregular installation of Tukaji Rao Holkar at Indore.
Lord Hardinge, Governor-General.
Crisis at Lahore.

1845 " Pagan Meng, king of Burma.
Murder of Matabar Singh.
Sikh army of the Khalsa invades British territory: first Sikh war.

1845 A.D.—Battles of Moodkee and Ferozeshahar.

1846 " Massacre at Khatmandu.

Jung Bahadur, prime minister.

Battle of Sobraon.

Close of the first Sikh war.

Jamu and Kashmir sold to Gholab Singh.

Temporary British occupation of the Punjab.

1848 " Lord Dalhousie, Governor-General.

Disaffection of Mulraj, Viceroy of Multan.

Treachery and murder at Multan.

Successes of Herbert Edwardes.

Second Sikh war.

Revolt of Sher Singh.

The Sikhs joined by Afghans.

Lapse of Satara to the British government.

1849 " Battle of Chillianwallah

Battle of Guzerat.

Annexation of the Punjab.

1851 " Mission of Commodore Lambert to Rangoon.

Second Burmese War.

Meng-don Meng, king of Burma.

Annexation of Pegu.

1853 " Sir John Lawrence, Chief Commissioner of the Punjab.

Annexation of Nagpore.

Cession of Berar to the British government.

1855 " Outbreak of hill-tribes, Koles and Santals.

English alliance with Dost Muhammad Khan.

1856 " Annexation of Oude.

Lord Canning, Governor-General.

Persian war.

Capture of Bushire and battle of Mohamrah.

1857 A.D.—Sepoy mutiny.

Mutiny at Barrackpore.

March 29th Outbreak of Mungal Pandy.

May 3d Explosion at Lukhnow.

" 10th Mutiny at Meerut.

" 11th The Rebels at Delhi.

" 30th Mutiny at Lukhnow.

June 4th Mutiny at Jhansi.

Mutiny at Cawnpore.

" 6th Siege of Cawnpore by Nana Sahib.

" 27th The massacre on the Ganges.

July 1st Coronation of Nana Sahib as Peishwa.

" 7th Advance of Havelock toward Cawnpore.

" 15th Massacre of women and children at Cawnpore.

Battle of Cawnpore.

" 17th Havelock's advance to Bithoor.

General insurrection in Oude.

Defence of the Residency at Lukhnow; death of Sir Henry Lawrence.

Havelock's victory at Bithoor.

Barnard's advance to Delhi.

Sept. 14th Storming of Delhi.

" 21st Arrest of the king; the two princes shot.

" 25th Relief of the Residency at Lukhnow by Havelock and Outram.

Nov. 23d Second relief by Sir Colin Campbell.

" 24th Death of Havelock.

Defeat of the Gwalior rebels.

1858 A.D.—Trial and transportation of Bahadur Shah.

Lord Clyde's campaign in Oude and Rohilkund.

Outram captures Lukhnow.

Sir Hugh Rose's campaign in Central India.

Sindia defeated by the Gwalior rebels.

1858 A.D.—Tantia Topi and the Gwalior rebels routed by Sir Hugh Rose.
The Queen's proclamation.
Hindustani fanatics driven out of Sitana.

1859 " Trial and execution of Tantia Topi.
End of the Oude rebellion.
Lord Canning's durbar at Agra.

1862 " Lord Elgin, Viceroy.
Sir Arthur Phayre, Chief Commissioner of British Burma, concludes a treaty with the king of Burma.

1863 " The Sitana campaign.
Sir William Denison, provisional Viceroy.
The Bhutan mission.
Death of Dost Muhammad Khan.
Sher Ali Khan recognized by the British government.

1864 " Sir John Lawrence, Viceroy.
Bhutan war.
Sher Ali treacherously imprisons his brother Afzal Khan.

1866 " Flight of Sher Ali to Kandahar: Afzal Khan proclaimed Amir.
Partition of Afghanistan.
Sir John Lawrence's recognition of Afzal Khan and Sher Ali Khan.

1867 " Sher Ali defeated by Azim Khan; his flight from Kandahar to Herat.

1867 A.D.—Death of Afzal Khan: accession of Azim Khan.
General Fytche, Chief Commissioner of British Burma, concludes a treaty with the king of Burma.

1868 " Sher Ali recovers the throne of Afghanistan.

1869 " Lord Mayo, Viceroy.
The Umballa conference.
Visit of H. R. H. the Duke of Edinburgh to India.

1872 " Lord Mayo visits Rangoon; assassinated at Port Blair.
Lord Northbrook, Viceroy.

1875 " Visit of H. R. H. the Prince of Wales to India.

1876 " Lord Lytton, Viceroy.

1877 " The Imperial Assemblage at Delhi on the 1st of January, 1877: proclamation of Her Majesty Queen Victoria as Empress of India.
Death of Jung Bahadur.

1878 " Sher Ali's rejection of a British mission.
Declaration of war against Afghanistan.

1879 " Death of Sher Ali.
Accession of Yakub Khan.
Attack on the British Residency at Kabul; massacre of the English mission.
British occupation of Afghanistan.

INDEX

INDEX

A

A'AYNGARS, a sect of worshippers of Vishnu in Southern India, 475; their distinctive creed, *ib.*

Abdalis, the legitimate Afghans, as opposed to the Ghilzais, or illegitimate branch, 622. *See* also Duranis and Barukzais.

Abdulla Khan, the elder brother of the two Saiyids, who enthroned Farrukh Siyar at Delhi, 246; hostile intrigues of Farrukh Siyar, 247, 248; revolution at Delhi, 250; assassination of his younger brother, 251; defeat and fall, 252. *See* also Saiyids.

Abdul Rahman Khan, son of Afzal Khan, helps to place his father on the throne of Kabul, 769; his rivalry with his uncle Azim Khan, 770; flight to Persian territory, *ib.*

Abul Fazl, the favorite and minister of Akbar, 166; engages Akbar in religious controversies, *ib.*; destroys the authority and power of the Ulama, 167; proclaims Akbar to be the "Lord of the period," who is to bring about the Muhammadan millennium, 168; assassinated, 171.

Adam, Mr., provisional Governor-General of India, 574; sends an obnoxious editor of a public journal to England, *ib.*; perished at sea, *ib.*

Adham Khan, revolts against Akbar in Malwa, 159; stabs the minister to death at Agra, *ib.*; executed by Akbar, *ib.*

Adoption, rite of, its religious significance, 700; its political bearings, 701; restricted by Lord Dalhousie, 702; conceded by Lord Canning, 757.

Adye, Major, at Cawnpore, 751 *note*; his narrative of the Sitana campaign, 759 *note*.

Afghanistan, description of, 620; highroad to India, 621.

Afghans, converted to Islam but rebel against the Arab domination, 95; found a dynasty at Ghor and drive the Turks out of the Punjab and Hindustan, 97; dynasty of the slave kings, 100–2; apparently of Jewish origin, 149; known as Patans, 150; establish a dominion in Hindustan under the Lodi dynasty, *ib.*; bad name and passion for revenge, 151; conquered by Baber the Moghul, 154; drive Humayun out of Bengal, 156; rule in Hindustan under Sher Khan, *ib.*; obsolete claims to Hindustan, 157; intermittent wars of Akbar, 158; treachery and disaffection of Afghan officers, 159; crushed by the resuscitation of the Rajputs, 160; revolt under a supposed brother of Aurangzeb, 210; treacherously massacred at Peshawar, *ib.*; throw off the Persian yoke and conquer Ispahan, 262; establish an empire in Central Asia under Ahmad Shah Abdali, 269; treacherous mercenaries in the service of Alivardi Khan, 314; revenge, *ib.*; invasion and plunder of Hindustan under Ahmad Shah Abdali, 328; found a principality in Rohilkund, *ib.*; supreme at Delhi, 338; massacre the Mahrattas at Paniput, 338, 392; threatened invasion of Hindustan under Zeman Shah in the days of Lord Wellesley, 495; Elphinstone's mission to Kabul sent by Lord Minto, 528 *note*; advance of Russia in Central Asia, 619; Afghan dominion to the south of the Oxus, 620; character of the Afghan people, 621; old contentions between Abdalis and Ghilzais, 622; later rivalries between Duranis and Barukzais, *ib.*; modern history of the Afghans, *ib.*; election and coronation of Ahmad Shah Durani, 623; hereditary ministry of the Barukzais, *ib.*; rise of the Kuzzilbashes, *ib.*; foundation of an Afghan empire, 624; reign of Timur Shah, *ib.*; disaffection in Balkh, *ib.*; Zeman Shah placed on the throne by Payendah Khan, chief of the Barukzais; 625; disaffection of the Sirdars, 626; transfer of the Punjab to the rule of Runjeet Singh, *ib.*; oppression of the Barukzais, 627; plots and massacres at Kandahar, *ib.*; rise of Futih Khan, the Barukzai Vizier, *ib.*; Zeman Shah dethroned and blinded, *ib.*; quarrels between the Sunnis and Shiahs, 628; slaughter of the Kuzzilbashes, *ib.*; Shah Shuja Durani seizes the throne at Kabul, 629; dethroned by Futih Khan Barukzai and escapes to British territory, *ib.*; rise of Dost Muhammad Khan, 630; cruel death of Futih Khan, 631; Durani puppets and Barukzai rulers, *ib.*; Dost Muhammad Khan Amir of Kabul, 632; Persian siege of Herat, 633; refusal of Lord Auckland to interfere between Dost Muhammad Khan and Runjeet Singh, 634; Russian mission at Kabul, *ib.*; first Afghan war, 635; British occupation of Afghanistan, 1839–41, 636–7; insurrection at Kabul and murder of Sir Alexander Burnes, 639; negotiations with rebel leaders, 640; murder of Sir William Macnaghten, *ib.*; destruction of the British army in the Khaiber, 641; advance of the avenging army under Pollock, 642; murder of Shah Shuja, *ib.*; siege of Jellalabad raised by Akbar Khan, *ib.*; Pollock's victory at Tezeen, 644; reoccupation of Kabul, *ib.*; return of avenging army to Hindustan, 645; hostility of the Afghans during the second Sikh war, 688; treaties of 1855 and 1857 with Dost Muhammad Khan, 715, 768; death of Dost Muhammad and recognition of Sher Ali Khan, *ib.*; fratricidal wars, 768, 770; policy of Sir John Lawrence, 771; Lord Mayo's conference with Sher Ali Khan at Umballa, 772; political difficulties, *ib.*; conciliatory policy of Lord Mayo, 773; estrangement of Sher Ali Khan, 775; dealings with Russia, *ib.*; mission of 1878 repulsed, *ib.*; massacre of Cavagnari's mission and British occupation, 776; probable destiny of the Afghan people as foreshadowed by Jewish history, 776 *note*.

Afghan-Turkistan, suzerainty established by Dost Muhammad Khan, 768; geographical meaning of the term, *ib. note*.

Afzal Khan, eldest son of Dost Muhammad Khan, 768; treacherously imprisoned by Sher Ali Khan, *ib.*; Amir of Kabul and Afghan-Turkistan, 769; his death, 770.

Agnew, Mr. Vans, accompanies Khan Singh to Multan, 686; his murder, *ib.*

Agni, god of fire, 56; subject to Ravana, *ib.*; testifies to the purity of Sita, 59; Vaidik idea of, 80.

Agra, sacked by Shah Jehan, 184; imperial road to Lahore, 220; condition in 1785 described, 448; the stronghold of Sindia, 459; captured by Lake, 505.

Ahadis, Moghul officers, 164.

Ahmad Shah Abdali, the Afghan conqueror, 269; interference in Delhi affairs, 328–9; intrigues with the king of Delhi, 338; enters Delhi, *ib.*; last invasion of Hindustan, 402; election and coronation as Ahmad Shah Durani, 623; his glorious reign, 624; a composer of psalms, 776 *note*.

Ahmadnagar, kingdom of, in the Dekhan, 118; conquered by Akbar, 171; revolt of Malik Amber the Abyssinian, 176; suppressed by Jehangir, 181.

Ailah Bai, daughter-in-law of Mulhar Rao Holkar, her administration of Indore, 397–8, 497.

Aix-la-Chapelle, treaty of, 287.

Ajmir, Roe's journey to, 177; imperial durbar at, *ib.*

Akalis or Sikh zealots, 673.

Akbar, son of Humayun, 157; the real founder of the Moghul empire, *ib.*; contemporary of Queen Elizabeth, *ib.*; becomes Padishah, 158; defeat of the Afghans, *ib.*; refuses to slay Hemu, *ib.*; discards Bairam Khan, *ib.*; wars and conquests, 158–9; his policy of equality of race and religion, 160; his policy toward the Rajput princes, 160–1; intermarriages with Rajputs, *ib.*; employs Rajputs against the Afghans, 162; personal characteristics of, 164; outwardly a Muhammadan, 165; religious collisions and controversies, 166–7; appears as a religious arbiter, 167; his apostasy, *ib.*; professes Christianity, *ib.*; founds a new religion known as the Divine Faith, 168; his ordinances, *ib.*; his cruelty, *ib.*; daily life, 168–9; division of lands, 170; conquest of Kabul and Kashmir, *ib.*; embassy to the Sultans of the Dekhan, 171; conquest of Ahmadnagar and Berar, *ib.*; death, *ib.*

Akbar, son of Aurangzeb, 214; his rebellion, *ib.*; the forged letter, *ib.*; flight, 215, 241.

Akbar Khan, eldest son of Dost Muhammad Khan, negotiates with Macnaghten, 640; his murderous treachery, *ib.*; massacre in the Khaiber pass, 641; forced to raise the siege of Jellalabad, 642; ruler of Kabul, 643; negotiations with Pollock, *ib.*; defeated at Tezeen, 644.

Akhoond of Swat, his religious character, 760; his behavior in the Sitana campaign, 761.

Alamghir, a puppet Padishah of Delhi, 328–9; intrigues with Ahmad Shah Abdali, 338, 391; murdered, *ib.*

Ala-ud-din, Sultan of Delhi, story of his early career, 102; governor of Karra, *ib.*; plunders the Buddhist temples at Bhilsa, *ib.*; Viceroy of Oude, *ib.*; expedition against the Mahratta Raja of Deoghur, 102–3; march into the Dekhan, 103; capture of Deoghur, *ib.*; assassination of his uncle, 104; proclaimed Sultan of Delhi, *ib.*; wholesale scattering of money, *ib.*; conquest of Guzerat, *ib.*; siege of Chitor, 105; stern measures of suppression at Delhi, 106; massacre of Moghuls, *ib.*; first Muhammadan conqueror in the Dekhan and Peninsula, *ib.*; plunder of Hindu temples in the south, 107; his death, 108.

Albuquerque, Alfonso de, Portuguese Viceroy in India, founds Goa and Malacca, 130; death, *ib.*

Alexander the Great, invades the Punjab, 64; passage of the Jhelum, *ib.*; defeat of Porus the elder, 65; builds a flotilla on the Jhelum, *ib.*; dealings with Porus the younger, *ib.*; compelled to retreat *via* the Jhelum and Indus, 66; harassed by the Brahmans, *ib.*; his vengeance, *ib.*; murder of Philip, his lieutenant, at Taxila, 67; his death, *ib.*; his dealings with Sandrokottos, the Hindu Chandra-gupta, *ib.*

Ali Bahadur, his mixed birth, Mahratta and Muhammadan, 452 *note*; sent by Nana Farnavese to help Sindia in Hindustan, *ib.*; associated with Himmut Bahadur, *ib.*; his recall to Poona demanded by Sindia, 459–60.

Alighur, Lake's victory at, 504.

Alivardi Khan, Nawab of Bengal, Behar, and Orissa, his early life, 310; his treachery, *ib.*; story of the baskets of human heads, 311; proclaimed Nawab, 313; treacherous assassination of Mahrattas, *ib.*; pays tribute to Mahrattas, 314; character and private life; 314–16; alarm at the French, 316; his death, *ib.*; described by Colonel Mill as a usurper, 337 *note.*

Allahabad, the ancient Prayaga, 49; the "field of happiness," 75; Clive's negotiations at, with Shah Alam and the Nawab Vizier of Oude, 362–3.

Allard, General, in the service of Runjeet Singh, 674.

Alompra the hunter, 589; drives the Talain kings of Pegu out of Ava, 590; conquers Pegu and establishes a port at Rangoon, *ib.*; his real name, Alom Phra, *ib. note.*

Alumbagh, garden of, in the suburbs of Lukhnow, Havelock defeats the rebels, 748–9; buried there, 750.

Alvarez Cabral, his expedition to India, 128; violence toward the Moors, *ib.*; cannonades Calicut, 129; alliance with the Raja of Cochin, *ib.*

Alves, Major, his narrow escape at Jaipur, 608.

Amar Singh, of Nipal, deprecates a war with England, 544; surrenders at Maloun, 547; advises a renewal of the war, 548.

Amar Singh, Raja of Tanjore, dethroned by Madras government, 488; suspected bribery of Tanjore pundits, *ib.*; pensioned, *ib.*

Amarapura, a Burmese capital, 591, 654.

Amboor, defeat of Anwar-ud-din at, 290.

Amherst, Lord, Governor-General of India, 574; forced into a war with Burma, 594; countermands the proceedings of Ochterlony at Bhurtpore, 598; retrieves his error, *ib.*; returns to England, 599; founds the sanatorium at Simla, *ib.*

Amildars, or governors of provinces, corruption of, 478.

Amirs, Moghul nobles, 164.

Amir Jumla, rebel minister of Golkonda, his close alliance with Aurangzeb, 191; defeats Shuja, the rebel brother of Aurangzeb, 195.

Amir Khan, the Afghan freebooter, interference in Indore, 523; his early career, 524; aggressions in Nagpore, *ib.*; interference in Rajputana between Jaipur and Jodhpur, 525; infamous proposal for ending the quarrel, 526; attitude during the Pindhari war, 555; his treaty with England, 557; founder of the Tonk dynasty, 558.

Amyatt, Mr., his factious opposition to Vansittart, 347; sent on a mission to Monghyr, 348; treacherously murdered, 350.

Ananda Bai, wife of Rughonath Rao, her part in the murder of Narain Rao Peishwa, 418.

Anandpal, son of Jaipal of Lahore, 95; league with the Rajput princes of Hindustan, *ib.*; defeated by Mahmud of Ghazni at Peshawar, 96.

Anderson, Lieut., accompanies Khan Singh to Multan, 686; his murder, *ib.*

Anderson, Mr., sent as Resident to Mahadaji Sindia's camp, 444, 448.

Andhra, ancient Hindu empire, 73.

Angrias, pirates of Gheria, rise of, 305, 390; surrender to Clive and Watson, *ib.*; escape from Gheria, *ib.*

Anson, General, Commander-in-chief at the outbreak of the sepoy mutinies, 742 *note.*

Anwar-ud-din appointed Nawab of the Carnatic by Nizam-ul-mulk, 284; forbids the English to make war on the French, 285; enraged at the duplicity of Dupleix, 286; defeat of his army by the French, *ib.*; defeated and slain by the Mahrattas at Amboor, 290.

Appa Sahib succeeds Rughoji Bhonsla as Raja of Nagpore, 563; his treachery toward the English, 564; appointed commander-in-chief by the Peishwa, *ib.*; warned by Mr. Jenkins, *ib.*; the battle of Sitabuldi, 565; double dealings, *ib.*; arrested for murder, 566; flight, *ib.*; takes refuge with the Raja of Jodphur, *ib.*; correspondence with the Raja of Satara, 703.

Apsaras, celestial nymphs from Indra's heaven in Swarga, 54.

Arabs conquer all Asia up to the Indus and Oxus, 95; Persian, Turkish, and Afghan revolt against their domination, *ib.*; Arab invasion of Sinde, *ib.*

Arakan, geographical position of, 575 *note*; conquered by Bhodau Phra, 590; ceded to the British government, 596.

Arcot, court and capital of the Nawabs of the Carnatic, 277; usurpation of Mortiz Ali, 283; settlement of affairs by Nizam-ul-mulk, *ib.*; capture and defence of Arcot by Clive. 299; visited by Buchanan, 477; titular Nawabs of, 490 *note*. *See* also Carnatic.

Argaum, battle of, 504; defeat of Sindia and the Bhonsla Raja by Colonel Wellesley, *ib.*

Arjuna, son of Pandu, by Kunti, 15; his skill with the bow, 17; his splendid archery at the exhibition of arms, 18–19; triumph at the Swayamvara of Draupadi, 23; leads away Draupadi as his bride, 24; his exile, 25; marries Subhadra and returns to Hastinapur, 26; at the court of Virata, 29; the dancing-master turned warrior, 31; discovered by the Kauravas, *ib.*; slays Bhishma, 34; and Karna, *ib.*

Armenians in Madras, 228.

Aryan colonies in the neighborhood of Hastinapur, 12; the Aryan immigrants from High Asia, *ib.*; treatment of the aborigines, *ib.*; frontier near Allahabad, 20; two castes of, 23 *note*; relics among the hill tribes, 78; worship of genii or spirits, 79.

Asia, Central, history of, 619.

Asof Jah. *See* Nizam-ul-mulk.

Asof Khan, brother-in-law of Jehangir, 178; plots with Shah Jehan to seize the imperial treasures at Agra, 183; installs Bulaki on the throne at Delhi, 185.

Asof-ud-daula, Nawab Vizier of Oude, 414; claims his father's treasures as state property, 415; negotiations with Warren Hastings, 435; tortures the servants of the two Begums, *ib.*; corrupt dealings with Warren Hastings, 442 *note*; his death, 465.

Asoka, Maharaja of Magadha, resembles Sandrokottos, 69; his reign and character, 69–70; a convert to Buddhism, 69; edicts of, *ib.*; sends Buddhist missions to foreign nations, 73.

Assam, conquered by the Burmese, 594; ceded to the British government after the first Burmese war, 596; tea cultivation introduced by Lord William Bentinck, 617.

Assaye, victory of General Wellesley at, 503–4.

Astrologers at Delhi, description of, 198.

Asuras and Rakshasas, demons and cannibals to the south and east of Allahabad, 20.

Aswamedha, or horse sacrifice in honor of Indra and the Sun, 37, 39.

Aswatthama, son of Drona, 17; his revenge, 35–6; the omen of the crows, 35; slaughters Dhrishta-dyumna and the sons of Draupadi, *ib.*

Auckland, Lord, Governor-General of India, 617; refuses to interfere between Dost Muhammad Khan and Runjeet Singh, 634; declares war against Dost Muhammad Khan for the restoration of Shah

Shuja, 635; anger at the withdrawal of Major Todd from Herat, 637; rupture of political relations with Ava, 655; policy toward Nipal, 662.
Aurangabad, founded by Aurangzeb, 191.
Aurangzeb, son of Shah Jehan, 190; a Sunni fanatic, 191; Viceroy of the Moghul Dekhan, *ib.*; ambitious projects, *ib.*; bait for Murad, 192; victory at Ujain, 193; defeat of Dara, *ib.*; captivity of his father, Shah Jehan, 194; ruin of Murad, *ib.*; installed as Padishah, *ib.*; fears and anxieties, 196; religious trimming, *ib.*; unamiable character, 197; maligns his tutor, *ib.*; his capital at Delhi, 197–9; alliance with Sivaji the Mahratta, 202; appoints Shaista Khan to be Viceroy of the Moghul Dekhan, *ib.*; suspicious of the Raja of Marwar, 203; suspected complicity in the death of Shah Jehan, 204; in Kashmir, *ib.*; fails to form a navy, *ib.*; threatened by Persia, *ib.*; return to Delhi, 205; intrigues against Sivaji, *ib.*; imposing durbar, 206; composure at the outbreak of Sivaji, *ib.*; reasons for his craft, 207; war against Sivaji, *ib.*; the sham rebellion, 207–8; renders future rebellion impossible, 208; prohibits history, 209; the Kabul revolt, 210; treachery and massacre, *ib.*; projected conversion of the Hindus to Islam, 212; policy, *ib.*; destruction of idolatry in Moghul India, *ib.*; forced impost of the Jezya, 213; operations in Rajputana, *ib.*; compromise with Marwar, 213–14; demands on the Rana of Udaipur rejected, 214; protracted wars, *ib.*; rebellion of Akbar, 214–15; retreat from Rajputana, 215; resolves to live in camp, 216; desultory wars, *ib.*; intrigues against Akbar foiled, *ib.*; bootless operations against the Mahrattas, 217; conquest of Bijapur and Golkonda, *ib.*; revival of Hindu nationality, *ib.*; able administration, 218; punishment of heinous criminals, *ib.*; collection of Jezya at Surat, 231; Hindu revolt in Bengal against his religious persecutions, 237–8; excitement at his death, 240; his dying fears, *ib.*; his persecution of the Sikhs, 242; execution of Guru Govind, 243.
Ava, or Burma proper, 575; capital of the kingdom, 591; English advance on, during first Burmese war, 596; mission of Crawfurd, *ib.*; ferment at, during the first Afghan war, 653; political relations with the British government under Phagyi-dau and Tharawadi, 654; insurrection of Pagan Meng, 655; second Burmese war, 697; settlement by Lord Dalhousie, 697–8.
Avitable, General, in the service of Runjeet Singh, 674, 676 *note*.
Ayodhya, or Oude, Aryan kingdom of, 12; Raj of, 20; the scene of the Ramayana, 42; known as Kosala, *ib.*; rejoicings at the expected installation of Rama, 43–4; conquered by the Maharaja of Magadha, 64; Raja of, engages Nala as his charioteer, 91.
Azam Shah, second son of Aurangzeb, 214, 241; defeated and slain by his elder brother, *ib.*
Azim Khan, son of Dost Muhammad Khan, and brother of Afzal Khan, captures Kabul, 769; his oppressive government, 770; defeats Sher Ali, *ib.*; succeeds Afzal Khan as Amir of Afghanistan, *ib.*; deposed, *ib.*; his subsequent fate, *ib.*

B

Baber, his invasion of India, 110; the founder of the Moghul empire, 152; descent and early life, *ib.*; character, *ib.*; conquers the Afghans of Delhi, 154; advances to Agra, *ib.*; defeats the Rajputs under the Rana of Chitor, *ib.*; his death, 155; a bad Muhammadan, *ib.*
Bahadur Shah, eldest son of Aurangzeb, succeeds to the throne of Delhi, 241; letters to Mr. Thomas Pitt, governor of Madras, *ib.*; revolt of

the Sikhs, 242; settlement with the Mahrattas, 243; death, 245. *See* also Shah Alam.

Bahadur Shah, last titular king of Delhi, 713; dealings with the British government, 713-14; makes common cause with the rebel sepoys, 724-5; held responsible for the massacre of Europeans at Delhi, 726; flight to the tomb of Humayun, 747; arrested by Hodson, *ib.*; sent as a state prisoner to Rangoon, 752; his death, *ib.*

Bahmani empire in the Dekhan, 114; dismembered into the five kingdoms of Ahmadnagar, Berar, Bider, Bijapur, and Golkonda, 118.

Bairam Khan, regent and minister of Akbar, 157; kills the Hindu Hemu, 158; discarded by Akbar, *ib.*; assassinated, *ib.*

Baiza Bai, widow of Daulat Rao Sindia, her ambitious designs on the throne of Gwalior, 606; refusal of Lord William Bentinck to interfere, *ib.*; forced to retire in favor of Jankoji Rao Sindia, *ib.*; her able administration, 648.

Baj-baj, curious capture of, 320 *note*.

Baji Rao, second Peishwa, rules the Mahratta empire from 1720 to 1740, as minister of Maharaja Sahu, 257, 386 *note*; dealings with Nizam-ul-mulk and the Moghul Padishah of Delhi, 259; extorts cessions of territory and tribute from Muhammad Shah, 259-60; advances on Agra and Delhi, 260; repulses by Saadut Ali Khan of Oude, *ib.*; his dealings with Nizam-ul-mulk, 261-3; his death, 269.

Baji Rao, son of Rughonath Rao, eighth and last Peishwa, his early struggles against Nana Farnavese, 463; intrigues with Daulat Rao Sindia, 464; permits Sindia to plunder Poona, 465; treacherous designs against Sindia, *ib.*; forced reconciliation with Nana Farnavese, 468; refuses to engage in a subsidiary alliance with the British government, 493; intrigues against Nana Farnavese, 497; cruelties at Poona, 498; defeated by Jaswant Rao Holkar, 499; flight into British territory, *ib.*; signs the treaty of Bassein proposed by Lord Wellesley, *ib.*; reduced to the condition of a feudatory of the British government, *ib.*; restored by the British to the throne of Poona, 500; his duplicity and treachery, *ib.*; intrigues against the British government during the administration of Lord Hastings, 550; underhand breaches of treaty, *ib.*; strange reception of Gungadhur Shastri, the minister from the Gaekwar of Baroda, 551; murder of the minister, 552; implication of Baji Rao and Trimbukji Dainglia, *ib.*; imprisonment and escape of Trimbukji, 552-3; fresh intrigues, 553; threats of Mr. Elphinstone, the British Resident, 554; treaty of Poona, *ib.*; desperate designs, 560; duplicity, *ib.*; outwits Sir John Malcolm, 561; treacherous movements, 562; repulsed by the British at Khirki, 563; flight from Poona, *ib.*; appoints Appa Sahib of Nagpore his commander-in-chief, 564; disgraceful repulse at Korygaum, 568; flight, *ib.*; final settlement, 570; death, 706.

Bakhtiyar, 101; captures Bihar and Nuddea, *ib.*; Viceroy of Bihar and Bengal, *ib.*

Bala Hissar, the "palace of kings" at Kabul, surrendered to Ahmad Shah Abdali by the Kuzzilbashes, 623; removal of the British garrison, 638.

Balaji Rao, third Mahratta Peishwa, 1740-61, 269; schemes to gain the sovereignty, 386; cruel treatment of Sukwar Bai, widow of Maharaja Sahu, *ib.*; behavior toward Tara Bai, *ib.*; removes the capital to Poona, 387; invasion of the Carnatic and Dekhan, 388; recalled to Satara, *ib.*; counterplots against Tara Bai, *ib.*; aggressions and outrages in the Dekhan and Carnatic, *ib.*; intrigues with the Moghul Court at Delhi, 389; general reconciliation with the Gaekwar and

Tara Bai, *ib.*; relations with Bombay, 390; the capture of Gheria, *ib.*; his wrath against the English, *ib.*; his administration, *ib.*; death, 393.
Balaji Visvanath, first Mahratta Peishwa, 386 *note*.
Bali, Raja of monkeys, 57; slain by Rama, *ib.*
Balkh, disaffection in, 624; its situation, *ib. note*.
Bandu Guru leads the Sikhs to vengeance, 243; his martyrdom, 250.
Bangalore, captured by Lord Cornwallis, 455; visited by Buchanan, 477; its foundation and history, 477–8.
Banghel, Raja of, his marriage with the queen of Olaza, 143; annexation of the Raj by Venk-tapa Naik, *ib.*
Banians, or Bunniahs, corresponding to the Vaisyas, 77 *note*; their attempt to ransom thugs, 218.
Bapoji Sindia, a treacherous ally of the English, 509–10.
Barace, the modern Baroche, an ancient Malabar port, 124–5 *note*.
Bari Doab, construction of the canal of, 694 *note*.
Barlow, Sir George, Governor-General, 517; his character, *ib.*; his political apostasy, *ib.*; mistaken concessions, 518; annulment of protective treaties with Rajput states, *ib.*; vain remonstrances with Nipal, 543.
Barnard, Sir Henry, advance to Delhi of, 743; his death, 742 *note*.
Baroche, a fort at the mouth of Nerbudda river, the ancient Barace, 124–5 *note*; ceded to the English by Rughonath Rao, 420; refusal of the Poonah council of regency to sanction the cession, 421; given back to Mahadaji Sindia by Warren Hastings with other cessions, 436, 502 *note*; fears of Lord Wellesley respecting a French landing, 502.
Baroda, the Gaekwar of, becomes a feudatory, 506. *See* Gaekwar.
Barrackpore, or "Chanuk," early English settlement at, 237; panic at, 717; incendiary fires, 719; mutiny, *ib.*; outbreak of Mungal Pandy, 720; previous mutiny during the first Burmese war, 727.
Barukzais, an Afghan tribe, an offshoot of the Abdalis, 622; plot at Kandahar against Zeman Shah, 627; slaughter of the conspirators, *ib.*; vain attempts to set up a Durani puppet as sovereign of Afghanistan, 631–2; struggles against the Duranis after the British retreat from Kabul, 642. *See* also Dost Muhammad Khan.
Barwell, Mr., a Company's civil servant appointed member of council, 412; sides with Warren Hastings against Clavering and Francis, 425; goes to England, 426; loses twenty thousand pounds at whist to Francis, 449.
Basalut Jung, son of Nizam-ul-mulk, 367 *note*; dealings with Governor Rumbold respecting Guntoor, 430.
Bassein, near Bombay, Portuguese fort there, 130; anxiously desired by the East India Company, 399; ceded to Bombay by Rughonath Rao, 420; restored to the Mahratta, 421.
Bassein, treaty of, concluded with Baji Rao Peishwa, 499; objections to the treaty, 500.
Bassein, in Burma, captured by the English, 697.
Bayley, Mr. Butterworth, provisional Governor-General. 600 *note*.
Behar or Bihar, 306 *note*; invaded by the Nawab Vizier of Oude and Shah Alam, 353.
Begums, the Oude, 415; preposterous claims to the state treasures of Oude, *ib.*; torturing of their servants with the cognizance of Warren Hastings, 435.
Benares, Raja of, conquered by Bhishma, 14 *note*; old name of Attock, *ib.*; Bulwunt Singh, Raja of, 355; acquisition of, carried out by

Philip Francis in opposition to Warren Hastings, 414–15; Cheit Singh, Raja of, pressed for money by Warren Hastings, 433–4; insurrection at Benares against Warren Hastings, 434. *See* Cheit Singh.

Benfield, Paul, his fabricated claims on Muhammad Ali, Nawab of the Carnatic, 427; his subsequent career, 440 *note*; appearance of his wife in London, *ib.*; denounced by Burke, 441 *note*.

Bengal, conquered by Bakhtiyar in the reign of Kutub-ud-din, 101; flight of the Raja of Nuddea, *ib.*; old capital at Gour, *ib.*; Portuguese mission to, in the sixteenth century, 181; horrible succession of tyrants, *ib.*; conquest of Sher Khan the Afghan, 156; English settlements in Bengal, 234; Mr. Job Charnock, governor, 235; fortifications and cannon prohibited by the Moghuls, *ib.*; English declare war against the Moghul Nawab, 236; flight of the English to Madras, *ib.*; foundation of Calcutta, 237; memories of Job Charnock, *ib.*; Hindu rebellion against the persecutions of Aurangzeb, *ib.*; notices of Bengal by Captain Hamilton, 238; refractory Rajas between Murshedabad and Patna, 289, 310; political isolation of the Nawabs of Bengal, Behar, and Orissa, 255; up-country factories, 308; rise of Murshed Kuli Khan, *ib.*; harsh treatment of Hindus, 309; rise of Alivardi Khan, 310; story of the baskets of human heads, 311; the Seth family insulted by Nawab Sarfaraz Khan, 312; destruction of Sarfaraz Khan, and proclamation of Alivardi Khan as Nawab, 312–13; Mahratta invasions, 313; treacherous assassinations, 314; Mahratta revenge, *ib.*; domestic life of the Nawab of Bengal, 315; hostility of his son, Suraj-ud-daula, 316; the young Nawab marches an army against Calcutta, 317; tragedy of the Black Hole, 318; alarm of the Nawab, 321; vacillations, *ib.*; plottings of Mir Jafir and the Seths against Suraj-ud-daula, 322; conspiracy joined by Clive, *ib.*; treachery of Omichund, *ib.*; battle of Plassy, 323; Mir Jafir installed Nawab, *ib.*; cessions to the English, *ib.*; incapacity of Mir Jafir, 324; general dependence on Clive, *ib.*; revolution of political ideas, 325; disaffection of Hindu grandees, 326; English blamed for non-interference, *ib.*; Mahrattas demand chout, *ib.*; territorial claims of the Shahzada, 327; his defeat and flight, 329; Clive appointed Governor of the English settlements, 336; succeeded by Holwell and Vansittart, *ib.*; necessity for a permanent European force, *ib.*; Clive's scheme for the acquisition of Bengal by the British nation, *ib.*; similar proposals of Colonel James Mill, 337 *note*; offer of the Dewani of Bengal, Behar, and Orissa to Clive, 337; objections of Mr. Pitt, *ib.*; dealings of Vansittart with Mir Jafir, 340; treaty with Mir Kasim, 341; Vansittart refuses a bribe, *ib.*; peaceful change of Nawabs, 342; installation of Shah Alam at Patna as the Great Moghul, 343; offer of the Dewani to Vansittart, 344; suspicions of Mir Kasim, *ib.*; secret preparations for war, *ib.*; quarrel about private trade, *ib.*; collision between the English and the Nawab's officers, 346; violence of the English at the up-country factories, 348; capture of Patna, 349; recovery of Patna by the Nawab's people, *ib.*; flight and surrender of the English, 349–50; elation of the Nawab, 350; murder of Amyatt, *ib.*; Mir Jafir proclaimed Nawab, 351; advance of an English army to Monghyr, *ib.*; massacre of the English at Patna, 352; flight of Mir Kasim into Oude, 353; battle of Buxar, 354; death of Mir Jafir, 357; corrupt sale of Bengal and Behar to his illegitimate son, *ib.*; return of Lord Clive to Calcutta, 359; his wrath at the sale, 360; introduces a system of double government, *ib.*; English sovereignty veiled by Moghul forms, *ib.*; office of Dewan of Bengal, Behar, and Orissa vested in East India Company, 362–3; political results, 363; golden prospects, 364; Clive succeeded by Verelst, 367; financial crisis, 370; evils of double government, 371; protection of a vicious system of native government, *ib.*; character of the Zemindars, 372; oppressive treatment of the Ryots, *ib.*; deputy Nawabs, 373; aggravation of evils under the double government, *ib.*; mock pageantry at Murshedabad, 374; Bengal drained of silver, *ib.*; Verelst's experiences of native administration, 375; appointment of English supervisors and committees, *ib.*; closer relation between the English and natives, *ib.*; native administration of justice, 376; Mr. George Vansittart gulled by Raja Shitab Rai at Patna, 377; results of the collision between Europeans and Hindus, 378; general corruption in Bengal, 380; native opinion turned against the English, *ib.*; horrible famine, 381; Warren Hastings appointed Governor, *ib.*; reforms in the revenue administration, 404; judicial reforms, 405; charges against the deputy Nawabs, *ib.*; transfer of the capital from Murshedabad to Calcutta, 406; flight of Shah Alam to Delhi severs the English from the Great Moghul, *ib.*; tribute for Bengal and Behar withheld by the English, 408; question of equity, *ib.*; reorganization of Bengal under a Governor-General, 412; creation of a Supreme Court at Calcutta, *ib.*; Philip Francis member of council, *ib.*; factious opposition to Hastings, 413; trial and execution of Nund-komar, 416; quarrel between Bengal and Bombay respecting the Mahratta war, 420; struggle between Hastings and Clavering for the post of Governor-General, 425; failure of the land settlement by five years' leases in Bengal, *ib.*; return of Philip Francis to Europe, 426; interference in Madras affairs, 431; spirited proceedings of Hastings, 433; empty treasury, *ib.*; return of Hastings to Europe, 441; permanent land settlement by Lord Cornwallis, 450.

Bentinck, Lord William, Governor of Madras, recalled in consequence of the mutiny at Vellore, 521; tardy redress, *ib.*; appointed Governor-General, 600; his successful domestic administration, 600–1; political relations with Mahrattas and Rajputs, 601; his political administration, 604; his forced interference in Gwalior affairs, 606; his interference in Indore affairs, 607; declines to interfere in Bundelkund affairs, *ib.*; or in Jaipur affairs, 608; threatens the king of Oude, 609; annexes Coorg, 613; his vacillations with regard to Mysore, 616; embarks for England, *ib.*; successful administration, 617.

Berar, Muhammadan kingdom of, in the northern Dekhan, 118; conquered by Akbar, 171; Berar and Nagpore formed into a feudatory Mahratta kingdom by the Bhonsla Raja, 384; plundered by the Mahratta Peishwa, 395; ceded to the English, 506; made over to Nizam Ali, *ib.*; restoration demanded by Rughoji Bhonsla, 519; ceded to the British government by the Nizam for the support of the Nizam's Contingent, 708. *See* Bhonsla and Nagpore.

Berhampore, sepoy mutiny at, 719.

Bernier, account of a false astrologer at Delhi, 198.

Bharadars, the Ghorka, 534; council of, at Khatmandu, 544, 546, 665.

Bharadwaja, his hermitage at Prayaga, 49; entertains Rama, *ib.*; wonderful miracle, 54 *note*.

Bharata, hero ancestor of Santanu, 12; all India called the land of Bharata, *ib.*; the Maha Bharata, *ib.*

Bharata, son of Dasaratha by Kaikeyi, 43; sent to Giri-vraja, *ib.*; possible representative of a Buddhist faction, *ib. note*; installed as Yuva-raja, 44; returns to Ayodhya, 50; celebrates funeral of Dasaratha, 51; performs the Sraddha, 52; refuses the Raj of Ayodhya, *ib.*;

marches to Chitra-kuta to seek Rama, *ib.*; passage of the Ganges, 53; meeting with Rama, 54; second return, 54–5.

Bharata, son of Dushyanta and Sakuntala, 88–9.

Bhils or Bheels, occupied the hills and jungles to the south, 12; an existing type of so-called aborigines, 78; their superstition, 17; legend of the Bhil prince and Drona, *ib.*; Sivaji's alliance with them, 203.

Bhilsa, Buddhist temples plundered by Ala-ud-din, 102.

Bhima, son of Kunti, 15; the second of the Pandavas, 16; jealousy of Duryodhana, *ib.*; his rivalry with Duryodhana at the exhibition of arms, 18; slays Hidimba and marries Hidimbi, 21; slays the cannibal Vaka, *ib.*; vows revenge against Duryodhana and Duhsasana, 27; serves as cook at the court of Virata, 29; slays Jimuta and Kichaka, 30; slays Duryodhana by a foul blow, 34; slays Duhsasana and fulfils his vow, *ib.*

Bhim Sein Thapa of Nipal accompanies Run Bahadur to Benares, 539; his return to Nipal, 541; the prime minister of Run Bahadur, *ib.*; orders a massacre at Khatmandu, 542; his relations with Run Bahadur's chief queen, *ib.*; summons a council of Bharadars at Khatmandu, 544; advises war, 544, 546; sues for peace, 547; renewal of war, 548; concludes the treaty of Segowlie, *ib.*; premier and paramour, 657; provokes the elder queen, 658; dealings with the Resident, *ib.*; his fall, 659; released from prison, 659–60; pensioned, 660; his condemnation, 661; his doom, *ib.*

Bhishma, son of Santanu, resigns all claim to the Raj of Hastinapur, 14; the dreadful vow, *ib.*; the faithful guardian, *ib.*; proposes the division of the Raj of Hastinapur between the Pandavas and Kauravas, 24; slain by Arjuna, 34; reappears in the Ganges, 40.

Bhodau Phra, king of Burma, reign of, 590; conquests and cruelties, *ib.*; pride and ignorance, 593.

Bhonsla family, rise of, 259.

Bhonsla, Rughoji, founds the feudatory kingdom of Berar and Nagpore under the suzerainty of Maharaja Sahu and the Peishwas, 384–5; his kinship to Sivaji, 386; suspicious of the designs of Balaji Rao Peishwa and the legitimacy of Raja Ram, 387; his death, 394.

Bhonsla, Janoji, succeeds Rughoji, claims chout for Bengal and Behar from Mir Jafir, 326 *note*; Clive inclined to yield, 365, 399; refusal of the Court of Directors, *ib.*; negotiations with Nizam Ali for getting the regency at Poona, 395; engages to desert Nizam Ali, 396; treacherous slaughter of half the Nizam's army, *ib.*; strange reconciliation, *ib.*; his death, 419 *note.*

Bhonsla, Mudaji, brother of Janoji, usurps the throne of Berar, 419 *note*; betrays the hostile confederacy of Hyder Ali, Nizam Ali, and the Mahrattas to Warren Hastings, and renews the demand for chout, 432; his neutrality secured, 433; his death, 500 *note.*

Bhonsla, Rughoji, the Second, succeeds to the throne of Berar, 500 *note*; joins in the war against Nizam Ali, 462–3; stupefaction at the treaty of Bassein, 500; anxious for the help of Jaswant Rao Holkar, 501; feeble operations in the field against Colonel Wellesley, 503; defeated at Assaye, *ib.*; his flight, *ib.*; cedes Cuttack and Berar to the British government, 506; demands their restoration, 519; his death, 563.

Bhonsla, Appa Sahib. *See* Appa Sahib, and Nagpore.

Bhopal, Pindhari chiefs settled in, 559; loyalty of the Begum during the sepoy mutiny, 742 *note.*

Bhowani, the goddess, 201 *note.*

Bhurtpore, Jat principality at, 400; feudatory to the British government, 506; the Raja throws off his allegiance, 511; the fortress besieged by Lake, *ib.*; the Raja frightened into submission, *ib.*; outbreak in, 597; growing danger, 598; capture of the fortress by Lord Combermere, 599.

Bhutan, 531; mission to, 762; country described, *ib.*; the people, 763; corrupt Buddhism, *ib.*; Dharma and Deva Rajas, *ib.*; Penlows, Jungpens, and Zingaffs, 763–4; constitutional element, 764; border aggressions, *ib.*; historical importance of the mission, *ib.*; civil war, *ib.*; dealings with England, 765–6; failure of the mission, 766–7; war with England, 767.

Bider, the ancient Vidarbha, 90 *note*; one of the five Muhammadan kingdoms of the Dekhan, 118.

Bihar, or Vihara, the land of Buddhist monasteries, anciently called Magadha, 64; captured by Bakhtiyar, 101. *See* Behar.

Bijapur, one of the five Muhammadan kingdoms of the Dekhan, 118; alliance of the Sultan of with Ram Rai, 121; flight of the Bijapur army, 202; conquered by Aurangzeb, 217.

Bithoor, Nana Sahib, Raja of, 732. *See* Nana Sahib.

Blackburne, Major, Resident at Tanjore, 486 *note*; investigation of dispute between the Tondiman and Sivaganga Rajas, *ib.*

Black Hole, tragedy of at Calcutta, 318–19.

Blake, Mr., murdered at Jaipur, 608.

Board of Control, created in 1784, 439; its constitution, *ib. note*; its orders with reference to the Carnatic, 440–1.

Bobili Raja, feud with the Raja of Vizianagram, 330–1; self-sacrifice of Rajputs, *ib.*

Bogle, his mission to Thibet, 536 *note*.

Bokhara, an Usbeg kingdom, 619; fate of Stoddart and Conolly at, 645–6; Russian advance to, 771.

Bombay, Portuguese fort at, 130 *note*; ceded to the English by the Portuguese, 230; gardens and terraces turned into ramparts, *ib.*; its situation, 388; relations with Poona, 417; negotiations with Rughonath Rao for the cession of Salsette and Bassein, 420; condemned by the Bengal government, *ib.*; sends an expedition to Poona, 422; convention of Wurgaum, 423.

Bonairs, their behavior in the Sitana campaign, 760–1.

Boscawen, Admiral, 287; raises the siege of Pondicherry, *ib.*; his return to England, 296.

Bowring, Sir Lewin, Chief Commissioner of Mysore, his account of the Coorg Raja, 611 *note*.

Brahma, worship of, 82.

Brahmans, priests and sages, 23 *note*; surprise at seeing a Brahman contend at a Swayamvara, 23; hatred of Buddhists, 21 *note*; the first of the four great castes, 25 *note*, 77; Brahman envoy at the court of Hastinapur, 31–2; persecuted by the Rakshasas, 55; excite the wrath of Alexander the Great, 66; rise and growth of their power, 83; Purohitas, Gurus and Swamis, 84; modern Brahmanism, 87, 113; Brahman element in Mahratta constitution, 244; their sects in Southern India, 474; distinction between spiritual and secular, Vaidikas and Lokikas, 476; officials of Tippu, 478; corrupt and oppressive, *ib.*; satires against, 482; Dubois' story of the four Brahmans, 482–5.

Brinjarries or carriers (*see* Manaris) engaged by Cornwallis, 456.

Bristow, Mr., supersedes Middleton as Resident at Lukhnow, 414; impolitic interference in the question of the Oude treasures, 415; supported by Francis, *ib.*

Brodie, Sergeant, his heroism during the Vellore mutiny, 520.
Brydon, Dr., his escape from the massacre in the Khaiber Pass, 641.
Buchanan, Dr., sent by Lord Wellesley from Madras to Malabar, 472-3; journey through Mysore, 472; sights and experiences, 472-82.
Buddhism, Kanishka, a liberal patron of, 71; missionaries sent out by Asoka, 73; Buddhist pilgrims from China, *ib.*; Buddhism, a revolt against the Brahmanical system of Manu, 87; doctrine of deliverance in annihilation, *ib.*; transplanted from Hindustan into Thibet, 581-2; rival sects of the red and yellow, 582 *note*; cheerful form of Buddhism in Burma, 576-7; corrupt form prevailing in Bhutan, 763.
Budge-budge. *See* Baj-baj.
Buhler's, Professor, *Introduction to the Vikramankakavya*, 88 *notes*.
Bulaki, son of Khuzru, 183; declared successor to the throne by Jehangir, *ib.*; his short reign, 185; his fate, 186.
Bulwunt Singh, Raja of Benares, detached from the cause of Shuja-ud-daula, Nawab Vizier of Oude, 355; father of Cheit Singh, 433.
Bundlekund, ceded by the Peishwa to the British government, 522; turbulence and anarchy suppressed by Lord Minto, *ib.*; evils of non-intervention, case of Sumpthur, 607.
Bundula, the Burmese general, invades the countries between Burma and Bengal, 594; repulsed at Rangoon, 595; his earthworks at Donabew, *ib.*; death, *ib.*
Burdwan, ceded to the English by Mir Kasim, 341, 343.
Burhanpur, Sir Thomas Roe at, 175-6.
Burke's denunciation of Benfield and Dundas, 441 *note*; his charges against Hastings, 441.
Burma, geography of, 575; its inhabitants described, 575-6; their life and manners, *ib.*; Buddhist institutions, 576-7; marriage institutions, 578; devastating wars, *ib.*; Portuguese adventurers, 579; a Burmese hero, *ib.*; his career, 579-87; public life of the kings, 590-1; the administration a network of officialism, 591; origin of the war with England, 593; pride and ignorance of the court, *ib.*; violence and insolence of officials, *ib.*; hostile incursions, 594; flight of the soldiery at the approach of the English, 595; the army repulsed at Rangoon, *ib.*; the panic at Donabew, *ib.*; the treaty of Yandabo, 596; second war with England, 697; capture of Rangoon, Bassein, and Prome, *ib.*; annexation of Pegu, *ib.*
Burma, British, formation of, 698; prosperity, *ib.*; visit of Lord Mayo, 773.
Burnes, Sir Alexander, at Kabul, 638; his defence against the Afghan outbreak at Kabul, 639; his murder, *ib.*
Burney, Colonel, Resident at Ava, 654; withdrawal, 655.
Bushire, captured by the English, 715.
Bussy, M., captures Jinji, 293; accompanies Muzaffir Jung, 295; proclaims Salabut Jung Nizam of the Dekhan, 296; his rupture with Salabut Jung, 306; marches to Hyderabad, *ib.*; letter to Alivardi Khan, 316; his wars against the Hindu Poligars, 330; sides with the Raja of Vizianagram against the Bobili Raja, 331; his successes against the English, 332; contrast with Clive, *ib.*; recalled by Lally, 333; reluctant obedience, *ib.*
Buxar, battle of, 354.
Byadeit, or privy council of the Burmese, 592.
Byeen-noung, a Burmese hero, 579; conquest of Pegu, 580; siege of Martaban, *ib.*; plunder and sack of Martaban, 583; his terrible vengeance on the ladies of Martaban, 584-6; he invades Siam, 586; recalled to Pegu, *ib.*; assassinated, 587; career of his foster-brother, 587-8; himself a type of Burmese conquerors, 589.

C

CACHAR, English acquisition of, 617.

Cæsar Frederic, his visit to Vijayanagar, 122.

Calcutta, foundation of the English settlement at, 237; fortifications round the factory, 238; social life of the English in the beginning of the eighteenth century, *ib.*; garrison of Fort William, *ib.*; English mission to Delhi, 248; government, 307; French and Dutch neighbors at Chandernagore and Chinsura, *ib.*; up-country factories, 308; experiences of Muhammadan rule, 311; the Mahratta ditch, 314; hostility of the young Nawab, Suraj-ud-daula, 316; attack on Calcutta, 317; inefficient defence of the English, 318; surrender of Fort William, *ib.*; tragedy of the Black Hole, 318–19; indifference of Asiatics, 319; recapture of Calcutta by Clive and Watson, 320; decisive battle of Plassy, 323; wild joy of the inhabitants of Calcutta, *ib.*; collision with Mir Kasim, 344; stormy councils, 346; deputation of Amyatt and Hay to Monghyr, 348; murder of Amyatt, 350; Mir Jafir proclaimed Nawab at Calcutta, 351; massacre of a hundred and fifty Englishmen at Patna, 352; corrupt proceedings of the Calcutta council at Murshedabad, 357; Lord Clive appointed governor, 359; introduces a double government, 363; political outlook of Calcutta in the eighteenth century, 382–3; relations with Delhi, 401; transfer of the capital of Bengal from Murshedabad to Calcutta, 406.

Calicut, court of the Zamorin, or suzerain of Malabar, 126; audience of Vasco de Gama in the palace, 127; hostility of the Muhammadan merchants, *ib.*; massacre of Portuguese by the Nairs, 129; Portuguese mission to the Zamorin, 144; description of the city and bazars, 146; Della Valle's audience with the Zamorin, *ib.*; scanty costume of ladies and courtiers, 146–7.

Calliaud, General, expedition to the Northern Circars, 367; treaty with Nizam Ali, *ib.*

Campbell, Sir Colin (Lord Clyde), Commander-in-chief, 748; his relief of Lukhnow, 749; defeats the Gwalior rebels at Cawnpore, 751; his campaign in Oude and Rohilkund, 752.

Cannanore, port of, 125.

Canning, Lord, Governor-General of India, 712; dealings with the Delhi family, 713–14; undisturbed by the rumors forerunning the mutiny, 715; sympathies with the sepoys, 727; vigorous measures, *ib.*; his durbar at Agra, 757; departure and death, *ib.*

Canning, Capt., his mission to Ava, 593.

Caravanserais in Moghul India, 221.

Carnac, Major, defeats the army of Shah Alam and the Nawab Vizier, 342; installs Shah Alam as the Great Moghul in the English factory at Patna, 342–3.

Carnac, Sir James, his dealings with the Raja of Satara, 703.

Carnatic, governed by a Nawab nominated by the Nizam of the Dekhan, subject to the confirmation of the Great Moghul, 275; geographical boundaries, *ib.*; politically divided by the river Koleroon, *ib.*; Moghul Carnatic and Hindu Carnatic, *ib.*; Rajas, *ib.*; Poligars, 276; Moghul rule more oppressive than the Hindu, *ib.*; ravages of the Mahrattas in the Upper Carnatic, *ib.*; succession of Nawabs, 277; revolution in the Hindu Carnatic, 278; old wars between Trichinopoly and Tanjore, *ib.*; Trichinopoly seized by Chunder Sahib, 279; Mahratta invasion, *ib.*; takes possession of Trichinopoly, 280; succession of Subder Ali as Nawab, 281; wrath of the Nizam, *ib.*; perplexities of the Nawab, *ib.*; assassination of Subder Ali, 282; settlement of affairs by Nizam-ul-mulk, 283–4; murder of the boy Nawab at a wedding feast, 284; Anwar-ud-din appointed Nawab, 285; war between England and France, *ib.*; defeat of the Nawab's army by the French, 286; peace between England and France, 287; restoration of Madras to the English, *ib.*; struggle between two rival Nawabs, 288; English and French take opposite sides, *ib.*; defeat and death of Anwar-ud-din at Amboor, 290; contest between Muhammad Ali and Chunder Sahib, *ib.*; interference of Nasir Jung, Nizam of the Dekhan, 293; brilliant success of the French, 295; bewilderment of the English, 296; crisis at Trichinopoly, 297; Clive's defence of Arcot, 299; triumph of the English and Muhammad Ali, 300; peace between the English and French, 304; invasion of Hyder Ali and Nizam Ali, 369; invasion of Balaji Rao Peishwa, 388; later invasions of Hyder Ali, 431; disasters of the English, 432–3; corrupt dealings of the English at Madras with the Nawab, Muhammad Ali, 426; claims of Paul Benfield, 427; Macartney's assumption of the revenue, 437; miscellaneous adventurers, 440 *note*; revenues restored to the Nawab, 441; settlement of the Nawab's debts, *ib.*; invasion of Tippu, 455; Carnatic brought under British administration by Lord Wellesley, 485; necessity for the transfer, 489; treacherous correspondence of the Nawab with Tippu of Mysore, *ib.*; final settlement by Lord Dalhousie, 706.

Cartier, governor of Bengal, 370.

Carumnassa river, 308 *note*; boundary of British territory in Bengal laid down to Lord Clive, 365.

Castes, division into four, 25 *note*, 77.

Catherine II. of Russia, Russian aggression in Persia during the reign of, 496 *note*.

Catholic missionaries, denunciations of cruelties of Hindu Rajas, 276 *note*.

Cawnpore, its history, 731; its garrison, 732; the place of refuge, 732; mutiny at, 733; besieged by Nana Sahib, 734; massacre in the boats, 735; imprisonment of women and children, 736; massacre of women and children, 738; defeat of Nana Sahib, *ib.*; entry of Havelock, *ib.*; occupied by the Gwalior rebels, 751; their defeat, *ib.*

Chakrantikam, ceremony of, 481.

Chamba lriver, 194, 241; boundary between Malwa and Rajputana, 421 *note*, 505.

Chamberlain, General Sir Neville, his conduct of the Sitana campaign, 759–61.

Chandernagore, founded by the French, 238, 307; captured by Clive and Watson, 321; restored to France, 361 *note*.

Chandra-gupta. *See* Sandrokottos.

Chandu Lal at the head of the Nizam's administration, 571; the sham loan, 572; resigns office, 708.

Charioteers, exercised political influence in ancient Hindu courts, 82 *note*.

Charnock, Job, governor of English settlements in Bengal, 235; arrested and scourged, 236; return to Calcutta, 237; the patriarch of Bengal, *ib.*

Cheit Singh, Raja of Benares, 433; his political status, 433–4; heavy demands of Hastings, 434; submission and rebellion, *ib.*; flight and deposition, *ib.*; one of the charges against Hastings, 441.

Chetu, a Pindhari leader, 527; killed by a tiger, 559.

Chilianwallah, the battle of, 688.

Chinsura, founded by the Dutch, 288, 307.
Chitor, old Rajput kingdom under the Rana, or Rajput suzerain, conquered by Ala-ud-din, 105; self-sacrifice of the Rajputs at, *ib.*; hostility of the Rana to Baber, 154; defeated, *ib.*; invaded by the Sultan of Guzerat, 155; headship of the Rajput league, 160–1; obstinate resistance to Akbar, 162; destruction of the city, *ib.*; Sir Thomas Roe's visit to the ruins, 177.
Chittagong, Portuguese mission to, 131; ceded to the English by Mir Kasim, 341.
Choultries, description of, 473.
Chout, collected by Sivaji, 211. *See* Mahrattas.
Chunder Sahib, son-in-law of Dost Ali, Nawab of the Carnatic, 278; gulls the Rani of Trichinopoly, *ib.*; imprisoned over six years at Satara by the Mahrattas, 280; liberated by the help of Dupleix, 288; proclaimed Nawab of the Carnatic, *ib.*; joins Muzaffir Jung, a claimant for the throne of Hyderabad, 290; delays at Tanjore, 292; flight to Pondicherry, 293; unexpected success, 295; surrender and murder, 300.
Clavering, General, a member of council at Calcutta, 412; contest with Warren Hastings for the post of Governor-General, 425; death, *ib.*
Clive, Robert, wins his first laurels at Pondicherry, 287; his early career, *ib.*; realizes the situation at Trichinopoly, 297; his plans, 298; his expedition to Arcot, *ib.*; defence at Arcot, 299; his career of conquest, *ib.*; leaves for England, 303; return to Bombay, 305; captures Gheria with Watson, 306; goes to Madras, *ib.*; recaptures Calcutta with Watson, 319–20; his anxiety for peace, 321; joins the conspiracy against Suraj-ud-daula, 322; deceives Omichund with a sham treaty, *ib.*; wins the battle of Plassy, 323; creates Mir Jafir Nawab, *ib.*; his jaghir, 324; his jackass, 325; his relations with the Moghul court at Delhi, 329; contrast to Bussy, 332; sends Colonel Forde to the Northern Circars, 333; appointed governor of Bengal, 336; his departure for England, *ib.*; convinced of the necessity of garrisoning Bengal, *ib.*; his scheme for the acquisition of Bengal, *ib.*; rejected by William Pitt, 337; his return to India, 357, 359; contemplated policy, 359–60; his wrath with Governor Spencer at Calcutta, 360; his negotiations at Murshedabad and Patna, *ib.*; his policy as regards the Great Moghul, 361; his restoration of Oude to the Nawab Vizier, *ib.*; his settlement with Shah Alam at Allahabad, 362; his office of Dewan, 363; results of his policy, 363–4; his external policy, 364; his misgivings about the Mahrattas, 365; his breach with Nizam Ali, *ib.*; obtains a firman from Shah Alam for the Northern Circars, 366; a Moghul Peishwa, *ib.*; thwarted by Madras, 367; leaves India for England, *ib.*; failure of his political system, 370–1; his double government and its results, 371–4.
Clyde, Lord. *See* Campbell, Sir Colin.
Cochin, ancient Cothinara, famous for pepper, 125 *note*; alliance with Portuguese, 129; feud with the Zamorin of Calicut, 145, 148.
Combermere, Lord, captures Bhurtpore, 599.
Company. *See* East India.
Conjeveram, or Kanchi-puram, visited by Buchanan, 473; its streets and houses, 474; the temple, *ib.*; headquarters of Ramanuja Acharya, 475 *note*.
Conolly, Captain, his fate at Bokhara, 645–6.
Cooper, Mr., military executions carried out by, 743 *note*.
Coorg, description of the country, 609; its isolation, *ib.*; warlike population, *ib.*; religious origin of the Raj, *ib.*; aggressions of Hyder

Ali, 610; and of Tippu, *ib.*; non-intervention of the British, *ib.*; mistaken interference in the succession, 611; madness of the Vira Raja, *ib.*; Chikka Vira Raja declares war against England, 612; valor of the Coorgs, *ib.*; their preference for British rule, 613; annexation, *ib.*; stipulation concerning cows, *ib. note.*

Coote, General Sir Eyre, defeats Lally at Wandiwash, 335; siege and capture of Pondicherry, *ib.*

Cornwallis, Lord, Governor-General of India, 449; introduces social reforms in Calcutta, *ib.*; permanent land settlement with the Bengal Zemindars, 450; judicial and administrative reforms, 450–1; war against Tippu, Sultan of Mysore, 454; dealings with Nizam Ali and the Mahrattas, 454–5; rebuffed by Mahadaji Sindia, 455; capture of Seringapatam, 457; attempts to establish a balance of power in India, 457–8; departure for England, 460; treaty with the Nawab of the Carnatic, 489; returns to India as Governor-General in succession to Lord Wellesley, 511; his extreme views, 516; his death, 517.

Coryat, Tom, his meeting with Roe at Chitor, 177; his travels, *ib.*

Cotton, Gen. Sir Sydney, drives Hindustani fanatics out of Sitana, 759.

Court, General, in the service of Runjeet Singh, 674, 676 *note.*

Cox, Captain, his mission to Ava, 593.

Crawfurd, Mr. John, his mission to Ava, 596.

Currie, Sir Frederic, Resident at Lahore, 685; accepts the resignation of Mulraj, *ib.*

Cuttack ceded to the English, 506.

D

DABUL in Konkan, Portuguese fort at, 181.

Dada Khasji, aspires to be premier of Gwalior, 649; his elevation by Tara Bai, 650; submission to the British government, 651.

Dacca, inland English factory at, 308; court of appeal at, 451.

Dalhousie, Lord, Governor-General, 685; resolves on the conquest of the Sikhs, 687–8; annexes the Punjab, 689–90; his genius, 691; administrative culture, *ib.*; creation of a government in the Punjab, 691–3; defence of the frontier westward of the Indus, 693–4; reduces the land revenue, 694; dealings with Burma, 695–8; annexes Pegu, 697; general energy and capacity, 698; suppression of barbarous usages in native states, 699; political dictum that no rightful opportunity should be lost of acquiring native territory, *ib.*; refuses to allow the right of adoption to cover a claim to the heirship of a principality in the case of dependent states, 702; case of the Raja of Satara, 703; recognition of the adopted son of the Kerauli Raja, 704; annexation of Nagpore, 706; dealings with the Carnatic and Tanjore families, *ib.*; dealings with Hyderabad and acquisition of Berar, 707–8; annexation of Oude, 710; deals with the Santals as Bentinck dealt with the Koles, 711; succeeded by Lord Canning, 712; agreement with the Moghul family at Delhi, 713.

Damaji Gaekwar, dynasty of, 384; espouses the cause of Tara Bai, 388; imprisoned by Balaji Rao, 388–9; joins Rughonath Rao, 395.

Damayanti. *See* Nala.

Dandaka, wilderness of, 49.

Dara, eldest son of Shah Jehan, 190; thwarts the projects of Aurangzeb, 191; defeated by Aurangzeb and Murad, 193; escape to the Punjab, 194; his second defeat, 195; assassination, *ib.*

Dasaratha, Maharaja of Ayodhya, 42; his four sons, *ib.*; cajoled by Kaikeyi, 44; his death, 50; funeral rites of, 51–2.

Daud Khan, 234; besieges Madras, *ib.*; Viceroy of Guzerat, 248; collision with Husain Ali Khan, *ib.*; death, *ib.*

De Boigne, General, in the service of Mahadaji Sindia, 446, 458; his return to Europe, 501.

De Gingen, Captain, 297.

Dekhan, conquests of Ala-ud-din, 103, 106; Sultans of (*see* Bahmani Sultans), 114; division of the Bahmani empire into five Muhammadan kingdoms, 118; Akbar's embassy to, 171; its failure, *ib.*; state of affairs in the time of Aurangzeb, 199; struggle for the throne of the Nizam, 289; acquisition by the French of the Northern Circars, 330; dealings of Bussy with Bobili and Vizianagram, 330–1; Lord Clive obtains the Northern Circars, 333–4, 366; Mahratta invasions, 387–8. *See* Mahrattas *and* Nizam.

Delhi, the Raja of, present at the Swayamvara of the princess of Kanouj, 98; capture of the city by the Afghans, *ib.*; rise of the Sultans of, 100; fatal removal of the capital to Deoghur in the Dekhan, 109; revolutions at the death of Jehangir, 185; sack of, by Nadir Shah's soldiery, 266; distractions between 1748 and 1758, history of, 327; struggles between the Afghans and Mahrattas at, 338; recovery of Delhi by the Mahrattas, 391; secret negotiations of Ahmad Shah Abdali with Alamghir, *ib.*; expulsion of the Mahrattas under Rughonath Rao and re-establishment of Afghan supremacy, 392; progress of affairs during the regency of Najib-ud-daula, 400; relations with Calcutta, 401; plots and assassinations under the Amir of Amirs, 444; ascendency of Mahadaji Sindia, 445; horrible excesses of Gholam Kadir, 451; General Lake's victory at, 504; audience with Shah Alam, *ib.*; treatment of the Moghul family by Lord Dalhousie, 713; tidings of the sepoy mutiny at Meerut, 724; approach of the mutineers, *ib.*; its defence by Brigadier Graves, 725; explosion of the magazine, *ib.*; tragedies in the palace, 726; flight of Europeans, *ib.*; the head-centre of revolt, 742; description of the defences, 744; the gates, *ib.*; the Ridge, 744–5; the old suburbs, 745; preparations for assault, 746; final assault, *ib.*; fighting inside the town, 747; reoccupation, 748; the Imperial Assemblage, 774.

Della Valle, his travels in India, 135; his account of the festival in honor of Hanuman, 57 *note*: his description of the war dances in the Dekhan, 116; description of Goa, 135–6; accompanies the Portuguese mission to Venk-tapa Naik, king of Ikkeri, 137–41; goes to Mangalore, 141; meeting with the queen of Olaza, 142–3; visits the king of the Yogis, 143; visits the city and bazar of Calicut, 145–6; audience with the Zamorin and the Malabar princesses, 146–7; departure from Calicut, 147.

Denison, Sir William, provisional Viceroy after the death of Lord Elgin, 761; orders the advance of the Bhutan mission, 765; his recognition of Sher Ali Khan, 768.

Deoghur, capital of a Mahratta kingdom in the Dekhan, captured by Ala-ud-din, 103; removal of the Muhammadan capital from Delhi by Muhammad Tughlak, 109; identified with the ancient Tagara, 125 *note*.

Deva Rai, assassination of his son, 117; submits to the Sultan of the Dekhan, *ib.*; marriage of his daughter, *ib.*; unpropitious parting with the Sultan of the Dekhan, *ib.*; defeats the Sultan, 118; his death, 119.

Deva or Deb Rajas in Bhutan, historical significance of the term, 763.

Devicotta in Tanjore, 287; ceded to the English, 288.

Dewal Devi, the Rajput princess of Guzerat, her strange adventures, 104–5.

Dewan, or accountant-general, 254; explanation of the term in reference to the Dewani of Bengal, 337, 344, 368.

Dhalimkote, Jungpen of, his conduct toward the Bhutan mission, 765.

Dharma Rajas in Bhutan, religious significance of the term, 763.

Dhian Singh, brother of Gholab Singh of Jamu, prime minister at Lahore, 675; dismissed by Kharak Singh and murders his successor, *ib.*; suspected of murdering the young Maharaja by the fall of an archway, *ib.*; checkmated by the queen-regent, 676; places Sher Singh on the throne, *ib.*; murdered. 677.

Dhrishta-dyumna, the brother of Draupadi, 23; slays Drona, 35; slain by Aswatthama, *ib.*; reappears in the Ganges, 41.

Dhritarashtra, the blind grandson of Santanu, married to Gandhari, 14; supplanted by his brother Pandu on account of his blindness, 15; becomes Maharaja of Hastinapur, *ib.*; his sons called the Kauravas, *ib.*; appoints Yudhishthira, eldest son of Pandu, to be Yuva-raja, 20; his vacillations, *ib.*; sends the Pandavas to Varanavata, and appoints his son Duryodhana to be Yuva-raja, *ib.*; sends his charioteer on a mission to the Pandavas, 32; affecting submission to the Pandavas, 36–7; retires with Gandhari to the banks of the Ganges, 37.

Dhulip Singh, infant son of Runjeet Singh, Maharaja of Lahore, 677; becomes a pensioner of the British government, 690.

Dhundu Punt. *See* Nana Sahib.

Diego Suarez, his extraordinary career in Burma, 588; murdered by the mob of Pegu, 589.

Digarchi, seat of the Teshu Lama, 532; temples of, plundered by the Ghorkas, 536.

Dinkur Rao, minister of Sindia, his conduct during the sepoy mutiny, 758.

Diu, Portuguese fort at, 130; repulse of the Turks at, by the Portuguese, 131.

Doab, grant of the revenue to Mahadaji Sindia, 459; its position, *ib.*

Donabew, on the river Irawadi, Bundula's stand at, 595; panic of the Burmese, *ib.*

Dost Ali, Nawab of the Carnatic, 277; withholds the tribute to the Nizam, *ib.*; appoints Chunder Sahib Dewan, *ib. note*; interferes in Trinchinopoly, 278; defeated and slain by the Mahrattas, 279.

Dost Muhammad Khan, first appearance of, 630; plunders the ladies of their jewels in the zenana at Herat, *ib.*; takes possession of Kabul, 631; proclaimed Amir, 632; his critical position, *ib.*; his anxiety to recover Peshawar, 634; applies for help to England and Russia, *ib.*; flight to Bokhara, 635; surrender, 636; an English prisoner, *ib.*; joins the Sikhs during the second Sikh war, 688; takes Peshawar and besieges Attock, *ib.*; driven out of Peshawar, 690; contends with Persia for Herat, 714; helped by England, 715; his death, 767; a faithful ally and successful ruler, 768; his treaty with Sir John Lawrence, 772; objections of Sher Ali Khan, *ib.*

Douglas, Captain, commandant of the palace guards at Delhi, killed in the sepoy mutiny, 726.

Doveton, Major, his futile mission to Tippu, 470.

Drake, Mr., governor of Calcutta, 317; demands of Suraj-ud-daula, *ib.*; escape from Calcutta, 318.

Draupadi, daughter of the Raja of Panchala, 22; her Swayamvara, *ib.*; rebuffs Karna, 23; won by Arjuna, *ib.*; her marriage, 24; gambled away by Yudhishthira. 27; her vow, 28; becomes a lady's-maid in the palace at Virata, 29; her Gandharva lovers, 30; saved from burning by Bhima, 30–1; her peril in the camp of the Kauravas, 35; her grief at the slaughter of her sons, 36; the funeral rites, *ib.*

Drona, the tutor of the Kauravas and the Pandavas, 16; his feud with the Raja of Panchala, *ib.*; marries a daughter of the house and educates the young princes at Hastinapur, *ib.*; his fame as a teacher of archery, 17; refuses to instruct the Bhil prince, *ib.*; worship of his image, *ib.*; his treatment of the Bhil prince, *ib.*; stops the combat between Duryodhana and Bhima at the exhibition of arms, 18; divides the Raj of Panchala with Drupada, 19; slays Drupada in the war of the Maha Bharata, 35; slain by Dhrishta-dyumna, *ib.*; re-appears in the Ganges, 40; difference of his exile from that of Rama, 48 *note*.

Drupada, Raja of Panchala, 16; his feud with Drona, *ib.*; defeated by Drona, 19; celebrates the Swayamvara of his daughter Draupadi, 22; sends an envoy in behalf of the Pandavas to Hastinapur, 31 slain by Drona, 34.

Dubois, Abbe, his description of a feud between the right and left hands, 480 *note*; reproduces the story of the four Brahmans, 482.

Duhsasana, treatment of Draupadi, 27; slain by Bhima, 34.

Dundas (Lord Melville) first president of the Board of Control, 439 *note*; denounced by Burke, 441 *note*.

Dupleix, governor of Pondicherry, 285; his alarm at the English fleet, *ib.*; deceives the Nawab of the Carnatic as regards Madras, 286; secures the release of Chunder Sahib from the Mahrattas, 288; schemes to make Chunder Sahib Nawab of the Carnatic in order to drive out the English, *ib.*; larger scheme regarding the Dekhan, 290; reception of Chunder Sahib and Muzaffir Jung at Pondicherry, *ib.*; worried by the delay at Tanjore, 292; checkmated by the invasion of Nasir Jung, 293; successful campaigns, *ib.*; cleverness of his wife, 294; sudden revolution at the death of Nasir Jung, 295; rejoicings at Pondicherry, *ib.*; appointed governor for the Great Moghul of all the countries to the south of the Kistna, *ib.*; sudden establishment of French ascendency in India, 296; misrepresentations as regards the English, 302; arrogates all the powers of a Nawab of the Carnatic, 303; refuses peace unless the English recognize his claims, *ib.*; sacrificed by the French government in Europe, 304; despair and death, *ib.*

Dupleix, Madame, her mixed parentage, 294; her knowledge of native languages and correspondence with native courts, *ib.*; known as Jan Begum, *ib. note*.

Durand, Sir Henry, at the storming of Ghazni, 635 *note*; political agent at Bhopal during the mutiny, 742 *note*.

Durani, modern name for the Abdalis, 622 *note*; dynasty of, founded by Ahmad Shah Abdali, 623.

Durani Shahs, and Barukzai Viziers, 629; expulsion of Shah Shuja, the Durani, 632; elevation of Dost Muhammad Khan, the Barukzai, *ib.*; restoration of Shah Shuja carried out by the English, 635; its failure, 639; murder of Shah Shuja, 642; civil war at Kabul between Barukzais and Duranis, *ib.*

Durbar, council of elders under the Raja, 11; hall of audience of Akbar, 169; Roe's audience with Jehangir at Ajmir, 177; wine-drinkers flogged at, 180; description of, at Delhi, 199; Sivaji at the durbar of Aurangzeb, 206.

Durga. *See* Kali.

Durjan Sal, of Bhurtpore, usurps the throne, 597–8; kept as a state prisoner, 599.

Duryodhana, the eldest of the Kauravas, 16; rivalry with Bhima at the exhibition of arms, 18; appointed Yuva-raja, 20; challenges

Yudhishthira to a gambling match, 26; wins the Raj and wife of the Pandavas, 27; mortally wounded by a foul blow from Bhima, 34; his death, 36; reappears in the Ganges, 41.
Dushyanta marries Sakuntala in Kalidasa's drama, 89; mythical father of Bharata, *ib.*; his bodyguard of Tartar women, 194 *note*.
Dustuck, or "permits" of the East India Company, 345; sale of dustucks by the Company's servants, *ib.*
Dutch at Pulicat and Sadras, 274; war with the English, 437 *note*.

E

EAST INDIA COMPANY, formation of, 173; checked by a Board of Control, 439; charter renewed in 1833, its results, 616; government of India transferred to the Crown, 756.
Edinburgh, visit to India of H.R.H. the Duke of, 774.
Edwardes, Lieutenant Herbert, successful operations against Multan, 686–7; deserted by Sher Singh, 687; left in charge of Multan, 689.
Egypt, Sultan of, interference with the Portuguese, 129–30.
Ekachakra, the modern Arrah, resting-place of the Pandavas, 21.
Elgin, Lord, Viceroy of India, 757; sanctions a mission to Bhutan, 764; his death, 761.
Ellenborough, Lord, Governor-General of India, 641; hesitates whether the English armies in Afghanistan should retreat or advance, 643; bombast and parade, 645; conquest of Sinde, 647; change of policy respecting Sindia and Holkar, 648; causes a regent of Gwalior to be appointed, 650; wrath at the action of Tara Bai, *ib.*; reduces Gwalior to tranquillity, 651; his contemplated measures against Indore, 652; his recall, *ib.*
Ellis, Mr., chief of the Patna factory, 348; violent conduct in connection with the private trade controversy, *ib.*; perilous position at Patna, 349; capture of Patna, *ib.*; flight and surrender, 350; perishes in the massacre, 352.
Elphinstone, Mr., his mission to Kabul, 523 *note*, 629; British Resident at Poona, 552; investigates the murder of Gungadhur Shastri, *ib.*; discovers the intrigues of the Peishwa and his minister, Trimbukji Dainglia, 553; rebukes and threatens Baji Rao Peishwa, 554; concludes the treaty of Poona, *ib.*; his scepticism of the professions of Baji Rao to Sir John Malcolm, 561; confirmed, 562; preparations for defence against the Peishwa, *ib.*; removes from the Residency to Khirki, *ib.*; destruction of his library, 563.
Elphinstone, General, succeeds Sir John Keane in command of the army at Kabul, 638; his vacillation, 640.
Eudemos, appointed by Alexander the Great in the room of Philip at Taxila, 67; murders Porus, *ib.*; driven out of the Punjab by Sandrokottos, *ib.*

F

FAH HIAN, pilgrimage of, 73; residence at Pataliputra, 74.
Faiz-ullah Khan, of Rohilkund, son of Hafiz Khan, 412; treaty with the Nawab Vizier of Oude, *ib.*
Fakirs among the Sikhs, 673 *note*.
Faria y Sousa, the Portuguese historian, 129 *note*.
Farrukh Siyar placed by the two Saiyids on the throne of Delhi, 246; incessant intrigues against the Saiyids, 247; duplicity respecting the Vice-royalty of the Dekhan, 248; connection with Dr. Hamilton, 249; tragic death, 250.

Ferozeshahar, the assault of, 680.
Firuz Shah, Sultan of Delhi, 110; burns a Brahman alive, *ib.*
Firuz, governor of Herat, 630; sends for aid to Kabul, *ib.*; taken prisoner, *ib.*
Fitzgerald, Captain, his brilliant charge at Sitabuldi, 565.
Foot-posts in India, 225.
Forbes, Mr., his primitive administration in Guzerat, 424–5; his regret at the restoration of Guzerat districts to Mahratta rule, 436.
Forde, Colonel, defeats the French under Conflans and recovers the English factories, 333; negotiations with Salabut Jung, 334; drives the French out of the Northern Circars, *ib.*
Fort St. David, English settlement at, 274, 286; captured by Lally, 333.
Fort St. George, origin of, 228; streets and houses, 229; English merchants of, propitiate Sivaji, 211; unsuccessful siege by Lally, 334. *See* Madras.
Fort William, garrison at, 238. *See* Calcutta.
Foujdars of districts, 226; their authority, *ib.*; at Hughli, 307.
Fra Joan, the pirate priest in Burma, 579.
Francis, Philip, appointed a member of the council at Calcutta, 412; author of the Letters of Junius. 413; his suspicions of the integrity of Warren Hastings, *ib.*; hostile measures, 414; ability, *ib.*; factious opposition, *ib.*; interference, *ib.*; acquisition of Benares, 414–15; sanctions the interference of Bristow in Oude affairs, 415; his charges against Hastings, 416; outwitted by Hastings, 416–17; the crisis at Calcutta, 425; plan of permanent land settlement in Bengal, *ib.*; duel with Hastings, 426; departure from India, *ib.*; excites national indignation against Hastings, 441; end, 442.
Fraser, Mr., Commissioner of Delhi, killed at the outbreak of the mutiny, 726.
French, their settlement at Pondicherry, 274; capture Madras, 285; defeat the Nawab's army, 286; war with the English, *ib.*; ascendency in India of, 296; besiege Arcot, 299; capitulate at Trichinopoly, 300; acquire the Northern Circars, 303; provisional treaty with the English, 304; loss of Chandernagore, 321; helpless condition in Hindustan, 330; desperate condition under Lally, 333–4 (*See* Lally); disasters in the Carnatic, 335; loss of military power in the Carnatic, *ib.*; intrigues at Poona, 421; agent at Poona, 446; French battalion in the service of Nizam Ali, 462; their conduct at the battle of Kurdla, 463; national hatred of the English, 467; Tippu an ally, *ib.*; Nizam Ali's French battalions disbanded, 468; French successes in the eastern waters, 526. *See* Perron *and* De Boigne.
Fryer, Dr., 226; his description of Masulipatam, 227; of Madras, 228; crossing the surf, 229; Fort St. George, *ib.*; description of Bombay, 230; of Surat, 230–1; return to Bombay, 231; adventures at Joonere, *ib.*; visit to Karwar, 233; leaves India, *ib.*
Futih Khan, Barukzai, son of Payendah Khan, of Kabul, 627; dethrones Zemau Shah, *ib.*; the real sovereign of Afghanistan, 628; puts down the Ghilzais, *ib.*; dismissed by Shah Shuja, 629; deposes Shah Shuja and sets up Mahmud Shah, *ib.*; seizes Herat, 630; blinded, *ib.*; cruelly murdered at Ghazni, 631.
Futtehgurh, mutiny at, 736; massacre of the fugitives at Cawnpore, 736–7.
Futtehpore, Havelock's defeat of mutineers and Mahrattas at, 737.
Fytche, General, Chief Commissioner of British Burma, his work on Burma, 596 *note*; his treaty with the king of Burma, 778.

G

Gaekwar of Baroda, rise of the family of, 258, 384; interference at Satara in behalf of Tara Bai, 388; treacherously imprisoned at Poona, *ib.*; released, 389; dealings with Baji Rao, 551; murder of his minister, Gungadhur Shastri, 552.

Gakkars, hill tribe of, desperate slaughter in the army of Mahmud of Ghazni, 96; assassinate Muhammad Ghori, 100.

Gandhara country, 15 *note*; Gandarians mentioned by Herodotus, *ib.*; Gandhari marries the blind prince of Hastinapur, 15; her conduct toward her blind husband, *ib.*; attends the exhibition of arms, 18; retires with her husband, Dhritarashtra, to the banks of the Ganges, 37.

Gandharvas, or ghosts, Draupadi's lovers, 30; present at the feast of Bharadwaja, 54; a hill tribe famous for its beautiful women, 54 *note*.

Ganesh, god of good luck, 82; worship of, *ib.*

Ganges, worship of by Sita, 49.

Garvock, General, his campaign against the tribes of the Mahabun mountains, 761.

Gayatri, or invocation of the sun, 481 *note*.

George II., Balaji Rao Peishwa sends angry letters to, 390.

Georgia, Russian aggression in, 496 *note*.

Ghats, the western, 125.

Ghazi-ud-din, a representative of the Sunnis, 327; appointed Vizier at Delhi, *ib.*; dethrones Ahmad Shah, *ib.*; places Alamghir on the throne, 327–8; removed by Ahmad Shah Abdali, 328; subverts the Afghan power, *ib.*, 389; a hereditary Sunni, 281 *note*; intrigues with Balaji Rao, 389; proceedings at Delhi, 391; puts Alamghir to death, *ib.*; flight and perpetual exile, 392.

Ghazni, the court of Mahmud, 95. *See* Mahmud.

Gheria, capital of the piratical Angrias, 306; expedition against, under Clive and Watson, 390; conduct of the Mahrattas, *ib.*

Ghilzais, children of a concubine, opposed to the Abdalis, 622; driven to the mountains, *ib.*; risings checked by Futih Kahn, 628; massacre the English in the Khaiber Pass, 641.

Ghor, Afghan fortress of, 97; reappearance of the name in Gour, 620 *note*.

Ghorkas. *See* Nipal.

Gholab Singh, the Jamu Raja, 675; his negotiations with Sir Henry Hardinge, 681; buys Kashmir and Jamu, 682; recognized as Maharaja, 683; his rebellious subjects, 684.

Gholam Husain Ali, his description of Shitab Rai, 376–8.

Gholam Kadir, horrible outrages committed at Delhi by, 451–2; his flight, capture, and death, 453.

Gillespie, General, prompt action at the Vellore mutiny, 521; death in the first Ghorka campaign, 546.

Giri-vraja, identical with Rajagriha, 43 *note*.

Goa, founded by Albuquerque, 130; Viceroy of, sends a mission to Bengal, 131; in the sixteenth century, 132–7; the exchange, 133; social life at, *ib.*; great commercial wealth, 134; expenditure in Goa, *ib.*; government, civil and ecclesiastical, 134–5; visit of Della Valle, 135; inhabitants, *ib.*; religious shows, 135–6; ecclesiastical influences in, 137.

Goddard, Colonel, sent by Warren Hastings from Calcutta through Central India to the Mahratta country, 422; his movements after the convention at Wurgaum, 423; operations in the first Mahratta war, *ib.*

Godwin, General, his expedition to Rangoon in the second Burmese war, 697.

Golkonda, a Muhammadan kingdom in the Dekhan, 118; alliance of the Sultan with Ram Rai of Vijayanagar, 121; conquered by Aurangzeb, 217; yearly rent to, paid by the English at Madras, 228–9.

Gomastas, or native agents, outrageous proceedings in Bengal, 345.

Gough, Sir Hugh, takes the field against Gwalior, 651; wins the battle of Maharajpore, *ib.*; battle of Moodkee, 680; postpones operations against the rebellion of Mulraj in Multan, 686; commands the English army at Ramnuggur and Chilianwallah, 688; wins the battle of Guzerat, 689.

Gour, Afghan capital of Bengal, 101; perhaps named from the Afghan stronghold of Ghor, 150 *note.*

Græko-Baktrian kings in Central Asia, 70.

Graves, Brigadier, at Delhi during the mutiny, 724–5; forced flight, 726.

Greathed, Brigadier, pursues the rebel sepoys from Delhi, 748.

Guggun Singh, paramour of the queen of Nipal, reported prime mover in the murder of Matabar Singh, 669; a member of the Chountria ministry, *ib.*; threatened by the heir-apparent, *ib.*; murdered, *ib.*

Guha, the Bhil Raja, entertains Rama, 49; his entertainment of Bharata, 53.

Gundlacama river, the real northern boundary of the Carnatic, 275 *note.*

Gungadhur Shastri, Brahman minister of the Gaekwar of Baroda, his mission to Poona, 551; his strange reception, *ib.*; his murder, 552.

Guntoor Circar, 367 *note*; rented to the English by Basalut Jung, 430; and to Muhammad Ali by the English, *ib.*; restored to the Nizam by Warren Hastings, 433.

Guptas, succeed to the dynasty of Kanishka, 71; possibly children of the Græko-Baktrians, *ib.*; join the Rajputs against the Indo-Scythians, 72; victory at Kahror, *ib.*; their disappearance, *ib.*

Guru Govind, or Tugh Bahadur, 243 *note*; his work among the Sikhs, 671; his execution, *ib.*

Gurus, religious teachers among the Brahmans, 84; Hindu saints, 223; their ceremonies of initiation and confirmation, 480–1; their money demands, 481; and visitations, *ib.*; satires against them, 482; Gurus among the Sikhs, 672.

Guzerat, conquered by Ala-ud-din, 104; Sultan of, calls in the Turks against the Portuguese, 131; defeat of the Turks, *ib.*; Sultan of, invades Chitor, 155; driven out by Humayun, 156; Jehangir's description of, 181; Gaekwar of, a Mahratta feudatory, 384; primitive administration of Mr. Forbes, 424; districts made over to Mahadaji Sindia, 436.

Guzerat, defeat of the Sikhs at the battle of, 689.

Gwalior, the capital of Sindia, 421 *note*; captured by Captain Popham, 424; non-intervention policy of Lord William Bentinck, 606; civil war stopped by intervention, *ib.*; the government remodelled by Lord Ellenborough, 651; appointment of a council of regency, *ib.*; reduction of the army and formation of a Gwalior Contingent, *ib.*; revolt of the Contingent, 751; defeat of the rebels, *ib.* *See* Sindia *and* Tantia Topi.

Gymnosophists, or naked philosophers, 66.

H

HAFIZ KHAN, the Rohilla Afghan ruler, his dealings with the Mahrattas 409; demands of Shuja-ud-daula, the Nawab Vizier of Oude, 409–10; interference of Warren Hastings, 410; defeat and death of, 411.

Haileybury, establishment of the College at, 513.

Haji Ahmad, the favorite of Shuja Khan, 310; jealousy of Mustafa Khan the Afghan, 314; horrible death at Patna, *ib.*

Hamilton, Captain, his description of Calcutta, 238; social life of the English, *ib.*; refractory Rajas in Bengal, 239.

Hamilton, Dr., accompanies the English mission from Calcutta to Delhi, 249; heals the disease of Farrukh Siyar, the Moghul king at Delhi, *ib.*; his death at Calcutta, *ib. note.*

Hanuman, the monkey hero, 57; helps Rama against Ravana, *ib.*; mission to Sita, *ib.*; worshipped as a god, *ib. note*; his burning tail, 58; dramatic representation of, *ib. note*; his temple on the western Ghats, 138.

Hardinge, Sir Henry, Governor-General of India, 652; unprepared for the Sikh invasion, 679; present at the battle of Moodkee, 680; his negotiations with Gholab Singh, Raja of Jamu, 681; raised to the peerage, 682; sells Kashmir to Gholab Singh, 683; refuses to create a subsidiary force, or to keep British troops in the Punjab, *ib.*; his compromise with the Lahore durbar, *ib.*; appointment of a British Resident at Lahore and council of regency, 684; miscellaneous measures, *ib.*; returns to England, *ib.*

Hari Pant, commander of the Mahratta contingent, 456; his grasping demands upon Lord Cornwallis, *ib.*

Hartley, Captain, accompanies the Bombay expedition to Poona, 423; repulses the Mahrattas, *ib.*; protests against the convention of Wurgaum, *ib.*

Harris, General, commands the British army in the last war against Tippu, Sultan of Mysore, 470.

Hastinapur, city of, where situated, 11; extent of Raj unknown, 12; occupied by Rajputs, *ib.*; to all appearance an Aryan colony, *ib.*; reign of Maharaja Santanu, *ib.*; succession of Pandu the pale, 15; of Dhritarashtra the blind, *ib.*; of Yudhishthira, 37; mythical presence of Krishna, 38.

Hastings, Warren, his simplicity and moderation, 332 *note*; sides with Vansittart in condemning the claim of the Company's servants to trade in Bengal duty free, 346; duel with a member of the Calcutta council, 348; appointed governor of Bengal, 381; confused history of his government, 404; his previous career, *ib.*; his reforms in the revenue administration, *ib.*; in the judicial, 405; refuses to restore Muhammad Reza Khan to the post of deputy Nawab, *ib.*; his dealings with the Nawab Vizier of Oude, 410; lays himself open to the charge of corruption, 411; not to blame for the Rohilla atrocities, 412; appoints Mr. Middleton Resident at Lukhnow, *ib.*; appointed Governor-General of India, *ib.*; three new members of council sent out from England, *ib.*; violent and vindictive opposition of Philip Francis, 414; out-voted, *ib.*; condemns the interference of Bristow, the successor of Middleton at Lukhnow, 415; accused by Nund-komar, 416; declines to meet the charges, *ib.*; action against Nund-komar, *ib.*; arrest and execution of Nund-komar for forgery, *ib.*; war with the Mahrattas, 420; secures a majority in the Calcutta council, 421; sends Goddard across India from Calcutta to the Mahratta country, 422; resigns the post of Governor-General and withdraws his resignation, 425; duel with Francis, 426; discovers the hostile confederacy of Hyder Ali, the Nizam, and the Mahrattas against the British government in India, 432; his spirited proceedings, 433; empty treasury, *ib.*; dealings with Cheit Singh, Raja of Benares, 434; narrow escape at Benares, *ib.*; suspicious negotiations with Asof-ud-daula, Nawab Vizier of Oude, 435; his return to Europe, 441; impeachment and acquittal, *ib.*; review of the charges, 441–2 and *note*; sends missions to Thibet, 586 *note*.

Hastings, Marquis of, Governor-General of India under the title of Lord Moira, 528; his conversion from a policy of non-intervention as laid down by the home authorities to that of a paramount power as laid down by Lord Wellesley, 529; remonstrances with the Ghorka rulers of Nipal, 543; recovers British districts from the Nipalese, 544; plans a campaign against Nipal, 546; receives the title of Marquis of Hastings, 548; treaty of Segowlie, *ib.*; resolves on the extinction of the Pindharies, 549; provoked at the intrigues of Baji Rao Peishwa, 553; his preparations against the Pindharies, 554; resolves on disarming the predatory powers—Sindia, Holkar, and Amir Khan, 556; negotiations with Sindia, *ib.*; ignores Sindia's treachery, 557; breaks up the Pindhari system, 558; thwarted by Baji Rao Peishwa, the Raja of Berar, and the army of Holkar, 560; constructs a new imperial system, 567; resolves on the extinction of the dominion of the Peishwas, 569; final decision, 570; his settlement of Holkar's state, *ib.*; success of his policy, 570–1; education of the natives, 571; dealings with the Nizam, *ib.*; sanctions the proceedings of Palmer & Co., 572; his error, 573; leaves India, *ib.*; reproached by the Directors, *ib.*; resuscitation of the Raja of Satara as a feudatory but not as a sovereign, 570, 702.

Havelock, General, joins Colonel Neill at Allahabad, 737; his early career and characteristics, *ib.*; his advance on Cawnpore, *ib.*; defeats Nana Sahib at Cawnpore, 738; enters the station, *ib.*; departure for Lukhnow, 739; fails to relieve Lukhnow, 740; his victory at Bithoor, 741; return to Cawnpore, *ib.*; joined by Sir James Outram, 748; advances to Lukhnow, *ib.*; relieves the garrison, 749; his death and burial, 750.

Hawkins, Captain, his mission to Jehangir, 174; forced return from Agra, *ib.*

Hay's (and Amyatt's) deputation to Monghyr, 348; kept as a hostage, 349; perishes in the massacre at Patna, 352.

Hearsey, General, expostulates with the sepoys at Barrackpore respecting the greased cartridges, 719; suppresses the mutiny of Mungal Pandy, 720.

Heath, commander of an English fleet in India, 236; his ill-judged naval operations against the Moghuls, 236–7.

Heber, Bishop, his translation of a Mahratta ballad, 553.

Hemu, Hindu minister of an Afghan sovereign, 156; killed by Bairam Khan, 158.

Herat conquered by Ahmad Shah Durani, 624; a bone of contention between Afghanistan and Persia, 630 and *note*; seized by Futih Khan, *ib.*; a bone of contention between Great Britain and Russia, 632; description of the fortress, *ib. note*; besieged by Persia, 633; complications at, 636; withdrawal of the English Envoy, *ib.*; difficulties between England and Persia respecting, 714; Yakub Khan governor, 769.

Herbert, Captain, defends Attock against the Afghans, 688.
Hidimba, a cannibal Asura, slain by Bhima, 21; his sister, Hidimbi, marries Bhima, *ib.*—an allegorical fiction expressing hostility against the Buddhists, *ib. note.*
Hill-tribes, non-Hindus, 78.
Himmut Bahadur, a military Guru, 452 *note*; associated with Ali Bahadur, *ib.*; deserts to the English, *ib.*
Hindus, their religion, 78; popular deities, 82–3.
Hindu literature, 87–93; its constituents (non-historical), 88; Hindu revolt at Delhi against Islam, 108; rebellion in Bengal against the persecutions of Aurangzeb, 237–8.
Hindu Rao, house of, at Delhi, 745; a forgotten celebrity, *ib. note.*
Hiouen-Thsang, a Buddhist monk from China, 74; his pilgrimage to India, *ib.*; his description of the people of India, *ib.*; memories of the Maha Bharata, *ib.*; present at the great festival of imperial almsgiving at Allahabad, 75; residence in the huge monastery at Nalanda, 76.
Hira Singh succeeds his father Dhian Singh as minister at Lahore, 677; places Dhulip Singh, infant son of Runjeet Singh, on the throne of Lahore, *ib.*; murdered, *ib.*
Hislop, Sir Thomas, commands the Madras army in the Pindhari war, 555; pursuit of the Pindharies, 566–7.
Hlot-dau, or supreme council of the Burmese, 592.
Hodgson, Mr., Resident at Khatmandu, 658; his entanglement, *ib.*
Hodson, Captain, arrests the Moghul king of Delhi, Bahadur Shah, 747; shoots the two princes, *ib.*
Holcombe, Captain, voyage to Patna, 311; baskets of human heads, *ib.*
Holkar, Mulhar Rao the First, founder of the family, 258, 397; his death, 397; his son's widow, Ailah Bai, *ib.*
Holkar, Tukaji Rao the First, commands the army of Ailah Bai, 397; sent to Sindia by Nana Farnavese, 452; Sindia demands his recall, 459; defeated by De Boigne, 460; his death, 497.
Holkar, Jaswant Rao, an illegitimate son of Tukaji Rao the First, 498; his early predatory exploits, *ib.*; defeats Sindia and the Peishwa in the battle of Poona, 499; sets up another Peishwa, *ib.*; invited by Daulat Rao Sindia and the Bhonsla Raja of Nagpore to join them in a war against the English, 501; craftiness of his proceedings, *ib.*; his position outside the pale of Wellesley's political system, 506; objections of the English to a protective alliance, 506–7; his predatory instincts, 507; his plundering ravages in Malwa and Rajputana, *ib.*; his alarm at the victories of the English, *ib.*; rebuffed by General Lake, 508; arrogant demands and threats, *ib.*; campaign of Lake in Rajputana, 509; retreat of Monson, *ib.*; Holkar's advance to Muttra, Delhi, and Bhurtpore, 510–11; defeated by General Lake, 511; unfortunate policy of Sir George Barlow, 517; arrogant pretensions of Jaswant Rao Holkar, 518; driven mad by brandy, 523; interference of Amir Khan, the Afghan, 524; his death, 526.
Holkar, Mulhar Rao the Second, adopted by the widow of Jaswant Rao, 526–7; regency of the widow, 527; sympathizes with the Pindharies, 554; the government at the mercy of the army, 558; beginning of hostilities, 560; murder of the queen-mother by the soldiery, 567; defeat of the army of Holkar by Sir John Malcolm at Mehidpore, *ib.*; settlement of the government of Indore by Lord Hastings, 570; death of Mulhar Rao Holkar the Second, 606.
Holkar, Hari Rao, claims to succeed Mulhar Rao on the throne of Indore, 607; recognized by Lord William Bentinck, *ib.*; his death, 651.

Holkar, Tukaji Rao the Second, irregular installation of, 652; the present Maharaja of Indore, *ib. note.*

Holwell, Mr. J. Z., voyage to Patna, 311; the baskets of human heads, *ib.*; present at Calcutta during the siege, 318; summoned before Suraj-ud-daula, *ib.*; survives the tragedy of the Black Hole, 319; succeeds Clive as governor of the English settlements in Bengal, 336.

Home, Lieutenant, blows up the Kashmir gate at Delhi, 746.

Honahwar. *See* Onore.

Hughli, English factory at, 234; removed to Calcutta, 237; headquarters of the Moghul Foujdar, 307; captured by Clive and Watson, 320; curious detail in the capture of, *ib. note.*

Humayun, son of Baber, succeeds to the throne of Hindustan, 155; a bad Muhammadan, *ib.*; gulled by Sher Khan the Afghan, *ib.*; interference in Rajput affairs, *ib.*; gift of the bracelet, *ib.*; defeated by Sher Khan and flies into Persia, 156; fifteen years' exile, *ib.*; return to Delhi, 157; death, *ib.*

Husain Ali Khan, the younger Saiyid, helps to place Farrukh Siyar on the throne of Delhi, 246; exposed to hostile intrigues of Farrukh Siyar, 247; expedition to Jaipur, *ib.*; appointed Viceroy of the Dekhan, 248; defeats Daud Khan, *ib.*; marches to Delhi with an army of Mahrattas, 250; assassinated, 251.

Hyderabad. *See* Nizam.

Hyder Ali, a Naik in the service of the Raja of Mysore, 300 *note*; excites the jealousy of the English by his leanings toward the French, 367; his rise to power, *ib.*; becomes master of the Raj of Mysore, 368; joined by Nizam Ali, 369; invasion of the Carnatic, *ib.*; the confederates defeated, *ib.*; plot and counterplot, *ib. note*; successes, 370; treaty at Madras, *ib.*; a natural enemy of the Mahrattas, 394–7 *note*; awkward diplomatic relations with the English, 399; becomes the most formidable power in the peninsula, 428; his wrath against the English, 429; reception of Swartz, the missionary, *ib.*; invades the Carnatic, 431–2; hostile confederacy with the Mahrattas and Nizam Ali, 432; his army, 431 *note*; defeated by Sir Eyre Coote, 433; death of, 436; character and home life, 436–7; fall of his dynasty, 471; alive to the value of Pariahs, 476 *note*; the founder of Bangalore, 477; aggressions on Coorg, 610.

I

Ikkeri, capital of Venk-tapa Naik, 138; visited by Della Valle, 138–41.

Impey, Sir Elijah, Chief Justice in Bengal, 416; trial and condemnation of Nund-komar, *ib.*; a judicial murder, 417.

India under the Rajas, 11; Greek and Roman knowledge of, 72–3; condition in the seventh century, 76; religious revolutions, *ib.*

Indore, the capital of Holkar, 421 *note*; foundation of, 497; mutiny at, 741; contemplated annexation by Lord Ellenborough, 648. *See* Holkar.

Indo-Scythian kings in India, 70–1; defeated by Rajputs and Guptas, 72.

Indra, Vaidik personification of the firmament, 80.

Indra-prasthra (Delhi), founded by the Pandavas, 25 and *note.*

Indus, river, crossed by Alexander the Great, 64; invoked as Saraswati in the Vaidik hymns, 83 *note.*

Irawadi, the river and valley of, 575.

J

JAGAT SETH, the great banker of Murshedabad, 812; his family insulted by Sarfaraz Khan, *ib.*; joins in a Hindu and Moghul plot for the destruction of Sarfaraz Khan and elevation of Alivardi Khan, *ib.*; joins with Mir Jafir at Plassy in the conspiracy against Suraj-ud-daula, 822.

Jaghir, an estate given in lieu of a salary, 170.

Jains, religion of, 112–13; conversion of Jain Rajas to Brahmanism, *ib.*

Jaipal, Raja of the Punjab, 95; defeated by Mahmud of Ghazni, *ib.*; suicide, *ib.*

Jaipur, Jai Singh, Raja of, his submission to Akbar, 161; vacillates during the wars between the sons of Shah Jehan, 192; deceived by Aurangzeb, 205; his son a hostage at Delhi, 207; plans the escape of Sivaji, *ib.*

Jaipur, Aurangzeb collects Jezya in, 213; submission to Farrukh Siyar, 247; contributions levied by Jaswant Rao Holkar, 518; the protective treaty with England annulled, *ib.*; quarrels with Jodhpur, 524–5; war and anarchy under the policy of non-intervention, 603; type of a dissolute Hindu Rani, *ib.*; forced interference of the British government, 604; council of Thakurs, a failure, *ib.*; infatuation of Bentinck, death of the Rani, and poisoning of the Maharaja, 608; murder of Mr. Blake, *ib.*

Jamu Rajas at the court of Lahore, 675; Jamu and Kashmir bought by Gholab Singh, 682.

Janoji Bhonsla. *See* Bhonsla.

Jaswant Singh, Raja of Marwar, marries a daughter of Shah Jehan, 193; fury of his queen on his flight from the battle of Ujain, *ib.*; accompanies Shaista Khan in the war against Sivaji the Mahratta, 208; suspected of treacherous dealings with Sivaji, *ib.*

Jats, Hinduized Scythians, threaten Delhi, 400; found a principality at Bhurtpore in Hindustan, *ib.*; Suraj Mal, the Jat hero of the eighteenth century, *ib.*; wars among his sons, 401; contributions levied by the Mahrattas, 402.

Java, Lord Minto's expedition to, 526; captured by the English and restored to the Dutch, *ib.*

Jehanabad, the new city of Delhi built by Shah Jehan, 188.

Jehandar Shah succeeds to the throne of Delhi, 245; a low drunkard under the tutelage of Zulfikar Khan, *ib.*; defeated and slain by Farrukh Siyar and the two Saiyids, 246.

Jehangir, or Selim, son of Akbar, 171; rebels against his father, *ib.*; implicated in the assassination of Abul Fazl, and poisoning of his father, *ib.*; his vices, 172; revenge on his son Khuzru, *ib.*; horrible execution of the followers of Khuzru, 173; infatuated by Nur Mahal, the "light of the harem," *ib.*; his reception of Captain Hawkins, 174; of Sir Thomas Roe, 175; becomes suspicious of the Khan Khanan, 178; shameless attempts at poisoning, *ib.*; drinking bout on his birthday, 179; punishment of wine-drinkers, 180; imperial progress from Ajmir toward the Dekhan, *ib.*; wonders of his camp, 181; return to Guzerat and Delhi, *ib.*; description of Guzerat, etc., 181–2; headquarters at Lahore, 182; his four sons, *ib.*; reported death, 183; defeat of Shah Jehan at Delhi, 184; capture of Jehangir by the Rajputs, 185; sudden death, *ib.*; nominates Bulaki, son of Khuzru, to succeed him as Padishah, *ib.*

Jews, parallelism between their history and that of the Afghans, 776 *note.*

Jeypore. *See* Jaipur.

Jezya, a religious capitation tax imposed by Aurangzeb, 213; attempts to collect it in Rajputana, *ib.*; collected by Aurangzeb at Surat, 231.
Jhansi lapses to the British government, 706 *note*; mutiny at, 730; treacherous massacre of Europeans by the Rani, *ib.*; death of the Rani in male attire, 754.
Jharokha, or public window of Akbar, 169; at Delhi, 199.
Jhota Ram, the Jain banker at Jaipur, the paramour of the Rani, 608; deludes Lord William Bentinck, 608; suspected of poisoning the Maharaja, *ib.*; forced to resign the post of minister, *ib.*; implicated in the murder of Mr. Blake, *ib.*
Jinjeera, Abyssinians of, 383; their hereditary chiefs, or Seedees, protect Mecca pilgrims against pirates, *ib.*
Jinji or Gingee, fortress of, in the Carnatic, a bone of contention between Zulfikar Khan and Ram Raja, 234; captured by Bussy, 293 and *note*; surrendered by the French, 335.
Jirgah, or council of elders among the mountain tribes of the Sulaiman mountains, 758.
Jodhpur, Rajput kingdom of. *See* Marwar.
Johur, Rajput rite of, performed at Chitor, 105, 155.
Joonere, a Mahratta fortress, the birthplace of Sivaji, 200; visited by Dr. Fryer, 231-2.
Jullunder Doab, in the Punjab, taken over by the British government after the first Sikh war, 683.
Jung Bahadur, the famous Ghorka chief at Khatmandu, excites the spite of the heir-apparent of Nipal, 664; boasts of the murder of Matabar Singh, 669; becomes military minister at Khatmandu, *ib.* *note*; all-powerful in Nipal, 670; subsequent career, *ib.*
Jungpens of Bhutan, 764.

K

KABUL, conquered by Akbar, 170; massacre of a Moghul army in the Khaiber Pass, 209; mysterious outbreak under the missing brother of Aurangzeb, 210; captured by Nadir Shah, 263; its surrender by the Kuzzilbashes to Ahmad Shah Abdali, 628; taken by Dost Muhammad Khan, 631; invaded by the English in the first Afghan war, 635; British occupation of, 636; insurrection at, 639; distractions in, 642; second British occupation under Pollock, 644; reception of a British mission refused by Sher Ali Khan, 775; and repulsed, *ib.*; treacherous attack on the British Residency, 776.
Kahror, battle of, 72.
Kaikeyi, youngest queen of Dasaratha, 43; her wrath at the installation of Rama as Yuva-raja, 44; cajoles Dasaratha, *ib.*
Kajar, reigning dynasty of Shahs of Persia, quarrels with the Zend party, 496; triumph of, *ib.*
Kalars, the caste of, 78; included in the people of Marawar, 486 *note.*
Kali (Parvati), her place in the worship of the Turanians, 78; worshipped by the Brahmans as a divine mother, 84; the mythical founder of the right and left "hands," 479.
Kalidasa, author of Sakuntala, 88.
Kama, Hindu god of love, 82.
Kam Baksh, youngest son of Aurangzeb, a Christian Sultan, 241; death in battle, 242.
Kampilya, the city of Drupada, 22; the modern Kampil, *ib. note.*
Kamran Mirza, son of Mahmud Shah, Amir of Kabul, his jealousy of the minister, Futih Khan, 630; blinds Futih Khan with hot needles, 631;

murder of Futih Khan, *ib.*; flight of Kamran to Herat, *ib.*; becomes ruler of Herat, 633; his treacherous plots, 634; his ingratitude toward the English, 636.

Kanara, kingdom of, 125; the country of Venk-tapa Naik, 137; a type of a Hindu Raj in Southern India, 138; Raja of, *see* Venk-tapa.

Kandahar captured by Nadir Shah, 263; plots of the Barukzais at, 627; massacre, *ib.*; captured by the English, 635.

Kanishka, or Kanerke, founder of the latest dynasty of Indo-Scythian kings, 71; brought Persian worship of the Sun into India, *ib.*; liberal patron of Buddhists, *ib.*

Kanouj on the Ganges, Aryan kingdom of, 12; the ancient Panchala, 16; empire of, 74; Maharaja of, lord paramount of the Rajputs, 98; celebrates the Swayamvara of his daughter, *ib.*; invites the Afghans to capture Delhi, *ib.*; overthrown by Muhammad Ghori, 100; rebellion in, 182.

Kapila, Raj of, associated with the early life of Sakya Muni, 61.

Karna, a friend of Duryodhana, 19; his ignoble birth as the son of a charioteer, *ib.*; challenges Arjuna at the exhibition of arms, *ib.*; is made a Raja by Duryodhana, *ib.*; rebuffed by the Pandavas, *ib.*; bends the bow at the Swayamvara of Draupadi, 28; rebuffed by Draupadi, *ib.*; killed by Arjuna, 34; reappears in the Ganges, 41.

Karnata, old empire of, 211 *note*.

Karra, Ala-ud-din governor of, 102; assassination of Jelal-ud-din, 104.

Kartakeia, god of war, 82.

Karwar, an English factory to the south of Goa, 233; visited by Fryer, *ib.*; Sivaji's government at, *ib.*

Kashmir, conquered by Akbar, 170; attempts of Aurangzeb to form a navy on the lake, 204; conquered by Ahmad Shah Durani, 624; bought from the English by Gholab Singh, 682; rebellion, 684.

Kassimbazar, inland English factory at, 308; captured by Nawab Suraj-ud-daula, 317; by Mir Kasim, 350.

Kathæi, revolt against Alexander, 65; customs of, 66–7.

Kauravas, rival kinsmen of the Pandavas, 11; jealousy of the Pandavas, 16; instructed in arms by Drona, *ib.*; compass the destruction of the Pandavas at Varanavata, 20; plot against the Pandavas with Sakuni, 26; the gambling match, *ib.*; invade Virata, 31; discover Arjuna, *ib.*; slaughtered by the Pandavas in the war of the Maha Bharata, 34.

Kausalya, eldest wife of Dasaratha and mother of Rama, 42; her anger at the exile of her son, 46; her vain remonstrances, *ib.*

Kaveri river, kept asunder from the Koleroon by an embankment, 278; delta of the two rivers in Tanjore, *ib.*

Kazi, or Muhammadan judge appointed to aid the Nawab, 226.

Keane, Sir John, commands the army for the occupation of Kabul, 635.

Kerauli, a Rajput principality, notices of, 704; question of adoption, *ib.*; conceded by the Court of Directors, *ib.*

Khaiber Pass, massacre of the Moghul army in, 209; destruction of the British army in, 641.

Khalifs, the successors of Muhammad, 94; Khalifs of Damascus and Bagdad, 95.

Khalsa, or holy brotherhood of the Sikhs, 671 and *note*; condition under Runjeet Singh, 673–4; growing disorders, 676; governed by councils of five, *ib.*; final overthrow of the Khalsa army, 689; its soldiers under British command, 690. *See also* Sikhs.

Khandava-prastha, an uncleared jungle round Delhi, 25; occupied by Nagas, *ib.*; Raj of, under the Pandavas, *ib.*

Khan Jehan, the Afghan general of Shah Jehan, 187.
Khan Khanan, his intrigues in the reign of Jehangir, 176; suspicions respecting, 178; attempts of Jehangir to poison him, *ib.*
Kharak Singh, eldest son of Runjeet Singh, succeeds his father as Maharaja at Lahore, 675; takes fright at the murder of his minister, *ib.*; his death, *ib.*
Khatmandu, revolution at, 537; mission of Kirkpatrick, 536; mission of Knox, 540; revolution at, 540–1; massacre, 542; ferment during the Kabul war, *ib.*; council of Bharadars at, 544, 546; frequent revolutions at, 657; ministerial complications at, 659; political compromise, *ib.*; tragedies. 662–3; a new ministry, 669; horrible massacre, 669–70.
Khirki, assaults of Baji Rao Peishwa, repulsed by the English, 563.
Khiva, an Usbeg kingdom, 619; Russian expedition to, 635.
Khokand on the Jaxartes inherited by Baber, 152; an Usbeg kingdom, 620; Russian advance to, 770–1.
Khurim, a Pindhari leader, 527; throws himself on the mercy of the English, 558.
Khuzru, eldest son of Jehangir, 172; favored by his grandfather, Akbar, *ib.*; excites the jealousy of his father, Jehangir, *ib.*; breaks out in revolt, *ib.*; its failure, *ib.*; horrible revenge of Jehangir, 172–3; his reconciliation with Jehangir, 180–1; his assassination by Shah Jehan, 183.
Kichaka, brother of the queen of Virata, 30; falls in love with Draupadi, *ib.*; slain by Bhima, *ib.*; his brothers try to burn Draupadi with his remains, *ib.*
Kinloch, Captain, futile expedition against the Ghorkas of Nipal, 534.
Kinnaras, singers in the heaven of Indra, present at the feast of Bharadwaja, 54.
Kirkpatrick, Colonel, his mission to Nipal, 536.
Knox, Captain, his mission to Khatmandu, 540; its failure, 541.
Koh-i-Baba, mountain system in Afghanistan, 620; includes the rock fortress of Zohak, the demon king, *ib. note.*
Kolhapore, a Mahratta principality, 384; family of the Rajas of, *ib. note*; intrigues of Nizam Ali, 395.
Koleroon river, dividing the Moghul Carnatic from the Hindu, 275.
Koles of Bengal, outbreak suppressed, 710–11.
Konkan, kingdom of, 125; Mahrattas of, 200.
Korygaum, glorious defence of, 568.
Kosala, Raj of, 42 *note.*
Kotwal, office of, in towns, 176, 226; criminal jurisdiction, *ib.*; office at Calcutta, 307.
Krishnaraj, Raja of Mysore. *See* Mysore.
Krories, revenue officials, introduced by Todar Mal, 170; their rapacity and oppression, *ib.*
Kshatriyas, the military caste in India, 23, 25; all who die in battle go to the heaven of Indra at Swarga, 41 *note*; one of the four great castes, 77.
Krishna, the incarnation of Vishnu, 38, 81; part played by him in the Maha Bharata, 38; supernatural appearance, *ib.*; expounds to Arjuna the doctrine of metempsychosis, *ib.*
Krishna Rai, Maharaja of Narsinga, 114; vengeance against the Sultan of the Dekhan, 114, 116.
Kubraj Pandey, in favor at Khatmandu, 665; his false step and fall, *ib.*
Kulbarga, capital city of the Bahmani Sultans, 114.
Kunti, one of the wives of Pandu, 15; her contest with Madri as to Sati, *ib.*; her sons, *ib.*

Kurdla, battle of, 468.
Kusa, son of Rama and Sita, 59.
Kutub-ud-din, Viceroy of Muhammad Ghori, 100; Sultan of Delhi, first of the slave-kings, *ib.*; builds the Kutub Minar, 100–1; his death, 101.
Kuru-kshetra, the plain of, the scene of the war of the Maha Bharata, 33; exaggeration and grandeur in the description of the battle, 39.
Kuvera, god of wealth, 82.
Kuzzilbashes, or Persian colonists, placed by Nidar Shah as a garrison in Kabul, 623; surrender the Bala Hissar to Ahmad Shah Abdali, *ib.*; protect Timur Shah, 625; slaughtered at Kabul by the Afghan Sunnis, 628.

L

LABOURDONNAIS, commander of a French squadron, captures Madras from the English, 285; his subsequent fate, 286 *note*.
Lahore, Jehangir's headquarters at, 182; massacre of princes at, 185; imperial road to Agra, 220; ferment during the Kabul war, 653–4; the court and capital of Runjeet Singh, 674; Sikh and Rajput factions at, 675; settlement of the government by Lord Hardinge, 683; compromise with Lord Hardinge, 683–4.
Lake, General, Lord Wellesley's instructions to, 502; his campaign in Hindustan, 504; its conclusion, 505; rebuffs Jaswant Rao Holkar, 508; preparations against Holkar, *ib.*; in Rajputana, 509; defeats Holkar and besieges Bhurtpore, 511; reduces Holkar to submission, 517; disgust at Holkar's pretensions, 508, 518; indignant at the annulment of the protective treaty with Jaipur, 518–19.
Lakshmana, second son of Dasaratha, 42; accompanies Rama on his exile, 47; drives Sita to Chitra-kuta, 59.
Lakshmi, the goddess of prosperity, 82; worship of, *ib.*
Lally, Count de, arrival at Pondicherry, 332; capture of Fort St. David, and recall of Bussy, 333; suspicious of Bussy, *ib.*; desperate situation at Pondicherry, 334; siege of Fort St. George, *ib.*; retreat, *ib.*; defeat at Wandiwash, 335; capitulation at Pondicherry, *ib.*; melancholy end, *ib.*
Lal Singh, paramour of the queen, and minister at Lahore, 678; his treachery to the Sikh army, 679; moves to Ferozeshahar, 680; flight at Moodkee, *ib.*; flight from Ferozeshahar, *ib.*; recognized as prime minister by Lord Hardinge, 683; his treachery in Kashmir, 684; his downfall, *ib.*
Lamas, or Buddhist abbots of Lhassa and Digarchi, 532.
Lambert, Commodore, his mission to Rangoon, 695; deceived and insulted by the Burmese officials, 696; begins the second Burmese war, *ib.*
Landour built on territory ceded by Nipal, 548.
Langhorn, Sir William, governor of Madras, 229.
Lanka, the modern Ceylon, the abode of Ravana, the demon Raja of the Rakshasas, 56.
Laswari, General Lake's victory at, 505.
Lava, son of Rama and Sita, 59.
Law, M., ex-governor of the French settlement at Chandernagore, supports the Shahzada and Nawab Vizier of Oude, 327; his helpless condition, 330.
Lawrence, George, a hostage in the first Afghan war, 683 *note*; carried off prisoner at Peshawar by Afghans and Sikhs, 688.
Lawrence, Henry, Major of the Bengal Artillery, afterward General

Sir Henry, 664 *note*, 692 *note*; Resident at Khatmandu, 668; prevents a massacre, *ib.*: Resident at Lahore, 683; suppresses a rebellion in Jamu and Kashmir, 684; proceeds to England, 685; President of the Board of Administration at Lahore, 692; his sympathies for the Sikh Sirdars, 693; retires from the Board, *ib.*; appointed Chief Commissioner of Oude, 713; prompt suppression of the outbreak at Lukhnow, 721; preparations for the defence of the British Residency at Lukhnow, 729; his death, 740.

Lawrence, Sir John, afterward Lord Lawrence, Commissioner of the Jullunder Doab, 683 *note*; civil member of the Board of Administration at Lahore, 692; first Chief Commissioner of the Punjab, 693; the savior of India during the sepoy mutiny, 743; Viceroy of India in succession to Lord Elgin, 762; policy in Afghanistan during the fratricidal war, 769–70; dealings with Sher Ali Khan, *ib.*; retirement and death, 771; his treaties with Dost Muhammad Khan, 772.

Lawrence, Major Stringer, takes the command of the East India Company's forces in India during the war against France, 286–7; goes to England, 296; returns to Madras, 300; operations at Trichinopoly, *ib.*; worried by the duplicity of Nawab Muhammad Ali, 301–2.

Lhassa, the residence of the Teshu Lama, 532; temples at, plundered by the Ghorkas, 536.

Littler, General Sir John, his position at Ferozepore at the breaking out of the first Sikh war, 679.

Lukhnow in 1857, sepoy mutiny of the 3d of May, 721; suppressed by Sir Henry Lawrence, *ib.*; preparations for defence, 728–9; the city and cantonment, 729; European and native forces, *ib.*; outbreak of the 30th of May, *ib.*; flight to Delhi, 730; defence against mutineers and rebels, 739; death of Henry Lawrence on the 4th of July, 740; assault of the 20th of July, *ib.*; failure of Havelock in August, *ib.*; heroism of the besieged, 749; first relief by Havelock, 750; second relief by Sir Colin Campbell, *ib.*; death of Havelock in November, *ib.*; burial in the Alumbagh, *ib.*; capture of Lukhnow by Outram, 752.

Lushington, Mr., perished in the massacre at Patna, 352.

Lytton, Lord, Viceroy of India, 774.

M

Macartney, Lord, governor of Madras, 437; treaty with Tippu, Sultan of Mysore, *ib.*; capture of Pulicat and Sadras, *ib. note*; assumption of the revenues of the Carnatic, 437; proposed reduction of the Nawab of the Carnatic to a pageant pensioner, 438; its dubious equity, 439; zeal of the Nawab's creditors, 440; restoration of the Carnatic ordered by the Board of Control, 440–1; his retirement, 441; declines the post of Governor-General, 449.

Macaulay, Lord, his imperfect story of Mir Jafir's jackass, 325 *note*; acquits Hastings of money corruption, 442 *note*.

Macnaghten, Sir William, appointed English minister and envoy at Kabul, 635; excites the disaffection of the Afghans by the abolition or reduction of subsidies, 637; imprudent removal of the British troops from the Bala Hissar, 638; vacillation during the insurrection at Kabul, 639; negotiations with the rebel leaders, 640–1; attacked and murdered by Akbar Khan, 640.

Macpherson, Sir John, provisional Governor-General in succession to Warren Hastings, 449.

Madras, visit of Fryer to, 228; origin of the town, *ib.*; yearly rent to

Golkonda, 229; surf-boats, *ib.*; Fort St. George, *ib.*; Sir William Langhorn governor, *ib.*; population, 230; threatened by Moghuls, 233; bribery of Zulfikar Khan, *ib.*; besieged by Moghuls under Daud Khan, 234; peace at Madras, *ib.*; growing commercial importance, 271; commercial establishment, 271–2; Governor in Council and Mayor's Court, 272; justices of peace and Pedda Naik, *ib.*; jealousy of the Dutch, *ib.*; "interlopers," 274; flourishing trade in cotton piece-goods, 277; isolation of traders, *ib.*; captured by the French under Labourdonnais, 285; restored to the English, 287; interference in Tanjore, *ib.*; wars with the French at Pondicherry, 288; treaty with Hyder Ali, 370; situation on the Coromandel coast, 382; its individuality, *ib.*; debts and difficulties of the Nawab of the Carnatic, 426; aggression of the Nawab on Tanjore, 427; Lord Pigot and Paul Benfield, *ib.*; imprisonment and death of Lord Pigot, 428; Sir Thomas Rumbold, governor, *ib.*; formidable power of Hyder Ali, *ib.*; mission of Swartz to Seringapatam, 429; troubles with the Nizam about Guntoor, 430; Mr. Whitehill, governor, 431; invasion of Hyder Ali of Mysore, *ib.*; Whitehill deposed by Warren Hastings, 433; victories of Sir Eyre Coote, *ib.*; Lord Macartney, governor, 437; troubles about the Nawab's debts, 440; orders of the Board of Control, 440–1; corruption and inaction under Governor Holland, 454; settlement of Tanjore, 485, 706; settlement of the Carnatic, 489, 706.

Madri, one of the wives of Pandu, 15; contest with Kunti, *ib.*; performs Sati, *ib.*; her two sons, *ib.*

Maduals, the sect of, in Southern India, 474, 476; their distinctions and creed, *ib.*

Magadha, the modern Behar, the cradle of Buddhism, corresponding with the country of the Rakshasas and Asuras, 20 *note*.

Mahabat Khan, 184; captures Jehangir, 185; sham burial of Shah Jehan, *ib.*

Maha Bharata, war of, told in an ancient Hindu epic written in Sanskrit, 11; probable date of the war, 12 *note*; character of the war, 33; composition of the poem, 37; religious teaching of, 38; grandeur and exaggerations of, 39; concluding scene at the Ganges, 40–1; memories of, in the time of Hiouen-Thsang, 74.

Mahabun mountain, inhabited by Hindustani fanatics, 759; English expedition under Sir Neville Chamberlain, *ib.*

Mahadaji Sindia. *See* Sindia.

Mahadeva. *See* Siva.

Maharaja, or "great Raja," 12.

Mahdu Rao, fourth Peishwa, succeeds his father Balaji Rao on the throne at Poona, 393; regency of his uncle, Rughonath Rao, *ib.*; farce of investiture at Satara, *ib.*; disaffection of the Mahratta feudatories, 394; quarrels with his uncle, *ib.*; imprisoned, *ib.*; reconciliation, 395; invades the territories of Hyder Ali, 397; fresh quarrels with his uncle inflamed by his mother and aunt, *ib.*; joins Nizam Ali in his invasion of Berar, *ib.*; his religious vagaries, 398; friendly advances of the English at Bombay, 399; refusal to part with Salsette or Bassein, *ib.*; awkward alliance between the English at Madras and Hyder Ali of Mysore, *ib.*; death by consumption, 403, 417; succeeded by his brother, Narain Rao, *ib.*

Mahdu Rao Narain, seventh Peishwa, infant son of Narain Rao, 419, 436; his suicide, 463.

Mahe, captured by the English, 429.

Mahmud of Ghazni, invades India, 96; twelve expeditions into Hindustan, *ib.*; defeats the Rajputs at Somnath, 97; destroys the idol pillar in the temple, *ib.*; returns to Ghazni, *ib.*; his death, *ib.*

Mahomet. *See* Muhammad.

Mahrattas, empire at Deoghur conquered by Ala-ud-din, 102–3; rise in the Konkan under Sivaji, 199; career of Sivaji, 200–1; organizes a system of blackmail or chout, 211; bootless operations of Aurangzeb against, 217; wars between Zulfikar Khan and Ram Raja, 233; settlement with Sahu Rao, the grandson of Sivaji, 243; his capital at Satara, *ib.*; indefinite claims to chout, 244; rise of the Brahman ministers or Peishwas, 245; their power and policy, 257; importance of Mahratta history, 258; military leaders subject to the Brahman Peishwas, 259; dealings with the Muhammadan powers, *ib.*; helplessness of the Moghul court at Delhi, *ib.*; secret relations between the Mahratta Peishwas and the Moghul Padishahs, 260–1; extensive ravages after the invasion of Nadir Shah, 269; invasion of the Carnatic, 279; dealings with the Nawab, 280; take Trichinopoly by surprise, *ib.*; imprison Chunder Sahib at Satara, *ib.*; merciless invasions of Bengal for the collection of chout, 313; treacherous massacre of Mahrattas by Nawab Alivardi Khan, *ib.*; quieted by the promise of the Nawab to pay yearly chout, 314; demand arrears of chout from Mir Jafir, 326; contest with the Afghans for the Moghul empire, 338, 392; horrible defeat and massacre at Paniput, 338, 392; demand chout for Bengal and Behar from the English, 365; Clive inclined to pay chout in return for Orissa, *ib.*; general view of the Mahratta empire and its feudatories, 383–4; three seats of home government —Poona, Satara, and Kolhapore, 384; four leading feudatories—the Gaekwar, Holkar, Sidia, and the Bhonsla Raja of Berar, *ib.*; transfer of power, after the death of Sahu, from the Raja of Satara to the Peishwa of Poona, 385–6; administration of Balaji Rao, the third Peishwa, 387–8; Mahratta wars from Mysore to the Punjab, 391; crushing defeat at Paniput, 392; Mahdu Rao, fourth Peishwa, 393; internal distractions, 394; wars against Hyder Ali and Nizam Ali, *ib.*; conduct Shah Alam to Delhi under Mahadaji Sindia, and establish the Mahratta ascendency in Hindustan, 403; wrath with the English at their refusal to pay tribute for Bengal, 408; threaten to march through the Rohilla country into Oude, 409; death of Mahdu Rao Peishwa, 417; accession and murder of Narain Rao, fifth Peishwa, 417–18; succession of Rughonath Rao, sixth Peishwa, 418; Mahdu Rao Narain, seventh Peishwa, 419, 436; negotiations with the English at Bombay, 420; condemned by the Bengal government, *ib.*; treaty of Purundhur (1776), 421; French intrigues at Poona, *ib.*; Bombay invited to restore Rughonath Rao, 422; Bombay expedition to Poona, *ib.*; convention of Wurgaum, 423; first Mahratta war, *ib.*; confederacy with Hyder Ali and Nizam Ali, 432; close of the first Mahratta war by the treaty of Salbai, 436; regarded as the most formidable power in India, 443; new Mahratta kingdom between the Jumna and Ganges founded by Mahadaji Sindia, 446; English Resident appointed at Poona, *ib.*; war between the Peishwa and Tippu Sultan, 448; rivalry between Nana Farnavese and Mahadaji Sindia, 452; dealings with Lord Cornwallis during the first war against Tippu, 454–5; grasping demands, 456; their treachery, 457; installation of the Peishwa as the deputy of the Great Moghul, 459; death of Mahadaji Sindia, 460; crushing demands on the Nizam for arrears of chout, 461; Mahratta envoy insulted at Hyderabad, 462; defeat of the Nizam at Kurdla, 463; suicide of Mahdu Rao Narain, *ib.*; Baji Rao, eighth Peishwa, *ib.*; intrigues between Baji

Rao, Daulat Rao Sindia, and Nana Farnavese, 464; reject Lord Mornington's offers of an English alliance, 468, 470; their rule in Tanjore described by Swartz, 487; replies of the Peishwa to the offers of Lord Wellesley, 493; Mahratta affairs, 497; defeat of Baji Rao at Poona by Jaswant Rao Holkar, 499; flight to the Bombay Presidency, *ib.*; conclusion of the treaty of Bassein, *ib.*; second Mahratta war, 500, 503; hostility of Sindia and the Bhonsla, 500, 502; campaign of Wellesley and Stevenson in the Dekhan, 502; English victories at Assaye and Argaum, 503–4; Lake's campaign in Hindustan, 504; English victories at Alighur and Delhi, *ib.*; Laswari, 505; Sindia and the Bhonsla become feudatories of the British government, *ib.*; difficulties with Jaswant Rao Holkar, 506–7; reduced to submission, 511, 517; reactionary policy of Cornwallis and Barlow, 516–17; brief interval of peace, 519; rise of the Pindharies, 527; projected conquest of the Pindharies by Lord Hastings, 549–50; intrigues of Baji Rao Peishwa, 550; murder of the Brahman minister of the Gaekwar, 552; imprisonment and escape of Trimbukji Dainglia, 552–3; remonstrances of the British Resident at Poona, 554; attitude of Sindia and Holkar, 555; submission of Sindia, 556; difficulties with Holkar, 558; duplicity of Baji Rao, 560; treachery, 562; hostilities begun by the Peishwa, 563; flight of the Peishwa, *ib.*; treachery of the Bhonsla of Nagpore, 564; battle of Sitabuldi, 565; Mr. Jenkins supreme, 566; defeat of the army of Holkar at Mehidpore, 567; extinction of the Peishwas, 569; settlement with Holkar, 570; success of Lord Hastings' policy, *ib.*; political relations during the administration of Lord Amherst and Lord William Bentinck, 601. *See also* Holkar *and* Sindia.

Malabar, Rajas of, 112; or western coast of India, 124; Malabar proper, 125; twelve kings of, *ib.*; pepper and pilgrims, 126; suzerainty of the Zamorin, 127; Malabar pirates, 130; visit of Della Valle to the court at Calicut, 146; Rajas sacred in battle, 147.

Malacca founded by Albuquerque, 130.

Malcolm, Captain John, his mission to Persia, 496; his early career, *ib. note*; negotiations with Daulat Rao Sindia, 505; story of "Old Brag," *ib. note*; his half-hearted treaty with Holkar, 517; sent by Lord Minto on a mission to Persia, 528 *note*; meets Baji Rao at Maholi, 561; outwitted, *ib.*; negotiations with Tulsi Bai, 567; defeats the army of Holkar at Mehidpore, *ib.*; final settlement of Baji Rao, 570.

Malik Amber, the Abyssinian minister of Ahmadnagar, 176; defeated by the Moghul army, 181.

Malik Kafur, general of Ala-ud-din, 107; plunders Hindu temples in the south, *ib.*; notably those of Madura and Mysore, *ib.*; a Hindu converted to Islam, 108.

Malwa, region of, 90; relative position of, toward Rajputana, 161 *note*; divided between Sindia and Holkar, 421 *note*.

Manaris, or hereditary oxen-drivers, 224; division into four tribes with caste marks, *ib.*; women tatooed with flowers, 224–5; identified with Brinjarries, 456.

Mandalay, present capital of Burma, 591.

Manel, residence of the queen of Olaza, 142.

Mangalore, Portuguese fort at, 131; treaty at, between Lord Macartney and Tippu Sultan, 437.

Manipura, ancient kingdom of, the modern Munipore, 26.

Manouchi, the Venetian physician, his memoirs of the reign of Aurangzeb, 209

Mansel, Mr., member of the Punjab Board of Administration, 692 *note.*
Man Singh, Raja of Jodhpur, claims the daughter of the Rana of Udaipur, 524; quarrels with Jaipur, 525. *See* Marwar.
Mansubdars, rank of, in the Moghul court, 164.
Manu, impersonality, laws of, 84; based on the transmigrations of the soul, 85; merits and demerits, *ib.*; heaven and hell, *ib.*; the divine spirit, *ib.*; deliverance of the soul in absorption, 86; four stages of life, *ib.*; Brahman prejudice concerning, 196 *note.*
Marawar country, a relic of Hindu antiquity associated with the legends of Rama, 486 *note.*
Marco Polo, his description of Coromandel and Malabar Rajas, 112.
Mariamma, the Malabar goddess, worshipped by the Portuguese ambassadors by mistake for the Virgin Mary, 127.
Martaban, in Burma, besieged by Byeen-noung, 580; surrendered, *ib.*; plundered and sacked, 583; revolting execution of the queen and her ladies, 584–6.
Maruts, Vaidik, personification of the winds, 80; followers of Indra, *ib.*
Marwar, Jaswant Singh, Raja of, marries a daughter of Shah Jehan, 193; wrath of his wife at his flight from the battle of Ujain, *ib.*; won over by Aurangzeb, 195; employed in the war against Sivaji, 208; suspected of treachery, *ib.*; his widow resists the collection of Jezya, 213; Man Singh claims the daughter of the Rana of Udaipur, 524; conflicts with refractory Thakurs, 604.
Masulipatam, Muhammadan port on the coast of Coromandel, visited by Fryer, 227; description of, 227–8; ceded to the French, 303; captured by the English, 334.
Matabar Singh, of Nipal, nephew of Bhim Sein Thapa, thrown into prison, 659; released and pardoned, 660; his mission to Lahore, 662; invited to return to Nipal, 667; wreaks his vengeance on the Pandeys at Khatmandu, *ib.*; appointed premier, *ib.*; his rash and overbearing conduct, 668; plots against the Maharaja, *ib.*; appointed premier for life, *ib.*; horribly murdered, *ib.*
Mathura, temple at, converted into a mosque by Aurangzeb, 212; plundered by the Afghans under Ahmad Shah Abdali, 328.
Mauritius taken from France by the British, 526.
Mayo, Lord, Viceroy of India, 771; his conference with Sher Ali at Umballa, 772; his conciliatory policy, 773; his interest in Burma affairs, *ib.*; visit to Rangoon, *ib.*; assassination, 774.
Max Muller, Professor, his edition of the Rik Vaidha, and translations of Vaidik hymns, 80 *note.*
Meade, Major, arrests Tantia Topi, 755.
Meanee, in Sinde, battle of, won by Sir Charles Napier, 647.
Mecca, Sherif of, repulses the envoys of Aurangzeb, 196.
Medows, General, his futile campaign against Tippu, 455.
Meerut, mutiny of the sepoys at, 721–2; terrible rising on Sunday, the 10th of May, 723; fatal delays, *ib.*; flight of the mutineers to Delhi and beginning of the revolt of the Bengal army, 724.
Megasthenes, the Greek ambassador at the court of Sandrokottos, 67; his description of the city of Pali-bothra, the modern Patna, 68; of the people of India, *ib.*
Mehidpore, battle of, 567.
Merivale, Mr. Herman, editor of the correspondence and journals of Philip Francis, 413 *note.*
Metcalfe, Mr., afterward Lord, his mission to Runjeet Singh, 523; conducts the negotiations with Amir Khan, 557; appointed Resident at Hyderabad, 572; condemns the bank of Palmer & Co., 572–3; con-

venes a council of Thakurs at Jaipur, 604; Governor-General of India, 617; grants liberty to the press, *ib.*

Metempsychosis, the dogma of, the transmigrations of the soul, 61; doctrine of deliverance from taught by Buddha, 62; doctrine of merits and deliverance taught by Manu, 85, 86.

Meywar. *See* Udaipur.

Middleton, Mr. superseded as Resident at Lukhnow by Mr. Bristow, 414.

Midnapore, ceded by Mir Kasim to the English, 341.

Mill, Mr., James, his groundless charges against Vansittart, 342 *note*; his opinion of Muhammad Reza Khan and Shitab Rai, 405 *note*.

Mill, Colonel James, proposed the conquest of Bengal long before Clive, 337 *note*.

Millennium, the Muhammadan, expected in the reign of Akbar, 167–8.

Minto, Lord, Governor-General of India, 521; his active policy, 522; despatches missions to Runjeet Singh, Persia, and Kabul, 523 and *note*; interferes to prevent the aggressions of Amir Khan on Nagpore, 524; active operations against the French and Dutch, 526; leaves India, 528; his remonstrances with Nipal, 530, 543; his ultimatum, 544.

Misls, or Sikh fraternities, 672; their decay, 673.

Misr Guru at Khatmandu, 659; forced to go on pilgrimage, 662; recalled from Benares, 665.

Mitchell, Colonel, his proceedings in the sepoy mutiny at Berhampore, 719.

Mithila, Raj of, the modern Tirhut, 43 *note*.

Mithra, or the Sun, worship of, imported into India by Kanishka, 71; corresponds with the Vaidik Surya, 80.

Mir Jafir, posted at Plassy by Nawab Suraj-ud-daula, 322; joins Jagat Seth in his conspiracy against Suraj-ud-daula, *ib.*; his dubious conduct at Plassy, 323; installed as Nawab by Colonel Clive, *ib.*; his money presents and cessions of territory, *ib.*; confers the quit-rent of the Company's territory on Clive, 324; origin of Clive's jaghir, *ib.*; his incapacity as a ruler, *ib.*; atrocities of his son Miran, 324–5; nicknamed "Colonel Clive's Jackass," 325; replaces Hindu commanders by Muhammadans, 326; Mahratta demands for chout, *ib.*; relations with the Shahzada, 327; becomes insufferable, 340; deposed by Vansittart in favor of his son-in-law, Mir Kasim, 341; restored to the throne by the Calcutta council, 351; his death, 357.

Mir Kasim, son-in-law of Mir Jafir, his dealings with Mr. Vansittart for the Nawabship of Bengal and Behar, 341; the preliminary treaty, *ib.*; his offer of twenty lakhs refused by Vansittart, *ib.*; proclaimed Nawab, 342; defeats the Moghul army under Shah Alam, *ib.*; secures letters of investiture from Shah Alam, 343; refuses to join in an English expedition to Delhi, *ib.*; suspicions of the English, 344; secret preparations for war, *ib.*; quarrel about private trade, 344, 346–7; his sudden abolition of all duties, 347; violence of the English council at Calcutta, *ib.*; reception of Amyatt and Hay at Monghyr, 348; stoppage of a boat-load of arms for the English factory at Patna, 349; puffed up with the recapture of Patna, 350; murder of Amyatt, *ib.*; flight to Patna, 352; massacre of 150 Englishmen at Patna, *ib.*; escape into Oude, 353; perishes in obscurity, 355.

Mlechhas, or barbarians, Hindu name for Guptas, 71.

Moghuls, their early invasions of India, 102; described as ugly nomads, *ib.*; massacred by Ala-ud-din, 106; invade the Punjab, 108; bribed by Muhammad Tughlak to go away, *ib.*; invasion of Timur, 150; Tartar origin of, 151; a ruling tribe, possibly representatives of the Royal Scythians described by Herodotus, 151 and *note*; religious

toleration, 151; approximate to the Persian type, 152; early life of Baber, *ib.*; invasion of India, 154; defeat of the Rana of Chitor, *ib.*; his death, 155; reign of Humayun, *ib.*; recovery of Hindustan by the Afghans, 156; exile of Humayun, *ib.*; returns to Delhi and dies, 157.

Moghul empire, founded by Akbar, 157; wars against the Afghans, 158; decay of the Muhammadan religion, 160; establishment of political and religious equality. *ib.*; efforts to amalgamate Moghuls and Rajputs, 160–1; introduction of a strong Rajput element, 162; Moghul aristocracy without hereditary rights, 163; hereditary aristocracy of the Rajputs, 164; antagonism of religion, a political gain, *ib.*; religion of Akbar, 168; public life of the Moghuls, 169; land-tenure, 170; reign of Jehangir. 172; English appear at Surat, 173: mission of Captain Hawkins to Agra, 174; mission of Sir Thomas Roe to Jehangir, 175; audience at Ajmir, 177; poisonings at the Moghul court, 178; festivals, 179; camp of the Great Moghul, 181; massacres of brigands and rebels, 181–2; Rajput wars, 182–3; death of Jehangir, 185; massacre of princes and accession of Shah Jehan, *ib.*; increasing antagonisms between Moghuls and Rajputs, 187; disaffection of tributary Rajas, 188; fratricidal wars between the four sons of Shah Jehan, 190; early career of Aurangzeb, 191; deceives his brother Murad, 192; succession of Aurangzeb to the Moghul throne, 195; description of Delhi, 197; early alliance with Sivaji and the Mahrattas, 202; conflicts with the Mahrattas, 203; suspicious death of Shah Jehan, 204; feigned rebellion, 207; history forbidden by public edict, 209; mysterious rebellion in Kabul, 210; treacherous massacre of Afghans, *ib.*; persecution of Hindus and destruction of idolatry, 212; imposition of the religious poll-tax, known as the Jezya, 213; religious wars in Rajputana, 214; splendid march of the Moghul army, 215; camp life of Aurangzeb, 216; conquest of Bijapur and Golkonda, 217; revival of Hindu nationality, *ib.*

Moghul empire, civilization of, 219; condition of the masses ignored, *ib.*; superior roads, 220; carriages, 221; caravanserais, *ib.*; dangers and inconveniences of travelling, 222; guards of horsemen, *ib.*; Thugs or stranglers, 223; absence of roads in Hindu kingdoms, *ib.*; hereditary oxen-drivers, 224; foot-posts in India, 225; administration of justice, *ib.*; Fryer's travels in India, 226–7; description of Masulipatam, 227; old Madras, 228; Bombay, 230; Surat, *ib.*; Joonere, 231; Karwar, 233; English settlements in Bengal, 234; refractory Rajas in Bengal and Behar, 239.

Moghul empire, story of its decline and fall, 240; fratricidal wars of the sons of Aurangzeb, 241; persecutions of the Sikhs, 242; growing independence of the Viceroys of provinces, 243; Mahratta claims to chout, 244; reign of Jehandar Shah, 245; rebellion of Farrukh Siyar and the two Saiyids, 246; constant plots and intrigues, 247; English mission from Calcutta to Delhi, 248; Mahrattas at Delhi, 250; assassination and revolution, *ib.*; decay of the empire, 252; cessation of the imperial progresses, *ib.*; latent force of court routine, 253; successions to local governments, *ib.*; the Padishah, the sole fountain of honor, rank, and title, *ib.*; provincial Dewans or Accountant-Generals, 254; general corruption, *ib.*; ostentatious reverence to the orders of the Padishah, 255; growing power of the Mahrattas, 257; secret relations between the Mahrattas and the Moghul court at Delhi, 260–1; invasion of Nadir Shah, 263; sack of Delhi, 266; horrible carnage, *ib.*; fall of the empire amid the contests between Mahrattas and Afghans, 269–70.

Monson, Colonel, appointed a member of the council of Calcutta, 412; his advance into Central India, in pursuit of Jaswant Rao Holkar, 509; disastrous retreat, 510.

Montgomery, Sir Robert, member of the Punjab Board of Administration, 692.

Moodkee, Hardinge and Gough's victory at, 680.

Moors, Arab Muhammadan traders so called, 126; intrigues against Portuguese, 127–8.

Morari, Rao, a Mahratta general at Trichinopoly, 280; declares against Mortiz Ali, 283; joins the regent of Mysore, 300; pretended mediation between Major Lawrence and Muhammad Ali, 301–3.

Mornington, Lord, succeeds Sir John Shore as Governor-General of India, 466; lands at Calcutta, 467; alarmed at the power of the French, *ib.*; abandons the idea of a balance of power, 467–8; alliance with Nizam Ali against Tippu, 468; futile negotiations with the Mahrattas, *ib.*; demands explanations from Tippu, 470; downfall of Tippu and settlement of Mysore, 471; created Marquis of Wellesley, *ib.* *See* Wellesley.

Mortiz Ali, brother-in-law of Nawab Subder Ali, commands Vellore, 281; resists demands of contribution, 282; implicated in the massacre of Subder Ali, *ib.*; proclaimed Nawab, 282–3; flight from Arcot, 283; implicated in the murder of the boy Nawab, 284.

Mostyn, Mr., English Resident at Poona, 444 *note.*

Mudaji Bhonsla. *See* Bhonsla.

Muhammad, the prophet of Arabia, his teaching and death, 94; succeeded by the four Khalifs, *ib.*; Arab conquest of Asia to the Indus and Oxus, 95.

Muhammadans, their conquest of Hindustan, 95–8; of Bengal, 101; of the Dekhan and Peninsula, 106; declining power, 110, 160; horrible rule in Bengal before the Moghul conquest, 131; antagonism toward Rajputs, 184–7.

Muhammadan Sultans of the Dekhan, 114; Bahmani dynasty of Kulbarga, 116; wars against the Hindu empire of Vijayanagar, 114–18; dismemberment into the five kingdoms of Ahmadnagar, Berar, Bider, Bijapur and Golkonda, 118; interference in the city of Vijayanagar, 119–20; bribed to retire, 120; unholy alliance with Ram Rai, 121; league of the Sultans against the Maharaja, *ib.*; decisive victory at Talikota, 121–2, 171; conquest of Ahmadnagar and Berar by Akbar, 171; invasion of Jehangir, 180–1; designs of Aurangzeb, 191; conquest of Bijapur and Golkonda, 217.

Muhammad Afzal Khan. *See* Afzal.

Muhammad Ali, Nawab of the Carnatic, appointed by the Nizam, 296; assisted by the English at Trichinopoly, 297; intrigues with Mysore, 300; his duplicity, 301; helped by the English in the reduction of rebellious Poligars, 305; his debts, 426; efforts to bribe the governor of Madras, 427; English adventurers at his court, 440 *note*; his death, 489; treachery of his son and successor, *ib.*; introduction of British administration into the Carnatic, 490; extinction of the titular Nawabship by Lord Dalhousie, 706.

Muhammad Azim Khan. *See* Azim.

Muhammad Ghori, his conquest of Hindustan, 98; stabbed to death by the Gakkars, 100.

Muhammad Reza Khan, bargaining with four members of the Calcutta council at Murshedabad, 357; becomes deputy Nawab of Bengal, *ib.*; wrath of Lord Clive, 360; corrupt collusion with English officials, 379; alleged misconduct during the famine, 381; arrested and brought to Calcutta, 405; his restoration refused by Warren Hastings, *ib.*

Muhammad Shah, succeeds to the throne of Delhi, 251; decline of the Moghul empire, 252; compelled to submit to Nadir Shah, 264; nominal sovereignty, 268; his death, 269.

Muhammad Tughlak, his disastrous reign, 108–9; bribes the Moghuls, 108; excessive taxation, 109; fatal removal of capital from Delhi to Deoghur, *ib.*; introduces copper counters for gold money, *ib.*; financial anarchy, 110; rebellions and revolutions, *ib.*; his death, *ib.*

Mulhar Rao Holkar. *See* Holkar.

Mulraj, Viceroy of Multan under Sikh rule, 685; his feigned resignation, *ib.*; murder of Mr. Vans Agnew and Lieutenant Anderson, 686; defeated by Herbert Edwardes, 686–7; suspicious of Sher Singh, 688; surrenders Multan, 689; imprisoned for life, 690.

Munro, Hector, his punishment of mutiny at Patna, 354; gains the battle of Buxar, *ib.*; disaster during Hyder Ali's invasion of the Carnatic, 432.

Murshedabad, capital of Bengal, moved from Dacca, 308; expenditure of the old Nawabs, 374; decline, 406.

Murshed Kuli Khan, becomes Nawab of Bengal, Behar and Orissa, 308; removes his capital from Dacca to Murshedabad, *ib.*; harsh treatment of Hindus, 309; hates his son-in-law, Shuja Khan, 310; his death, *ib.*

Muzaffir Jung. *See* Nizam.

Mysore, Hindu government of, 300 *note*; cession of Trichinopoly to the Hindu regent, 301; Hindu regent joins the French, 302; rise of Hyder Ali, 367; his invasion of the Carnatic, 369; offensive and defensive treaty with the English, 370; his formidable power, 428; mission of Swartz, 429; invasion of the Carnatic, 432; death of Hyder Ali, 436; palace life at Seringapatam, *ib.*; succession of Tippu, son of Hyder, 437; treaty of Mangalore, *ib.*; aggressions of Tippu on the lines of Travancore, 454; campaigns of Lord Cornwallis, 455–7; submission of Tippu, 457; hostile negotiations of Tippu with the French, 467, 470; last war against Mysore, 470; downfall and death of Tippu, 471; resuscitation of a Hindu dynasty by Lord Wellesley, *ib.*; travels of Buchanan in Mysore, 472; description of Bangalore, 477; government of Purnea, 479, 613; aspires to be a Peishwa, 614; enthronement of Krishnaraj, *ib.*; ruinous profligacy, 615; fruitless warnings, *ib.*; rebellion in Mysore, *ib.*; deposition of the Raja, 616; prosperity under British rule, *ib.*

N

Nadir Shah, or Nadir Kuli Khan, his rise in Persia, 262; assists Shah Tahmasp, *ib.*; usurps the throne of Persia, 263; unsuccessful embassies to the Moghul, *ib.*; captures Kandahar and Kabul, *ib.*; reported intercourse with Saadut Ali Khan and Nizam-ul-mulk, *ib.*; intrigues, *ib.*; march through the Punjab, 264; defeats the Moghuls at Kurnal, *ib.*; submission of Muhammad Shah, *ib.*; negotiations with the Nizam, *ib.*; march to Delhi, 265; gloomy entry into Delhi, *ib.*; massacre of Nadir Shah's soldiery, *ib.*; his revenge, 266; Nadir Shah in the mosque, *ib.*; collection of the subsidy, 267; spoils, 268; intermarriage and ceded territory, *ib.*; resuscitation of the Moghul, *ib.*; return to Persia, *ib.*; declaration of the Sunni faith, *ib.*; assassination, *ib.*; effects of his invasion, 269; his death the commencement of Afghan history, 622.

Nagas, or snake-worshippers, 12; a Scythic tribe occupying Khandavaprastha, 25; an existing type of the so-called aborigines, 78.

Nagpore, Raja of, demands the restoration of Cuttack and Berar, 519; Amir Khan's aggressions on, 524; treachery of Raja Appa Sahib, 563; espouses the cause of Baji Rao Peishwa, 564; defeat and flight of Appa Sahib, 566; succession of a boy Raja, *ib.*; mixed administration of Mr. Jenkins, 601, 704; deterioration under native rule, 705; annexation of Nagpore, 706.

Naiks, or deputy Hindu rulers, 123.

Nairs, the military caste in Malabar, 125; massacre of the Portuguese at Calicut, 129.

Najaf Khan, career of, 446 *note*; his son, Afrasiab Khan, *ib.*

Najib-ud-daula, appointed by Ahmad Shah Abdali to be guardian of the Moghul king at Delhi, 328; a Rohilla Afghan, *ib.*; driven out by Ghazi-ud-din, *ib.*; regent guardian at Delhi under the title of Amir of Amirs, 392, 400; dealings with Suraj Mal, the Jat Raja, 401; intrigues with the English at Calcutta, *ib.*; behavior toward Ahmad Shah Abdali, 402; overtures to the Mahrattas, *ib.*; his death, 402, 406 *note.*

Nala and Damayanti, the poem of, 89–91; Swayamvara of Damayanti, 90; the royal gambler, *ib.*; exile in the jungle, *ib.*; flight of Nala, and agony of Damayanti, 91; reconciliation, *ib.*; characteristics of the poem, *ib.*

Nalanda, the Buddhist university of, visited by the Chinese pilgrims, 76.

Nana Farnavese, the Brahman minister at the court of Poona, 418; favors St. Lubin, the French adventurer at Poona, 421; plots and intrigues, *ib.*; origin of influence, 422 *note*; supported by Mahadaji Sindia, 422; his action in the convention of Wurgaum, 423; dread of Hyder Ali, 435; ratifies the treaty of Salbai, 436; becomes the real head of affairs at Poona, 443; schemes for checking Sindia, 452; plays a double game with Tippu and Cornwallis, 455; attempts to prevent the installation of the Peishwa as deputy of the Great Moghul, 459; antagonism toward Mahadaji Sindia, *ib.*; calls upon Sindia for the revenues of the conquered provinces in Hindustan, 460; the rivalry closed by the death of Mahadaji Sindia, *ib.*; height of prosperity, 463; distractions arising from the suicide of the Peishwa, *ib.*; discovers the intrigues of Baji Rao, and declares him to be Peishwa, 464; flies to Satara, *ib.*; return and imprisonment, *ib.*; forced reconciliation with Baji Rao, 468; evades an alliance with the British government, 470; grounds of his refusal, 493; his death, 497.

Nana Sahib, the adopted heir of Baji Rao Peishwa, 707; claims to inherit the pension granted to Baji Rao, *ib.*; residence at Bithoor, 732; his deceitful professions, *ib.*; his wild dreams of restoring the extinct Mahratta empire of the Peishwa, 733; joins the mutineers, *ib.*; his threatening letter to General Wheeler, *ib.*; besieges Cawnpore, 734; his treacherous proposals, *ib.*; negotiations, 735; massacre on the river Ganges, 735–6; installation as Peishwa, 736; defeated by Havelock, 737; orders the massacre of women and children at Cawnpore, 738; flight from Cawnpore, *ib.*; reoccupies Bithoor, 740; defeated by Havelock, 741.

Nanuk Guru, founder of the Sikh brotherhood, or commonwealth, in the Punjab. 242, 671.

Nao Nihal Singh, grandson of Runjeet Singh, Maharaja at Lahore, 675; his death at his father's funeral, *ib.*

Napier, Sir Charles, his campaign in Sindia, 647; wins the battles of

Meanee and Hyderabad, *ib.*; controversy with Outram, 647–8; appointed Commander-in-chief of the Bengal army in succession to Lord Gough, 689.

Napier, Colonel Robert (Lord Napier of Magdala), his engineering work in the Punjab, 694 *note*; his dashing charge on the retreating army of Tantia Topi, 754.

Napoleon Bonaparte, his supposed designs on India, 467, 501–2.

Narain Rao Peishwa, succeeds his father, Mahdu Rao, on the throne of Poona, 417; his murder, *ib.*

Narayana, or Para Brahma, the supreme god of the Smartals, 475.

Narsingh Acharya, successor of Sankhara Acharya, 474 *note.*

Narsinga, or Vijayanagar, Hindu empire of, 118. *See* Vijayanagar.

Nasir Jung. *See* Nizam.

Nasik, visited by Rama, 55 *note.*

Naths and Swamis, worshipped as gods, 84, 540.

Nawab, or governor, a Moghul officer, 225; civil administration, 226.

Nawabs of Bengal and the Carnatic. *See* Bengal *and* Carnatic.

Nawab of Joonere, the birthplace of Sivaji, 231; discourses with Dr. Fryer, 232; a type of a Moghul fortress, *ib.*; a converted Brahman appointed to the command by Aurangzeb, *ib.*

Nawab Nazim, duties of, 361 *note*; distinguished from the Dewan, *ib.*, 363; reduced to a pageant, *ib.*; reduction of allowances, *ib. note.*

Negrais, English factory at, 590; massacre of English by the Burmese under Alompra, *ib.*

Neill, Colonel, his advance from Calcutta to Lukhnow, 737; delayed at Benares and Allahabad, *ib.*; joined by a column under Havelock, *ib.*; proceeds to Cawnpore, 739; difficulties at Cawnpore, 740; killed at the relief of Lukhnow, 749.

Newars, Buddhist Rajas of Nipal, 533; conquered by the Ghorkas, *ib.*

Nicholson, Brigadier John, arrival at the siege of Delhi, 746; commands an assaulting column, *ib.*; his death, 747.

Niebuhr, Karsten, his prophecy respecting the English East India Company, 716 *note.*

Nipal, history of, 531; description of the Nipal valley, 532; occupied by the Newars, or Hindu Buddhists, 533; conquered by the Ghorkas, *ib.*; atrocities of Prithi Narain, 534; Ghorka constitution, *ib.*; military organization, 535; early Ghorka Maharajas, *ib.*; plunder of the temples of Lhassa and Digarchi, 536; Chinese invasion, *ib.*; Ghorkas conclude a treaty with the English, *ib.*; apply for help against China, *ib.*; refused by Lord Cornwallis, *ib.*; defeat and humiliation of the Ghorkas by the Chinese, 536–7; mission of Kirkpatrick, 536; its failure, 537; revolution at Khatmandu, *ib.*; Run Bahadur, the Nero of Nipal, *ib.*; his madness, 538; conspiracy of the Pandeys, 539; flight of Run Bahadur to Benares, *ib.*; dealings of Lord Wellesley with Run Bahadur, *ib.*; mission of Captain Knox, 540; revolution headed by the chief queen, *ib.*; failure of Knox's mission, 541; return of Run Bahadur to Nipal, *ib.*; downfall of the Pandeys, *ib.*; counter conspiracy, *ib.*; murder of Run Bahadur, 542; massacre at Khatmandu, *ib.*; triumph of Bhim Sein Thapa and the chief queen, *ib.*; aggressions on British territory, 543; ultimatum of Lord Minto, 544; of Lord Moira (Hastings), *ib.*; council of Bharadars at Khatmandu, *ib.*; Ghorka debates, peace or war, *ib.*; slaughter of British police, 546; disastrous campaign of 1814, *ib.*, retrieved by General Ochterlony, 547; fall of Maloun, *ib.*; vacillation of the Ghorkas, *ib.*; treaty of Segowlie, 548; differences about the Terai, *ib.*; subsequent history of Nipal, 657; infant Maharajas, *ib.*; Bhim Sein Thapa thwarted by an ambitious queen, 658; entanglement of the British Resident, *ib.*; fall of Bhim Sein Thapa, 659; ministerial complications, *ib.*; political compromise, *ib.*; quarrel between the two queens, 660; great temple of Pusput Nath, *ib.*; tragedies at Khatmandu, 661; condemnation and suicide of Bhim Sein Thapa, *ib.*; threatening attitude toward the English, 662; action of Lord Auckland, *ib.*; violence of the elder queen, *ib.*; her death, 663; wrath of the Maharaja at English newspapers, *ib.*; mad freaks of the heir-apparent, *ib.*; dangerous treatment of Jung Bahadur and others, 664; reaction against the British government, 665; great state trial of the Pandeys, *ib.*; national movement against the heir-apparent, *ib.*; Maharaja faces the revolutionary party, *ib.*; petition of advice and remonstrance, 666; attempted arrest of revolutionary leaders, *ib.*; regency of the queen, 667; return of Matabar Singh, a nephew of Bhim Sein Thapa, to Khatmandu, *ib.*; revenge of the Thapas on the Pandeys, *ib.*; threatened massacre prevented by Henry Lawrence, 668; murder of Matabar Singh, *ib.*; new ministry at Khatmandu, 669; terrible massacre, 669–70; rise of Jung Bahadur, 670; installation of heir-apparent, *ib.*

Nirvana, eternal sleep or annihilation, Buddhist dogma of, 62, 87.

Nizams of Hyderabad, rise of Chin Kulich Khan, afterward known as Nizam-ul-mulk, 255; incurs the wrath of Jehandar Shah, 256; saved by Zulfikar Khan, 257; appointed Subahdar of the Dekhan, *ib.*; wars with the Mahrattas, 259 *et seq.*; negotiations with Nadir Shah, 264; implores him to stop the massacre at Delhi, 266; anger at the growing independence of the Nawabs of the Carnatic, 277; demands arrears of tribute from Dost Ali, 281; advances an overwhelming army to Arcot, 283; settles the Nawabship, 284; receives an English deputation at Trichinopoly, *ib.*; returns to Hyderabad, *ib.*; his death, 287; distractions in his family, 289.

Nizam Nasir Jung, the second son of Nizam-ul-mulk, seizes the throne, 289; claims of Muzaffir Jung, the grandson, 290; cause of the grandson espoused by Dupleix, *ib.*; Nasir Jung at Arcot, 293; alarm at the capture of Jinji by the French, 294; sudden murder, 295; Nizam Muzaffir Jung, grandson of Nizam-ul-mulk, succeeds to the throne, 295; appoints Dupleix to be governor of the Peninsula for the Great Moghul, *ib.*; murdered, 296.

Nizam Salabut Jung, placed on the throne by M. Bussy, 296; cedes the Northern Circars to the French, 303; rupture, 306; conquests of Bussy in the Northern Circars, 330; story of the Poligars of Bobili and Vizianagram, 330–1; recall of Bussy by Lally, 333; conquests of Colonel Forde in the Northern Circars, *ib.*; imprisonment and death of Salabut Jung, 334; cedes the Northern Circars to the French and then to the English, 366 *note*.

Nizam Ali succeeds to the throne of Hyderabad, 334; invades the Carnatic, 359; proposed alliance by Clive, rejected by the Court of Directors, 365; Clive claims the Northern Circars by right of a firman from Shah Alam, 366; conclusion of a separate treaty with Nizam Ali by the Madras government, 367; promised yearly tribute for the Northern Circars, *ib.*; joint expedition of Nizam Ali and the English against Hyder Ali, *ib.*; treachery of Nizam Ali, 368; secret intrigues with Hyder Ali, 369; deserts Hyder and makes peace with the English, *ib.*; English obtain from Shah Alam a blank firman for all the dominions of the Nizam, *ib.*; intermittent wars and intrigues with the Mahrattas, 395; plunders Poona, *ib.*; strange reconciliation with Rughonath Rao, the sixth Peishwa, 396; further dealings,

419; exasperated at the English occupation of Guntoor, 430; confederates with Hyder Ali and the Mahrattas against the English, 432; allies with Lord Cornwallis against Tippu, 454–5; inaction, 455–6; Mahratta claims for arrears of chout, 458, 461; English decline to interfere, 461; seeks the aid of the French, 462; insults the Mahratta envoy at Hyderabad, *ib.*; utterly defeated by the Mahrattas at Kurdla, 463; submits to every demand, *ib.*; allies with Lord Mornington against Tippu, 468; disbandment of the French battalions at Hyderabad, *ib.*; becomes a feudatory under the subsidiary system of Lord Wellesley, 493; his dominions threatened by Daulat Rao Sindia and Rughoji Bhonsla, 502–3; receives Berar as a pure gift from Lord Wellesley, 506.

Nizams (modern history), territories ravaged by the Pindharies, 528; secret negotiations of Baji Rao Peishwa, 551; Charles Metcalfe Resident at Hyderabad, 572; affairs of Palmer & Co., *ib.*; debts defrayed out of the tribute for the Northern Circars, 573; negotiations respecting the Nizam's Contingent, 707–8; cession of Berar, 708.

Northbrook, Lord, Viceroy of India, 774.

Northern Circars, cession of, to the French, 308; Bussy's conquests of the Poligars, 330–1; cession to the English, 365–6 and *note*; granted to the English by the firman of Shah Alam, 366; Madras government agree to pay a yearly tribute, 367; money appropriated to the payment of the Nizam's debts to Palmer & Co., 573.

Nott, General, commands the English force at Kandahar, 635; his wrath at the order to retreat, 643; marches to Kabul with the gates of Somnath, 644.

Nuddea, the old capital of Bengal, 101 and *note*; surprised by Bakhtiyar and his horsemen, *ib.*; flight of the Raja to Jagganath, *ib.*

Nur Mahal, or the "Light of the Harem," the favorite wife of Jehangir, story of, 178; her intrigues respecting her daughter, 182; baffled by the Rajputs and her brother, Asof Khan, 184–5.

Nund-komar, his charges against Warren Hastings, 416; his infamous character, *ib.*; tried and executed on a charge of forgery, *ib.*; a judicial murder, 417; its results, *ib.*

Nynee Tal, hill station of, built on territory ceded by Nipal, 548.

O

OCHTERLONY, COLONEL, afterward General Sir David, placed in charge of Delhi by General Lake, 505; his successful defence of Delhi against Jaswant Rao Holkar, 511; his victorious campaign against Nipal, 547; capture of Maloun, *ib.*; active proceedings at Bhurtpore on the outbreak of Durjan Sal, 598; condemned by Lord Amherst, *ib.*; his mortification and death, *ib.*

Olaza, the Kanarese queen of, 141; her interview with Della Valle, 142; her strange behavior, 143.

Omichund, threatens to divulge the conspiracy of Jagat Seth, Mir Jafir, and Colonel Clive, to Nawab Suraj-ud-daula, 322; duped by Clive with a sham treaty, *ib.*; the chief blot on the character of Clive, *ib. note.*

Omrahs, answering to the Amirs at the Moghul court, 164 *note*.

Onore, 131; the type of a Portuguese settlement and fortress, 138.

Oude, the ancient Ayodhya, the principal scene of the Ramayana, 42 *et seq.*; the frontier at Sungroor, 48–9, 53; return of Rama and Sita, 59; Ala-ud-din appointed Viceroy by his uncle, the Sultan of Delhi, 102; murder of the Sultan on the Ganges, 104; Nawab Viziers of, *see* **Saadut Ali Khan, Shuja-ud-daula,** *and* **Asof-ud-daula;** conquered and occupied by the English, 356; restored to the Nawab Vizier by Lord Clive, 361; reasons for the restoration, 361–2; satisfaction of Shuja-ud-daula, 362; payment of tribute refused to Shah Alam at Delhi, 408; threatened by the Mahrattas, 409; hostile claims on the Rohillas, *ib.*; obtains the services of a brigade from Warren Hastings, 410; conquest of the Rohillas, 411; cession of the suzerainty of Benares to the British government, 414; claim of the two Begums to the state treasures, 415; Warren Hastings declines to interfere, *ib.*; Philip Francis interferes in behalf of the Begums, *ib.*; settlement by Hastings, 435; cruel usage of the servants of the Begums by the Nawab Vizier, *ib.*; charges against Warren Hastings, 441; threatened invasion of the Afghans under Zeman Shah, 494; alarm of Lord Wellesley, *ib.*; his demands on the Nawab Vizier, 495; territorial cessions to the British government, *ib.*; threats of Lord Amherst, 709; of Lord William Bentinck, 609, 709; of Lord Hardinge, 709; Sleeman's report, *ib.*; tenderness of Lord Dalhousie toward the king of Oude, 710; annexation ordered by the Court of Directors, *ib.*; English administration, early mistakes, 712; appointment of Sir Henry Lawrence to be Chief Commissioner, 713; general insurrection, 739; Lord Clyde's campaign, 752; end of the rebellion, 756–7.

Outram, Major, afterward General Sir James, his controversy with General Sir Charles Napier respecting Sinde, 647–8; commands an expedition against Persia, 714; joins Havelock at Cawnpore, 748; waives his right to command in favor of Havelock, *ib.*; advance on Lukhnow, *ib.*; assumes the command, 750; left at Lukhnow by Campbell, *ib.*; drives the rebels out of Lukhnow, 752.

Oxus river, the natural boundary between the Usbegs and Afghans, 619–20.

P

PADISHHA, Moghul, equivalent for emperor, 157 *note*; fountain head of Moghul aristocracy, 163; ostentatious reverence to, 255.

Pagan Meng, king of Burma, 655; his low character, 656; deposed, 697.

Paget, Sir Edward, suppresses a sepoy mutiny at Barrackpore with grapeshot, 727.

Pali taught in Burma, 577.

Palmer & Co., bankers of Hyderabad, 572; their proceedings condemned by Metcalfe, 572–3; their insolvency, 573.

Panchala, kingdom of, mentioned in the Maha Bharata, 16; its frontiers, *ib. note*; identified by Manu with Kanouj, *ib.*

Pandavas, rival kinsmen of the Kauravas, 11; the sons of Pandu, 16; jealousy of the Kauravas, *ib.*; the instructions of Drona, *ib.*; narrow escape at Varanavata, 20; adventures in the disguise of Brahmans among the Rakshasas and Asuras, 21; journey to Ekachakra, *ib.*; attend the Swayamvara of Draupadi, 22; alliance with Drupada, 24; obtain the Raj of Khandava-prastha; 25; found Indraprastha, *ib.*; celebrate the Raja-suya, 26; gambling-match with the Kauravas, *ib.*; become the slaves of Duryodhana, 27; second exile, 28; at Virata, in disguise, 29; send an envoy to Hastinapur, 32; triumph over the Kauravas, 34–7; celebration of the Aswamedha, 39–40.

Pandey, a leading Ghorka family, its rise to power in Nipal, 539; Damodur Pandey, premier, *ib.*; flight of Run Bahadur and Bhim Sein Thapa to Benares, *ib.*; downfall of the family, 541; imprisonment and execution of Damodur Pandey, *ib.*; rise of Runjung Pandey, son of Damodur, 658; supported by the elder queen, *ib.*; appointed premier, 659; removed from office, *ib.*; flies with the elder queen to the temple of Pusput Nath, 660; restoration to power, 661; intrigues against the British government, 662; dismissed from office, *ib.*; return from exile, 665; revives old charges that the elder queen had been poisoned, *ib.*; state trial at Khatmandu, *ib.*; conviction and punishment of Kubraj Pandey, *ib.*; execution of members of the family, 667.

Pandu, the pale-complexioned grandson of Santanu, 14; marries Kunti and Madri, 15; installed on the throne of Hastinapur, *ib.*; reigns as Maharaja, *ib.*; retires to the jungle, *ib.*; death and Sati, *ib.*; his sons known as the five Pandavas, 16.

Pandya or Pandion, identified with Madura, 73; king of, sends an embassy to Augustus Cæsar, *ib. note.*

Paniput, battle of, horrible slaughter of Mahrattas by the Afghans under Ahmad Shah Abdali, 388, 392.

Panjani, annual Ghorka festival in Nipal, 585; yearly redistribution of all offices and commands, *ib.*

Para Brahma. *See* Narayana.

Pariahs, or outcasts, 77–8, 476 *note*; the right and left "hands," 479–80 *note.*

Parwiz, son of Jehangir, his command in the Dekhan, 176; his reception of Sir Thomas Roe, the English ambassador, *ib.*; recalled by Jehangir, 178.

Patali-putra, the modern Patna, 68; centre of Buddhism in the time of Fah Hian, 74.

Patan kings of Delhi, 150.

Patell, or head-man of a village, 459.

Patna, Pali-bothra, or Patali-putra, captured by Sandrokottos, 67; description of, 67–9; magistrates, 68; capital of Asoka, 69 *note*; English settlement at, 235; inland English factory for saltpetre, raw silk, cotton piece goods, and opium, *ib.*, 308; installation of the Great Moghul (Shah Alam) at, 342; captured by the English under Mr. Ellis, 349; recaptured by the troops of Nawab Mir Kasim, 349–50; massacre of 150 Englishmen at, 352; taken by the English, 358; court of appeal at, 451.

Paul, the Emperor, recalls the Russian army from Georgia, 496 *note.*

Payendah Khan, hereditary chief of the Barukzais, 624; procures the succession of Zeman Shah to the throne of Afghanistan, 625–6; removed from his posts, 626; slaughtered in the presence of Zeman Shah, 627.

Pegu, distinguished from Ava, 575; desolating wars between the Talains of Pegu and the Burmese of Ava, 578; conquered by Byeen-noung, a Burmese warrior of the sixteenth century, 579–80; revolt of the royal monk, 586; massacre of Burmans, 587; assassination of Byeen-noung, *ib.*; recovery of Pegu by a foster-brother of Byeen-noung, *ib.*; execution of the royal monk, 588; Diego Suarez appointed governor of Pegu, *ib.*; outrage on a marriage procession, *ib.*; stoned to death by the mob of Pegu, 589; Talain conquest of Ava in the eighteenth century, *ib.*; conquest of Pegu by Alompra, 590; British conquest of Pegu, 697; administrative changes, *ib.*; glorious future, *ib.*

Peishwas, hereditary Brahman ministers of the Mahrattas, their rise to power, 245; important element in Mahratta history, 258; Balaji Visvanath, first Peishwa, 257; his policy, *ib.*; Baji Rao, second Peishwa, *ib.*; his dealings with the Nizam and Padishah, 259; Balaji Rao, third Peishwa, 369, 386; schemes for the sovereignty of the Mahratta empire, 386; leaves a puppet Maharaja at Satara, and removes the capital to Poona, 387; Mahdu Rao, fourth Peishwa, 393; Narain Rao, fifth Peishwa, 403, 417; murdered, 418; Rughonath Rao, sixth Peishwa, *ib.*; birth of Mahdu Rao Narain, seventh Peishwa, 419; Rughonath Rao applies to the English for help, 420; beginning of the first Mahratta war, *ib.*, 423; suicide of Mahdu Rao Narain, 463; Baji Rao, eighth Peishwa, 464; flies to Bombay presidency, 499; concludes the treaty of Bassein with the British government, *ib.*; second Mahratta war, 502–3; extinction of the Peishwas, 569. *See also* Mahrattas.

Penlows, or governors, in Bhutan, 763–4.

Pennakonda, court of the Narsinga Rajas at, removed from Vijayanagar, 123.

Perron, succeeds De Boigne in the command of Sindia's French battalions, 501; collects the revenues of the Doab, *ib.*; excites the alarm of Lord Wellesley, *ib.*; defeat of his cavalry by General Lake at Alighur, 504; retires into British territory with his private fortune, 505.

Persia, Shah of, refuses to give up Bulaki to Shah Jehan, 186; wars with the Moghul about Kandahar, 189; threatens Aurangzeb, 204; modern history of, 261; dynasty of Sufi Shiahs, *ib.*; usurpation of Nadir Shah, 263; Persian invasion of Hindustan, 263–4; Persian affairs after the death of Nadir Shah, 496; threatens Herat, 633; siege of Herat, *ib.*; war with England, 714–15.

Peshawar, defeat of the Rajput league by Mahmud of Ghazni, 96; massacre of Afghans at, 210; revolt against Timur Shah, 625; occupied by Runjeet Singh, 632; anxieties of Dost Muhammad for its restoration, *ib.*, 634; the key of the British frontier, 758.

Phagyi-dau, king of Burma, successor of Bhodau Phra, reigning during the first Burmese war, 590; dethroned in favor of Tharawadi, 654.

Phayre, Sir Arthur, Commissioner of Pegu, 697; Chief Commissioner of British Burma, 698; his treaty with the king of Burma, 773.

Philip, lieutenant of Alexander at Taxila, 67; murdered by Hindu mercenaries, *ib.*; succeeded by Eudemos, *ib.*

Pigot, Lord, governor of Madras, 427; restores Tanjore to the Raja, *ib.*; refuses a bribe from Muhammad Ali, Nawab of the Carnatic, *ib.*; resists the claims of Paul Benfield, 428; arrested by the opposition members of the Madras council, *ib.*; dies in confinement, *ib.*; his inconvenient pledge to the Tanjore Raja, 487.

Pindharies, low freebooters attached to the Mahratta armies during the wars of the eighteenth century, 527; present at Paniput, *ib.*; dependent on Sindia and Holkar, *ib.*; supported by grants of land to different leaders, *ib.*; Chetu and Khurim, *ib.*; depredations in Rajputana and Malwa, *ib.*; in the Dekhan, 528; their periodical incursions described by Captain Sydenham, Resident at Hyderabad, *ib.*; induce Lord Moira (Hastings) to adopt the policy of Lord Wellesley, 529; opposition of the home authorities out of dread of the Mahrattas, *ib.*; extend their raids to British territories, 549; resolution of Lord Hastings to exterminate them, *ib.*; revulsion of public opinion in England on account of Pindhari atrocities, 550; British cabinet authorize hostilities against any native power that protects the Pindharies, *ib.*; attitude of Sindia, Holkar and Amir Khan, 555; preparations of Lord Hastings, 554–6; destruction of the Pindharies and extinction of the predatory system, 558–9.

Pinto, Fernam Mendez, present at the siege of Martaban by Byeen-noung, 581; his veracity as regards what he saw, *ib. note*; his description of the surrender of the king, queen and ladies of Martaban, 581–2; sack of Martaban, 583; execution of a hundred and forty ladies, 584–5; drowning of the king and sixty male captives, 586; story of rebellions in Pegu, 586–8; execution of a royal monk, 588; stoning to death of Diego Suarez in the market-place of Pegu, 589.

Pitt, Thomas, grandfather of the Earl of Chatham, governor of Madras, 234; besieged for three months by Daud Khan, Nawab of the Moghul conquests in Southern India, *ib.*; pays a demand for ten thousand pagodas, *ib.*; his relations with Bahadur Shah, son and successor of Aurangzeb, 241.

Pitt, William, proposal of Clive that the British nation, and not the East India Company, should take possession of Bengal, Behar, and Orissa, 336; rejected on the ground that it would render the British Crown too powerful, 337–8; creates a Board of Control, 439; refuses to recommend Warren Hastings for a peerage, or for employment under the Crown, 442; justified, *ib.*

Place, Mr., a Madras civilian, his measures in the Company's Jaghir, 472–3.

Plassy, decisive battle on the 23d of June, 1757, won by Clive, 323; its immediate results, *ib.*; its remarkable effect on Balaji Rao, Peishwa of the Mahrattas, 390.

Pliny, his accounts of the coast of Malabar, and the voyages of Roman merchants thither, 124.

Poligars, minor chiefs of the Carnatic, held their lands by military tenure, 276; of the Northern Circars, conquered by Bussy, 330; mortal feud between Bobili and Vizianagram, 330–1.

Pollock, General Sir George, commands the force for the relief of General Sale at Jellalabad, 641; victorious march through the Khaiber Pass, 642; negotiates with Akbar Khan for the liberation of the prisoners in Kabul, 643; incensed at the orders to retreat, *ib.*; defeats Akbar Khan at Tezeen, 644; return of the avenging army to India, 645.

Pondicherry, a hundred miles to the south of Madras, French settlement at, 274; Dupleix, the governor, persuades the Nawab of the Carnatic to prohibit the English from all hostilities, 285; insists on keeping possession of Madras, 286; unsuccessful siege under Admiral Boscawen, 287; meeting at, between Dupleix, Chunder Sahib, and Muzaffir Jung, 290; reverses, 293; rejoicings at the death of Nasir Jung, 295; treaty of 1775 at Pondicherry, 305; arrival of a French force in 1758 under Count de Lally, 332; rejoicings of the French at the retreat of Lally from Madras, 334; siege and capture of Pondicherry by Colonel Eyre Coote, 335; restored to the French under the treaty of Paris, 361 *note*; recaptured by the English, 429; third English occupation, 461.

Poona, old Mahratta fortress of, 200; description of, 384; becomes the capital of the Mahratta Peishwas, 387; plundered by Nizam Ali and the Bhonsla, 395; revolution against Rughonath Rao, 419; Bombay expedition to, frustrated by another revolution, 422; plundered by Daulat Rao Sindia, 464; cruelties of Baji Rao Peishwa, 498; defeat of Baji Rao by Jaswant Rao Holkar, 499; flight of Baji Rao to Bassein, *ib.*; restored to Poona by the English, *ib.*; treaty of, between Mr. Elphinstone and Baji Rao, 554; final extinction of the Peishwas, 569.

Port Blair, assassination of Lord Mayo at, 774.

Porto Novo, victory of Sir Eyre Coote against Hyder Ali, 433.

Portuguese, early appearance off the coast of Malabar, 124; fleet under Vasco de Gama, 126; audience with the Zamorin of Calicut, 127; worship the goddess Mariamma by mistake for the Virgin Mary, *ib.*; expedition under Alvarez Cabral, 128; violent proceedings, *ib.*; massacre of Portuguese by the Nairs, 129; cannonade Calicut, *ib.*; treaty with the Raja of Cochin, *ib.*; hostilities and atrocities committed on Muhammadan ships, *ib.*; anger of the Sultan of Egypt, *ib.*; foundation of Goa and Malacca by Alfonso de Albuquerque, 130; build forts impregnable to native powers, *ib.*; mission to Bengal, 131; repel the Turks at Diu, *ib.*; conquered like Christians but triumphed like Pagans, 132; description of Goa, *ib.*; social life, 133; wealth, 134; government, civil and ecclesiastical, 134–5; visit of Della Valle, 135; pepper dealings with Venk-tapa, Raja of Kanara, 137; mission to Ikkeri, 138; typical Portuguese fort at Onore, *ib.*; court of Ikkeri, 139; embassy to the Zamorin of Calicut, 144; hostility toward the early English traders, 173–4; settlement at Hughli captured hy Shah Jehan, 186; doom of the inhabitants, *ib.*; adventurers in Burma, 579–85.

Porus the elder, suzerain of the Punjab, 64; defeated by Alexander, 65; murdered by Eudemos, 67.

Porus the younger, vassal of Porus the elder, 64; flies at the approach of Alexander, 65.

Pottinger, Lieutenant, his gallant conduct at the siege of Herat, 634.

Prayaga, the modern Allahabad, sacred ground, 49; Rama entertained there, *ib.*; the field of happiness, 75.

Prithi Narain, Maharaja of Nipal, the Ghorka hero, 534; his bloodthirsty atrocities, *ib.*; his death, 535.

Prome, conquered by Byeen-noung, 586; British advance to, 596; captured by the English, 697.

Ptolemy, mention of Plithana and Tagara, 124–5 *note*.

Pulicat, Dutch settlement at, 274; captured by Lord Macartney, 437 *note*.

Punakha, the capital of Bhutan, 764.

Punchayet, or jury of five, 671; govern the Sikh army of the Khalsa, 676.

Punjab, invaded by Alexander, 64; distributed among Rajas, *ib.*; flourishing state in time of Alexander, 66; Tartar and Moghul invasions of, 110–11; Sikh revolt in, 242; temporary supremacy of the Mahrattas, 391; Mahrattas driven out by Afghans, 392; conquered by Ahmad Shah Durani, 624; revolts against Zeman Shah, 626; its pacification, *ib.*; a political volcano after the death of Runjeet Singh, 649; rise of the Sikh commonwealth (*see* Sikhs), 671; career of Runjeet Singh, 673; history of his successors, 675; dangerous power of the Sikh army of the Khalsa, 676; history of the first Sikh war under Lord Hardinge, 679; settlement of the government, 683; rebellion of Mulraj at Multan, 685; second Sikh war, 688; British administration, 692; contrasted with native administration, 693; military defence of the frontier, *ib.*; its possession the salvation of the empire during the sepoy mutinies, 743.

Purdhans, or ministers in the Mahratta constitution, 387.

Purnea, the Brahman Dewan of Tippu of Mysore, 478; proposed conversion to Islam, *ib.*; his administration in Mysore, 479; its character, 614; aspires to be a Peishwa, *ib.*; his death, *ib.*

Purundhur, treaty at, with the council of regency at Poona, 421; condemned by the Court of Directors, *ib.*

Pusput Nath, the great temple at Khatmandu, 660–1.

R

RAJAS of Malabar, the twelve, 125; sacred in battle, 147.
Rajagriha, or Giri-vraja, the capital of Magadha, 62 *note*.
Raja Ram, his claims to succeed Sahu Rao as Raja of Satara, 269; supported by Tara Bai, 385; deserted and imprisoned by Tara Bai, 388; his subsequent life as a state prisoner, 389, 393.
Rajasthan. *See* Rajputana.
Rajasuya, or royal sacrifice, celebrated by the Pandavas, 26.
Rajas, Rajput, 164 *note*.
Rajmahal, hill-ranges of, inhabited by the Santals, 711.
Rajputana, funereal pomp in the exile of princes, 48; founded by Rajputs, 100; invasion of, by Ala-ud-din, 105; wars of Akbar, 161; of Aurangzeb, 213; Moghul retreat from, 215; Hindu revolt in, 242; quarrels between Jodhpur and Jaipur, 524–5; shattered condition of, 602; distractions in, 607.
Rajputs, claim to be Kshatriyas, 23 *note*; defeat the Indo-Scythians, 72; descended from Surya or the sun, 81; league against the Turks, 95–6; defeated by Mahmud at Peshawar, 96; afterward at Somnath, 97; perform the Johur, or solemn self-sacrifice, at Chitor, 105; divided into children of the sun and children of the moon, *ib. note*; defeated by Baber, 154.
Rajput political system, league of princes under the suzerainty of Chitor cemented by intermarriages, 160; policy of Akbar, 161; incorporation of the Rajput league with the Moghul empire, 162; growing antagonism between Rajputs and Muhammadans during the reigns of Jehangir and Shah Jehan, 184, 188; climax in the reign of Aurangzeb, 212–15.
Rakshasas, a term of reproach applied to the aborigines of India, 14 *note*; represented as Asuras, demons and cannibals to the south and east of Allahabad, 20; inhabit Magadha, the modern Behar, *ib. note*; connection with Buddhism, 21 *note*; persecute the Brahmans at Chitra-kuta, 55; wars with Rama, *ib.*; pictures of Rakshasas, 55–6; identified with Buddhists, 56, 60.
Rama, approximate date of, 42 *note*; the son of Dasaratha, by Kausalya, 43; marries Sita, *ib.*; preparation for his instalment as Yuvaraja, *ib.*; appears as the champion of the Brahmans, *ib. note*; condemned to exile, 46; his obedience to his father, *ib.*; historical significance of the story of his exile, 47; contradictions in the story, *ib.*; a political exile, not a religious devotee, 48; difference between his exile and that of Drona, 48 *note*; journeys to Sringavera, *ib.*; meeting with Bharata, 54; performs the Sraddha, *ib.*; refuses the Raj, *ib.*; wars with the Rakshasas, 55–6; represented as an incarnation of Vishnu, 56; prepares for war against Ravana, *ib.*; helps Sugriva against Bali, whom he slays, 57; helped by Hanuman, the hero of the monkeys, *ib.*; his miraculous bridge built by monkeys, 58 *note*; slays Ravana, *ib.*; triumphant return to Ayodhya, 59; performs the Aswamedha, *ib.*; his cruelty to Sita, *ib.*; discovery of Sita and her two sons, 59; reconciliation, 60; wild distortion of his character in order to serve a religious purpose, *ib.*; an incarnation of Vishnu, 81.
Ramanand, a disciple of Ramanuja Acharya, 475 *note*; his teaching, *ib.*
Ramanuja Acharya, the apostle of the Vaishnavas and A'ayngars, 475 and *note*.
Ramayana reveals a higher stage of civilization than the Maha Bharata, 42; its conclusion, a religious parable, 56; religious significance of, 59–60.

Ramisseram, the modern Manaar, its association with Rama's miraculous bridge, 58 *note*; procession to, 223.
Ramnad, estate of, granted to the ancestors of the great Marawar for the protection of the pilgrims to Ramisseram, 486 *note*.
Ramnuggur, Gough's indecisive action at, 688.
Rampoora, captured by the English, 509; restored to Jaswant Rao Holkar, 518.
Ram Rai, son of Timma the minister, becomes Maharaja of Vijayanagar, 119; his pride and insolence, *ib.*; dethroned by the revolt of Termal Rai, *ib.*; deceives Termal Rai by pretended submission, 120; recovers the throne, 121; alliance with the Muhammadan Sultans of Bijapur and Golkonda, *ib.*; sacrilege of his Hindu soldiery in Muhammadan territory, *ib.*; defeated and slain in the decisive battle of Talikota, 122; breaking up of the empire, 123.
Ram Raja. *See* Raja Ram.
Ram Shastri and Mahdu Rao, story of, 398; the upright Brahman, *ib.*; investigates the murder of Narain Rao, 418; retires from Poona, 419.
Rangoon, maritime capital of Burma, founded by Alompra, 590; British expedition to, 594; repulse of Bundula, 595; advance of Tharawadi, 655; casting of the big bell, *ib.*; petty oppressions of European and American strangers, 656; oppression of British merchants, 695; captured by British troops, 697; visit of Lord Mayo, 773.
Rani, or queen, 11; influence over a Raja, *ib.*
Ranjit Singh, the Jat, 401. *See* also Runjeet Singh.
Ranuji Sindia, dynasty of, 385; menial duty performed by, 402; rise to rank and wealth, *ib.* *See* Sindia.
Ravana, Raja of Rakshasas, 56; oppressor of the gods, *ib.*; carries off Sita, *ib.*; slain by Rama, 58.
Rawlinson, Sir H., at Kandahar, 635; the question of retreat or advance, 643–4; his opinion of the gates of Somnath, 644 *note*.
Raymond, the French general in the service of Nizam Ali, 462; his conduct at the battle of Kurdla, 463.
Reed, General, Commander-in-chief in 1857, his resignation, 742 *note*.
Reinhardt, *alias* Somers, Sombre, and Sumru, 352–3.
Ripon, Lord, Viceroy of India, 777.
Rituparna, Raja of Ayodhya, 42 *note*.
Roads of the Moghul empire, 220–1.
Roe, Sir Thomas, his embassy from James the First to the Great Moghul, 175; landing at Surat, *ib.*; visit to Parwiz at Burhanpur, 176; journey to Ajmir, 177; visit to Chitor, *ib.*; meeting with Coryat, *ib.*; audience with Jehangir, *ib.*; failure of mission, 178; Moghul festivals, 179; warnings to the Company, 180.
Rohilkund, Lord Clyde's campaign in, 752.
Rohilla Afghans, political situation of, 409–10; negotiations of Warren Hastings with the Nawab Vizier of Oude, 410; Rohillas defeated by the English, 411; unfortunate association of the English in the Rohilla war, 412; condemnation of the war by Clavering, Monson, and Francis, 413; charges against Warren Hastings, 441.
Rose, Sir Hugh, his brilliant campaign in Central India, 752–3; defeats Tantia Topi, 754; his energeric action in the Sitana campaign, 761.
Rughoji Bhonsla, Raja of Berar, 384; family of, 419 *note*; his help implored by Baji Rao, 500; his stupefaction at the treaty of Bassein, *ib.*; his coalition with Daulat Rao Sindia, 501–3; defeated at Assaye and Argaum, 504; sues for peace, *ib.*; becomes a feudatory of the British government, 505–6; demands the restoration of Cuttack and Berar, 519; his death, 563. *See also* Bhonsla.

Rughonath Pundit, leader of the moderate party at Khatmandu, 659; made prime minister, *ib.*; his retirement, 661.

Rughonath Rao, afterward sixth Peishwa, commander of the Mahratta army, 390; supports Ghazi-ud-din at Delhi, 391; advance to Lahore, *ib.*; driven out of the Punjab by the Afghans, 392; quarrels with Mahdu Rao, 394; violet conduct of, *ib.*; plunders Berar and Hyderabad, 395; secret correspondence with Janoji Bhonsla, *ib.*; treacherous slaughter of half the Nizam's army, 396; reconciliation with Nizam Ali, *ib.*; fresh quarrels with Mahdu Rao, 397; imprisonment, *ib.*; opposes Mahadaji Sindia, 403; release of, 417; supported by Sakaram Bapu, 417–18; second imprisonment, 418; murder of Narain Rao, *ib.*; implication, *ib.*; sixth Peishwa, 418–19 and *note*; befooled by Nizam Ali, 419; the revolution at Poona, *ib.*; applies for help to Bombay, 420; treaty with the English at Surat, *ib.*; intrigues and proceedings for his restoration to Poona, 421–3; throws himself on the protection of Sindia, 423; set aside and pensioned under the treaty of Salbai, 436.

Rumbold, Sir Thomas, governor of Madras, 428; refuses to recall the expedition to Mahe, 429; sends Swartz on a mission of peace to Hyder Ali, *ib.*; dealings with Basalut Jung respecting Guntoor, 430; inopportune demands upon Nizam Ali, *ib.*; return to England, 431.

Run Bahadur, Maharaja of Nipal, grandson of Prithi Narain, 535; overthrows his regent uncle, 537; the Nero of Nipal, *ib.*; his madness, 538; feigned abdication, *ib.*; flight to Benares, 539; his dealings with the English, 539–40; pledges himself to become a Swami, 540; his return to Nipal, 541; his murder, 542.

Runjeet Singh, rise of, 522; aggressions on the Cis-Sutlej states, 523; mission of Charles Metcalfe, *ib.*; cajoled by Zeman Shah, 626; occupies Peshawar, 632; refuses to allow the English army to pass through the Punjab, 635; his administration of the Punjab, 693.

Russian aggression in Persia and Georgia, 496 and *note*; extension of power and influence in Central Asia, 618; advances toward the Usbegs, 619; designs on Herat, 632; expedition to Khiva, 635–6; advances in Central Asia, 767; dealings with Sher Ali, 775.

S

SAADUT ALI KHAN, Subahdar of Oude, 255; a Persian Shiah, 256; drives back the Mahrattas, 260; joins the Moghul imperial army, *ib.*; growing power, 261; rivalry with Nizam-ul-mulk, 263; reported secret correspondence with Nadir Shah, *ib.*; captured at Kurnal, 264; treachery, *ib.*; suicide, 265.

Saadut Ali, enthroned by Sir John Shore as Nawab Vizier of Oude, 466; hoarding of money, *ib.*

Sadras, Dutch settlement at, 274; captured by Lord Macartney, 437 *note*.

Sahu Rao, Maharaja of the Mahrattas, 243; vassal of the Moghul, *ib.*; his effeminate training, 244; death of, 269, 287, 385; his imbecility, *ib.*

Saiyids, the two, conspire for the elevation of Farrukh Siyar to the throne of Delhi, 246; successful rebellion, *ib.*; hostile intrigues of Farrukh Siyar, 247; their supremacy at Delhi, 251; their fall, *ib.*; their jealousy of Nizam-ul-mulk, 257.

Saka, era of, 72.

Sakaram Bapu, supports Rughonath Rao at Poona, 417–18; intrigues for the return of Rughonath Rao, 421; ultimate fate of, 422.

Sakuni, brother of Gandhari and uncle of the Kauravas, 26; a gambler, the thrower of false dice, *ib.*; throws the dice for Duryodhana, *ib.*; reappears in the Ganges, 41.
Sakuntala, the drama of, written by Kalidasa, 88; marriage of a Raja with a Brahman's daughter, 89; supernatural incidents, *ib.*; characteristics, *ib.*
Sakya Muni, or Gotama Buddha, 61; his parentage and domestic circumstances, *ib.*; his vision, *ib.*; old age, disease, and death, *ib.*; his era, *ib. note*; sees the religious mendicant, *ib.*; becomes a mendicant, a recluse, and a Buddha, 62; his teaching, *ib.*
Salabut Jung, Nizam of Hyderabad, 296; cedes the Northern Circars to the French, 303; rupture with Bussy, 306: implores the help of the English, *ib.*; critical position in the Dekhan, 334; dethroned and confined, *ib.*; subsequent fate, *ib. note.*
Salbai, the treaty of, 436; Mahadaji Sindia's attempted violation of, 446.
Sale, General Sir Robert, at Jellalabad, 639; relieved by Pollock, 641.
Salivahana, era of, 72.
Salkeld, Lieutenant, at the siege of Delhi, 746.
Salsette, island of, coveted by the English, 399; ceded to Bombay by Rughonath Rao, 420; and by the Mahratta council of regency, 421; retained by Bombay in accordance with the treaty of Salbai, 436.
Sambhaji the First, son of Sivaji, 217; betrayed to Aurangzeb, *ib.*; succeeds to the kingdom of Konkan, 234 *note.*
Sambhaji the Second, Raja of Kolhapore, 384 *note.*
Sandrokottos, drives Eudemos out of Taxila, 67; identified with Chandragupta, *ib.*; his adventures, *ib.*; ascends the throne of Magadha and drives the Greeks out of India, *ib.*; alliance with Seleukos, *ib.*; marriage with the daughter of Seleukos, *ib.*; his palace, 69; bodyguard of Tartar women, 194 *note.*
Sangermano, Father, authentic details of the atrocities of Bhodau Phra in Burma, 590.
Sanjaya, minister and charioteer, his mission to the Pandavas, 82; his position, *ib. note*; failure of the mission, 83.
Sankhara Acharya, the apostle of the Smartals, 474 and *note.*
Santals, revolt of, 771; suppression, *ib.*
Santanu, Maharaji of Hastinapur, 12; claimed descent from Bharata, *ib.*; marriage with a young damsel, *ib.*; the dreadful vow of his son Bhishma, 14.
Sarfaraz Khan, son of Shuja Khan, 309–10; favorite grandson of Murshed Kuli Khan, 310; outwitted by his father, *ib.*; succeeds to the throne of Murshedabad, 312; insolent tyranny, *ib.*; insults the family of Jagat Seth, *ib.*; destruction, *ib.*
Saraswati, goddess of learning and mythical wife of Brahma, 82; conception and worship of, 83; identified with the Indus river, *ib. note.*
Sarayu, river, the modern Gogra, 42, 48 *note.*
Satara, the capital of Sahu, the grandson of Sivaji, 384; Tara Bai's intrigues at, 388; invested by Balaji Rao's troops, 389; the pageant Raja of, brought to Baji Rao's camp, 567; his proposed elevation by the British government, 569; territory assigned for his support, 570; partially resuscitated, 702; his extravagant pretensions, 702–3; dethroned, 703; adoption refused to his successor, *ib.*; lapse of the Raj, *ib.*
Sati, or Suttee, absence of, in the war of the Maha Bharata, 36 *note.*
Satrughna, third son of Dasaratha, 43.
Sawant Waree, 384 *note.*

Saymbrumbaukum, the great water-tank of, 473.
Scythians, the Royal, 151 *note*; probably the Moghuls, 151.
Seedees or Sidis of Jinjeera and Surat, 383 and *note*.
Segowlie, the treaty of, 548.
Seistan, Sher Ali's grievances respecting, 775.
Seleukos, alliance with Sandrokottos, 67; marriage of his daughter, *ib.*
Selim, Prince, son of Akbar. *See* Jehangir.
Selimghur, the state prison at Delhi, 251, 744.
Serais, 221.
Serfoji, adopted son of the Raja of Tanjore, his claims to the throne of, 487–8; imprisoned by Amar Singh, 488; suspected bribery of Madras pundits, *ib.*; a cipher Raja, *ib.*
Seringapatam, Hyder Ali's life at, 436; captured by Cornwallis, 457; stormed by General Harris, 471.
Serpent-worship, among the Manaris, 225.
Sethipati, title of, granted to the ancestors of the great Marawar, 486 *note*.
Shah Abbas the Second, of Persia, threatens Aurangzeb, 204.
Shah Alam, eldest son of Aurangzeb, 207; commander of the Muhammadan army against Sivaji, *ib.*; the sham rebellion, 207–8; takes a part in the war in Rajputana, 214; struggles with Azam Shah, 241; ascends the throne under the name of Bahadur Shah, *ib.*; relations with Madras, *ib.*; reign, 242; operations against the Sikhs, 243; death, *ib.*
Shah Alam, eldest son of Ahmad Shah, and known as the Shahzada, 327; threatens Bengal, *ib.*; Clive's dealings with, 329; proclaimed Padishah under the name of Shah Alam, 340; threatens Patna, *ib.*; defeated by Mir Kasim, 342; negotiations with Carnac, *ib.*; installation at Patna, *ib.*; letters of investiture, 343; secret negotiations with Vansittart, 344; accompanies Shuja-ud-daula into Behar, 353; joins the English, 354; converted by Clive into an imperial idol for the resuscitation of the Moghul empire, 361; dealings with Clive at Allahabad, 362; becomes a puppet Padishah, 366; his firman to Clive, *ib.*; the second firman, 369; dealings with Hyder Ali, *ib. note*; throws himself into the hands of the Mahrattas and returns to Delhi, 370; Mahadaji Sindia's ambitious designs on, 403; political results of his flight from Allahabad to Delhi, 406; severance of all political ties with the English, *ib.*; forfeiture of his claim to tribute, 408; weak dependence on the Amir of Amirs, 444; invites Mahadaji Sindia to Delhi, 445; disavows Sindia's demands for chout, 446; a state prisoner at Muttra, 448; interviews with Mr. Charles Malet, *ib.*; his fallen state, *ib.*; leaves Muttra for Delhi, 451; blinded by Gholam Kadir, 452; taken by General Lake under the protection of the British government, 504.
Shah Jehan, son of Jehangir, reported intrigues against his elder brother, Khuzru, 180; his character, *ib.*; aspirations for the throne, 182; takes charge of Khuzru, 183; implicated in the murder of his brother, *ib.*; excites the wrath of Jehangir, *ib.*; plots with Asof Khan for seizing the imperial treasures at Agra, *ib.*; sack of Agra, 184; defeat at Delhi, *ib.*; ravages in Bengal, *ib.*; flight to the south, *ib.*; sham death and burial, 185; proclaimed Padishah, *ib.*; sends an embassy to Persia to demand Bulaki, 186; obscurity of his reign, *ib.*; his love of flattery, *ib.*; spite against the Portuguese, *ib.*; wreaks his vengeance on Hughli, *ib.*; builds the new city of Jehanabad, near old Delhi, 188; builds the Taj Mahal, *ib.*; zenana influences, 189–90; his four sons, 190; his rumored death, 191; his captivity at

Agra, 194; imprisoned for life by his son Aurangzeb, 195; his mysterious death, 204.

Shah Shuja, Amir of Afghanistan, his reception of Elphinstone's mission at Peshawar, 523 *note*; previously appointed governor of Peshawar by Zeman Shah, 626; supplants his brother Mahmud on the throne of Kabul, 629; driven out by Mahmud and the Barukzais, *ib.*; becomes a pensioner of the British government at Ludhiana, *ib.*; refuses to be a puppet king in the hands of the Barukzais, 631; supplanted on the throne of Kabul by Dost Muhammad, 632; British government dethrone the Dost and restore Shah Shuja to Kabul, 634–5; his unpopular rule, 637; monopolizes the Bala Hissar, 638; his perilous position, 642; murdered by the Barukzais, *ib.*

Shahs of Persia, their rule, 261.

Shahryar, youngest son of Jehangir, 182; intrigues of Nur Mahal, *ib.*; his expedition to Persia, 183; captured and blinded, 185.

Shahzada, his claims to Bengal, Behar, and Orissa, 327; flight from Delhi, 329; correspondence with Clive, *ib.*; defeat and flight, *ib.*; generosity of Clive, *ib.*; becomes Padishah. *See* Shah Alam.

Shaista Khan, uncle of Aurangzeb, appointed Viceroy of the Dekhan, 202; captures Poona, *ib.*; attacked by Sivaji, *ib.*; his suspicions of Jaswant Singh, *ib.*

Shastri, Head, his importance in the Mahratta constitution, 387 and *note*.

Shelton, Brigadier, in Afghanistan, 638; fails to enter Kabul, 639.

Sher Khan the Afghan, 155; gulls Humayun, *ib.*; defeats Humayun, 156; his rule in Hindustan, *ib.*

Sher Ali Khan, Amir of Afghanistan, Jewish features of, 149 *note*; his rivalry with Afzal Khan, 768; his recognition by the British government, *ib.*; treacherous imprisonment of Afzal Khan, *ib.*; madness at the murder of his first-born, 769; flight to Kandahar, *ib.*; recognized by Sir John Lawrence as ruler of Kandahar, *ib.*; his futile effort to recover his throne, 770; flight to Herat, *ib.*; his sudden restoration to the throne at Kabul, *ib.*; dealings with Sir John Lawrence, 771; conference at Umballa with Lord Mayo, 772; his grievances, *ib.*; estrangement, 775; dealings with Russia, *ib.*; war with England, *ib.*; death, *ib.*

Sher Singh, reputed son of Runjeet Singh, becomes Maharaja of Lahore, 676; begs English help against the army of the Khalsa, 677; his violent death, *ib.*

Sher Singh, an influential Sikh Sidar, sent to co-operate with Edwardes against Mulraj at Multan, 687; deserts the English, *ib.*; his cold reception by Mulraj, 688; goes to Lahore, *ib.*; doubtful battle of Chilianwallah, 688–9; the final defeat at Guzerat, 689.

Shiahs, antagonism with Sunnis, 190; their tenets, 190–1; in Persia, 261.

Shitab Rai, rise of, 355; his proceedings in Oude, 356; negotiations between the Nawab Vizier, Shuja-ud-daula, and the English, *ib.*; becomes deputy Nawab at Patna, 360, 371, 374; alarm at the coming of Mr. George Vansittart, 376; artful behavior, 377; failings, 377–8; origin and rise, 378–9; labors to alleviate the famine in Bengal, 381; charges against, 405; acquittal, *ib.*; death, *ib.*; Mill's acceptance of the acquittal, *ib. note*.

Shore, Sir John (Lord Teignmouth), works out the permanent land settlement, 450; Governor-General, 461; his capacity, *ib.*; refuses to help Nizam Ali against the Mahrattas, *ib.*; his weakness, 465; turns attention to Oude, *ib.*; embarks for Europe, 466; return to the policy of, 516; gives up Burmese political refugees, 593.

Showers, Brigadier, pursuit of the rebels by, 748.

Shuja, son of Shah Jehan, 190; Viceroy of Bengal, *ib.*; a Shiah, *ib.*; defeated by Sulaiman and Jai Singh, 192; by Amir Jumla, 195; flight to Arakan, *ib.*; his alleged death, *ib.*; supposed reappearance in Afghanistan, 210.

Shuja Khan, profligate son-in-law of Murshed Kuli Khan, 809–10; outwits his son at Murshedabad, 810; easy reign, *ib.*; death, 812.

Shuja-ud-daula, Nawab Vizier of Oude, son and successor of Sufdar Jung, 327 *note*; harbors the Shahzada, 329; his ambitious views, *ib.*; schemes to secure the Bengal provinces, 353; repulsed at Patna, *ib.*; further schemes and return to Oude, 353–4; defeated at Buxar by Hector Munro, 354; flight to the Rohilla country, *ib.*; negotiations with the English, 355; final defeat and surrender, 356; the restoration of Oude to, 361–2; converted by Lord Clive into an ally of the English, 364; threatened by the Mahrattas, 409; claims against the Rohillas, *ib.*; applies for an English brigade, 410; negotiations with Warren Hastings at Benares, *ib.*; his cowardice and cruelty in the Rohilla war, 411; treaty with Faiz-ullah Khan, the Rohilla, 412; his death, 414; his apparent bribe of ten lakhs to Warren Hastings, 442 *note*.

Siah Koh, mountains of Afghanistan, 620 and *note*.

Siam, invaded by the king of Burma, 586.

Sikhs, foundation of a brotherhood, 242; religious tenets, *ib.*; vengeance against persecution, 243; operations of Bahadur Shah, *ib.*; defeat and wholesale executions, 250; invasion of Hindustan, 669; dangerous power of the army of the Khalsa, 676; invade British territory, 678; cross the Sutlej in force, 679; treacherous generals, *ib.*; defeated at Moodkee, 680; ousted from Ferozeshahar, *ib.*; flight to the Sutlej, *ib.*; hostilities renewed, *ib.*; defeated at Aliwal, 681; defeated at Sobraon, 681–2; close of the first war with England, 682; growing disaffection, 685; general outbreak, 687; joined by Afghans, 688; fight the battle of Chilianwallah, 688–9; defeated at Guzerat, 689. *See* Punjab *and* Runjeet Singh.

Sikri, defeat of Rajputs by Baber, 154.

Siladitya, empire of, 74; "Maharaja Adhiraj," *ib.*; his tolerance in religion, *ib.*; the field of happiness at Prayaga, 75; imperial almsgiving, *ib.*

Simla, built on territory ceded by Nipal, 548.

Sinde, Arab invasion of, 95; conquered by Ahmad Shah Durani, 624; its history previous to the English conquest, 647; cause and conduct of the war, *ib.*; conquest of, by Sir Charles Napier, *ib.*; annexation, *ib.*

Sindias of Gwalior, rise of the family, 258, 384.

Sindia, Ranuji, founder of the family, originally keeper of the Peishwa's slippers, 402.

Sindia, Mahadaji, an illegitimate son of Ranuji, his rise to power, 402; conducts Shah Alam from Allahabad to Delhi, 403; places him on the throne of Delhi, 406; calls on the English to pay tribute for Bengal, 408; refused, *ib.*; interferes in Poona affairs, 421; capture of Gwalior by Captain Popham, 424; negotiates the treaty of Salbai, 436; rewarded with the cession of English conquests in Guzerat, *ib.*; guarantee for the treaty of Salbai, 444; his designs on Delhi and Poona, *ib.*; invited to Delhi, 445; murder of Afrasiab, 445 and *note*; founds a new Mahratta kingdom in the Doab, 446; his French battalions under De Boigne, *ib.*; demands chout for Bengal and Behar, *ib.*; rebuffed by the English, *ib.*; hurt by the appointment of a Resident at Poona, *ib.*; compelled to retreat from Muttra to Gwalior, 451;

refuses to join Cornwallis against Tippu, 455; his commanding position, 458; installation of the Peishwa at Poona as deputy of the Great Moghul, 459; persists in holding the Peishwa's slippers, *ib.*; mock humility, *ib.*; his demands on the Peishwa, *ib.*; counter demands of Nana Farnavese, 460; his death, *ib.*

Sindia, Daulat Rao, succeeds Mahadaji Sindia as Maharaja of Gwalior, 460; his intrigues with Baji Rao Peishwa, 464; plunders Poona, 465; narrow escape from assassination, *ib.*; prevents Baji Rao from forming an alliance with Lord Wellesley, 468; stubbornly resists all overtures from the English to join in the defence of India against the Afghans under Zeman Shah, 494; helps Baji Rao against Holkar, 499; decisive defeat of the united armies at Poona, *ib.*; stupefied at the treaty of Bassein, 500; forms a junction with the Bhonsla Raja of Berar, *ib.*; fails to induce Jaswant Rao Holkar to join them, 501; excites the alarm of Lord Wellesley by his French battalions, *ib.*; vacillating dealings with Colonel Arthur Wellesley, 503; defeated at Assaye, *ib.*; at Argaum, 504; negotiations with Wellesley and Malcolm, 505 *note*; story of his minister, "Old Brag," *ib.*; offers to co-operate with the English against Jaswant Rao Holkar, 509; treachery of his officers, 510; declares for Jaswant Rao Holkar, 511; brought to his senses, *ib.*; difficulty with his overgrown army, 520; ravages Udaipur, 525; entertains Pindharies, 527; dreaded by the Court of Directors, 529; his evasive attitude, 555; outwitted by Lord Hastings, 556; ultimatum of the British government, 556–7; unlucky discovery of his treacherous negotiations with Nipal, 557; concludes a new treaty with the British government, *ib.*; dies without heirs, 605.

Sindia, Jankoji Rao, adopted by Baiza Bai, the widow of Daulat Rao, 606; Baiza Bai bent on being queen regent for life, *ib.*; civil war, *ib.*; Lord William Bentinck refuses to interfere, *ib.*; recognition of Jankoji Rao by the British government, *ib.*; settlement of Gwalior affairs, *ib.*; weak and distracted government, 648–9; overgrown army, 649; dies without heirs, 650.

Sindia, Jyaji Rao, adopted by Tara Bai, the widow of Jankoji Rao, 649–50; disputes about the regency, 650; Lord Ellenborough outwitted by Tara Bai, *ib.*; defeat of the army of Gwalior at Maharajpore and Punniar, 651; settlement of Gwalior affairs, *ib.*; loyalty of Jyaji Rao during the sepoy mutiny, 741.

Singhs, the Sikh lion-warriors of Guru Govind, 671.

Sirdars, the Afghan, in the service of Nadir Shah, 623; leave the Persian army and return to Kandahar, *ib.*; elect Ahmad Abdali to be their Shah, *ib.*; prosperity under Ahmad Shah Durani, 624; starved and imprisoned by Payendah Shah, 625–6; the leaders of the Sikh Misls, 672; Puritan and Pindhari types of, 672–3. *See also* Timur Shah *and* Zeman Shah.

Sita, wife of Rama, 43; accompanies Rama on his exile, 47; worships the Ganges, 49; worships the Jumna, *ib.*; her abduction by Ravana, 56; her ordeal of purity, 58–9; cruelly abandoned by Rama, 59; residence at Chitra-kuta, *ib.*; her two sons, *ib.*; reconciliation with Rama, 60.

Sitabuldi, battle of, 565.

Sitana, the villages of, 758–9; inhabited by Hindu fanatics, 759; the British campaign under Sir Neville Chamberlain, 759–61.

Siva, or Mahadeva, his place in the religion of the Turanians, 78; in modern Hindu belief, 82; resolved by the Brahmans into the Supreme Being, 84; idol pillar of, at Somnath, 96; destroyed by

Mahmud, 97; worship of at Conjeveram, 474; worshipped by the Smartals, 475; and by the Maduals, 476; abhorred by the Vaishnavas and A'ayngars, 475.
Sivaganga Raja, or little Marawar, 486 *note*; feud with the Tondiman, *ib.*
Sivaji the Mahratta, his appearance as a rebel and a freebooter in the mountains of the Konkan, 199; his early career in the neighborhood of Poona, 200; Rajput origin, *ib.*; a worshipper of Siva and Bhowani, *ib.*; reverence for Brahmans, *ib.*; genius for creating an army, 201; exploit with the tiger's claws, 201–2; alliance with Aurangzeb, 202; compromise with Bijapur, *ib.*; aggressions on the Moghuls, *ib.*; night attack on Shaista Khan, 203; capture and plunder of Surat, 203–4; calls Surat his treasury, 204; scheme of Aurangzeb for entrapping the mountain rat, 205; Sivaji flattered and duped, *ib.*; audience with Aurangzeb at Delhi, 206; wrath at his reception, *ib.*; strange escape from Delhi, 207; attacked by a force of Moghuls and Rajputs under Shah Alam, *ib.*; a sham rebellion, *ib.*; wariness of Sivaji, 208; organizes a system of blackmail, or chout, 211; installed as Maharaja of the Konkan, *ib.*; conquests in the Lower Carnatic, *ib.*; his death, *ib.*
Slave-kings, Afghan dynasty of, 100–1.
Sleeman, Colonel, his report on Oude, 709.
Smartal Brahmans, the sect of, 474; creed and distinctions, 475; non-practice of the Chakrantikam, 481 *note*.
Smith, General, commanding the Poona Subsidiary Force, 562; his appearance at Poona, 563; sets out in pursuit of Baji Rao, *ib.*; defeats the army of Baji Rao at Ashti, 568.
Smith, Sir Harry, defeats the Sikhs at Aliwal, 681.
Smith, Colonel Baird, Chief Engineer at the siege of Delhi, 748 *note*.
Sobraon, the battle of, 681–2.
Somnath, 96; the great temple at, *ib.*; battle of, 97; recovery of the sandalwood gates captured by Mahmud, 644.
Spencer, Mr., succeeds Vansittart as governor at Calcutta, 356; his corrupt bargaining with Muhammad Reza Khan respecting the succession of the Nawabship of Bengal and Behar, *ib. note*, and 357; Clive's anger at, 360.
Sraddha, performed by Bharata, 52; description of, *ib. note*.
Sringavera, the modern Sungroor, etc., 48; the Aryan barrier, *ib.*
Staunton, Captain, his brilliant defence of Korygaum, 568.
Stevenson, Colonel, moves up the Hyderabad Subsidiary Force toward Poona, 500; co-operates with Colonel Wellesley against Sindia and Rughoji Bhousla, 500, 502.
St. Lubin, arrives at Poona as ambassador from the King of France, 421; attentions of Nana Farnavese, *ib.*
St. Thome, Portuguese settlement at, 229; captured by the generals of the Sultan of Golkonda, *ib.*; by the French, *ib.*
Stoddart, Colonel, his public execution at Bokhara, 646.
Subahdar, 217; the common name for Viceroy of a province, 226 *note*.
Subder Ali, son of Dost Ali, Nawab of the Carnatic, 278; outwitted by Chunder Sahib, 279; alarm at the Mahrattas, *ib.*; agreement with the Mahrattas, 280; proclaimed Nawab, 281; threatened by Nizam-ul-mulk, *ib.*; perplexity, 281–2; levies contributions for the Mahrattas, 282; assassination, *ib.*
Subhadra, the sister of Krishna, marries Arjuna, 26.
Subzi Mundi, or vegetable market, an old suburb at Delhi, 745.
Sudder, or Company's judicial courts, 413 *note*.

Sudras, or cultivators, one of the four great castes, 77; not "wearers of the thread," *ib.*; probably of Turanian origin, *ib.*; contemned by the Smartals, 475; separate quarters in towns, 476.
Sufdar Jung, Nawab of Oude. 327 *note*.
Sugriva, the monkey Raja, his alliance with Rama, 57.
Sukwar Bai, wife of Maharaja Sahu, her intrigues and vow, 385–6; cruel death by Sati, 386.
Sulaiman, mountains of, the northwest frontier adopted by Lord Dalhousie, 758.
Sulaiman, son of Dara, 192; escapes to Kashmir, 195; betrayal, *ib.*
Sumru, his massacre of the English at Patna, 352–3; his flight into Oude, 353; his surrender demanded from the Nawab Vizier, 355; subsequent career, *ib. note*.
Sumpthur, death of the Raja of, 607; civil wars, *ib.*; refusal of Lord William Bentinck to interfere, *ib.*; terrible catastrophe, *ib.*
Sunnis, their tenets, 190; antagonism with the Shiahs, *ib.*; fierce contest with Shiahs at Kabul, 628; slaughter of Kuzzilbashes, *ib.*
Supreme Courts of Judicature created at the three Presidency capitals, 412–13 and *note*.
Suraj Mal, the Jat hero, 400; his dealings with the Moghuls, 401; surrounded and slain, *ib.*
Suraj-ud-daula, grandson of Alivardi Khan, 316; evil character, *ib.*; bitterness against the English, *ib.*; succeeds his grandfather as Nawab at Murshedabad, 316–17; marches against Calcutta, 317; entry into the captured town, 318; author of the tragedy of the Black Hole, 318–19; alarm at the advance of the English, 321; vacillations, *ib.*; hostility toward the English, 322; general conspiracy against the Nawab, *ib.*; defeat at Plassy, 323; taken prisoner and murdered, 325.
Surat, appearance of English at, 173–4; landing of Sir Thomas Roe, 175; captured by Mahrattas, 203; called the treasury of Sivaji, 204; described by Dr. Fryer in the reign of Aurangzeb, 230–1; factory at, removed to Bombay, 236; successful war operations of the English against the Moghuls, *ib.*; Abyssinian admirals, or Seedees, of, 383; treaty at, between Rughonath Rao and the English at Bombay, 420.
Surya, the sun-god, Vaidik worship of, 80; ancestor of the Rajputs, 81.
Suttee, abolition of, by Lord William Bentinck, 617.
Swamis, worshipped as gods by Brahmans, 84; their ceremonies of initiation and confirmation, 480–1.
Swarga, the heaven of Indra, 41 *note*, 80.
Swartz, the missionary in Tanjore, his mission to Hyder Ali, 429; his description of Hyder Ali's palace life and administration at Seringapatam, 436–7; his description of Mahratta rule in Tanjore, 487.
Swatis, their behavior in the Sitana campaign, 760–1; interference of the Akhoond, 761.
Swayamvara, or "self-choice," an ancient marriage festival, 22; that of Draupadi, a Rajput romance, 22–3; that of Damayanti, 89–90; that of the princess of Kanouj, 98; modern relic of, 161.
Sydenham, Captain, Resident at Hyderabad, his description of the Pindharies, 528.
Symes, Colonel, his mission to Ava, 593.

T

Tagara, the modern Deoghur, 124–5 *note*.

Taj Mahal at Agra, description of, 188; built by Shah Jehan as the mausoleum of his favorite wife, 189; occupied by Mr. Malet, 448.

Talains, people of the lower Irawadi. *See* Pegu.

Talukdars of Oude, 465 and *note*; their oppressive rule in Oude, 710; harshly treated after the annexation, 712; general insurrection during the sepoy mutiny, 739.

Talikota, decisive battle of, between the Muhammadan Sultans of the Dekhan and the Hindu Raja of Vijayanagar, 121–2.

Tamil country, 107; language, *ib. note*.

Tanjore, kingdom of, south of the Koleroon, 275; Rajas of, originally Naiks or viceroys, under the Maharajas of Vijayanagar, *ib.*; water supply dependent on Trichinopoly, 278, 485; conquered by the Mahrattas in the seventeenth century, 485; English aggressions on, 287–8; hostile demands of Chunder Sahib and Muzaffir Jung, 292; delays of the Raja, *ib.*; aggressions of Nawab Muhammad Ali, 427; restored to the Raja by Lord Pigot, *ib.*; brought under British rule, 485; death of the Raja, 487; disputed succession, 487–8; Raja reduced to a pageant, 488; extinction of the dynasty, 706.

Tantia Topi, the Mahratta Brahman in the service of Nana Sahib, 741; his military genius, *ib. note*; defeats General Windham at Cawnpore, 751; routed by Sir Hugh Rose, 753; intrigues at Gwalior, *ib.*; raises a new rebel army, 753–4; defeated, 754; pursued, captured, and executed, 755; a type of the old Peishwas, *ib.*

Tantras, mystic literature of the Turanians, 79.

Tara Bai, widow of Raja Ram, her intrigues at Satara, 385 and *note*; her career, *ib.*; befooled by Balaji Rao, 386; the ordeal of Raja Ram, 387; her obstinacy, 389; general reconciliation, *ib.*; death of, 393 and *note*.

Tara Bai, widow of Jankoji Rao Sindia, 649; adopts Jyaji Rao, 650; assumes the regency, *ib.*; excites the wrath of Lord Ellenborough, *ib.*; war against the army of Gwalior, 651; the regency intrusted to a council of six nobles, *ib.*

Tartar invasions, 102; Tartars under Timur Shah, 110; ruling tribe known as the Moghuls, 151.

Tartar women, imperial bodyguard of, 194 and *note*.

Tavernier, his description of Indian travel, 221, 224.

Taxiles, his kingdom in the Punjab, 64; his submission to Alexander, *ib.*; his city of Taxila identified with Attock, 759 *note*.

Tej Singh, commander of the army of the Khalsa, 678; his treachery, 679; left to watch General Littler at Ferozepore, 680; flight from Ferozeshahar, 681; flight at Sobraon, 682.

Telinga country, situated in the eastern Dekhan, 107; conquered by Ala-ud-din, *ib.*; seat of the Telugu language, *ib. note*.

Tenasserim, province of British Burma, its position, 575 *note*; ceded to the English, 596.

Terai, the forest at the base of the lower Himalayan slopes, 532; cause of dispute in the negotiations between England and Nipal, 547–8.

Termal Rai, the mad Maharaja of Vijayanagar, 119; calls in the Muhammadans, 120; does homage to the Sultan of Bijapur, *ib.*; betrayed by Ram Rai, *ib.*; outrageous proceedings in the palace, 121; his suicide, *ib.*

Thakurs, or feudatory nobles of Rajputana, their refractory character, 602; their conflicting councils, 604; contest with Jhota Ram at Jaipur, 608.

Thapa family of Nipal. *See* Bhim Sein Thapa.
Tharawadi, brother of the king of Burma, his absurd boasting in the first Burmese war, 596; becomes king of Burma, 654; expels the British Residency, 655; his empty threats, *ib.*; his disappearance, *ib.*
Thibet, geographical position of, 531; invaded by the Ghorkas, 536; Bogle's mission to, *ib. note*; Turner's mission, *ib.*
Thugs, or stranglers, execution of, 218; male and female, 223.
Timur Mirza, Shah of Afghanistan, 624; his rebellious subjects, 625; his vengeance, *ib.*; remorse, madness, and death, *ib.*
Timur Shah, invades the Punjab and Hindustan, 110; invades India, 150.
Tippu, Sultan, son of Hyder Ali, 437; treaty with Lord Macartney, *ib.*; war with the Peishwa, 448; dangerous power of, 453; enmity against the English, *ib.*; dealings with Nizam Ali, the French and Mahrattas, *ib.*; attack on Travancore, 453–4; desolates the Carnatic, 455; bewilderment and submission to Lord Cornwallis, 457; an ally of France, 467; a hostile alliance, 468; displays open hostility, 470; refuses explanations, *ib.*; overwhelmed, *ib.*; refuses humiliation, 471; death and character, *ib.*; his palace and administration, described by Buchanan, 478; his aggressions in Coorg, 610.
Todar Mal, employed by Akbar to carry out the revenue settlement, 170.
Tod, Captain, afterward Colonel, his active interference in Rajputana, 602; his *Annals and Antiquities of Rajasthan*, *ib. note*.
Todd, Major D'Arcy, his withdrawal from Herat, 636–7; his fate, 687.
Tondiman, Poligar, helps Major Lawrence and Nawab Muhammad Ali during the siege of Trichinopoly by the French, 300; his wrath at the Nawab's dealings with the Mysore regent, 302; his feud with the Sivaganga Rajas, 486 *note*.
Tongso Penlow, or governor of eastern Bhutan, 764, 766 *note*.
Tonk, principality of, founded by Amir Khan, 524, 558.
Tonk Rampoora. *See* Rampoora.
Toungoo, its position in the interior of Burma, 579 *note*.
Toy-cart, the Sanskrit drama of, 91; story of, 91–2; unsatisfactory denouement, 93.
Travancore, Raja of, attacked by Tippu Sultan, 453–4.
Trichinopoly, kingdom of, 275; war of the succession, 278; interference of the Nawab of the Carnatic, *ib.*; treacherously seized by Chunder Sahib, 279; occupied by Muhammad Ali, 296; closely besieged by Chunder Sahib and the French, *ib.*; relieved by Clive's occupation of Arcot, 298; English triumphant, 300; importance of, as the key to the Hindu Carnatic, 301.
Trimbukji Dainglia, the minister of Baji Rao, 550; implication in the murder of Gungadhur Shastri, 552; surrendered to the English and confined, *ib.*; his romantic escape, 553; his army of rebels, *ib.*; captured and confined, 570.
Trivadi, victory of Dupleix at, 293.
Tughlakabad, capital of the Tughlak Sultans, 108.
Tughlak, Turkish governor of Punjab, 108; captures Delhi, *ib.*; founder of the dynasty of Tughlak Sultans, *ib.* *See* Muhammad Tughlak.
Tukaji Holkar. *See* Holkar.
Tulsi Bai assumes the government of Indore, 528; declares for the Peishwa, 566; barbarously murdered, 567.
Turanians, relics of, 78; their religion turning on the mysteries of life and death, *ib.*
Turkey, Sultan of, makes war on the Portuguese in India, 181–2.
Turks and Afghans, 94 *et seq.*
Turner, his mission to Thibet, 536 *note*.

U

Udaipur, or Oodeypore, foundation of, 162; Rana of, maintains his independence, 208; rejects the insolent demands of Aurangzeb, 214; quarrel between Jaipur and Jodhpur respecting the Rana's daughter, 524–5; unsuccessful appeals of the Rana for British interference, 525; murder of the princess, 526.

Udai Singh, Rana of Chitor, 162; founds Udaipur, *ib.*; his vow, *ib.*

Ujain, kingdom of, 71; scene of the Toy-cart, 91; victory of Aurangzeb at, 193.

Ulama, the collective body of Muhammadan lawyers and divines, 165; hated by Abul Fazl, 166; their authority derided and usurped by Akbar, 167.

Umballa, conference between Lord Mayo and Sher Ali at, 772.

Umbeyla Pass, position of the British army during the Sitana campaign, 759–60.

Umra Singh, prince of Jodhpur, his refractory conduct at the court of Shah Jehan, 187–8.

Umritsir, the religious centre of the Sikhs, 672.

Upadasa imparted by Gurus, 480–1 and *note.*

Upton, Colonel, sent to Poona as agent of the Bengal government, 420.

Usbegs, drive Baber out of Bokhara, 152; the foes of Persia, 262; serve in the army of Nadir Shah, 265; states of Khiva, Bokhara, and Khokand, 619; Russian advances, *ib.*

V

Vaidik hymns and Vaidik gods, 79–82; moral influence, 81.

Vaidika Brahmans, 476.

Vaishnavas, the sect of, 474, 475; their creed and distinctions, *ib.*

Vaisyas, or merchants, one of the four great castes, 25 *note.*

Vaka, a cannibal Asura slain by Bhima, 21; the story apparently an allegorical fiction, *ib. note.*

Vallabhi Rajas supplant the Guptas, 72.

Valmiki, his hermitage, 49; the mythical author of the Ramayana, 49, 59.

Vansittart, Mr., succeeds Holwell as governor of Bengal, 336, 340; vacillating proposals for a deputy Nawab, 340–1; his relations with Mir Jafir and Mir Kasim, 341; refusal of a bribe, *ib.*; the proposed advance of the English to Delhi, 343; secret negotiations, 344; the debates about private trade, 346–7; failure as an arbitrator, 346; factious opposition, 347; proposes to make terms with the Nawab, 351; returns to England, 356.

Vansittart, George, sent to overlook the native administration at Patna, 376; gulled by Raja Shitab Rai, *ib.*

Varanavata, the ancient Prayaga and modern Allahabad, 20.

Varuna, the Vaidik god of the sea, 80.

Vasco de Gama, leaves Lisbon with a fleet, 126; anchorage off Calicut, *ib.*; audience with the Zamorin, 127; fails to establish a trade in Calicut, 128; returns to Portugal, *ib.*

Vayu, Vaidik god of wind, 56; subject to Ravana, *ib.*; personification, 80.

Vellore, fortress of, twelve miles from Arcot, 279; assassination of Subder Ali at, 281–2; visited by Buchanan, 477; sepoy mutiny at, 520; cause of the mutiny, 521.

Venk-tapa Naik, Raja of Kanara, 137; receives the Portuguese ambassadors, 138; annexes the Raj of Banghel, 143.

Ventura, General, in the service of Runjeet Singh, 674.
Verelst, Mr., governor of Bengal, 367; obtains the blank firman for the government of Hyderabad from Shah Alam, 369; returns to England, 370; his experiences of native administration, 375.
Victoria, Queen, assumes the direct government of India, 756; proclaimed Empress of India at the Imperial Assemblage at Delhi, 774.
Vidarbha, residence of Nala and Damayanti, 90.
Vijayanagar, ancient Hindu empire at, associated with the worship of Vishnu, 113; same as Narsinga, *ib.*; city of, 114; Krishna Rai insulted by the Bahmani Sultan, *ib.*; marriage of the Hindu princess to a Muhammadan Sultan, 117; atrocities at the court, 118; rebellion of Termal, 119; recovery of the throne by Ram Rai, 121; hostile confederacy of the Muhammadan Sultans of the Dekhan, *ib.*; terrible defeat at Talikota, 122; dismemberment of the empire, 123.
Vikramaditya, era of, 72 *note*.
Virata, the resting-place of the Pandavas, 29; the modern Bairat, *ib. note*; story of the Raja of Virata, *ib.*
Vishnu, his worship, a development of that of Surya the sun, 81; in modern Hindu belief, 82; the Supreme Spirit in modern Brahmanism, 87; worshipped at Conjeveram, 474; worshipped by the Vaishnavas and A'ayngars, 475.
Viswakarma, the architect of the gods, helps Bharadwaja, 53.
Vizagapatam, English driven out of, 332.
Vizianagram, Raja of, his feud with Bobili Raja, 331; assassinated by Rajputs, *ib.*
Vizier Ali, recognized by Sir John Shore as Nawab Vizier of Oude, 465–6; deposed on the score of illegitimacy, 466.
Vyasa, "the arranger," 37; part played by him in the Maha Bharata, 38; appears on the banks of the Ganges, 40; invokes the dead warriors of the Maha Bharata, *ib.*

W

WAHABIS, sect of, located on the Mahabun mountain, 759. *See* Sitana.
Wakiahnawis, court or news-writers of Aurangzeb, 218, 225.
Wales, H.R.H. the Prince of, his visit to India, 774.
Wandiwash, battle of, 335.
Watson, Admiral, joined by Clive, 305; destruction of Gheria, 306; joint recapture of Calcutta, 319–20; joint capture of Chandernagore, 321.
Wellesley, Colonel, afterward Duke of Wellington, accompanies the Madras army in the last war against Tippu, 470; commands the Madras army after the restoration of Baji Rao to Poona, 500; watches Daulat Rao Sindia and the Bhonsla, 500–1; stops the vacillations of Sindia, 503; glorious victory at Assaye, 503–4; victory at Argaum, 504; negotiations with Sindia, 505; story of "Old Brag," *ib. note*.
Wellesley, Marquis of, appointed Governor-General of India as Lord Mornington, 467; alarm at the French, 467–8, 470, 496, 501–2; seeks to establish a balance of power, 467; an impossibility, *ib.*; alliance with Nizam Ali, 468; insists on the disbandment of the French battalions at Hyderabad, *ib.*; rebuffed by the Mahratta powers, *ib.*; demands explanations from Tippu of Mysore, 470; conquest of Mysore, 471; deputes Buchanan on a journey through Mysore and Malabar, 472; assumes the direct administration of Tanjore, 485; of the Carnatic, 489; abandons the policy of a balance of power, and

adopts that of a paramount power with subsidiary alliances, 492; dealings with the Nizam, 493; proposals rejected by the Peishwa and Daulat Rao Sindia, 493–4; alarm at the threatened invasion of the Afghans under Zeman Shah, 494; demands on the Nawab Vizier of Oude, 495; sends Captain John Malcolm on a mission to Persia, 496; defeat of Baji Rao Peishwa at Poona by Jaswant Rao Holkar, 499; treaty of Bassein forced on the Peishwa, *ib.*; objections to the treaty, 500; alarm at the French battalions of Daulat Rao Sindia, and the designs of Napoleon, 502; campaign of Arthur Wellesley in the Dekhan, 503; of General Lake in Hindustan, 504; Great Moghul taken under British protection, *ib.*; protective treaties with Rajput and other native princes, 505–6; cedes Berar to the Nizam, 506; difficulties with Jaswant Rao Holkar, 506–7; military operations against Holkar, 508; disastrous retreat of Colonel Monson, 509–10; unexpected successes of Holkar, 511; return of Lord Wellesley to England, *ib.*; compared with Akbar, 512; his errors the outcome of genius, *ib.*; remodels the Indian civil service, 513; reaction against his policy, 514–15; his errors, 516; his mortification, *ib.*; his dealings with Nipal, 539–41; his policy adopted by Lord Hastings, 529.

Wheeler, General Sir Hugh, commanding at Cawnpore, 731; his preparations for defence, 732; receives a threatening letter from Nana Sahib, 733; negotiations with Nana Sahib, 735; the massacre at Cawnpore, 735–6.

Wheler, Mr., a member of council under Warren Hastings, 425.

Whish, General, retires from Multan, 687; captures Multan, 689; joins Gough against Sher Singh, *ib.*

Whitehill, Mr., governor of Madras, 431; evil administration, *ib.*; invasion of Hyder Ali, *ib.*; deposed by Warren Hastings, 433.

Willoughby, Lieutenant, gallantry in blowing up the arsenal at Delhi, 725–6; his death, 726.

Wilson, General, Commander-in-chief at the siege of Delhi, 742 *note*; capture of Delhi, 743.

Windham, left at Cawnpore by Sir Colin Campbell, 750; defeated by Tantia Topi, 751; abandons Cawnpore to the Gwalior rebels, *ib.*

Wurgaum, convention of, 423.

Wylde, General, his expedition against the Afghan tribes on the Black Mountain, 762 *note.*

Wynch, governor of Madras, turned out of the service by the Court of Directors, 427.

Y

Yakub Khan, son of Sher Ali Khan, governor of Herat, 769; restores his father to the throne of Kabul, 770; imprisoned by Sher Ali Khan, 775; his accession to the throne of Afghanistan, *ib.*; abdication, 776.

Yama, the judge of the dead in the Vaidik mythology, 56, 81.

Yandabo, treaty of, with Burma, 596.

Yar Muhammad Khan, the real ruler of Herat, 633; his antagonism to Persia, *ib.*; helped by British gold, 636; treacherous correspondence with Persia, *ib.*; his death, 714.

Yogis and their king described by Della Valle, 143–4.

Yudhishthira, son of Kunti, 15; the eldest of the Pandavas, 16; his jealousies, *ib.*; appointed Yuva-raja, 20; loses his wife in a gambling match, 27; takes possession of Hastinapur, 37; celebrates the Aswamedha, 39.

Yuva-raja, or little **Raja**, custom of appointing as heir-apparent, still prevailing in Hindu courts, 19–20; similar custom among the Jews, 20 *note*.

Z

ZABITA KHAN, the Rohilla, succeeds his father, Najib-ud-daula, as Amir of Amirs at Delhi, 402; flight to the Rohilla country, 403; his death, 451.

Zamorin of Calicut, 126; receives the Portuguese ambassadors, 127; Portuguese embassy to, 144; his troubles, 145; appearance of, 147; cause of his feud with the Raja of Cochin, 148.

Zeman Shah, Amir of Afghanistan, desires to invade India, 494; his invasion a bugbear, 495; his fate, *ib.*; story of his reign, 625–8; the pacification of the Punjab, 626.

Zemindars, their judicial and administrative powers, 372; checked by the right of petition to the Nawab, 373; authority transferred to European collectors, 405; change of prospects under the permanent land settlement of Lord Cornwallis, 450.

Zend party in Persia, their quarrels with the Kajar, 496.

Zingaffs of Bhutan, corresponding to messengers or chuprassies, 764.

Zulfikar Khan, Nawab of the conquests of Aurangzeb in the Dekhan and Peninsula, 233–4; bribed by the English at Madras, 234; his wars with Ram Raja, the Mahratta, *ib.*; defeats Kam Baksh, 241; political supremacy at Delhi, 245; advances against Farrukh Siyar, 246; submission and assassination, *ib.*; saves the life of Nizam-ul-mulk, 257.